PRIVATE SECURITY AND THE INVESTIGATIVE PROCESS

Third Edition

PRIVATE SECURITY AND THE INVESTIGATIVE PROCESS

Third Edition

Charles P. Nemeth

CRC Press is an imprint of the
Taylor & Francis Group, an **informa** business

Auerbach Publications
Taylor & Francis Group
6000 Broken Sound Parkway NW, Suite 300
Boca Raton, FL 33487-2742

Printed in the United States of America on acid-free paper
10 9 8 7 6 5 4 3 2 1

International Standard Book Number: 978-1-4200-8569-3 (Hardback)

Library of Congress Cataloging-in-Publication Data

Nemeth, Charles P., 1951-
Private security and the investigative process / Charles P. Nemeth. -- 3rd ed.
p. cm.
Includes bibliographical references and index.
ISBN 978-1-4200-8569-3 (hardcover : alk. paper)
1. Private investigators--United States. 2. Criminal investigation--United States. I. Title.

HV8091.N46 2010
363.28'9--dc22 2009046418

Visit the Taylor & Francis Web site at
http://www.taylorandfrancis.com

and the Auerbach Web site at
http://www.auerbach-publications.com

Contents

Preface

Works of this kind serve multiple purposes: education and enhancement of the security profession; training for field operations; as a research and database; or to disseminate new practices and procedures in a massive industry. It is my hope that a little of all of these have been accomplished in the authorship of this text, but of primary importance is that the text be a product for the practitioner, both entry level and experienced. At its best, this compilation is a working tool, filled with forms, checklists, guides—documentation that is useful in general and specific cases. Practitioners will want it as a resource filled with references to other sources, ideas, and suggestions for tactics and security strategy and as a refresher on methods in a most complex field. Private security is by no means a dull undertaking. The stereotype of the bank guard who sleeps on the job has little or no truth to it. If one disagrees, merely examine the contents of this work.

In Chapter 1, the phenomenon of privatization of once-public law enforcement functions is fully analyzed. The future expansion of private security is inevitable given this tendency. Additionally, our world needs an inexhaustible supply of information, especially accurate and verified, about people, places, and things. The investigative process serves this end.

Chapter 2 highlights the traits, characteristics, professional skills, and personal attributes so essential to the competent investigator.

How to conduct an initial interview adeptly is the subject matter of Chapter 3. Initial impressions of both clients and their cases and the importance of an objective case evaluation are thoroughly reviewed.

Witnesses, whether lay or expert, are discussed in Chapter 4. Methods of dealing with testimonial evidence, its content, and quality cannot be overemphasized.

One of the text's larger chapters is Chapter 5, "Collection of Information," covering what is clearly an a priori condition of being a good practitioner in the security industry. Topics include leads and their development, public and private sources of information—databases and publications—and computer services. Specific practical applications are also included.

The text's most comprehensive chapter, Chapter 6, "Collection of Evidence and Preservation of the Scene," continues this direction. Subjects include investigative kits, physical evidence and its collection, scene sketches, photographic evidence, and documentary applications.

In Chapter 7 surveillance techniques, whether singular, on foot, or in a patrol car, are examined and graphically reproduced.

Understanding the dynamics of report writing, with specific forms and documentation, is the prime purpose of Chapter 8. Just as in public law enforcement, security professionals are increasingly burdened by paperwork.

Commencing with Chapter 9, the text takes an applied direction. Using the varied skills and competencies discussed in the previous eight chapters, the text sets out to apply these generic principles in specialized case situations. Chapter 9 is dedicated to theft and property offenses. Covering insurance cases, whether workers' compensation or personal injury reviews, is the intent of Chapter 10. Substantial attention is given to vehicular and accident investigation and reconstruction. In Chapter 11, the diverse means of investigating personal backgrounds are catalogued.

Finally, Chapter 12 gives a rudimentary assessment of administrative requirements in the operation of a security office. Topics includng billing, letters of introduction, filing, and expense billing are covered.

To my readers go earnest thanks for your patience and trust, and, as always, I look forward to your input and professional insights.

1 Introduction to the Private Security Industry and the Investigative Process

I. THE TREND TOWARD PRIVATIZATION

Although public perceptions tend to see the justice model as a public function, there is a long history and tradition involving private operatives providing justice services. In fact, most of our national history displays a preference for private justice and police services. Using state, federal, or local officials to provide protection services was a new paradigm commencing in the late nineteenth century. Even with this recognition, life has come full circle since so many once public services are being returned to private control. In courts, parking authorities, public housing projects, federal installations, detective services and traffic control, private sector justice has reemerged. The growth of private sector justice is a phenomenon that manifests unlimited growth. Undoubtedly, a movement toward privatized justice systems and operations is under way. The *Hallcrest Report II*, the well-regarded qualitative and quantitative study of private security, computes this staggering trend in Figure 1.1.[1]

At every level, one witnesses this orientation to the private. Even criminal investigative practice is not immune to this change. The industry at large expends nearly $66 billion per annum[2] and "plays a major protective role in the Nation's life. It employs an estimated 1.1 million persons, and total expenditures for its products and services are estimated at $22 billion for 1980. In 1979, federal, state, and local enforcement expenditures were only $14 billion."[3]

The industry's robust growth is also well documented by the Bureau of Census and Bureau of Labor Statistics as outlined in Figure 1.2.[4]

The National Center for Policy Analysis (NCPA) foretells a further expansion of private justice function. Since the mid-1960s the economic impact of private sector justice has been significant by any measure, as the NCPA notes:

- There are nearly three times as many private security guards as public law enforcement officers, 1.5 million in 1990, and the private sector spends almost twice as much on private security as we pay in taxes to support the public police.
- Private bounty hunters, or bail enforcement agents, make the private bail bonding system work for persons accused of crimes by tracking down and apprehending those who try to flee.
- And the private sector on occasion has been used innovatively in other ways to prepare cases for district attorneys, to prosecute criminal cases, and to employ prisoners behind bars.[5]

William Cunningham, John J. Strauchs, and Clifford W. Van Meter, authors of the seminal work on the private security industry, "The Hallcrest Report II: Private Security Trends: 1970–2000," confirm this impetus:

> After reviewing the literature covering possible reasons for the steady growth of private protection over the past 2 to 3 decades, the Hallcrest staff believes that 4 interrelated factors largely explain the greater

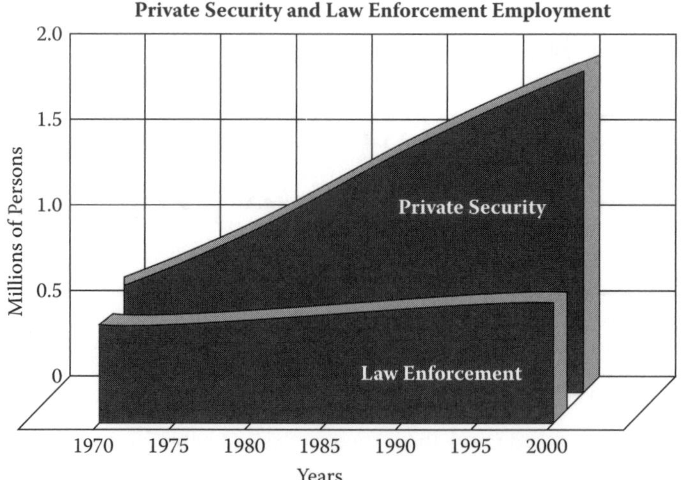

FIGURE 1.1

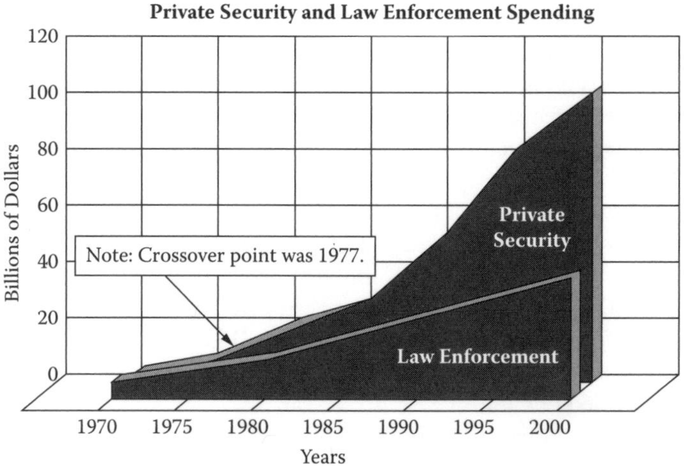

FIGURE 1.2

> employment and expenditure shift from public to private protection and the increasing growth of private security, while public protection has limited or no growth. These 4 major reasons for growth are: (1) an increase in crimes in the workplace, (2) an increase in fear (real or perceived) of crime, (3) the "fiscal crises of the state" has limited public protection, and (4) an increased public and business awareness and use of the more cost effective private security products and services.[6]

The picture for private sector justice is exceptionally bright. The Bureau of Labor Statistics paints an average 18 percent growth rate for private detectives and investigators until 2016, as shown in Figure 1.3.[7] When security guards and gaming surveillance officers are evaluated, the projections keep on the upward trend with little resistance. Gaming has delivered another avenue of growth for the private sector justice. The statistics are shown in Figure 1.4.[8]

In short, the justice sector, both its civil and criminal components, witnesses a shift from the public mentality to the private contribution. This movement is sometimes referred to as privatization. Privatization is the trend of making services and functions traditionally performed by public entities, the province of private, for-profit entities, usually companies. In order to understand

Projections Data from the National Employment Matrix

Occupational Title	SOC Code	Employment, 2006	Projected Employment, 2016	Change, 2006–16	
				Number	Percent
Private detectives and investigators	33-9021	52,000	61,000	9,400	18

NOTE: Data in this table are rounded. See the discussion of the employment projections table in the *Handbook* introductory chapter on Occupational Information Included in the Handbook.

FIGURE 1.3

Projections Data from the National Employment Matrix

Occupational Title	SOC Code	Employment, 2006	Projected Employment, 2016	Change, 2006–16	
				Number	Percent
Security guards and gaming surveillance officers	33-9030	1,049,000	1,227,000	178,000	17
Gaming surveillance officers and gaming investigators	33-9031	8,700	12,000	2,900	34
Security guards	33-9032	1,040,000	1,216,000	175,000	17

NOTE: Data in this table are rounded. See the discussion of the employment projections table in the *Handbook* introductory chapter on Occupational Information Included in the Handbook.

FIGURE 1.4

privatization, one must distinguish between public and private functions. Public law enforcement is and has always been saddled with attending to the needs of the public good. Few private security companies have to be concerned with domestic disputes, the transportation of the deceased, stray animals, or protection of the homeless.[9] *The Private Security Advisory Council* characterized police work as a public interest function. Public police have "a wide range of responsibilities to protect essentially public concerns, and their efforts are closely tied to statutorily mandated duties and the criminal justice system."[10]

> **Web Exercise:** The trend towards privatization has been unmistakable in all corners of government, from water to airports, and most other governmental functions. Visit http://www.reason.org/apr2006

The *Advisory Council* further relates that police are burdened with constitutional limitations and must interpret and implement certain guidelines in the performance of their law enforcement duties, causing natural inefficiencies not experienced by private sector operatives. Public policing is further restrained by public budgeting and financing processes that are inevitably tied to political influence.

Police administrators must evaluate and allocate resources according to the needs and demands presently operating within their community structure.[11] Norman Spain and Gary Elkin, in an article titled "Private and Public Security: There Is a Difference," note that:

> One of the traditional functions of the public police is to deter crime. In reality, their ability to do this is drastically limited. The primary reasons are that the police have little authority to change the conditions that foster crime. They have no authority to decide who will reside in their jurisdiction, whom they will police. Private security forces, on the other hand, may alter—at times drastically—the environment in which they operate. They can have walls and fences erected, doors sealed, windows screened, lights put up, and intrusion detectors installed. They can often play a decisive role in determining whom they have to monitor—who is to be an employee of the company—by conducting background investigations of potential employees.[12]

Such differences are difficult to debate, for private security is primarily concerned with the private concerns of private property assets and particular individuals. Individuals and privately funded organizations and businesses undertake measures to provide protection for the perceived security needs, which involve their private interests, not in the public domain. Private security is an option exercised to provide an additional or increased level of protection than that afforded by public law enforcement, which must respond to the larger concerns of the public.[13]

What forces have prompted this shift to the private? There are numerous explanations for this movement in the paradigm, though most relate to, first, a growing perception, whether actual or perceived, about rising crime rates in America; and, second, the cost/benefit supremacy of private law enforcement versus public operations. In the former instance, there is widespread agreement that crime is out of control in the American landscape. Even though studies may indicate minor drops in the murder rate, the reality of crime spreads in just about every sector of American life, from the corporate boardroom to the local grocery store. The world has witnessed the daily avalanche of crime in the community. Both qualitatively and quantitatively, crime has a tendency to trend upward. This is a perennial problem and is especially evident over the past 50 years. Although a recent decrease can be seen in overall rates, the rate is at an historic high. The Bureau of Justice Statistics targets homicide as evidence of crime's ascendency.

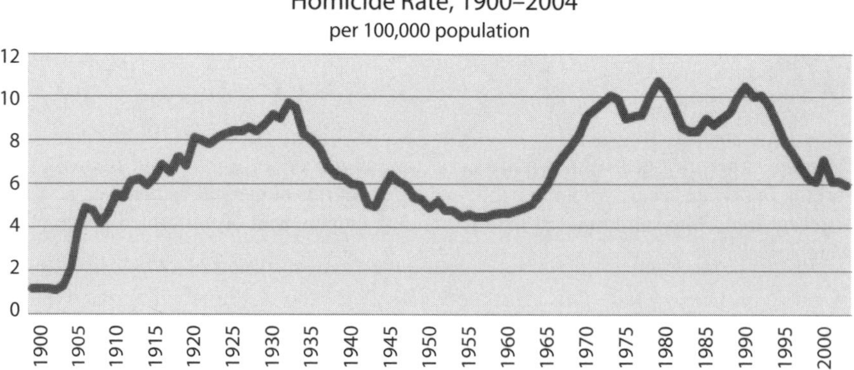

Note: The 2001 rate includes deaths attributed to the 9/11 terrorism attacks.

Source: National Center for Health Statistics, data available from the Bureau of Justic Statistics at http://www.ojp.usdoj.gov/bjs/glance/hmrt.htm.

It can also be safely argued that the post-9/11 world of terrorism has directly driven growth in the private sector. The task of homeland security is rightly construed in the context of a public-private partnership with the Department of Homeland Security (DHS) fully advancing cooperation.[15] Private security plays key roles in developing security plans for corporations and health facilities, parking authorities, and entertainment complexes. The list of corporate and business interests in need of protection and coordinated plans of response with public authority are simply too long to delineate.

> **Web Exercise:** See the DHS "Best Practices on Public Private Partnerships" at http://oja.wi.gov/docview.asp?docid=14758&locid=97

Aside from this victimization perspective, the economic aspects of crime also drive the movement to privatization. Business, industry, and the corporate world measure crime in dollar terms and evaluate how the bottom line feels the pain and pinch of a crime-ridden world. The effects of crime upon business are many and varied:

- Increased costs of insurance and security protection;
- Costs of internal audit activities to detect crime;
- Cost of investigation and prosecution of suspects measured in terms of lost time of security and management personnel;
- Reduced profits;
- Increased selling prices and weakened competitive standing;
- Loss of productivity;
- Loss of business reputation;
- Deterioration in quality of service;
- Threats to the survival of small business;
- Cost of crime prevention programs;
- Cost of crime reporting and mandated security programs;
- Loss of tax revenue;
- Increased costs of consumer goods and services to offset crime losses;
- Loss of investor equity;
- Increased taxes;
- Reduced employment due to business failures;
- Increased costs for technological equipment.[16]

The coupling of economic influences with the tidal wave of criminal victimization gives the private security industry legitimacy and poignancy that it would not have otherwise. Not everyone is pleased. Howard Rice critiques not only the growth of private security, but also the striking entanglement resulting from the private employment of public police as both entities carry out their responsibilities:

> In recent trends, private security has outstripped the growth of the public police; more people are now working in private security than in public policing. Yet this numerical comparison fails to reflect another recent trend: the substantial growth in off-duty employment of uniformed police officers by private employers.[17]

With these dual forces at work, the thrust toward privatization is inevitable. In a climate of growing frustration regarding crime and the criminal justice system, private security will certainly flourish.[18]

II. THE INVESTIGATIVE PROCESS: PRIVATE SECURITY'S ROLE

Investigation is the process of factual assimilation and the systematic collection of evidence. It is a process of observation, inspection, and analysis, involving continuous and regular inquiry into a specific subject. It requires balancing the theories of investigative practice and the information in policy manuals and textbooks with experience and "street smarts." Investigative practice depends on facts and hard information. Without these, an investigation rests on an uneasy and tenuous foundation. A successful private investigator must provide the information necessary to support or refute a claim, cause of action, or criminal prosecution. Solid investigative practices usually rely on the following traits:

- Energy and alertness.
- Knowledge of the law.
- Ability to set realistic objectives.
- Methodical approach.
- Knowledge of human nature.
- Observation and deduction abilities.
- Ability to maintain meaningful notes.

Solid investigative practice operates under an investigative plan, creates a theoretical framework that underlines the investigative process, and proposes a cause or case in law that relates to the investigative regimen.

The investigative process must reconstruct events, conditions, or (as is often stated) the "truth" itself. Finding the truth can be a challenge for even the most seasoned investigators. Objective and fully reliable information is hard to come by. To reconstruct events and circumstances, the investigator will engage many parties and practices including witnesses, physical and real evidence, documents, forensic science, demonstrative evidence, and the sophistication of expert opinion. In a sense, the investigator reconstructs history for the present. James Davidson and Mark Lytle's *After the Fact* suggests that the investigative process is really a journey into the historical past:

> "History is what happened in the past." That statement is the everyday view of the matter. … The everyday view recognizes that this task is often difficult. But historians are said to succeed if they bring back the facts without distorting them or forcing a new perspective on them. In effect, historians are seen as couriers between the past and present. Like all good messengers, they are expected simply to deliver their information without adding to it.[19]

In sum, the process of investigation requires the conversion of alleged acts into real and useful evidence.[20]

The functions of investigation are many and multifaceted. From its Latin derivative, *vestigare*, investigation implies a tracking, a search, an assimilation, or collection of information and facts. Russell Colling, in his work *Hospital Security*, concludes that the differences between the investigative protocol of the public officer from the private officer are really one of form and mission, and indeed the missions are very complementary.

> It is techniques and varying purposes that differentiate the security investigation from that of a law enforcement agency. This is not to say that the security investigation always has a different focus. A police investigation is conducted basically for the purpose of apprehending the perpetrator of a crime and locating evidence for the successful prosecution of a case. Security investigations, on the other hand, may involve, in addition to crimes, the gathering of information in regards to the violation of organizational rules and regulations; a job applicant's background, for conditions that may lead to criminal violations; the need for new security controls and procedures; liability claims or potential claims; unsafe conditions; or evidence needed to prove or disprove certain allegations.[21]

The American Society for Industrial Security recognizes the expanding investigative role that private security is playing:

> Along with this burgeoning of the prevention role, investigative responsibilities have grown as well, calling for more expert investigators using more sophisticated techniques.

> Today, many business firms and other organizations employ investigators directly as part of their in-house security programs. Others retain outside investigators for temporary assignments or on a more permanent basis through contractual arrangements. Some organizations delegate security and investigative duties to employees having assignments in other fields, for example, personnel, safety, or insurance. Others call on persons with law enforcement experience but little or no exposure to private security to perform these tasks. Private investigative agencies and in-house security departments must sometimes employ persons with limited background in the private investigatory arena to meet the demand for security services.[22]

The broad spectrum of individuals and entities in need of private security's investigative skills can only impress those once unaware of this contribution. For those laboring in the field it is a given that these relationships are part and parcel of the private sector function. The following is taken from Pinkerton's *Investigations Department Training Manual*:

Public Prosecutors and Law Enforcement Agencies
- Investigation of crimes.
- Locating fugitives and witnesses.
- Securing evidence and surveillance.
- Public/private coordination and planning for Homeland Security.

Lawyers
- Investigation of cases in preparation of trial or adjudication.
- Locating witnesses and missing heirs, etc.
- Locating concealed assets and serving papers.

Patent Attorneys
- Investigation of infringements.
- Establishing facts in respect of adoption, use and abandonment.

Publishers
- Investigation to defend libel actions.
- Investigation of unfair competition.
- Investigation of copyright infringement.

Banks
- Investigation of crimes.
- Investigation of applicants and employees considered for advancement to positions of trust and responsibility.
- Protection of transportation of valuable property.
- Surveillance of employees and others suspected of improprieties.
- Verification of reported assets.
- Checking the operation of business enterprises.
- Investigation of credit applicants.
- Investigation of computer and e-transaction fraud.

Insurance Companies and Self-Insurers
- Investigation of defalcations [embezzlement], robberies, burglaries, thefts, losses, fires and other casualty claims.
- Investigation of life, accident, malpractice, compensation and other claims.
- Shadowing claimants to establish extent of their disabilities.

Railway, Bus and Airline Companies
- Honesty and service inspections.
- Investigation of claims.
- Terrorist threats.

Motor Freight, Warehouse and Freight Terminal Companies
- Investigation of thefts, etc.
- Investigation of claims.

Stores
- Store detectives.
- Investigation of thefts, etc.
- Locating credit skips and frauds.

Manufacturing and Wholesale Distributing Companies

- Investigation of product liability claims.
- Investigation of unfair competition, willful attempts to damage products' reputation, fraudulent disclosure of trade secrets and violation of trade agreements.
- Homeland defense plans.

Hotels

- Hotel detectives; investigations of thefts, etc.
- Inspection of service in various departments for honesty, efficiency, waste and violation of regulations.

Character Investigations

- Investigations to establish reputation, confirm residence address, present and/or prior employment or business, marital status, habits, mode of living, income, financial and credit responsibility, social and business connections, police record and other details as desired.

Surveillance

- Establishing movements, associates, attention to duty during business hours and mode of living, etc.
- Video recording service to document activities of personal injury claimants.

Plant and Store Surveillance

- Over weekends, on holidays, and during night hours, keeping premises under surveillance to detect removal of property, attempted depredations, admittance of unauthorized persons and other improper acts.

Undercover Investigations

- Investigation of employees to expose dishonesty, waste, carelessness, inefficiency, willful neglect, violation of safety rules, favoritism, employee discrimination, lowered morale, sabotage, and other irregularities.[23]

A. Types of Investigative Activities

The investigative process serves many purposes in both the criminal and civil justice systems, including:

1. To determine if there is sufficient factual evidence to support or defeat each element of a cause of action.
2. To accumulate the necessary factual evidence to prove or defeat a case at trial or to form the basis for a settlement.
3. To locate leads to additional evidence.
4. To locate persons or property.
5. To find evidence that might be used to discredit (impeach) a witness or the opponent.[24]

The role of private security in the investigative process is also determined by the subject matter of the investigation. Professor Thomas Eimermann affirms how the subject matter of an investigation, and its corresponding methodology, will depend upon the subject matter of that investigation.

> The nature of the investigation will, of course, vary considerably with the area of law involved, as well as with the particular facts of the case at hand. Negligence cases require a great deal of investigative work. Damaged cars, broken machines, and injured persons all have to be examined. Witnesses have to be interviewed at length in order to determine the existence of negligence on the part of one or more parties to the accident. In work[ers'] compensation cases, negligence is not an issue, but the extent of damage is. Likewise, the extent to which an injury was work-related becomes an important aspect of the investigation. In probate, an investigation could involve either locating missing heirs or attempting to determine what the mental state of the deceased was at the time the will was written. The underlying skills in all areas are basically the same.[25]

The range and scope of investigative practice is as varied as the multiplicity of subject matters. A representative list might include:

- Claims investigation.
- Divorce investigation.
- Location of missing persons.
- Location of heirs and assigns.
- Civil investigation.
- Criminal investigation.
- Credit investigation.
- Background investigation.
- Undercover investigation.
- Insurance investigation.
- Personal injury investigation.
- Traffic accident investigation.
- Property loss investigation.
- Medical malpractice investigation.
- Government agency investigation.
- Fire, Safety, and Occupational Safety and Health Administration (OSHA) investigations.
- Domestic relations investigation.
- Patent and trademark investigations.
- Organized crime investigation.
- Fraud and white-collar crime investigations.
- Employee investigation.
- Polygraph investigation.
- Housing code investigation.
- Building trades investigation.
- Surveillance activities.
- Witness location.
- Workers' compensation cases.
- Corporate investigation.
- Judgment investigation.
- Product liability and consumer claims.
- Public record searches.
- Title searches.
- Marine investigation.
- Construction accident investigation.
- Toxic tort investigation.
- Psychological and psychiatric investigation.
- Questioned document investigation.

The above list is a partial attempt to cover investigative strategy, since the nature and extent of investigative work and practice in the security industry is impossible to categorize fully. As technological, scientific, and other advances occur, for example, in the areas of forensic science, DNA, or computer forensics, the need for skilled investigators will mirror the emerging fields. Both investigation method and the investigators who carry out the investigation will come to depend on not only an expertise but also a recognizable field. In this sense, investigative practice is forever changing. For an outline of the various functions of private security personnel see Figure 1.5.[26] Security firms reflect this multifaceted approach to investigating. See Figures 1.6[27] and 1.7.[28]

The *Hallcrest Report* confirms private security's markedly involved role in investigative functions in both the civil and criminal contexts. Figure 1.8[29] indicates the breadth and depth of investigative practice.

FUNCTIONS OF PRIVATE SECURITY PERSONNEL

Guard and Patrol Services and Personnel

Guard and patrol services include the provision of personnel who perform the following functions, either contractually or internally, at such places and facilities as industrial plants, financial institutions, education institutions, office buildings, retainment establishments, commercial complexes (including hotels and motels), health care facilities, recreation facilities, libraries and museums, residential and housing developments, charitable institutions, transportation vehicles and facilities (public and common carriers), and warehouses and goods distribution depots:

- Prevention and/or detection of intrusion, unauthorized entry or activity, vandalism, or trespass on private property;
- Prevention and/or detection of theft, loss, embezzlement, misappropriation or concealment or merchandise, money, bonds, stocks, notes, or other valuable documents or papers;
- Control, regulation, or direction of the flow or movements of the public, whether by vehicle or otherwise, to ensure the protection of property;
- Protection of individuals from bodily harm; and
- Enforcement of rules, regulations, and policies related to crime reduction.

Investigative Services and Personnel

The major services provided by the investigative component of private security may be provided contractually or internally at places and facilities, such as industrial plants, financial institutions, educational institutions, retail establishments, commercial complexes, hotels and motels, and health care facilities. The services are provided for a variety of clients, including insurance companies, law firms, retailers, and individuals. Investigative personnel are primarily concerned with obtaining information with reference to any of the following matters:

- Crime or wrongs committed or threatened;
- The identity, habits, conduct, movements, whereabouts, affiliations, associations, transactions, reputation, or character of any person, group of persons, association or organization, society, other group of persons or partnerships or corporation;
- Preemployment background checks of personnel applicants;
- The conduct, honesty, efficiency, loyalty, or activities of employees, agents, contractors, and subcontractors;
- Incidents and illicit or illegal activities by persons against the employer or employer's property;
- Retail shoplifting;
- Internal theft by employees or other employee crime;
- The truth or falsity of any statement or representation;
- The whereabouts of missing persons;
- The location or recovery of lost or stolen property;
- The causes and origin of or responsibility for fires, libels or slanders, losses, accidents, damage, or injuries to property;
- The credibility of informants, witnesses, or other persons; and
- The securing of evidence to be used before investigating committees, boards of award or arbitration, or in the trial of civil or criminal cases and the preparation thereof.

FIGURE 1.5 Reprinted from *Principles of Security*, 2nd ed. with permission. Copyright 1988 Matthew Bender & Company, Inc., a member of the Lexis/Nexis Group. All rights reserved.

B. General Investigative Methods

With these thoughts in mind, there are certain universal characteristics and traits necessary in the investigative process. First, the hallmark of any investigation is the ability to gather facts. The Association of Trial Lawyers of America makes this point abundantly clear:

> The principles of investigation are the same for the professional investigator or the attorney. ... It is common knowledge among experienced lawyers that the case may be won or lost in the investigation. It is therefore essential that the investigator be both well trained in the art of conducting an investigation and carefully briefed in the specific objectives of his investigation of a particular case.[30]

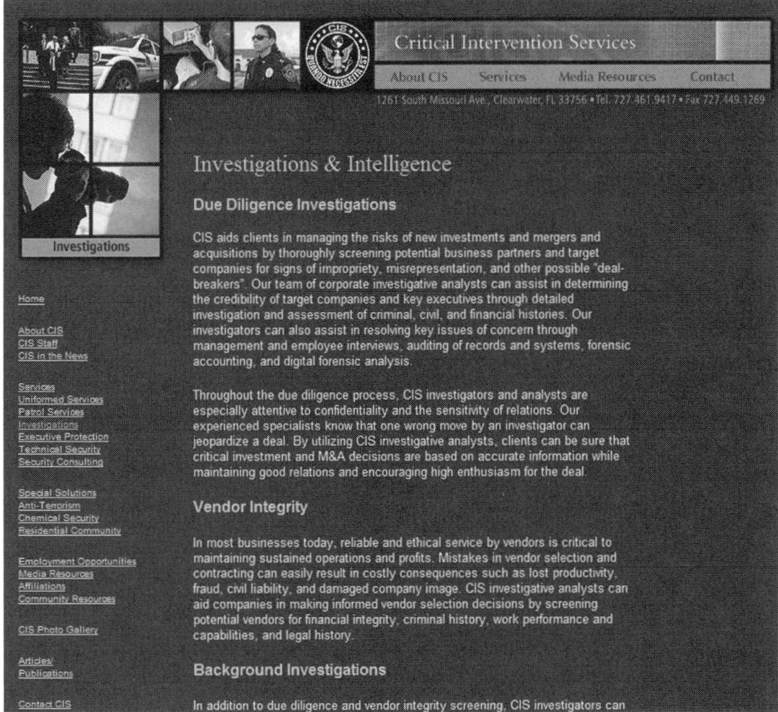

FIGURE 1.6 Reprinted from www.cisworldservices.org/index.html and www.cisworldservices.org/investigations.html. With permission.

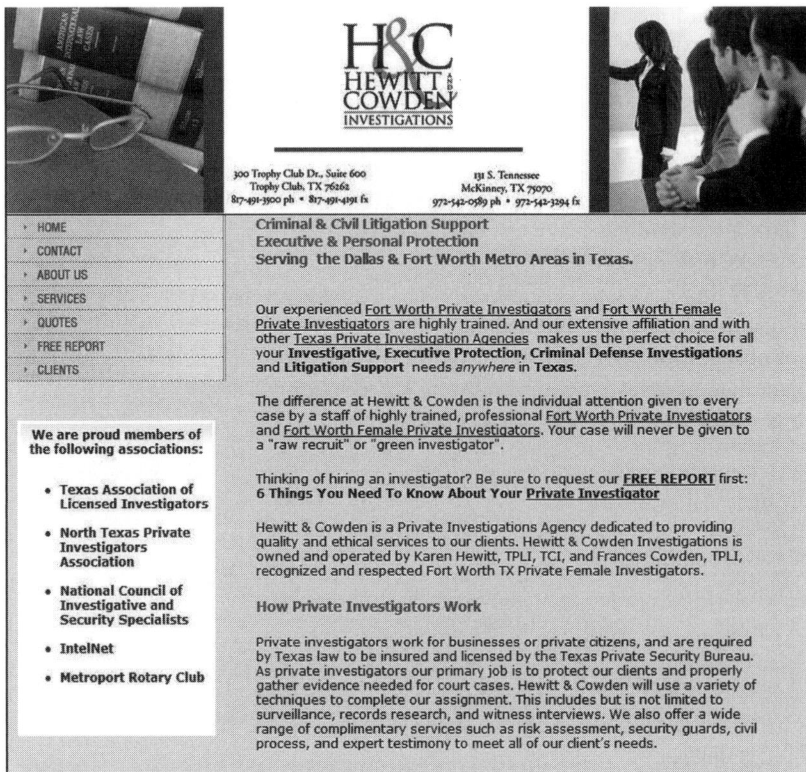

FIGURE 1.7 http://www.dallas-pi.com/. With permission.

Private Sector Crime Investigation

Rank Order of Investigation Frequency

1. Pilferage/employee theft
2. Vandalism
3. Burglary
4. Check fraud
5. Shoplifting
6. Robbery
7. Embezzlement
8. Drug abuse
9. Credit card fraud
10. Receiving stolen property
11. Cargo theft
12. Arson
13. Terrorism
14. Insurance fraud
15. Industrial espionage
16. Computer related
17. Commercial bribery
18. Extortion
19. Securities theft/fraud
20. Bankruptcy fraud

FIGURE 1.8

Continuing this line of reasoning, Art Buckwalter, in his amply documented work, *Investigative Methods*, comments on this reality:

> No list can possibly cover all potentialities. Constantly new situations and complexities develop, calling for special investigative assignments. One of the realities for investigators is the persistence of variable factors that make every case and every career different. These variables of personalities and situations

> can never be standardized. They spring from the nature of the human heart and mind and from the conflicts and complexities of our modern life.[31]

No matter what the case or subject matter, security professionals who hope to attain a high level of professional standing must be competent investigators. Business, industry, attorneys, agencies at the federal, state, and local levels, and other employers look to the security investigator to collect information and to resolve factual disputes and confusing data. In a general sense, the security investigator lays a foundation, a conceptual framework, upon which cases can be evaluated, decisions can be made, or eventual action and policymaking can be formulated.

Investigation is the process of fact assimilation. Investigation is the systematic collection of evidence necessary to support or refute a claim, whether civil or criminal in nature. Investigation is the process of observation, close inspection and analysis, and continuous and regular inquiry into a specific subject matter. Investigation is the search and journey toward the reconstruction of events and conditions pertinent to a client's needs and interests:

> Successful investigation involves a balance between the scientific knowledge of the investigative process acquired by study and experience and the skills acquired by the artful application of learned techniques.[32]

In sum, without obtaining facts, data, and real evidence, the investigator has not performed effectively. The security professional who desires to be considered successful must provide the information requested, rather than operate by conjecture or hunch. Sound investigative practice cannot rely upon the assertions and allegations of a client, but rather a corroboration of the same.

Therefore, astute investigative practice must include these uniform practices:

1. A logical sequence must be followed.
2. Real, physical evidence must be legally obtained.
3. Real, physical evidence must be properly stored and preserved.
4. Witnesses must be identified, interviewed, and prepared for any potential or actual litigation.
5. Leads must be developed.
6. Reports and documentation must be collected.
7. Information must be accurately and completely recorded.
8. Evidence collected must correlate to the claim, cause of action, or offense charged.[33]

In the end, the security investigator practice must have an end, a goal, and a relationship between cause and effect. Security specialist C. A. Roper communicates some timeless advice on finding a purpose for the security plan:

1. The use of electronic security systems to reduce the vulnerability to any perceived or identifiable threat and to reduce the reliance on fixed-station security forces.
2. Integrating physical security into various organizational contingency plans, mission planning, and the testing of these physical security procedures and measures.
3. Coordination with each organizational element and/or facility area in applying physical security applications to the concepts and procedures involved in security and personnel protection and also those involved in a set protection. This should be performed in an integrated and coherent manner.
4. Training all security personnel to respond to attempted unauthorized entries at facilities and to respond to indicators and occurrences within the facility.
5. Creating and sustaining an awareness of physical security for all personnel throughout the organization via a security education, training, and motivation program.
6. Identifying those resources that will enhance and/or increase the current level of physical security at an installation or facility.[34]

The investigative process must comprehensively reconstruct events, conditions, or, as is often stated, the truth itself. Finding the truth is often an elusive undertaking. In the process of finding truth, investigators must evaluate, gauge, and assess witnesses, physical and real evidence, documents, testimony, and the entire array of evidentiary considerations in the formulation of a case. *Simply put, the process of investigation requires the conversion of alleged acts into real and useful evidence.*[35]

The underlying purpose of this book is to provide a comprehensive, practical, and authoritative resource manual to the industry and its practitioners and to those seeking a career in the private security industry. By reading its contents, the security professional should gain insight into the fundamental competency skills necessary to function as an investigator.

NOTES

1. William Cunningham, John J. Strauchs, and Clifford W. Van Meter, "Private Security Trends 1970–2000, The Hallcrest Report II" (1990), Figure 7.2 at 237.
2. "High Growth Reported for the US Private Security Services Market," Reuters, August 5, 2008, at http://www.reuters.com/article/pressRelease/idUS168856+05-Aug-2008+MW20080805, visited August 27, 2009.
3. U.S. Department of Justice, National Institute of Justice, *The Growing Role of Private Security* (U.S. Government Printing Office, 1984), 1.
4. "The Hallcrest Report II," *supra* note 1, Figure 7.3 at 239.
5. Morgan O. Reynolds, Using the Private Sector to Deter Crime—NCPA Policy Report No. 181, at Executive Summary, National Center for Policy Analysis, 1994, at http://www.ncpa.org/pdfs/st181.pdf, visited August 27, 2009.
6. "The Hallcrest Report II," *supra* note 1, at 236.
7. U.S. Department of Labor, Bureau of Labor Statistics: Occupational Outlook Handbook 2008–2009, at http://www.bls.gov/oco/ocos157.htm#projections_data, visited August 27, 2009.
8. *Id.* at 7.
9. Richard W. Lukins, "Training for the Security Guard," *Security Mgmt.* 20 (1976), 32.
10. National Advisory Committee on Criminal Justice Standards and Goals, Private Security: Report of the Task Force on Private Security 5 (1976).
11. *Id.* at 10.
12. Norman Spain and Gary Elkin, "Private and Public Security: There Is a Difference," *Security World* 16 (1979), 32.
13. National Advisory Committee, *supra* note 10.
14. Federal Bureau of Investigation, *Crime in the United States, Uniform Crime Reports* (U.S. Government Printing Office, 2007), Table 1A.
15. The federal government, at the both the executive and legislative levels, have made support for public-private cooperation a key policy goal. Public-private partnerships have been recognized by several presidential directives and national strategies as a necessary element of preparedness: Homeland Security Presidential Directive (HSPD) 7 (LLIS.gov ID# 9937), issued by President George W. Bush on December 17, 2003, tasks the Department of Homeland Security (DHS) and various federal agencies with coordinating information sharing and other protective measures with the private sector; Homeland Security Presidential Directive 9 (LLIS.gov ID# 9938), also issued by President Bush on January 30, 2004, establishes public-private information sharing as part of a national policy to protect the nation's agriculture and food systems; The National Preparedness Standard on Disaster/Emergency Management and Business Continuity (National Fire Protection Association 1600) (http://www.nfpa.org/PDF/nfpa1600.pdf?src=nfpa), 2004 edition, recommends cross-sector cooperation on a number of issues; The National Response Plan (LLIS.gov ID# 11904), released December 1, 2004, outlines the roles and responsibilities of the private sector in emergency response, including coordination with public sector responders; the National Strategy for Homeland Security (LLIS.gov ID# 138), released on July 1, 2002, states that "government at the federal, state, and local level must actively collaborate and partner with the private sector"; the National Strategy for the Physical Protection of Critical Infrastructure and Key Assets (LLIS.gov ID# 11888), released in February 2003, states that "local communities play critical roles in … engaging their public and private leadership in the development of coordinated local and regional plans to assure the protection of residents and businesses."
16. National Advisory Committee, *supra* note 10, at 19.

17. U.S. Department of Justice, *National Institute of Justice, Private Employment of Public Police* (U.S. Government Printing Office, 1988), 1.
18. J. R. Greene, T. M. Seamon, P. R. Levy, "Merging Public and Private Security for Collective Benefit: Philadelphia's Center City District," *Am. J. Police*. 14(1995), 3–20.
19. James Davidson and Mark Lytle, *After the Fact: The Art of Historical Detection*, 5th ed. (McGraw-Hill, 2005), xv.
20. Patricia W. Kittredge, "Guideposts for the Investigation of a Negligence Case," *Prac. Law.* 90 (1973), 55; J. Stannar Baker, "Reconstruction of Accidents," *Traffic Dig. Rev.* 17 (1969), 9; P. Magarick, "Investigating the Civil Case: General Principles," *Am. Jur. Trials* 1 (1987), 361.
21. Russell Colling, *Hospital Security* (Butterworth Publishers, 1982), 211.
22. American Society for Industrial Security, *Basic Guidelines for Security Investigation* (1981), 1.
23. Pinkerton's, Inc., *Investigations Department Training Manual* (1990), 30–31.
24. James Mccord, *The Litigation Paralegal* (West Publishing, 1988), 69.
25. Thomas Eimermann, *Fundamentals of Paralegalism* (Little, Brown, 1980), 102–103.
26. T. Ricks, B. Tillett, and C. Vanmeter, *Principles of Security*, 2nd ed. (Anderson Publishing, 988), 173–174.
27. Critical Intervention Services, Inc., http://www.cisworldservices.org/index.html, visited Nov. 5, 2009.
28. Hewitt & Cowden Investigaitons, http://www.txinvestigators.com, visited Nov. 4, 2009.
29. "The Hallcrest Report II," *supra* note 1, at 26.
30. The Association of Trial Lawyers of America, *The Anatomy of a Personal Injury Lawsuit, A Handbook of Basic Trial Advocacy*, 2d. ed. 1981), 14–15.
31. Art Buckwalter, *Investigative Methods* (Butterworth Publishers, 1984), 22.
32. W. Bennett and K. Hess, *Criminal Investigation* (West Publishing, 1981), 9.
33. *Id.* at 9.
34. C. A. Roper, *Physical Security and the Inspection Process* (Butterworth-Heinemann/Elsevier, 1997), 2.
35. Kittredge, "Guideposts for the Investigation of a Negligence Case," 55; Baker, "Reconstruction of Accidents," 9; Magarick, "Investigating the Civil Case: General Principles," 357.

2 General Characteristics of a Competent Investigator

I. INTRODUCTION

In the investigative realm, as in any other occupation, certain skills, qualities, and competencies are essential to success. Although differing personalities, styles of operation, and skill levels exist, there are common traits that constitute the professional investigator. Although there is variation in how to accomplish the investigative task, there is a sort of "investigative DNA." Russell Colling, in his text, *Hospital Security*, portrays the solid investigator as a "natural."

> The really good investigator has a natural aptitude and is intrigued by the investigative process coupled with the human relations involved. An investigation offers a challenge and will often succeed or fail in direct relation to the degree of competence and enthusiasm displayed.[1]

Colling further indicates that adept investigators must possess these attributes:

- Energy and alertness
- Knowledge of the law
- Ability to set realistic objectives
- Methodical approach
- Knowledge of human nature
- Observation and deduction abilities
- Ability to maintain meaningful notes.[2]

Undoubtedly, the competent investigator, whether public or private, encompasses all these traits and more. This chapter highlights the types of traits and skill levels needed to succeed in the world of investigative practice.

II. OBJECTIVITY AND INVESTIGATIVE PRACTICE

Good investigators are driven by facts rather than by emotions, preconceptions, biases, or opinions that lack a factual basis. "Once an investigator loses sight of the facts and commences to be led by opinions, he no longer maintains the necessary objectivity."[3] Investigators who commence the process of fact-gathering and assimilation with preconceptions and preconceived conclusions are destined to produce a faulty result. Therefore, the investigator's strongest suit is an open-minded, hypothesis-driven, scientific approach to the case. Only when an investigator purges personal feelings and preconceptions will the investigative process have integrity, for facts are what drive the investigator and comprise the subject matter of the investigation itself.

Fact gathering must become the hallmark of the security operative's investigative process. If it does, the investigator's actions will inspire others to believe in the integrity of the process and to see judgments as reliable and credible. A recent job description for an investigator stresses these capacities:

- Analyze problems to identify significant factors, gather pertinent data, and recognize solutions;
- Plan and organize work; and
- Communicate effectively orally and in writing.

These skills develop a professional approach in the investigator and produce a "confident, business-like"[4] investigator working in the field. This allegiance to objective fact-gathering is not always easy. Security investigators are often placed in situations that are emotional by design. Domestic disputes, labor unrest, public protest, to name a few settings, represent the types of cases involving heightened emotions.[5] The ability to keep your head in these scenarios is professionally demanding. Adhering to objective method, remaining emotionally detached, and carrying out the assigned task without animus is a tall order. Norman Bottom and John Kostanoski's *Introduction to Security and Loss Control* emphasizes the role objectivity plays in investigative method.

> Few private investigators rely overmuch on technology. Their primary trade is extracting information from the willing and unwilling, and locating records and documents. Some investigators have good technical skills in one or more of the following categories: photography, computer usage, eavesdropping equipment (technical intelligence-gathering), accident investigation, lighting measurements, marine transportation, and so on.[6]

In the final analysis, the effective investigator searches for objective reality and records it.[7]

III. LOGIC AND INVESTIGATIVE PRACTICE

Aside from the emotional control just discussed, the competent investigator must depend upon a logical method and protocol. Fact gathering and deductive reasoning about the facts, conditions, and circumstances of a given case demand a logical mind. Logic can best be described as the orderly and sensible review of facts, conditions, and events in a consistent and sequential order. To do so the investigator must devise appropriate inquiry techniques. Simply, *ask the right questions in the right order!* Since logic is an exercise of pure reason, facts can be evaluated by direct, deductive, inferential, or reverse forms of reasoning. Queries in a general sense will be:

- *Who* was responsible for this information?
- *What* does the information mean?
- *Where* was this information gathered?
- *When* was this information collected?
- *How* was this information acquired?
- *What* other parties or individuals might be responsible for this information?
- *Why* was this information found in this location?

In this way, the investigator looks for correlations. "All possible cause and effect relations must be examined, links found, and conclusions drawn, but only after thoroughly exploring all alternatives."[8]

As an illustration, consider a claim of food poisoning alleged against a restaurant and hotel establishment. Assume that you are a security officer assigned to investigate the claim. What types of logical inquiries should be made? Walter J. Buzby and David Paine, in *Hotel and Motel Security Management*, suggest these various lines of inquiry:

1. When did the victim become ill? (date and hour)
2. What was the nature of the illness? (pains, vomiting, dizziness, etc.)
3. How long did the illness continue?
4. Was a doctor consulted or any medicine taken? If a doctor was consulted, a copy of his findings should be secured.
5. What food or foods does the victim claim caused his illness?

6. Why does he feel that these foods caused the illness? Did they have a particular odor, taste, or appearance that caused suspicion?
7. What activities did the victim engage in prior to eating the suspected foods? Had he been to any parties, consumed any alcohol, medicine? Had he been in the company of any other persons? If so, get names and addresses so they may be contacted for statements.
8. Had the victim sustained any traumatic experience prior to eating? If so, get full details.
9. If the victim is unable to pinpoint any particular item of food that is suspicious, secure a complete list of all food eaten.
10. Check hotel records (restaurant records) as to number of servings of each item consumed by the victim that were served that day.
11. Check records for any other reports of illnesses on that particular day.[9]

This type of logical processing is often described as the *Who, What, Where, When, How, and Why* questioning sequence. Adept investigators who ask the right questions, in the right order, will find the facts that are essential to successful case resolution. In a criminal or civil context, the standard 5W and H lines of questioning look like this:

Who Questions
- Who discovered the incident or crime?
- Who reported the incident or crime?
- Who saw or heard anything of importance?
- Who had a motive or other reason for participation?
- Who was responsible for the incident or crime?
- Who can be considered an aider, abetter, coconspirator, codefendant, or coplaintiff?
- With whom did the defendant associate?
- Who are the witnesses?

What Questions
- What occurred during this incident or crime?
- What are the incidents or crimes in question?
- What are the elements of these causes of action or crimes?
- What are the facts and actions committed by the defendant or suspect?
- What do the witnesses know?
- What evidence has been obtained?
- What was done with the evidence?
- What tools and other instruments were employed?
- What weapons or other real evidence exists?
- What means of transportation was used in the incident or commission of the crime?
- What was the modus operandi (method of operation)?

Where Questions
- Where was the incident or crime discovered?
- Where was the incident or crime committed?
- Where were the suspects or defendants seen?
- Where were the witnesses during the event?
- Where was the victim found?
- Where were the tools and other instruments obtained?
- Where does the suspect or defendant live?
- Where does/did the victim live?
- Where is the suspect or defendant now?
- Where is the suspect or defendant likely to frequent?
- Where was the suspect or defendant tracked down?

When Questions

- When did the incident or crime take place?
- When was the incident or crime discovered?
- When were appropriate parties notified of the incident or crime?
- When did the police arrive at the scene?
- When was the victim last seen?
- When was the suspect apprehended?

How Questions

- How did the incident or crime take place?
- How did the suspect or defendant get to the scene?
- How did the suspect or defendant depart from the scene?
- How did the suspect or defendant get the necessary information to commit the wrongful act?
- How much damage was done?
- How much property was stolen?
- How much skill, knowledge, and personal expertise was necessary for this incident or crime to take place?

Why Questions

- Why did the incident or crime take place?
- Why were particular tools or instruments utilized?
- Why was there a particular method employed?
- Why did the witnesses talk?
- Why did the witnesses show reluctance in talking?

Investigative documentation, like the Security Department Incident Report in Figure 2.1,[10] mirrors this logical penchant necessary for effective investigation.

Any investigative report should be objective and logical—in most cases a standardized report form will aid the investigator in collecting the who, what, where, when, how, and why information. In investigative practice, the search for truth, through the reconstruction of events and conditions, requires that the facts be carefully collected and studied.

Investigative logic is an exercise of both the intellect and the imagination. However, it is not fabrication or some type of delusion. Instead, it is the capacity and ability to draw natural inferences based on logic and reality from well-grounded facts. The investigator must be able to distinguish, compare, and contrast the reliable from the conjectural, and just as importantly, be willing to change, modify, and therefore adjust one's basic theory to the facts as the case evolves. E. Smith, in his book *A Practical Guide for Investigators*, concurs with the view of logical flexibility.

> The theory must be abandoned as soon as proof shows it is inconsistent with facts uncovered. Every theory should be investigated to an end. Nothing should be taken for granted. When discarding a theory, it should not be entirely eliminated from the mind. The ability to judge when a theory should be abandoned is a valuable asset to the investigator.[11]

IV. PERSEVERANCE, DILIGENCE, AND INVESTIGATIVE PRACTICE

"Stick-to-itiveness," the professional and personal obsession with getting the facts right, and the corresponding desire to discern the proper resolution of a case are mandatory attributes of a good investigator. Cases are rarely resolved by chance but rather by hard work. The investigator must be not only a collector and assimilator of information and facts, who subjects those facts to deductive and inferential analysis, but also a person of enormous perseverance. Since most investigations

SECURITY DEPARTMENT INCIDENT REPORT

OFFENSE CATEGORY		DATE-TIME RECEIVED	DAY OF WEEK	DATE MO DAY YR	TIME AM. PM.	INVESTIGATION NO.
FORCED ENTRY		COMPLAINANT'S NAME				HOME PHONE
THEFT	PERS.PROP.					
	COMPANY PROP.	ADDRESS				BUSINESS PHONE
	COIN MACHINE					
	AUTO	STATUS ☐ VISITOR ☐ EMPLOYEE ☐ OTHER (SPECIFY)				
ROBBERY						
ASSAULT		DATE-TIME OF OFFENSE	DAY OF WEEK		DATE MO DAY YR	TIME AM. PM.
RAPE						
MANSLAUGHTER		PLACE	WEAPON USED			
DISTURBANCE						
VANDALISM						
TRAFFIC		TRADEMARK				
OTHER (SPECIFY)						

VICTIM'S NAME			ADDRESS
SEX ☐ M ☐ F	AGE	RACE	STATUS ☐VISITOR ☐EMPLOYEE ☐OTHER (SPECIFY)

MEDICAL TREATMENT ☐ YES (EXPLAIN) ☐ NO	DESCRIPTION OF LOST PROPERTY	VALUE

DESCRIPTION OF OFFENDERS

NO.1	SEX ☐ M ☐ F	RACE	HEIGHT	BUILD	EYES	HAIR	GLASSES ☐ Y ☐ N	COMPLEXION
	MARKS				AGE	HAT	COAT	SHIRT
NO.2	SEX ☐ M ☐ F	RACE	HEIGHT	BUILD	EYES	HAIR	GLASSES ☐ Y ☐ N	COMPLEXION
	MARKS				AGE	HAT	COAT	SHIRT

WITNESS NAME	ADDRESS	TELEPHONE
WITNESS NAME	ADDRESS	TELEPHONE

LAW ENFORCEMENT AGENCY NOTIFIED	TIME	PERSON
1.	☐ AM	
	☐ PM	
2.	☐ AM	
	☐ PM	

NAME OF PERSON ARRESTED 1.	ADDRESS
NAME OF PERSON ARRESTED 2.	ADDRESS

CHARGES

1.	2.

WAS PHYSICAL FORCE USED? ☐ YES ☐ NO

SIGNATURE OF REPORTING OFFICER	DATE	FOR SECURITY OFFICE USE ONLY APPROVED ____________ DATE NAME CARD COMPLETED ____________

FIGURE 2.1 Sample incident report form.

NARRATIVE – BE SPECIFIC IN WRITING OF THIS REPORT. BE SURE TO USE THE GUIDELINES: WHO, WHAT, WHEN, WHY, WHERE AND HOW. DESCRIBE OFFENSE IN DETAIL, INCLUDE INITIAL STATEMENTS UTTERED BY VICTIM, WITNESSES AND SUSPECTS. EXAMPLE: IN CAR THEFT, WHAT WAS VICTIM'S RESPONSE TO DIRECT QUESTION, "WAS CAR LOCKED?" DESCRIBE SCENE OF OFFENSE AND CONTRIBUTORY CONDITIONS SUCH AS POOR LIGHTING, EXTREME ISOLATION, ETC. LIST EVIDENCE FOUND AT SCENE AND ALL OTHER RELEVANT INFORMATION SUCH AS SOBRIETY OF VICTIM, WITNESSES AND SUSPECTS. SAFEGUARD REPORT FOR REFERENCE.	
FOR SECURITY DEPARTMENT USE ONLY	
THIS OFFENSE IS DECLARED: UNFOUNDED CLEARED BY ARREST EXCEPTIONALLY CLEARED INACTIVE (NOT CLEARED)	SIGNED________________ DATE ________ SECURITY DIRECTOR

FIGURE 2.1 (continued).

do not move forward in a straight line and are likely to have impediments placed in the path of resolution, an intense desire to reach proper conclusions can only aid the investigator. The security specialist must be able to handle adversity, dead ends, frustrations and setbacks, and a wide array of unexpected and even surprising contingencies. Perseverance can be described as a deliberateness that withstands excuse or mitigating factors. Perseverance can also take the form of mental and physical endurance that is not readily swayed. These qualities are particularly essential when the private security operative is involved in cases of terrorism, hostage negotiation, and the design and implementation of executive protection systems.

Perseverance generates a steady stream of leads such as witnesses during the investigative process. "Occasionally, the investigator may be able to produce an unknown or unsuspected witness, but the discovery of such a witness cannot usually be credited to chance."[12] Instead, the witness will be discovered because the investigator has followed a lead with persistence. In every aspect of the investigative process, this dedication to task and result reaps fruit in the long run. Despite the tediousness of much investigative work, the security specialist must stay resolved and attuned to the overreaching goal. The practices of surveillance, inventory, and warehouse searches, auditing techniques, records analysis, and title, tax, and record abstraction are hardly exciting activities, yet each of these practices may yield remarkable results. The investigator must remain steadfast in the mission and fully recognize that while the investigative process is slow and deliberate, in time it will generate laudable leads.

For example, in building a case for divorce based upon infidelity, adultery, cruelty, or abuse, the investigator must find and evaluate the circumstances, events, and conditions supporting the client's position. The investigator must also accord the opposing party an objective view and not simply believe the allegations and affirmations of any client, but confirm the claims. In short, the investigative perspective requires looking at the whole picture—all parties and evidence that bear upon a case. To do so requires a persevering and diligent personality. "Investigation often involves hours, or even days, of waiting and watching, of performing tedious, boring assignments that may or may not yield information or evidence helpful to the case. Nonetheless, patience and perseverance are often the key to successful investigation."[13] Be mindful, however, that perseverance and diligence are not equated with stubbornness and intractability. Perseverance must be tempered with and complemented by an intellectual and personal flexibility.

V. HUMAN RELATIONS SKILLS AND INVESTIGATIVE PRACTICE

Because so much of an investigator's success depends upon the ability to collect information, one's capacity for human interaction adds to this competency. Investigators who cannot relate to clients, witnesses, agency heads, government employees, the police system and social service personnel, and insurance and claims adjusters will be less than proficient. Interpersonal skills promote the acquisition of information and provide a steady stream of intelligence worthy of collection.

An investigator who alienates a witness loses valuable information. If an investigator cannot express or communicate in clear, understandable terms, questions will not be answered. In this sense being an educated person is crucial to the operation, one must have the ability to express ideas and do so while engendering ease in the party interviewed.[14] If an investigator makes people feel ill at ease, offended, or defensive, the ability to collect information will be substantially impaired. Ideally, private investigators must have personal characteristics that attract and motivate the opposition. "The investigator's career is totally people oriented. Investigation is concerned, directly and indirectly, with and about people. Thus, private investigators need to feel at home with them, understand, motivate, and communicate with them."[15] Without sufficient human relations skills, security specialists operate at a continuous disadvantage. At a minimum, an investigator must be able to accomplish the following:

1. To express positive attitudes towards others.
2. To be able to manifest interest in others.
3. To be able to build a good human relations.
4. To be able to express empathy and concern for others.
5. To be able to establish a good rapport with others.
6. To be able to adapt to different personalities and circumstances.
7. To be able to communicate effectively with others.
8. To be a believable personality.
9. To be clear and accurate in communications with others.
10. To be able to persuade and motivate other people.
11. To be able to effectively manage conversations and to elicit information.
12. To understand the emotional strengths and weaknesses of others.
13. To exercise control of one's emotions.
14. To be able to make friends rather than enemies.[16]

Another measure of human relations skills is the art of communication itself. Most people think of communication as verbal or written; however, nonverbal communication also plays a role in investigative practice. Nonverbal communication includes body language and an awareness of sensory perceptions, such as sight, smell, taste, hearing, and touch. Investigators must be attuned to human and environmental conditions. "'Why' people instinctively like or dislike others; trust or fear them; are attracted to or repelled by others is too complex for us to study definitively. [Investigators] must be aware that their total communication effort is affected by the impression they give others, whether in the form of body odors (good or bad), facial expressions, 'body language,' voice tone, phrasing, and vocabulary, or writing style and technique."[17]

Common sense dictates that information-gathering and fact assimilation and collection will be easier for those who can skillfully interact with others. From another perspective, certain personality traits plainly benefit an investigator. A partial listing of those personality traits and characteristics and part of a solid investigator has been posed by Art Buckwalter, in his very worthy work *Investigative Methods*:

- *Alert*—ready and quick to understand or act; aware
- *Believable*—one whom other persons can believe and trust
- *Calm*—able to control emotions; free from agitation and excitement
- *Common sense*—down-to-earth, good judgment
- *Dependable*—worthy of being depended on; reliable and trustworthy
- *Determined*—resolute; able to see an investigation through to its finish
- *Honest*—truthful, frank, honorable, and straightforward in conduct or speech
- *Impartial*—unbiased, equitable, free from favoritism, fair
- *Ingenious*—possessed of inventive ingenuity, shrewd, capable of creating a clever and effective solution to an investigative problem
- *Law-abiding*—conforms to or lives in accordance with the law
- *Level-headed*—has sound judgment, balanced reasoning
- *Objective*—able to concentrate on facts and external aspects of investigation without focusing on subjective feelings
- *Observant*—takes careful notice; with keen powers of observation
- *Patient*—capable of calm waiting and forbearance under provocation; undaunted by obstacles and delays
- *Perceptive*—discerning, aware; has alert senses
- *Persistent*—tenacious, dogged, able to see the problem through
- *Prudent*—capable of directing and conducting oneself wisely and judiciously; discreet, sensible, reasonable, and skillful in the application of capabilities
- *Remembers well*—capable of recollection and recall
- *Responsible*—accountable, reliable; able to answer for own conduct and obligations and to assume trust
- *Resourceful*—able to fall back on other sources or strategies when the usual means are not effective; has reserve abilities and alternative resources
- *Thorough*—able to carry things through to completion; painstaking, exact, and careful about details
- *Versatile*—has many aptitudes, circumstances, and situations that require change in tactics or positions[18]

See Figure 2.2 from Denver Security Services, which emphasizes these traits.

VI. ETHICS AND THE INVESTIGATIVE PROCESS

The qualities of objectivity, logic, perseverance, and diligence, along with formidable interpersonal skills, represent mandatory attributes of the competent investigator. However, these traits need to be coupled with an ethical and professional philosophy. In short, the security specialist must have an ethical compass that guides these practices. Ethics are the stuff of good and moral conduct. In most cases, the security professional inherently knows what correct conduct is. Even so, this same

FIGURE 2.2 Denver Security Services Website.

specialist must learn to weigh and evaluate the ethical parameters of each action chosen during the investigative operation. Ethics must always be in the forefront of security practice.[19] Without ethical parameters, investigative practice may lose its legal and moral legitimacy. Those who disregard principles of civilized conduct, who fail to adhere to moral and legal values, and disregard professional behavior that is consistent with democratic notions cause both individual and collective harm. Aside from abridging a particular legal or human right, a lack of ethics undermines the legitimacy of a particular investigation and calls into question its legality. The security industry fully recognizes the correlation between ethics and acceptable investigative practice. Pinkerton's, Inc., the premier security firm, publishes rules of conduct for all employees. See Figure 2.3.[20]

Pinkerton's is highly concerned with the ethical dimensions of its employees. Pinkerton's strives to hire individuals of good character who possess the attributes of truthfulness, honesty, and loyalty. Given the contemporary decline of universal perceptions of what is moral, good, and true, and the emergence of conflicting ethical schemes, it has become a more complex task to ensure ethical individual and institutional conduct. Attempts have been made, at the legislative level, to promulgate minimum ethical standards. Government authorities are increasingly involved in delienating acceptable practices in the security industry. The State of Illinois defines good character and professionalism by defining various types of unprofessional conduct. See Figure 2.4.[21]

Similarly, the National Advisory Committee on Criminal Justice Standards and Goals, in its report "The Task Force on Private Security," presented in Figure 2.5,[22] has promulgated a Code of Ethics for the security firm managers.

The American Society for Industrial Security (ASIS), since renamed ASIS International, the premier professional association of the security industry, promulgates a Code of Ethics that guides the industry and the particulars of investigative practice. See Figure 2.6.[23] Previous to this promulgation, ASIS heavily depended upon its 1980 Code, which is reproduced in Figure 2.7 for historical purposes.

The question of ethics is both a moral and practical one. The security industry has had chronic difficulties with the high attrition rates of personnel and the low quality of both applicants and currently employed personnel. This revolving door of personnel is a vicious circle, usually triggered by low salaries and little or no training, which in turn translates into the hiring of marginal personnel.

The Company and its employees shall not:

1. Engage in any unlawful activity or use unethical or reprehensible practices to obtain information, or engage in any controversial or scandalous case which might damage the Company's reputation.
2. Accept business from persons with disreputable reputations, or from those engaged in an illegitimate, disreputable, or questionable enterprise.
3. Induce a person to commit a crime entrapment.
4. Knowingly engage in work for one client against the interest of another client.
5. Guarantee success, or accept business for a fee contingent upon success.
6. Accept rewards or gratuities or permit its employees to do so.
7. Engage in work in behalf of a defendant in a criminal action.
8. Compromise with felons, or negotiate for the return of stolen property.
9. Seize repossess property without due process of law.
10. Obtain secret formulas, processes, designs, records, the names of customers, or other private business information.
11. Represent claimants against insurance companies and self-insurers.
12. Shadow jurors.
13. Engage in wiretapping.
14. Collect amounts.
15. Investigate the morals of women, except in criminal cases or on behalf of their employers.
16. Obtain information or evidence for use in divorce actions.
17. Investigate public officers in the performance of their official duties.
18. Investigate a political party for another.
19. Investigate the lawful activities of a labor union.
20. Report the union affiliations of employees or prospective employees.
21. Report the events transpiring at labor union meetings or conventions, except those open to the public without restrictions.
22. Shadow officers, organizers, or members of a labor union for the purpose of reporting their lawful union organizing, or other lawful activities.
23. Supply the names of union members, officers, organizers, or sympathizers.
24. Report to employers the reaction and attitude of employees and union officers and representatives expressed or implied, with respect to union organizing or bargaining processes.
25. Arrange to report on the lawful organizational activities of employees and their collective bargaining processes, irrespective of whether the report be made to an employee of the Company or indirectly to the client.
26. Supply persons to take the place of those on strike.
27. Furnish armed guards upon the highways for persons involved in labor disputes.
28. Interfere with or prevent lawful picketing during labor controversies.
29. Transport in interstate commerce any person with the intent of employing such person to obstruct or interfere with lawful picketing.
30. Furnish to employers any arms or ammunition, etc.

FIGURE 2.3 Pinkerton ethical guidelines.

With substandard employees comes substandard investigative practice. The industry is fully aware of its compelling need to increase the ethical and professional demands on its personnel. So pressing is this issue that the U.S. Department of Justice formulated a National Task Force and Advisory Committee on the status of private security, focusing on both the industry and its employees, that sets forth some minimal standards of qualification, conduct, and goals. Standard 1.8, reprinted in Figure 2.8,[24] outlines the preemployment screening qualifications.

It is unlawful to:

1. Interfere with, restrain, or coerce employees to join or assist any labor union.
2. Interfere with or hinder the lawful collective bargaining between employees and employers.
3. Pay, offer, or give any money, gratuity, favor, consideration, or anything of value, directly or indirectly, to any person for any oral or written report of the membership meetings, or lawful activities of any labor union, or for any written or oral report of the lawful activities of employees in their collective bargaining processes in the exercise of their right of self-organization.
4. Advise orally or in writing anyone of the membership of an individual in a labor organization.
5. Supply persons to take the place of those on strike.
6. Furnish armed guards upon the highways for persons involved in labor disputes.
7. Interfere with or prevent lawful picketing during labor disputes.
8. Transport in interstate commerce any person with the intent to employ such person to obstruct or interfere with peaceful picketing.
9. Furnish to employers arms or munitions, etc.
10. Attempt to influence anyone to disclose records or information made secret by law and not available to the public.
11. Obtain business secrets.
12. Obtain names of customers.
13. Tap wires.
14. Eavesdrop.
15. Possess or carry a weapon without being licensed to do so. (In some states.)
16. Impersonate a law enforcement officer.
17. Shadow jurors.
18. Compound a felony.
19. Collect accounts. In some states.
20. Report on the race, color, religion, and place or origin of any person. (In some states.)
21. Wear a Military Uniform without authority.

FIGURE 2.3 (continued).

Robert J. Gallati attacks the issue of personnel qualification head on:

> Personnel issues are raised, relative to the selection of qualified personnel in both the proprietary and contract security area. Inadequate salaries and the lack of career-development emphasis create high attrition rates, with the consequent need to hire more and more persons. …
>
> Due to the highly competitive nature of contract security, plus the high turnover rates, the cost of adequate training becomes a factor in the bidding process. …
>
> Should there be mandatory qualifications for every security employee? Should these qualifications apply to both the selection and training …? Should there be federal minimum standards, or state or local regulations? How would such regulations be enforced?[25]

The questions and problems posed by Gallati, as well as numerous other experts in the field of private security, are becoming commonplace critiques. It is a fact that the industry suffers from internal turnover and early career plateaus.[26] It is a fact that pay scales are low, even though improving. It is a fact that investigators who have the perseverance, diligence, logic, objectivity, and enhanced skills of human relations will not fully develop these attributes if they are not well trained, well compensated, and guided on a path of high ethical expectations. "The industry itself should zealously rectify any deficiencies in the matter of regulation. Its credibility depends upon enactment."[27] Bottom and Kostanoski concur:

Sec. 40-10. Disciplinary sanctions.

(a) The Department may deny issuance, refuse to renew, or restore or may reprimand, place on probation, suspend, revoke, or take other disciplinary or non-disciplinary action against any license, registration, permanent employee registration card, canine handler authorization card, canine trainer authorization card, or firearm control card, and may impose a fine not to exceed $10,000 for each violation for any of the following:

(1) Fraud or deception in obtaining or renewing of a license or registration.

(2) Professional incompetence as manifested by poor standards of service.

(3) Engaging in dishonorable, unethical, or unprofessional conduct of a character likely to deceive, defraud, or harm the public.

(4) Conviction of or entry of a plea of guilty or nolo contendere in Illinois or another state of any crime that is a felony under the laws of Illinois; a felony in a federal court; a misdemeanor, an essential element of which is dishonesty; or directly related to professional practice.

(5) Performing any services in a grossly negligent manner or permitting any of a licensee's employees to perform services in a grossly negligent manner, regardless of whether actual damage to the public is established.

(6) Continued practice, although the person has become unfit to practice due to any of the following:

(A) Physical illness, mental illness, or other impairment, including, but not limited to, deterioration through the aging process or loss of motor skills that results in the inability to serve the public with reasonable judgment, skill, or safety.

(B) Mental disability demonstrated by the entry of an order or judgment by a court that a person is in need of mental treatment or is incompetent.

(C) Addiction to or dependency on alcohol or drugs that is likely to endanger the public. If the Department has reasonable cause to believe that a person is addicted to or dependent on alcohol or drugs that may endanger the public, the Department may require the person to undergo an examination to determine the extent of the addiction or dependency.

(7) Receiving, directly or indirectly, compensation for any services not rendered.

(8) Willfully deceiving or defrauding the public on a material matter.

(9) Failing to account for or remit any moneys or documents coming into the licensee's possession that belong to another person or entity.

(10) Discipline by another United States jurisdiction or foreign nation, if at least one of the grounds for the discipline is the same or substantially equivalent to those set forth in this Act.

(11) Giving differential treatment to a person that is to that person's detriment because of race, color, creed, sex, religion, or national origin.

(12) Engaging in false or misleading advertising.

(13) Aiding, assisting, or willingly permitting another person to violate this Act or rules promulgated under it.

(14) Performing and charging for services without authorization to do so from the person or entity serviced.

FIGURE 2.4 State of Illinois' definitions of unprofessional conduct.

(15) Directly or indirectly offering or accepting any benefit to or from any employee, agent, or fiduciary without the consent of the latter's employer or principal with intent to or the understanding that this action will influence his or her conduct in relation to his or her employer's or principal's affairs.
(16) Violation of any disciplinary order imposed on a licensee by the Department.
(17) Failing to comply with any provision of this Act or rule promulgated under it.
(18) Conducting an agency without a valid license.
(19) Revealing confidential information, except as required by law, including but not limited to information available under Section 2-123 of the Illinois Vehicle Code.
(20) Failing to make available to the Department, upon request, any books, records, or forms required by this Act.
(21) Failing, within 30 days, to respond to a written request for information from the Department.
(22) Failing to provide employment information or experience information required by the Department regarding an applicant for licensure.
(23) Failing to make available to the Department at the time of the request any indicia of licensure or registration issued under this Act.
(24) Purporting to be a licensee-in-charge of an agency without active participation in the agency.

(b) The Department shall seek to be consistent in the application of disciplinary sanctions.

(c) The Department shall adopt rules that set forth standards of service for the following:

(i) acceptable error rate in the transmission of fingerprint images and other data to the Department of State Police;
(ii) acceptable error rate in the collection and documentation of information used to generate fingerprint work orders; and
(iii) any other standard of service that affects fingerprinting services as determined by the Department.

(Source: P.A. 95-613, eff. 9-11-07.)

FIGURE 2.4 (continued).

> Ethical problems give security and loss control an image problem. Often, it is the employer who needs an ethical overhaul. Business, in general, has an image problem. …
>
> Security and loss control is responsive to the demands of the employer. If the employer lacks ethics, it cannot be surprising that the security department has ethical shortcomings. Even if the security department has no part in the unethical conduct, the public is likely to tar all employees with the same brush.[28]

No investigative process can reach its full potential if its operatives are viewed as downtrodden or second-rate professionals. Public respect plays an integral role in the investigator's ability to function. If private security operatives are continually under suspicion, both occupationally and personally, their access to facilities and information will be substantially restricted. This image problem must be cleared up if public respect is to be gained. The challenge is to improve the image of this industry and convince the public that security and loss control is more than a uniformed guard leaning against a mall interior.

CODE OF ETHICS FOR PRIVATE SECURITY MANAGEMENT

As managers of private security functions and employees, we pledge:

I. To recognize that our principal responsibilities are, in the service of our organizations and clients, to protect life and property as well as to prevent and reduce crime against our business, industry, or other organizations and institutions; and in the public interest, to uphold the law and to respect the constitutional rights of all persons.
II. To be guided by a sense of integrity, honor, justice and morality in the conduct of business; in all personnel matters; in relationships with government agencies, clients, and employers; and in responsibilities to the general public.
III. To strive faithfully to render security services of the highest quality and to work continuously to improve our knowledge and skills and thereby improve the overall effectiveness of private security.
IV. To uphold the trust of our employers, our clients, and the public by performing our functions within the law, not ordering or condoning violations of the law, and ensuring that our security personnel conduct their assigned duties lawfully and with proper regard for the rights of others.
V. To respect the reputation and practice of others in private security, but to expose to the proper authorities any conduct that is unethical or unlawful.
VI. To apply uniform and equitable standards of employment in recruiting and selecting personnel regardless of race, creed, color, sex, or age, and in providing salaries commensurate with job responsibilities and with training, education, and experience.
VII. To cooperate with recognized and responsible law enforcement and other criminal justice agencies; to comply with security licensing and registration laws and other statutory requirements that pertain to our business.
VIII. To respect and protect the confidential and privileged information of employers and clients beyond the term of our employment, except where their interests are contrary to law or to this Code of Ethics.
IX. To maintain a professional posture in all business relationships with employers and clients, with others in the private security field, and with members of other professions; and to insist that our personnel adhere to the highest standards of professional conduct.
X. To encourage the professional advancement of our personnel by assisting them to acquire appropriate security knowledge, education, and training.

FIGURE 2.5 Code of ethics for private security managers and employees.

The National Task Force and Advisory Committee, at Goal 2.1, holds:

> The responsibilities assumed by private security personnel in the protection of persons and property require training. Training should be instituted at all levels to insure that personnel are fully prepared to exercise the responsibilities effectively and efficiently.[29]

Goal 3.1 of the same Advisory Committee calls for a Code of Ethics to be adopted and enforced by all private security personnel and their employers. Finally, Standard 3.2 holds that private security personnel should perform their security functions within the generally recognized guidelines for the protection of individual rights. See Figure 2.9.[30]

In sum, the private security industry needs to address both the ethical and professional dimensions of its undertaking. Practitioners, academicians, management, and legislators all concur on these and other challenges in the industry's future.

Code Of Ethics

Aware that the quality of professional security activity ultimately depends upon the willingness of practitioners to observe special standards of conduct and to manifest good faith in professional relationships, ASIS International (ASIS) adopts the following Code of Ethics and mandates its conscientious observance as a binding condition of membership in or affiliation with the organization:

ARTICLE I

A member shall perform professional duties in accordance with the law and the highest moral principles.

ARTICLE II

A member shall observe the precepts of truthfulness, honesty, and integrity.

ARTICLE III

A member shall be faithful and diligent in discharging professional responsibilities.

ARTICLE IV

A member shall be competent in discharging professional responsibilities.

ARTICLE V

A member shall safeguard confidential information and exercise due care to prevent its improper disclosure.

ARTICLE VI

A member shall not maliciously injure the professional reputation or practice of colleagues, clients, or employers.

NOTE: *Reference Policy 1080 from Policy & Procedures Manual*

FIGURE 2.6 ASIS International code of ethics. ASIS was previously known as the American Society for Industrial Security.

ASIS Code of Ethics and Ethical Considerations

Approved June 27, 1980

Preamble

Aware that the quality of professional security activity ultimately depends upon the willingness of practitioners to observe special standards of conduct and to manifest good faith in professional relationships, the American Society for Industrial Security adopts the following Code of Ethics and mandates its conscientious observance as a binding condition of membership in or affiliation with the society.

Code of Ethics

I. A member shall perform professional duties in accordance with the law and the highest moral principles.
II. A member shall observe the precepts of truthfulness, honesty, and integrity.
III. A member shall be faithful and diligent in discharging professional responsibilities.
IV. A member shall be competent in discharging professional responsibilities.
V. A member shall safeguard confidential information and exercise due care to prevent its improper disclosure.
VI. A member shall not maliciously injure the professional reputation or practice of colleagues, clients, or employers.

Ethical Considerations on Article I

I-1. A member shall abide by the law of the land in which the services are rendered and perform all duties in an honorable manner.
I-2. A member shall not knowingly become associated in responsibility for work with colleagues who do not conform to the law and these ethical standards.
I-3. A member shall be just and respect the rights of others in performing professional responsibilities.

Ethical Considerations on Article II

II-1. A member shall disclose all relevant information to those having a right to know.
II-2. A right to know is a legally enforceable claim or demand by a person for disclosure of information by a member. Such a right does not depend upon prior knowledge by the person of the existence of the information to be disclosed.
II-3. A member shall not knowingly release misleading information, nor encourage or otherwise participate in the release of such information.

Ethical Considerations on Article III

III-1. A member is faithful when fair and steadfast in adherence to promises and commitments.
III-2. A member is diligent when employing best efforts in an assignment.
III-3. A member shall not act in matters involving conflicts of interest without appropriate disclosure and approval.
III-4. A member shall represent services or products fairly and truthfully.

FIGURE 2.7 ASIS code of ethics and ethical considerations. With permission.

Ethical Considerations on Article IV

IV-1. A member is competent who possesses and applies the skills and knowledge required for the task.

IV-2. A member shall not accept a task beyond the member's competence nor shall competence be claimed when not possessed.

Ethical Considerations on Article V

V-1. Confidential information is non-public information the disclosure of which is restricted.

V-2. Due care requires that the professional must not knowingly reveal confidential information or use a confidence to the disadvantage of the principal or to the advantage of the member or a third person unless the principal consents after full disclosure of all the facts. This confidentiality continues after the business relationship between the member and his principal has terminated.

V-3. A member who receives information and has not agreed to be bound by confidentiality is not bound from disclosing it. A member is not bound by confidential disclosures made of acts or omissions that constitute a violation of the law.

V-4. Confidential disclosures made by a principal to a member are not recognized by law as privileged in a legal proceeding. The member may be required to testify in a legal proceeding to information received in confidence from his principal over the objection of his principal's counsel.

V-5. A member shall not disclose confidential information for personal gain without appropriate authorization.

Ethical Considerations on Article VI

VI-1. A member shall not comment falsely and with malice concerning a colleague's competence, performance, or professional capabilities.

VI-2. A member who knows, or has reasonable grounds to believe, that another member has failed to conform to the Society's Code of Ethics shall present such information to the Ethical Standards Committee in accordance with Article XIV of the Society's Bylaws.

FIGURE 2.7 (continued).

Standard 1.8

Minimum Pre-employment Screening Qualifications

The following minimum pre-employment screening qualifications should be established for private security personnel:

1. Minimum age of 18;
2. High school diploma or equivalent written examination;
3. Written examination to determine ability to understand and perform duties assigned;
4. No record of conviction, as stated in Standard 1.7;
5. Minimum physical standards;
   a. Armed personnel—vision correctable to 20/20 (Snellen) in each eye and capable of hearing ordinary conversation at a distance of 10 feet with each ear without benefit of a hearing aid.
   b. Others—no physical defects that would hinder job performance.

FIGURE 2.8 Private security personnel minimum pre-employment screening qualifications.

Advisory Committee Goals 3.1 and 3.2

Goal 3.1—Code of Ethics

A code of ethics should be adopted and enforced for private security personnel and employers.

Goal 3.2—Conduct of Private Security Personnel

Private security personnel should perform their security functions within generally recognized guidelines for the protection of individual rights.

FIGURE 2.9 Advisory committee goals.

NOTES

1. Russell Colling, *Hospital Security* (Butterworth Publishers, 1982), 221.
2. *Id.*; see also the historic role investigative services have played in the world of private security and private protection in Charles P. Nemeth and K. C. Poulin, *Private Security and Public Safety: A Community Based Approach* (Pearson-Prentice Hall, 2005), 22.
3. A. Markle, *Criminal Investigation and Presentation of Evidence* 1 (West Publishing, 1976), 1.
4. Art Buckwalter, *Investigative Methods* (Butterworth Publishers, 1984), 36.
5. Karl Ask and Pär Anders Granhag, "Hot Cognition in Investigative Judgments: The Differential Influence of Anger and Sadness," *Law Hum. Behav.* 31 (2007), 537–551.
6. Norman R. Bottom and John Kostanoski, *Introduction to Security and Loss Control* (Prentice Hall, 1990), 26.
7. Rick Sarre, Book Review, *Crim. J. Rev.* 34 (2009), 142 (reviewing Frank MacHovec, *Private Investigation and Security Science: A Scientific Approach*, 3rd ed. [Charles C. Thomas, 2006]).
8. Wayne W. Bennett and Karen M. Hess, *Criminal Investigation* (West Publishing, 1976), 11.
9. Walter J. Buzby and David Paine, *Hotel and Motel Security Management* (Butterworth Publishers, 1976), 122–123.
10. Edward T. Guy, John J. Merrigan, and John S. Wanat, *Forms for Safety and Security Management* (Butterworth Publishers, 1981), 128.
11. E. Smith, *Practical Guide for Investigators* (Paladin Press, 1982), 34.
12. Patricia W. Kittredge, "Guideposts for the Investigation of a Negligence Case," *Prac. Law.* 90 (1973), 55; J. Stannar Baker, "Reconstruction of Accidents," *Traffic Dig. Rev.* 17 (1969), 9; P. Magarick, "Investigating the Civil Case: General Principles," *Am. Jur. Trials* 1 (1987), 361.
13. *Am. Jur. Trials.* 1 (1987), 357, 365.
14. Bennett and Hess, *supra* note 8, at 13.
15. Questions regarding the value of education in human interaction have been long analyzed in the criminal justice sector, in both the public and private setting. See Philip Carlan, "Do Officers Value Their Degrees?" *Law Order.* (December 2006), 59.
16. Buckwalter, *supra* note 4, at 36.
17. *Id.* at 35–47.
18. National Association of Legal Assistants, *Manual for Legal Assistants* (West Publishing, 1979), 10.
19. Buckwalter, *supra* note 4, at 47–49.
20. Robert D. McCrie, "ASIS Intl. Takes Risks with Guidelines Commission Strategy," Security Letter, November 15, 2003; "ASIS Publishes Standards for Professionals," Corporate Security, January 31, 2003 (2001); Mary Lynn Garcia, "Personal Opinion: Raising the Bar for Security Professionals," *Security J.* 13 (2000), 79.
21. Courtesy of Pinkerton's, Inc.
22. 225 Ill. Comp. Stat. 447/40-10 (2004).

23. U.S. Department of Justice, LEAA, National Advisory Committee on Criminal Justice Standards and Goals, Report of the Task Force on Private Security (1976). U.S. Gov't. Printing Office, Washington, DC.
24. See ASIS International, Code of Ethics, available at http://www.asisonline.org/membership/resources/codeofethics.pdf, visited August 28, 2009.
25. National Advisory Committee on Criminal Justice Standards and Goals, *Private Security: Report of the Task Force on Private Security* (U.S. Department of Justice, Law Enforcement Assistance Administration, 1976), 82.
26. Robert R. Gallati, *Introduction to Private Security* (Prentice Hall, 1983), 269.
27. "Executive Security Focus of New Course," *Forensic Examiner.* 17 (2008), 64; Dennis W. Bowman, "Comparing Law Enforcement Accreditation and Private Security Standards," *J. Security.* 26 (2003), 17; Bruce Mandelblit, "A Sorry State of Security?" *Security.* (April 2003), 54.
28. Nemeth and Poulin, *supra* note 2, at 308.
29. Bottom and Kostanoski, *supra* note 6, at 37–38.
30. National Advisory Committee, *supra* note 24, at 89.
31. *Id.* at 123, 126.

3 Initial Interview and Case Evaluation

I. INTRODUCTION

Communication skills, especially during interviews with a prospective or existing client, witness, suspect, or other party, are a core competency for the investigator. How to ask questions and gain information should not be assumed to be an easy skill to master. In fact, it is safe to say that the art of investigation and questioning takes years to perfect. Interviews are but one of those stages where the questions mean a great deal. An interview can encompass many purposes, including an initial visitation with a prospective client, an ongoing dialogue with a long-term client, an observational review and analysis of a witness or suspect statement, an interrogation of a suspected wrongdoer, a character assessment by a suspect's neighbor, or a background information check. In any of these scenarios, the private investigator must gauge his or her time and energy wisely. Knowing the difference between idle chitchat and productive discussion is essential.

At a minimum, an interview is a conversation designed to garner facts and clarify issues. Viewed positively, the interview is human interaction between the interviewer and the respondent. "Properly handled, an interview is an accurate communication of information; improperly handled, it can become a serious source of bias restricting or distorting the communication flow."[1]

Whatever the circumstances and conditions surrounding the interview process, certain practices are universal.

1. Select a time and a place that is mutually convenient.
2. Prepare in advance for an interview.
3. Begin the interview on a cooperative and pleasant note.
4. Establish rapport with the respondent or interviewee.

Without preparation, the interview will be a flawed exercise from the outset. Knowing what to ask, how the issues course through the selected questions, and being able to conduct a meaningful post-assessment of the interview are just a few parts of the interview protocol. "The issues to be discussed and the questions to be asked must be clear before the interview. In complicated discussions, the investigator may decide to list objectives and questions in advance, but the list should not be used during the actual interview."[2]

On a practical note, information is more easily acquired when the investigator acts professionally and treats the respondent with the courtesy and dignity that all people expect and to which they are entitled. See Figure 3.1 for an example of the importance of these traits in an actual company.

II. INITIAL INTERVIEW

Many times, the first step in a investigation is the interview of either a client, suspect, victim, witness, plaintiff, or defendant. At the initial interview, the security officer's interactive talents are put to the test. At this stage, the investigator sets the tone for the upcoming investigative process. Success in the initial interview depends on the following principles:

FIGURE 3.1 Able Investigations Website.

1. That a client's confidences are respected.
2. That a client's cooperation is secured.
3. That the investigator is friendly, courteous, and polite at all times.
4. That the investigator practices the art of conversation.
5. That the investigator exudes confidence and reassures the client.
6. That the investigator promotes a good, positive attitude on behalf of the firm he or she represents.
7. That all information collected is an accurate presentation of the client's representations.
8. That regular and constant communication is necessary to insure subsequent releases of information called for in the initial interview.[3]

Letting the client, witness, or other interested party subject to the interview know that he or she is both welcome and needed promotes a positive interview environment. "An attitude of superiority on the part of the investigator should be avoided. Many people may not have had the educational opportunities that may have been offered to the investigator and nothing antagonizes these people more quickly than a patronizing attitude. Therefore, the investigator should try to meet everyone on as close to an equal level as possible and should show friendship toward those whom he intends to interview."[4]

Whether or not information is free-flowing and naturally forthcoming largely depends on the investigator's capacity to create an environment conducive to discussion. Although an oral exchange can be both pleasant and easy to manage, it is an inadequate way of obtaining formal information and the foundational support necessary for case development. Because of this, the best practice that security investigators can adopt is the use of forms, checklists, fact-gathering sheets, and other written instruments for the purpose of initial information collection.

Major contract or proprietary security firms have implemented uniform, standardized procedures. Pinkerton's "Schedule of Investigation Service" (SOIS), shown in Figure 3.2, organizes preliminary personal, financial, and contractual terms and obligations that are required. The reverse side of the document contains terms and conditions related to fees and costs, loss liability, and general rights and obligations of the parties. This document is a critical component of the initial interview for prospective or existing clients.

SCHEDULE OF INVESTIGATION SERVICE

DISTRICT NAME DISTRICT NUMBER

CLIENT NO. DATE

NEW CHANGE CANCEL

CLIENT PURCHASE ORDER NUMBER

OPERATION

CLAIM NUMBER

SEND REPORTS AND BILLS TO:

COMPANY NAME

STREET ADDRESS

CITY, STATE, ZIP

ATTENTION OF:

TITLE

( ) –

TELEPHONE

PERSONAL AND CONFIDENTIAL ____________

CLIENT BUSINESS ADDRESS

COMPANY NAME

STREET ADDRESS

CITY, STATE, ZIP

( ) –

TELEPHONE

REMARKS/CAUTIONS ____________

SERVICE RATES/SUPPLEMENTAL CHARGES

SERVICE RATE/HOUR $____________

AUTO EXPENSE/MILE $____________

MAX. TELEPHONE & EXP $____________

RETAINER $____________

ADDITIONAL EXPENSES ____________

REVENUES: ☐ TAXABLE ☐ NON-TAXABLE STATE/COUNTY/CITY ____________

INVOICES: ______ # COPIES ________ ______ DL BEST & ASSOCIATES ______ **REPORTS:** ______ # COPIES FORM ______

SUBJECT DESCRIPTION:

NAME

STREET ADDRESS

CITY, STATE, ZIP

TELEPHONE

☐ CURRENT ☐ LAST KNOWN

SEX ______ OTHER ______

COLOR ______ MARITAL STATUS ______

AGE/DOB ______ SSN ______

HEIGHT ______ AUTOMOBILE ______

WEIGHT ______ LIC. NO. ______

OCCUPATION CURRENT/LAST EMPLOYER

PROBLEMS REFERRED TO DISTRICT NAME/NUMBER ____________

DETAILED

INVESTIGATION SERVICE ACCEPTED SUBJECT TO TERMS AND CONDITIONS CONTAINED ON REVERSE

NAME OF CLIENT

AUTHORIZED REPRESENTATIVE

TITLE DATE

AUTHORIZED REPRESENTATIVE

TITLE DATE

SALES

DISTRICT SECURITY OFFICE ☐ DIRECT SALES ☐ REFERRAL ☐ OTHER ☐ PREVIOUS CLIENT ☐
TELEPHONE DIRECTORY ☐ HOUSE ☐

FIGURE 3.2 Investigation service schedule.

TERMS AND CONDITIONS

I. INVESTIGATIVE SERVICES

a. Client and _________'s Inc. (hereinafter described as "_________") hereby mutually agree that _________ shall furnish investigative services of the type, and at the rate, and at the location described on the reverse side hereof. Such service will be provided in accordance with and shall be subject to all of the terms and conditions hereof.

II. SCOPE OF SERVICE

a. The conduct and scope of responsibility of all investigators assigned to Client and the scope of investigative services and Client's objectives shall be set forth in and governed by this agreement and any letter or memorandum of understanding mutually agreed to by both parties, which may be revised and supplemented at any time in writing upon mutual agreement of both parties.
b. Should Client unilaterally attempt to alter this agreement, prepare any related letter or memorandum of understanding, give directions to the investigator, or assume any supervision of the investigator, Client shall be solely responsible for any and all consequences arising therefrom.
c. No information will be developed or supplied dealing with the lawful organizational activities and collective bargaining processes of Client's employees or of any labor union.

III. FEES AND COSTS

a. Client shall pay _________ for its investigative services in accordance with the fees contained on the reverse side hereof. Client also agrees to reimburse to _________ all costs and expenses incurred by _________ in the performance of its services as set forth in _________ invoices.
b. All of _________ invoices are payable by Client to _________ upon presentation to Client, without offset of any kind or nature whatsoever. In the event of an error or dispute on an invoice, Client agrees to promptly pay the undisputed portion of the invoice. Client agrees to pay _________ one and one-half percent (1 ½%) per month interest or such maximum amount as permitted by law, whichever is less, on any invoice not paid within thirty (30) days of invoice date. In the event that legal action is necessary to enforce this or any other provision of this agreement, Client agrees to pay the costs and attorney's fees of _________.

IV. RESPONSIBILITY FOR LOSS

a. _________ will use its best efforts in the performance of the requested services, however, _________ does not make any representations or guarantee concerning the result of its investigative services, and no warranty, express or implied, is included in this contract or otherwise made by _________.
b. _________ shall be responsible only for the content of and the methods of obtaining the information supplied to Client and not for the usage of that information by Client. Client agrees to defend, indemnify and hold _________ harmless from any and all legal actions, losses, claims, demands, liabilities, causes of action, judgments, costs or expenses imposed upon _________ as a result of Client's utilization of information supplied by _________.

V. UNDERCOVER

a. In the event Client requires the use of one or more employees of _________ working undercover, Client agrees to the usage of such undercover personnel and expressly authorizes _________ to place such person in Client's business. Said undercover personal shall at all times remain solely under the employ of _________ while appearing to be an employee of Client. Client agrees to provide any and all credentials and means of identification which may be necessary to give such undercover personnel the appearance of being employees of Client. It is understood and acknowledged by Client that said undercover personnel may be at risk during such simulated employment and that their safety may be seriously endangered if their true capacity is discovered by regular employees of Client. Therefore, Client agrees that both during and after any undercover operation, to use all possible discretion and secrecy to protect the identity of undercover personnel and to reveal such identity only to such persons as are necessary and consistent with the performance of the undercover operation. Client agrees to indemnify and hold _________ harmless from and against any and all claims, damages, actions, losses, demands, liabilities, causes of actions, judgments, costs or expenses of any kind which _________ may sustain as a result of injuries to undercover personnel resulting from the negligence or other fault of Client or of Client's employees.

VI. GENERAL

a. _________ shall retain the right in its sole discretion to subcontract any or all of its services under this contract and to delegate responsibility for performance of services. _________ may at its own expense retain the assistance of such other persons or entities as it may deem necessary or advisable.
b. This contract and the services covered thereunder may be terminated immediately by either party without cause and without penalty upon written notification to the other.
c. This agreement is entered into solely for the mutual benefits of the signatory parties, and no benefits, rights, duties, or obligations are intended or created by this agreement as to any third parties.
d. Client and _________ agree that if any of the terms and provisions of this agreement shall be invalid or inoperative, all the remaining terms and provisions shall remain in full force and effect.
e. The entire agreement of the parties is expressed herein, and no understandings, agreements, purchase orders, work orders, or other documents shall modify the terms and conditions of this agreement. _________ expressly limits acceptance to the terms and conditions herein, which acceptance may be evidenced by either representative of Client executing this agreement or by Client accepting the services performed by _________.
f. No modifications of the terms and conditions of this agreement shall be binding upon _________ unless approved in writing by an authorized representative of _________.
g. This agreement must be signed by an authorized representative of Client before investigation reports are released.
h. The obligations of Client pursuant to Articles III, IVb, and V, shall survive the expiration, completion, and/or earlier termination of this agreement.
i. _________ is an equal opportunity employer. All federal EEO and affirmative action requirements in reference to race, sex, religion, national origin, handicap and Vietnam veterans or disabled veterans status as found in 41 CFR 60-1.4, 60-250.3 and 60-741.3 are herein incorporated by reference.

FIGURE 3.2 (continued).

A. Miscellaneous Matters at Initial Interview

1. Authorization and Release

Information gathering depends not only on knowing what information is desired but also on having access to it. An Authority to Release Information form should be completed during the initial interview stage, which grants the authorized party access to every record listed at Figure 3.3.

2. Information or Fact Sheets

Before conducting any interview, make sure of the objectives of the interview. If the security officer has been hired by another, it is important to evaluate the request closely and accurately. As an example, the insurance industry contracts with proprietary security firms for claims investigation. A requisition document, general to the industry, portrays the parameters of information to be gathered in the initial interview. See Figure 3.4.

The initial interview may focus more narrowly on the specific action or investigative purpose. The Personal Injury Information Worksheet, shown in Figure 3.5, is used for the compilation of background information, pertinent data on the client's legal representation, economic and personal injury losses, and insurance policy information.

1. Investigators are frequently asked to identify, list, and discover parties in a personal injury lawsuit. What types of parties, that is, plaintiffs and defendants, are possible?
2. In a property, vehicular, or related claim, the defendant's insurance policies are reviewed for policy limits. Why is the plaintiff's policy only viewed for purposes of uninsured limit?
3. What is a salutation, and why is it important to put it in?

An abridged version of an accident fact sheet is provided in Figure 3.6. This type of document should be placed in the beginning of the file or permanently affixed to the inside cover of the file for easy access for other parties who need to examine the file.

Auto accidents generate an early need for reliable information. Information-gathering at the initial interview sets the stage for all subsequent investigative activities. Figure 3.7 calculates the extent and severity of personal injuries resulting from an auto accident.

1. Why does the form distinguish between immediate injuries and permanent ones?
2. Why are Questions 4 and 5 important?
3. Which questions on the form are geared to a common insurer's defense, namely, a preexisting condition?
4. Which questions attempt to quantify the economic cost of this physical injury?

Figure 3.8 lays out initial questioning in a case of product defect and corresponding liability or defense. Insurance companies hire private investigators to determine the authenticity of claims under product liability actions. Is the injury feigned? Is the product actually defective? Was the product being misused? Was the user following or disregarding the instructions for product usage?

1. Question 16 solicits information regarding how a product was being used. Why is that important?
2. In Question 21, the client's awareness of danger in relation to the product is examined. Do you know why?
3. Why are Questions 29 and 30 important in a product liability case?

In the law of domestic relations, fact gathering takes on heightened importance since emotions tend to distort reality. The reliability, credibility, and veracity of any party's claim must be critically examined. A reputable form series, from initial interview to final disposition, is an absolute must

Authority to Release Information

To Whom It May Concern:

I hereby authorize any investigator or other authorized representative of ________________ ____________ bearing this release or copy thereof within one year of its date, to obtain any information in your files pertaining to my employment, military, educational records (including, but not limited to, academic achievement, attendance, athletic, personal history, and disciplinary records), medical records, credit records (including credit card and payment device numbers), and law enforcement records (including, but not limited to, any record of charge, prosecution or conviction for criminal or civil offenses). Thereby direct you to release such information upon request to the bearer. This release is executed with full knowledge and understanding that the information is for the official use of ________ __________________________. Consent is granted for ______________________________ to furnish such information, as is described above, to third parties, in the course of fulfilling its official responsibilities. I hereby release you as the custodian of such records, and any school, college, university, or other educational institution, hospital or other repository of medical records, credit bureau, lending institution, consumer reporting agency, retail business establishment, law enforcement agency, or criminal justice agency, including its officers, employees, or related personnel, both individually and collectively, from any and all liability for damages of whatever kind, which may at any time result to me, my heirs, family or associates because of compliance with this authorization and request to release information, or any attempt to comply with it. I am furnishing my Social Security Account Number on a voluntary basis with the understanding such is not required by Federal statute or regulation. I have been advised that ___________________________________ will utilize this number only to facilitate the location of employment, military, credit, and educational records concerning me, in connection with this application. Should there be any question as to the validity of this release, you may contact me as indicated below.

Full Name: ____
(Signature) include maiden & any other previously used name

Full Name: ____
(Typed or printed) include maiden & any other previously used name

Social Security #: ____

Parent or Guardian: ____
(if under 18 years of age)

Date: ____

Current Address: ____

____

____

Telephone Number: ____

Cellular: ____

Witness: ____

FIGURE 3.3 Client's form authorizing release of information.

Insurance Claim Investigation Form

Date: ____________________

Company ______________________ Address ______________________

Report to ______________________ Telephone ______________________

Assured ______________________

Claim No. ______________________

Claimant ______________________

Address ______________________

Description: Sex__________ Marital Status__________ Age__________ Race__________

Height__________ Weight__________ Occupation ______________________

Last Employer ______________________

Automobile______________________ License No. ______________________

Date of Accident ______________________

Description of Accident ______________________

____

____

____

____

Nature of alleged disability______________________

Extent of Injury Claimed ( ) Partial ( ) Continuing ( ) Permanent

Desired: ( ) Activities checked (Through personal inquiry: Yes___; No ___)

( ) Dependency Status

( ) Investigation of accident, including statements

( ) Activities through observation. (Specific authorization will be requested beyond 2 days)

( ) Video, if active.

( ) Previous medical history.

Rate: ( ) Flat Rate ______________________ ( ) Hourly Rate ______________________

Remarks ______________________

____

____

____

____

FIGURE 3.4 Insurance claim investigation form.

Personal Injury Questionnaire

Please tell us how you preferred to be contacted:

Name ______________________________

Address 1 ______________________________

Address 2 ______________________________

City ______________________________

State______________________________

Zip Code ______________________________

Home Phone ______________________________

Work Phone ______________________________

Cell Number ______________________________

Special Contact Information ______________________________

Incident Information:

Date and Time of Incident: ______________________________

Location of Incident:______________________________

Did the incident occur within the scope of your employment? ☐ Yes ☐ No

If yes, describe:______________________________

Did the incident occur within the scope of the responsible party's employment? ☐ Yes ☐ No

If yes, describe:______________________________

Tell us what you believe happened: ______________________________

____

____

Are there any photographs or video of the scene, people, vehicles or anything else? ☐ Yes ☐ No

If yes, describe:______________________________

____

____

Immediate Injury Information

Please list all of your injuries from the incident and describe in detail:______________________________

____

____

Describe all medical treatment you have had as a result your injury: ______________________________

____

____

Are you still treating? With who?______________________________

____

____

FIGURE 3.5 Personal injury questionnaire.

Personal Injury Questionnaire

NOTE: Skip to ONE of the four categories below that best describes the incident: (1) Motor vehicle accident (injured in a car accident); (2) Product Liability (injured by a product); (3) Premises Liability (injured on someone's property); or (4) Malpractice (injured by a medical provider).

(Motor Vehicle Case)

Where were you in vehicle? ____________________

Name and address of investigating authority (Police Dept., Sheriff, Highway Patrol, etc.): ____________________

____

____

Did you or the other driver(s) receive any citation? ☐ Yes ☐ No

If yes, explain what (you) (other driver) were cited for: ____________________

____

What were the weather and road conditions like? ____________________

Provide accident report if you have it: ☐ Yes ☐ No

Had you or anyone else been drinking or taking drugs to your knowledge? ☐ Yes ☐ No

If yes, describe: ____________________

How did you leave the scene? ____________________

____

(Product Liability Cases)

Describe in detail the product that you believe injured you: ____________________

____

Who owns the product? ____________________

Where is the product? ____________________

Do you have access to the product? ____________________

How old is the product? ____________________

Do you or does anyone else to your knowledge have any photographs of the product taken shortly after the incident? ☐ Yes ☐ No

If yes, where are the photographs? ____________________

____

(Premises Liability Cases)

To whom was the incident reported? ____________________

Were any photographs taken of the scene or the cause of the incident shortly afterwards? ☐ Yes ☐ No

If yes, where are the photographs? ____________________

What were you wearing, including your shoes? ____________________

Do you still have your clothing and shoes? ☐ Yes ☐ No

Did the incident occur outside or inside? ☐ Yes ☐ No

(Medical Negligence Cases)

Name, address and telephone number of every person or entity who you believe was the cause of your injuries or illness and why you believe that. ____________________

____

FIGURE 3.5 (continued).

Personal Injury Questionnaire

GENERAL INFORMATION—please fill out all questions below, regardless of case type.

Employment History & Lost wages

Current Employer's Name: ____________________

Were you employed here at time of accident? ____________________

Address: ____________________

Title: ____________________

Job Duties: ____________________

Wages/Earnings: ____________________

Dates of employment: ____________________

Did you lose any time from work as a result of the injury you sustained from the incident? ☐ Yes ☐ No

If yes, give the dates you were unable to work: ____________________

Did you lose earnings or have any other losses as a result of being unable to work? ☐ Yes ☐ No

If yes, state the amount of earnings lost: ____________________ $

Past Claims History:

Have you ever been involved in any lawsuits? ☐ Yes ☐ No

If yes, please provide the following information:

Nature and reason for case: ____________________

Outcome: ____________________

Have you ever filed a Workers' Compensation claim? ☐ Yes ☐ No

If yes, please provide the following information: ____________________

For what type of injury: ____________________

Date of claim: ____________________

Outcome: ____________________

Past Medical History

Please provide the following information:

1. Your prior health status (circle one): ☐ Excellent ☐ Good ☐ Fair ☐ Poor
2. Prior health history, including any prior hospitalizations or injuries, including approximate dates: ____________________

FIGURE 3.5 (continued).

Accident Fact Sheet

Client Personal Information

Client Name	Date of Birth
Address	Home Phone
City, State, Zip code	Social Security No.

Client Accident Information

Date/Time of Accident

Location of Accident

Description of Accident

Medical Information

Bodily Injuries

Name of Ambulance Company	Cost

Name and Address of Hospital

Name of Treating Physician(s)

Client Insurance Information

Insurance Company	Phone Number
Address	Contact Person
Vehicle Owner	Claim Number
Name of Insured	

Defendant Insurance Information

Insurance Company	Phone Number
Address	Contact Person
Vehicle Owner	Claim Number
Name of Insured	

FIGURE 3.6 Form used to report details of accident.

Personal Injury Case -
Medical and Consequential Loss

INTERVIEW GUIDE
Use with 475 M.V. (Motor Vehicle), 485 A.C. (Accident Case) or with 490 P.L. (Products Liability)

File No.__________

Client__________ Date__________ Time______ To______

Interviewed by__________ Fee Arrangement__________

Referred by__________ Date of Accident__________

Statute of Limitations expires__________

(Where space is found insufficient use blank sheet and refer to question number)

PERSONAL INJURIES

1. Nature and extent of injuries__________

2. Immediate effect of injuries (unconsciousness, pain, inability to move or walk, cuts, abrasions, lacerations, bleeding, fractures and other physical discomforts)__________

3. Permanent injuries: list all permanent injuries, including scars, disfigurements, possibility of plastic or remedial surgery__________

4. Identify ambulances or other emergency vehicles__________

5. First aid or other medical treatment at scene, nature of assistance and names and addresses of those rendering assistance__________

480S - Personal Injury Initial Interview Guide
Rev. 9/97 P12/99

 Page 1

FIGURE 3.7 Guide for use when interviewing client for information pertaining to injuries and costs related to injuries. With permission.

6. If taken to hospital: (a) by what means and by whom (b) name and address of hospital (c) date of admission (d) date of discharge (e) treatment received and from whom ________________

7. If taken elsewhere than to hospital, where, by what means and by whom ________________

8. X-rays, EEG, EKG and other tests: (a) by whom and where ________________

(b) parts of body x-rayed and what x-rays disclosed ________________

(c) results of EEG, EKG and other tests ________________

9. Treatment by doctors and paramedical personnel: (a) name and address of each and nature of specialty (orthopedic, therapeutic, surgical, psychiatric, general medical, dental, etc.) (b) nature and extent of treatments and where given ________________

10. Outpatient treatment: name and address of hospital, date and nature of each treatment, name and address of each doctor, nurse or paramedical personnel ________________

11. Medical expenses: where and by whom, dates, total charges, amounts paid to date and by whom paid (hospital, treating and consulting doctors, nurses, paramedics, laboratories, x-rays, appliances, special clothing, etc.) ________________

480S - Personal Injury Initial Interview Guide
Rev. 9/97 P12/99

 Page 2

FIGURE 3.7 (continued).

12. Future or anticipated medical treatments: nature, for how long and estimate of cost

13. Dates of home confinement

14. Home nursing care: name, address, phone of each person, nature of services, dates performed and amount paid

15. Household help: name, address, phone of each person, nature of services, dates performed and amount paid

16. Present complaints

17. Activities limited by injury (hobbies, chores, day-to-day activities, walking, etc.)

18. If client refused to accept any medical care or treatment recommended by doctors, show the care or treatment refused, doctor involved, date of each refusal and reasons for refusal

PREVIOUS MEDICAL HISTORY

19. General condition of health in last 10 years

20. Nature, dates, extent of injuries from prior accidents, diseases or other disabling illnesses (heart, lung, brain, kidney, blood, vascular, sight, hearing, speech, dental, surgery, etc.)

480S - Personal Injury Initial Interview Guide
Rev. 9/97 P12/99

 Page 3

FIGURE 3.7 (continued).

21. Names and addresses of doctors involved (include x-rays, EEG, EKG and other tests)________

22. If hospitalized, names and locations of hospitals, duration and dates of hospitalization ________

23. Aggravation or effect of present injuries on any existing or prior physical or mental condition ________

24. Physical examinations: for insurance, military employment or for other purposes, results and whether insurance, employment or military service denied ________

25. Previous accident or injury claims: names and addresses of attorneys, insurance companies, disposition of each claim (including Workers' Comp.) ________

EMPLOYMENT AND INCOME PRIOR TO ACCIDENT

26. Name, address and phone of employer ________

27. Employer's business ________

28. Positions held and duties ________

29. Hours worked: per day ______ per week ______ hourly pay $ ______

30. Average weekly earnings for preceding 12 months $________

31. Earnings reported on income tax returns for past 2 years (show breakdown if more than one employer or business)________

EMPLOYMENT AND INCOME FOLLOWING ACCIDENT

32. Time lost from work (itemize)________

4808 - Personal Injury Initial Interview Guide
Rev. 9/97 P12/99

 Page 4

FIGURE 3.7 (continued).

33. If client returned to work after accident, for each employment show: (a) name, address, phone and business of employer ______________________________

____

(b) positions held and duties ______________________________

(c) hours worked: per day ____________ per week ____________ hourly rate $____________

(d) average weekly earnings $ ______________________________

34. Date of return to full employment ______________________________

35. If client did not return to work, explain ______________________________

____

____

36. If injuries impaired or in any manner restricted ability to perform duties of employment or business, explain

____

____

____

____

37. Lost time since returning to work (dates, periods, reason, income lost, sick leave used) ____________

____

____

____

38. If a promotion or increase in salary was expected at the time of the accident but did not materialize, give details ______________________________

____

____

39. If injuries resulted in loss of business income, explain ______________________________

____

____

____

40. If substitute help was required in client's business to perform all or part of client's duties, give names, addresses and phone numbers of each person, nature of services, dates performed and amount paid

____

____

____

41. List fellow employees, supervisors or business associates who have knowledge regarding client's employment and what each knows ______________________________

____

480S - Personal Injury Initial Interview Guide
Rev. 9/97 P12/99

 Page 5

FIGURE 3.7 (continued).

42. If client lost any rights or benefits related to employment (such as seniority or pension rights), explain

43. Nature, extent and source of any other income or pecuniary loss

RÉSUMÉ OF EMPLOYMENT HISTORY FOR 5 YEARS PRECEDING THIS ACCIDENT

44. Employer, position or nature of employment, period, average earnings

EDUCATION AND TRAINING

45. Educational background (schools attended, major subjects, degrees)

46. Special skills or licenses

47. If client's plans or prospects for further education or employment changed as a result of this accident, explain

48. If nature of employment at time of accident was different, inferior to or in a field other than that for which client had been previously engaged in or trained for (a) explain (lessening of demand for specific professional personnel etc.) (b) show resulting reduction in earnings

SUBSEQUENT INJURIES

49. If client has been injured since the date of the injury in question, indicate what the injury was, how it was received and the hospitals and treating physicians involved

480S - Personal Injury Initial Interview Guide
Rev. 9/97 P12/99

FIGURE 3.7 (continued).

Product Liability -
Factual Information (Including Property Damage)

INTERVIEW GUIDE

(For personal injuries and related damages use with form 480S)

File No. ______

Interviewed by ______ Date ______ Time ______ To ______

Referred by ______ Fee Arrangement ______

Date of Accident ______

Statute of Limitations expires ______

CLIENT - SPOUSE - CHILDREN

1. Full name ______ SSN ______
2. Other names used ______ Birthdate ______
3. Residence ______
   Municipality ______ County ______ State ______ Zip ______
4. Telephone: Home ______ Business ______ Fax No. ______
5. If a minor or incompetent: names, addresses, and phone of parents and name, address, relationship and phone of guardian ______

SPOUSE

6. Full name ______ SSN ______
7. Other names used ______ Birthdate ______
8. Residence if different ______
   Municipality ______ County ______ State/Zip ______
   Telephone No. ______ Fax No. ______

CHILDREN

9. Name, sex, age and residence of minor children ______

DESCRIPTION OF PRODUCT

10. Name of product ______
11. Trade name and/or manufacturer ______
12. Model number and other identification ______

490 P.L. - Product Liability
Initial Interview Guide
Rev. 9/97

 Page 1

FIGURE 3.8 Guide for interviewing client and/or family members when investigating a product liability case.

13. Description of product and use for which intended ______

14. Availability of copies of advertisements ______

PRODUCT FAILURE

15. Date and place of accident or period of exposure to product ______

16. How product was being used ______

17. Describe what happened ______

18. What did product do or fail to do that caused injury or damage ______

19. Cause of the product failure or malfunction (indicate presence or absence of any safety devices) ______

20. If instructions and warnings were not fully followed, explain any deviations ______

21. Client's awareness of danger in use of or exposure to product ______

490 P.L. - Product Liability
Initial Interview Guide
Rev. 9/97

 Page 2

FIGURE 3.8 (continued).

22. Is the product or similar products made with safety devices? If so, were they available and in use? Explain

WITNESSES

23. Name, address, and phone number of each. Indicate family or other relationship to anyone involved in accident

24. Location of witnesses in proximity to scene of accident

25. Conversations, remarks and oral statements made at scene of accident, by and to whom, and in whose presence

26. Statements made to police: identify officer, date, time, in whose presence and details

27. Statements made at hospital, by and to whom, date, time, in whose presence and details

28. Location and availability of copies of all written statements (identify)

PURCHASE OF PRODUCT

29. Product was purchased on ______ for $ ______ new ☐ used ☐

30. Name, address and phone number of seller

490 P.L. - Product Liability
Initial Interview Guide
Rev. 9/97

 Page 3

FIGURE 3.8 (continued).

31. Name and address of salesperson ______________________

32. If not purchased by client, then by whom and relationship to client ______________________

33. If not purchased, how acquired by client (rented, borrowed) explain ______________________

34. Describe containers, instructions, warnings and manufacturer's warranty which came with product ______________________

35. Availability of above ______________________

36. Verbal representations made at time of purchase, by and to whom, in whose presence and details ______________________

PRODUCT HISTORY

37. Ownership and control from original purchase to time of accident ______________________

38. Trace usage from original purchase to time of accident ______________________

39. Care and maintenance of and repairs to the product from original purchase to time of accident ______________________

40. Describe any trouble or difficulty with prior use of product ______________________

FIGURE 3.8 (continued).

LOCATION OF PRODUCT

41. Present location of product and person in control ______

42. Present condition of product ______

43. Availability of same or similar products for inspection and testing ______

INVESTIGATION

44. Full details of any investigation of the incident, by whom and for whom. Availability of reports of investigation ______

45. If a report or complaint was made, give full details (to whom, by whom, dates, obtain copy and indicate response) ______

46. Details of experiences of others with this or similar products ______

PROPERTY DAMAGE

(If personal injuries are involved use form 480S for medical and related damages, lost wages, future earnings, etc.)

47. Describe in detail what property was damaged ______

490 P.L. - Product Liability
Initial Interview Guide
Rev. 9/97

 Page 5

FIGURE 3.8 (continued).

48. Name and address of party making repairs. Attach copy of repair bills or estimates if no repairs made (indicate which were paid) ______

______

______

49. If any damaged items were sold or otherwise disposed of, enter name and address of person to whom sold or transferred, date and consideration received ______

______

______

______

______

50. Market value of damaged items prior to accident $ ______ before repairs $ ______ after repairs $ ______

51. Itemize and explain additional expenses incurred, such as costs of replacement, storage charges, additional living expenses, etc. ______

______

______

______

______

______

INSURANCE

52. If there is insurance covering any of the damages, provide full details (i.e., homeowners, accident, medical insurance) ______

______

______

______

______

______

FOR OFFICE USE ONLY
Received

- ☐ Retainer Agreement
- ☐ Police Report Authorization
- ☐ Police Report
- ☐ Photographs
- ☐ Other
- ☐ Hospital and Medical Reports
- ☐ Medical and related bills
- ☐ Rental of appliances, etc.

490 P.L. - Product Liability
Initial Interview Guide
Rev. 9/97

 Page 6

FIGURE 3.8 (continued).

for investigators laboring in divorce practice. Figure 3.9, or a similar form, should be inserted at the beginning of the file. Essential background information is collected, such as petitioner's name, address, and phone numbers, and the names of the children. A small space for notes is provided.

A more comprehensive example, which deals with grounds for divorce, is reproduced at Figure 3.10.

1. Question 12 requests a marriage certificate. Why?
2. What other domestic relations cause of action within the present marriage could possibly be pending before a court of local jurisdiction?
3. This form does not assume a no-fault situation. Where are grounds of fault discussed?
4. Question 50 deals with the question of reconciliation. Do you think this is an important point in the initial interview process? Explain.

3. Follow-Up Letter

It is sound practice to follow up any witness, client, or other party interviewed with a letter that recites the scope and content of the interview. See Figure 3.11.

One's skill and expertise in eliciting information from witnesses and clients depends on numerous factors. Remember that the investigator is conducting and controlling the interview, setting the tone and pace of informational response. Therefore, the burden rests upon the interviewer. The process of collecting information often involves the art of compromise and conciliation. "To minimize the stress, avoid conduct that can be interpreted by the witness as creating a 'pressure situation.' Give an impression of relaxed efficiency, not nervous haste. Smile and demonstrate real interest; not gloom, worry or distraction. Be thoughtful, courteous, and responsive; not inconsiderate, rude, or remote."[5]

With new clients, the investigator must create a positive first impression and recognize that the initial interview is, hopefully, the gateway to a long-term relationship. Correspondence and other explanatory documentation teach the new client about investigative dynamics.

B. Recording Interview Impressions

The success of the initial interview process and subsequent interaction between the client and the investigator is a recurring concern of security management and administrative personnel. Most well-managed security firms contact clients directly regarding the type of treatment they receive by using a Client Contact Report (see Figure 3.12) or similar form.

III. CASE EVALUATION

After the information is gathered, it should be assessed for quality and reliability, and this evaluation will lead to the conclusion about a particular case or claim. The integrity, credibility, and merit of an underlying claim or investigative purpose can often be gleaned from the initial interchange between investigator and client. Over time, the investigator develops a sixth sense about the merits of a client's claim.

The interview process may, and often does, assist the investigator in dealing with individuals and cases that are suspect. Examples of cases and clients you want to avoid are:

1. Clients who are trying to make a change in society.
2. Clients who are crusaders.
3. Clients who simply want revenge.
4. Clients who have a "pot-of-gold-at-the-end-of-the-rainbow" mentality.
5. Clients who are mentally or emotionally disturbed.
6. Clients who proclaim too much the merits of their case.
7. Clients who are shoppers for professional services.
8. Clients who have other underlying and unknown motivations.[6]

Divorce Case Notes

Client Information

Client Name			Date of Birth
Address			Home Phone
City, State, Zip code			Social Security No.
Employer	Income	Occupation	
Employer's Address	City, State, Zip code		Phone
Education			
Maiden Name	Military Service		Discharge Date
Date & Place of marriage			Separation Date

Spouse's Information

Client Name			Date of Birth
Address			Home Phone
City, State, Zip code			Social Security No.
Employer	Income	Occupation	
Employer's Address	City, State, Zip code		Phone
Education			
Maiden Name	Military Service		Discharge Date

Children

Name	Age	Birthdate

Notes

FIGURE 3.9 Divorce case notes.

Matrimonial Interview Information Record

(To be completed in conjunction with Form No. 830S)

File No. ______________ Case No. ______________

Interviewed by ______________________________ Date ______________ Time: ________ To ________

Referred by ______________________________ Fee Arrangement ______________________________

(Where space is found insufficient use blank sheet and refer to question number.)

CLIENT

1. Full Name ______________________________
2. Maiden name ______________________________
3. Other names used ______________________________
4. (a) Res. Phone ______________________________ (b) Bus. Phone ______________________________

   Fax Number ______________________________ Eye Color ______________

SPOUSE

5. (a) Full Name ______________________________ (b) S.S. # ______________
6. Maiden name ______________________________
7. Other names used ______________________________
8. Physical Description: Height ________ Weight ________ Color eyes ________ Color hair ________

   Glasses ________ Scars or Marks ______________ Other ______________

PRESENT MARRIAGE

9. Date ______________ Place ______________________________
10. Availability of marriage certificate ______________________________
11. Residences since marriage (show dates) ______________________________

CHILDREN OF PRESENT MARRIAGE

12. (a) Minor Child ______________________________

    (b) School ______________________________

829S - Matrimonial Interview Information Record
Rev. 3/98 P3/98

 Page 1

FIGURE 3.10 Matrimonial interview information record. With permission.

Experience teaches investigators that certain cases are naturally suspect. However, each case should be judged individually; the investigator must "listen and observe how the client tells the story. Proving the case may require that this person be a witness."[7] Determining whether or not the case is worth the trouble largely depends on the client's sincerity and authenticity. "Clients may be abrasive, dull, neurotic, alcoholic, nervous, argumentative, or entirely inarticulate, yet still be able to

13. Names, birth dates and residence of adult children and school currently attending ______________________

____

14. Which children are adopted (a) ______________________ Date __________

(b) ______________________ Date __________

15. Health status and nature of physical or other disability of each child ______________________

____

16. Monthly (4.3 weeks) support received or paid for any children (a) ______________________

(b) ______________________

17. Voluntary ☐ or by Court Order ☐ (if by Court Order give details) ______________________

____

PRIOR MARRIAGE (answer on a separate page if more than one)

18. Party involved: Client ☐ Spouse ☐ Date __________ Place ______________________

19. Prior marriage name ______________________ Name of prior spouse ______________________

20. Cause of dissolution ______________________

21. Court and date of dissolution ______________________

22. Copy of judgment attached ☐ ______________________

OTHER CHILDREN OF CLIENT OR SPOUSE

23. Names and birth dates of minor or handicapped children (and name of parent) ______________________

____

24. Residence and Custody ______________________

25. Names, birth dates and residence of adult children and school currently being attended (name parent) ______________________

____

26. Health status and nature of physical or other disability ______________________

____

27. Support received or paid for any children ______________________

____

28. Voluntary ☐ or by Court Order ☐ (if by Court Order, give details) ______________________

____

8298 - Matrimonial Interview Information Record
Rev. 3/98 P3/98

 Page 2

FIGURE 3.10 (continued).

testify effectively about potentially winning claims that the attorney can accept."[8] The investigator who conducts a professional initial interview will filter out the troublesome clients.

Finally, the investigator must take his or her interviewees as he or she finds them. One cannot assume that a client will necessarily be cooperative, friendly, or generally receptive to any type of questions. Witnesses, clients, suspects, or other parties will all exhibit personal traits and characteristics that are sometimes hard to predict. "When witnesses appear to be reluctant to cooperate, the

EMPLOYMENT - CLIENT

29. Occupation ______________ Job title ______________ How long employed ________

30. Tel. No. ______________ Fax No. ______________

31. Work days and hours ______________

32. Union ☐ Non-Union ☐ Union Name ______________ Union Card No. ________

EMPLOYMENT - SPOUSE

33. Occupation ______________ Job title ______________ How long employed ________

34. Employer's name, address & phone # ______________

35. Work days and hours ______________

36. Union ☐ Non-Union ☐ Union Name ______________ Union Card No. ________

OTHER FAMILY ACTIONS–PRESENT MARRIAGE

37. List Court, docket number, nature of proceedings, dates, by whom instituted, disposition, and names of attorneys involved. Include all family actions involving support, custody or domestic violence (pending and closed)

CAUSE OF ACTION

38. Desertion ☐ Separation ☐ Extreme Cruelty ☐ Adultery or Deviant Sexual Conduct ☐
Drug Addiction or Drunkenness ☐ Imprisonment ☐ Institutionalization for Mental Illness ☐
Other ☐

FACTS AND CIRCUMSTANCES

39. Provide, on separate sheets, a chronological statement detailing all events, reasons and causes for divorce or dissolution of marriage. Include names and addresses of witnesses and each person who participated in the incidents or acts.

40. Likelihood of reconciliation ______________

8298 - Matrimonial Interview Information Record
Rev. 3/98 P3/98

 Page 3

FIGURE 3.10 (continued).

investigator should attempt to determine the cause for this reluctance: Are they friends of the other party or the victim? Do they fear some sort of retaliation? Are they simply afraid of being called to testify at the trial stage?"[9]

The investigator will also be dealing with individuals who may be characterized as hostile, adverse, friendly, or expert in nature. These types of witnesses are covered in detail in Chapter 4.

Remember these general suggestions:

CUSTODY

41. Reasons for custody of minor children as expressed by client: ____________________

____

____

(a) Type of custody ____________________

☐ Joint legal custody with ____________________ parent having primary residential care

☐ Joint physical custody

☐ Sole custody to one parent, visitation by the other

42. Reasons why a party should or should not have custody of children ____________________

____

____

VISITATION **M = Mother** **F = Father** (Note by "M" or "F" for each category)

a. Holidays/School Break

	CURRENT	PROPOSED		CURRENT	PROPOSED		CURRENT	PROPOSED		CURRENT	PROPOSED
New Year's Day			2nd Night Passover			1st Evening			Mother's Day		
Martin Luther King Day			Memorial Day			Hanukkah			Father's Day		
President's Day			July 4th			Christmas Eve			Summer		
President's Week			Labor Day			Christmas Day			Vacation		
Good Friday			Rosh Hashanah			Christmas Week			Other		
Easter Sunday			Yom Kupper			New Year's Day					
1st Night Passover			Thanksgiving Day								

8298 - Matrimonial Interview Information Record
Rev. 3/98 P3/98

©1998 by ALL-STATE LEGAL®
A Division of ALL-STATE International, Inc.
www.aslegal.com 800.222.0510 Page 4

FIGURE 3.10 (continued).

1. Interview witnesses in a timely fashion.
2. Solicit as much factual information from witnesses as is possible.
3. Utilize witnesses as leads to other potential sources of information.
4. Convert all witnesses' statements to writing.
5. Befriend witnesses and avoid antagonism at all costs.
6. Keep in touch with witnesses as the case progresses.[10]

[Date]

[Name of Client]
[Address]

Dear [client]:

When we discussed your claim the other day, I am sure that much of the information was new and unfamiliar to you. I am writing at this time to go over some of the items we discussed and the way we handle the investigation of injury claims. This also can serve as a reference for you in the future if a question arises as to how an investigation proceeds.

Preparation and Investigation

We already have begun the information-acquisition procedure. In the future, if you receive any calls from another party or any insurance company, you should refer the call directly to us. Do not answer any of their questions or provide any information. Members of your family or others who are likely to answer your phone should be given the same instruction.

I will attempt to acquire witness statements from individuals who have information about how the injury occurred. If you learn of any additional names of witnesses, please contact us immediately. If anyone calls you with information, please make sure to get the party's name, telephone number, and address before giving him or her our number to call.

I have written for medical information concerning the injuries involved. It will be important for you to keep me advised of any new doctor that you see. Please be sure to keep all receipts for drugs or any type of medical apparatus that you purchase. It would be quite helpful if you could send to us copies of all medical bills that you receive. This information is very important as it advises us of your medical expenses and the dates of treatment and the type of services that have been rendered. If a hospital admission is anticipated for any procedure of any nature, call to let us know in advance. If the hospital does not give you a copy of a bill, attempt to retain your patient number which can be found on your identification bracelet. This helps us locate your medical records.

If there is any significant change in your medical condition, please let us know. If you are going to be out of town for any length of time, please give us a call with a forwarding number in case it becomes necessary to contact you.

Sincerely,

[Name of Investigator]

FIGURE 3.11 Witness follow up letter.

Client Contact Report

Office______________________________ Operation______________________

Client______________________________ Date Commenced ________________

	Contacted			Initiated by		
Date	**In person**	**phone**	**email**	**client**	**Invest.**	**Briefly describe discussion**

FIGURE 3.12 Client contact report.

Be especially attentive to legal and ethical issues that can arise during the interview process. Privacy statutes or civil rights violations, sexual harassment, or misrepresentation or other falsehood should perpetually guide the suitability of questions and interrogation tactic chosen. In most cases, pretext interviews are entirely improper. "Outright misrepresentation should be avoided and impersonation of law enforcement or other government officials should never take place."[11]

NOTES

1. American Society for Industrial Security, *Basic Guidelines for Security Investigations* (1981), 45.
2. *Id.* at 46.
3. Carol Bruno, *Paralegal's Litigation Handbook* (Delmar Thomson Learning, 1980), 68–83.
4. Patricia W. Kittredge, "Guideposts for the Investigation of a Negligence Case," *Prac. Law*. 90 (1973), 55; J. Stannar Baker, "Reconstruction of Accidents," *Traffic Dig. Rev*. 17 (1969), 9; P. Magarick, "Investigating the Civil Case: General Principles," *Am. Jur. Trials* 1 (1987), 361.
5. *Am. Jur. Trials* 1 (1987), 357, 374.
6. National Association of Legal Assistants, *Manual for Legal Assistants* (1979), 246.
7. Lawrence Charfoos and David Christensen, *Personal Injury Practice: Technique and Technology* (Lawyer's Co-Operative, 1988), 428.
8. *Id.* at 433; see also Julius Glickman, "Persuasion in Litigation," *Litigation*. 8 (1982), 30; David Horowitz, "How to Handle a New Client," *Prac. Law.* 21 (1975), 11–12.
9. *Id.*
10. Thomas Eimermann, *Fundamentals of Paralegalism* (Aspen Publishers, 1980), 117.
11. Mark Weinstein, *Introduction to Civil Litigation* (West Publishing, 1986), 54–55.
12. American Society for Industrial Security, *supra* note 1, at 52.

4 Witnesses

I. THE PURPOSE OF WITNESSES

In trial litigation, testimonial evidence (that given by people under oath) is generally one of the more useful means of proof. Of course, the testimony of any witness is subject to attack for its credibility, veracity, or sometimes even admissibility.

Keep in mind that witnesses can and do serve a useful purpose to the investigator outside of the courtroom as well. Most witnesses provide information, leads, and other insights into the case as a whole, without ever testifying in court. Investigators see the value of witnesses in diverse ways:

- Identification of suspects.
- Narration of facts and conditions surrounding the case.
- Discussion of motive and modus operandi.
- A tool of quality control by eliminating remote suspects.
- Proof of a hunch, guess, or professional conjecture.
- Direct eyewitness information.[1]

Ralph F. Brislin's remarkable manual, *The Effective Security Officer's Training Manual*, relays intelligently:

> Upon arrival at the scene and once you have determined who requires first aid, attempt to identify anyone and everyone who may have knowledge of what occurred. Ask witnesses to remain in the area until you have had a chance to talk to them. It is critical in this situation that you have a notebook and pen at your disposal. Attempt to interview those persons who were actually involved, whether they are the alleged victims or perpetrators.[2]

II. TYPES OF WITNESSES

Witnesses generally fall into two categories: lay and expert. An expert witness has a specialized knowledge upon which his or her testimony emerges, such as a chemist, a DNA specialist, or a ballistics examiner. All other witnesses are labeled lay witnesses, those who testify to objective reality without a scientific vein or purpose.[3] To illustrate, in a speeding case, a lay witness relays "He was going fast." While the expert, holding radar results, states "The radar reading was 101 mph." But witnesses in the street serve as many purposes as there are cases. The list includes:

- A witness may be the actual victim of an intentional deed.
- A witness may be a victim of a crime.
- A witness may be a personally injured party in a negligence or medical malpractice case or similar tort.
- A witness may be an eyewitness, that is, an individual who personally witnessed the event and can testify to the facts and conditions.

- A witness can also be described as a character witness—he or she is capable of attesting to the good, bad, or indifferent nature of an individual's character or, at least, the community's perception of that character.
- A witness may also be expert in nature, having the capacity to testify as to certain fields of expertise that are beyond the scope of the normal lay person.
- Witnesses who give factual recitations and, in some cases, opinions, are also typified as lay witnesses.
- Witnesses can be further described as friendly to one's case or viewed as being adverse, unfriendly, or hostile.

A. Missing or Unknown Witnesses

Investigators often operate under the false assumption that witnesses are available and accessible. "Missing witnesses or parties (sometimes referred to as skips) are generally divided into two categories. The first and most common type is the unintentional skip, whose whereabouts are unknown because he has moved without leaving a forwarding address, and the passage of time has left his trail cold. The second type is the intentional skip, who leaves no forwarding address when he moves in order to avoid contact with his past. Often, the intentional skip may be seeking escape from an unpleasant situation, such as a domestic or creditor problem."[4]

Finding an unknown or missing witness can be difficult, particularly in criminal matters. Missing witnesses sometimes have submerged into an underground hiding system, particularly in major metropolitan areas. In domestic relations cases, especially in the prosecution of individuals who neglect support or alimony obligations, investigators have to track down individuals who move from jurisdiction to jurisdiction and create new, illegal identities. Despite the difficulties, witnesses can and usually are found.

Some suggested steps to tracking missing witnesses are:

1. *Client Interview*: Often forgotten is the client himself. He will often have secondary addresses, hiding places, or insights into customs and habits regarding travel and possible location of a given individual.
2. *Telephone Books*: Scan all available telephone books for names or aliases that might match the individual in question. Also, look in earlier phone books, since it is common for names that were once listed to become unlisted pending or during certain legal difficulties. Also, if a number is secured, try to call and use fictitious, though not illegal, circumstances to introduce oneself to determine the location of a specific person.
3. *Mail and Telegrams*: The use of certified mail, Western Union telegrams, or other electronic means can be a practical and useful way of tracking a witness. If a last known address is found, a subpoena or summons to serve on a witness will satisfy most jurisdictional requirements.
4. *Police Reports or Other Documents*: The investigator can assume that other parties who were in attendance at a crime or accident scene may have taken the names of other witnesses down in some type of report or documentation.
5. *Canvass Community*: With a picture or other identification aid in hand, investigators can often spend productive time canvassing businesses, shops, restaurants, and people of the community. This is a typical and long-standing investigative technique.
6. *Newspaper and Other Media Sources*: Frequently at scenes of crimes or personal injury litigation, a newspaper reporter will have taken pictures or made some record of the case.
7. *Public Transportation Carriers*: Checking with bus, taxi, train, and trolley drivers and other individuals who provide regular service to the public may lead to identification of a specific witness.

8. *City Address Directories*: If a name is not available, a street address can sometimes be cross-referenced with a specific name if a telephone company provides such information. City directories also can provide information and are available at most public libraries.
9. *Postal Service*: Registered or certified mail or other means of address authentication are useful ways of verifying the location of a specific witness. While postal regulations do not provide for the direct disclosure of forwarding addresses, these are indirect methods of finding the location of a specific witness. In criminal actions, and under the authority of postal inspector activities, access to this traditionally confidential information is made available to public law enforcement representatives.
10. *Other Leads*: Check any of the following: social clubs, union halls, professional organizations, schools and educational institutions, utility companies, veterans offices, government agencies, welfare offices, recreational organizations, public record depositories, department of motor vehicles, voter registration records, marriage, birth and death records, police records, National Crime Information Center (NCIC) records.

It is also essential that investigators develop relationships with firms that locate missing heirs, witnesses, and judgment debtors, particularly companies that specialize in the areas of estates and trusts, criminal law and litigation, and debtor, creditor, and collection practices. See Figure 4.1[5] for a Missing Persons Posting Submission Form from one of these firms.

B. Lay Witnesses

A lay witness, simply defined, is any witness who is not an expert. A lay witness must have the general capacity to testify, record, recollect, narrate, attest to, and affirm certain conditions and facts. In this way, the witness is construed as competent enough to testify. Federal Rule of Evidence (FRE) 601 outlines the theme of competence:

> Every person is competent to be a witness except as otherwise provided in these rules. However, in civil actions and proceedings, with respect to an element of a claim or defense as to which State law supplies the rule of decision, the competency of a witness shall be determined in accordance with State law.[6]

Additionally, he or she must have the requisite level of mental capacity and emotional competency to outline in some logical and sensible sequence the facts, conditions, and events. In formal litigation, lay witness's testimony "is limited to those opinions or inferences that are (a) rationally based on the perception of the witness and (b) helpful to a clear understanding of the witness' testimony or the determination of a fact in issue."[7] Generally, lay opinions are frowned upon; however, opinions based on personal observation and perception (such as those related to alcohol intoxication, speed at which a vehicle was moving, height, distance, etc.) are readily accepted.[8] "Minimally, witnesses can testify to facts or truths personally experienced. Lay witnesses can and do go beyond mechanical recitation of data and expand the scope of testimony by giving opinions on actually observed events."[9]

The Federal Rules of Evidence, at 701, clearly delineate the lay witness's testimonial capacity:

> If the witness is not testifying as an expert, the witness' testimony in the form of opinions or inferences is limited to those opinions or inferences which are (a) rationally based on the perception of the witness and (b) helpful to a clear understanding of the witness' testimony or the determination of a fact in issue, and (c) not based on scientific, technical, or other specialized knowledge within the scope of Rule 702.10.

Despite these limitations, the role of lay witness's testimony should never be minimized in the litigation sphere.[11] "A popular notion among most lay people is that expert testimony is the only

Things to get ready or do -

- **FILL IN THE FORM BELOW IN DETAIL !**
- the information you send is going from the boxes below directly onto the internet.

Keep in mind that the site is not associated with any law enforcement entity, or organizations, public, private, or federal.

You have as much space as you need, and as much contact with me that it takes to get it online. The most important thing to remember is the need for good, correct information to publish.

Please fill out this form of request with as much detail as possible, the bottom box should be endless. The site is run by one person, as soon as I personally see your information, you'll know via email.

The photos - 3 maximum - as soon as you fill out the form, email the photo or photos to **admin@someoneismissing.com.**

PLEASE FILL THIS OUT

Your Name -

Email -

Phone -

State - USA ONLY — Pick One

City - ALL COUNTRIES

Country — Pick One

UK and AU Regions - — Pick One

Missing Person's Info -

Name -

Sex - — Pick One

Age -

Height -

Hair - — Pick One

Eyes - — Pick One

Weight - — Pick One

Last Seen -

Date - DAY-MONTH-YEAR

City last seen in -

FIGURE 4.1 www.someoneismissing.com/noreport.htm. With permission.

State last seen in - Pick One

Country last seen in - Pick One

UK and AU Regions - Pick One

Reward Offered - yes no

If So - How Much

Tattoo's, Scars or Birthmarks -

Vehicle Details if applicable -

Other information - Put what you would like the flyer to say here - 3 to 4 sentences as you wish. Take a look at some of the flyers on the front page and you can about how much you can say.

Submit Reset

FIGURE 4.1 (continued).

form of evidence admissible in a criminal or civil action. This perception is a result of many factors, such as media coverage of flamboyant witnesses and other fringe litigation. However, the bulk of testimony given in any criminal or civil action is fundamentally 'lay' in nature."[12] Just as in expert testimony, the lay witness needs to meet certain criteria for testimonial admissibility.

In any investigative process, the investigator should corroborate the reliability of the testimony. A lay witness may testify about what he or she has perceived, understood, or experienced, but the testimony need be credible. While the testimony of lay witnesses is unacceptable in matters requiring expert opinion, the statements of lay witnesses serve a variety of purposes during investigation, from corroboration of facts to elimination of a suspected party. Always use lay testimony as a source for leads.

C. Expert Witnesses

The role of expert witnesses in the investigative process is unquestionably significant. Experts scrutinize evidence, perform a quality control function, and provide insights into cases that are under investigation. Just as the courts have increasingly relied on expert testimony as a form of explanation and understanding, so too does the security industry in the assessment of cases. "If scientific, technical, or other specialized knowledge will assist the trier of fact to understand the evidence or to determine a fact in issue, a witness qualified as an expert may testify thereto in the form of an opinion or otherwise."[13] "An expert witness is considered to be one who is qualified to speak with authority by reason of his or her special or unique training, skills or familiarity with a particular subject. An expert witness is allowed to render opinions and draw opinions and draw conclusions (in contrast, witnesses not qualified as experts are generally not allowed such latitude)."[14]

It is generally accepted that an expert has a certain level of knowledge, understanding, and experience that exceeds that of the ordinary layperson. Standards of education, personal qualification, experiential activities, scholarly publication, and production indicate whether a witness is properly qualified as an expert.

1. *Qualifications of the Expert*

a. Experience Once the determination has been made that the subject matter of the witness's testimony has "crossed the barrier of judicial acceptability" and is a discipline that passes credible review with respected scientific researchers and assists the tribunal, the next issue is the qualification and character of the proposed expert witness. Under FRE Rule 702, an expert should be "qualified as an expert by knowledge, skill, and experience."[15] A finding of suitable qualification can depend on the following criteria:

- The witness has specialized training in the field of his expertise.
- The witness has acquired advanced degrees from educational institutions
- The witness has practiced in the field for a substantial period of time.
- The witness taught courses in the particular field.
- The witness has published books or articles in the particular field.
- The witness belongs to professional societies or organizations in a particular field.
- The witness has previously testified and has been qualified as an expert before a court or administrative body on the particular subject to which he has been asked to render an opinion.[16]

Degreed and intellectually advanced persons do not automatically qualify as experts. Qualifications bear a foundational relationship to the evidence being proffered. For example, in *Will v. Richardson-Merrell, Inc.*,[17] a plastic surgeon's testimony regarding the influence and effects of a drug called Benidictin was declared improper since the expertise of the plastic surgeon was pharmacological. Although knowledge is an a priori expert qualification, the extent of an expert's knowledge is demonstrated under these lines of inquiry:

- How many times has the expert acted as a consultant?
- In how many cases has the expert actually testified?
- Were the issues in previous cases similar to the issues in the case before the bar?
- Has the expert ever been employed by the opposing counsel?
- What percentage of the expert's previous trial work was done on behalf of plaintiff's cases and what percentage was on behalf of defendant's cases?
- What record-keeping method does the expert use to insure against conflict of interest problems?
- Has the expert written or published any articles, papers, or treatises concerning the subject matter involved in your case?[18]

Witnesses without a remarkable experiential history can hardly be taken seriously as experts. Weight given the expert evidence largely depends on the credibility of the expert's testimony. An expert with no experiential base is less believable than one with a substantial history.

b. Education and Training Experience is merely one aspect of qualification. Another facet is the academic background of the proposed expert. Does the proposed expert have advanced degrees from a college or university? Aside from a baccalaureate degree, most experts possess a minimum of a master's degree. In many scientific fields, a doctorate is required. Psychiatric evaluations call for an medical degree with postdoctoral training in psychiatry. Certain other fields such as ballistics and fingerprint analysis do not necessarily call for postbaccalaureate study and are usually manned by law enforcement forensic experts. Plainly though, more degrees lead to the proposition, rightly or wrongly, that the witness's education makes the witness's testimony more credible. Degrees are in some ways merely pieces of paper. Look to the grantor of the degree since some institutions are suspect. Less-than-honorable degree-granting institutions of higher learning that commonly advertise in periodicals, magazines, and newspapers need to be avoided.

Unfortunately, a negative stereotype is often applied to certain degree-granting state and religiously affiliated schools. This author has been a long-term critic of the legal profession's heavy and unwarranted emphasis on Ivy League degrees. Being a graduate of an Ivy League institution is no assurance of expertise or superior intelligence. In selecting experts, extreme positions at either end of the educational spectrum are to be shunned. An expert whose educational preparedness is based on a "matchbook" university will be given very little weight if the testimony is admitted at all. On the other hand, a jury and the court alike should resist dogmatic acceptance of the testimony of expert witnesses from historically prestigious institutions. There is an amazing diversity of expertise in the modern world based on both experience and academic training, from graduates of the smallest of religiously affiliated institutions to the largest of state universities to the ivy-covered halls.

c. Professional Associations and Other Memberships Membership in professional groups or organizations is a supposed sign that the expert is currently maintaining the expertise espoused. Membership in professional organizations and scientific groups keeps the expert on the cutting edge of his or her developing discipline.

In discerning the utility of an expert witness, consideration is carefully given to memberships. An impressive membership history will shape jurors' perceptions. "[T]he jurors will form their initial impressions regarding the expert's demeanor and credibility, and those impressions will determine their overall empathy and identification with the expert then testifying."[19]

Pay significant attention to whether the proposed expert has all required licensure and certifications in a proclaimed specialization, is in receipt of a certificate of training or other documentation, or has been admitted to any professional associations or groups, which attest to the specialized nature of the expertise.

d. Publications, Conferences, and Presentations Expert witnesses become even more compelling when publications—whether books, studies, or periodical articles—are highlighted during qualification questioning. Whether misplaced or not, the lay person perceives a publication record as evidence of an enlightened professional. Publications, especially those that are found in refereed or edited journals, manifest the general academic community's acceptance of the expert's theoretical posturing. Practice, in and of itself, is less persuasive than the expert who frames theoretical problems in publicly published forums. The true expert, the more believable one, is that witness who has written and researched in his field as a complement to pure experience. Not to be forgotten are textbook publications, authored participation in legal materials, or editorial contributions to legal advisory committee reports and documents. The formality and permanency of writing indelibly impress the fact finder.

Indicative of expertise is the expert's record of attendance at continuing education seminars, conferences, and conventions. These actions impress upon the jury the expert's commitment to excellence, the expert's willingness to be in the scientific forefront, and the expert's recognition that his or her field of study is constantly changing, maturing, and intellectually developing. In medical and scientific fields, this approach is mandatory.

What the attorney wants in all cases is the most technically competent expert, with the most exemplary credentials obtainable in the field. In general, credentials should show that the expert has devoted a substantial part of his or her professional experiences to his or her fields of specialization. Among the matters to investigate are education, licensure or board certification, if acceptable, and practical experience. Experience should be evaluated in terms of quality as well as quantity. Factors affecting quality include exposure to authorities in the field or recognition by peers through awards or honors or membership in professional societies. Authorship of articles and applicable trade or professional publications is also impressive, and any articles should be reviewed for content to determine what positions the expert has gone on record as taking. The more education or practical experience the expert has the better the expert is, both from the standpoint of evaluating the case and the ultimate testimony at trial.[20]

Undoubtedly, certain experts will be stronger in some of these criteria than others. In a perfect world, all of these qualifications would be met. Generally, keep in mind the following suggestions to determine whether an expert is worthy of hire:

1. Previous experience with the witness, if any.
2. Reputation amongst other experts.
3. Degree of specialization and technical areas.
4. Publications.
5. Previous testimony recorded in transcripts, newspaper articles or other information about the witness.
6. Catalogs or other types of university or college literature indicating the witness is on faculty.
7. Professional advertising literature that is published by the expert.
8. The expert's resume.
9. Previous depositions of the expert.[21]

Employ the checklist at Figure 4.2 as a screening and qualification device.

The areas of expertise are only limited by a judicial decision as to what is scientifically acceptable and what is not.[22] Courts have long construed certain disciplines as having "crossed the barrier of judicial acceptability,"[23] while barring the admissibility of those fields deemed untried or untrue. For example, the fields of astrology or parasensory perception have still not developed sufficient scientific support, nor is it likely to occur, to be viewed as legitimate scientific endeavors.[24]

But this mentality has been under siege since the 1990s. Instead of scientific rigor, the U.S. Supreme Court has issued two rulings, *Daubert*[25] and *Kumho*,[26] both of which effectively end the reign of *Frye* in the federal system.

The federal courts, by and through a pivotal ruling, *Daubert v. Merrell Dow Pharmaceuticals*,[27] have effectively made the *Frye* rule moot in their jurisdiction. *Daubert* has been the primary support of those hoping to achieve the admissibility of "sciences" once scorned. Strict reliance on the general consensus test of *Frye* is being replaced with a "more searching and flexible inquiry about the reliability and relevance of the offered evidence."[28] Under *Daubert*, judges are "gatekeepers" now performing dual functions; screening "expert scientific testimony not merely to assure that the expert is qualified, but also to assure that the expert methodology is 'reliable.'"[29] Judges were to determine whether "the scientific evidence had sufficient testing, peer review and publication."[30] *Daubert*'s suggestions were toothless, and, as a result, unpredictability at the lower courts became normal. It is questionable whether judges are even capable of performing the latter function.[31] Like it or not, until and when *Daubert* is modified, judges have taken on an increasing screening role in scientific evidence.[32]

Daubert's lenient and inconsistent results have generated enormous criticism. The U.S. Supreme Court's 1999 ruling, in *Kumho Tire Co. v. Carmichael*,[33] accelerated the gate-keeping role of the judge when it comes to the quality and content of expert evidence. Not only are the questions of qualification and field pertinent, but also the methodology behind the results testified to.[34] *Kumho* is a valiant attempt to banish a burgeoning "junk science" industry from the courtroom. Expert evidence should be primarily rooted in a "real science"[35] that only arises from "careful and controlled experimentation."[36]

Expert Witness Questionnaire

Name: ________________________________

Address: ________________________________

____

Home Phone: Work Phone: ________________________________

Fax Number: E-mail Address: ________________________________

Business or Occupation: ________________________________

Name of Organization: ________________________________

Length of Time in Business: ________________________________

Position Held in Organization: ________________________________

Prior Positions: ________________________________

Education:

Under Graduate Degree: Institution: ________________________________

Graduate Degree: Institution: ________________________________

Post Graduate: Institution: ________________________________

Specialized Training:

Courses: ________________________________

Licenses and Certifications: ________________________________

Professional Associations and Organizations: ________________________________

____

Academic Background: ________________________________

____

Expert Witness Experience: ________________________________

____

Specializations: ________________________________

____

FIGURE 4.2 Expert witness questionnaire.

For private security operatives, the liberalization of the scientific rules, replaced with the vagaries of helpfulness and the like, was once thought to be friendly to some industry practices. For example, in the investigative realm, polygraphs and other truth-measuring devices have never crossed the barrier of judicial acceptability, and legislation restricts their use. Traditional *Frye* rules shut that door.[37] But many argue that *Daubert* opens up the new vista of admissibility, making it more likely than not, at least over time, that the polygraph may see the light of day.[38] On the other hand, psychiatry and psychology, although imprecise disciplines, are accepted as areas of expert testimony by the judicial system. Yet even if a field is never formally admitted into court, its use of the investigative end of a case may still be wise and warranted. Polygraphs are a solid example of a useful, yet non-judicially recognized, form of expert evidence.

For most evaluators, scientific, medical, and technical experts giving testimony in reputable fields can be rightfully depended on and upon whom private security investigators might call in the analysis of their assignments. Some of the more typical fields might be:

Actuaries	Criminalists	Microscopic Specialists
Agriculturalists	Electrical Contractors	Nuclear Scientists
Anthropologists	Engineers	Psychologists
Appraisers	Environmentalists	Physicists
Archaeologists	Foresters	Psychiatrists
Aviation Safety Experts	Geologists	Radiologists
Biologists	Meteorologists	Security Analysts
Botanists	Metallurgists	Surveyors
Chemists		

Expert witnesses come from many quarters. Paul Kirk's "Locating Scientific and Technical Experts" assembles expertise through many avenues including educational groups, associations, scientific bodies, and boards that are surely to have members with the needed backgrounds.[39] *The Lawyer's Desk Reference Manual* also contains pertinent information on expert groups and associations.[40] There are a host of possible avenues for locating expert witnesses.

Seen regularly in the legal community are published directories that compile listings of experts and their intellectual endeavor. Some examples are:

- *The Directory of Medical Specialists*, A. N. Marquis Co., 200 East Ohio Street, Chicago, IL, 60611;
- *Consultants and Consulting Organization Directory*, Consultant's Project, Box 428, College Park, MD, 20740;
- "Locating Scientific and Technical Experts," *Am. Jur. Trials.* 2 (1987), 302–356;
- "Locating Medical Experts," *Am. Jur. Trials.* 2 (1987), 112–133; and,
- *The Lawyer's Guide to Legal Consultants, Expert Witnesses, Services, Books and Products*, Attorney's Profiles International, 30700 Bainbridge Road, Suite H, Solon, OH 44139-2291.

Consult *Who's Who* directories for specific fields from the law, engineering, biochemistry, geology, mathematics, psychology, psychiatry, and related fields. Most reference librarians will be happy to assist in sorting out and discovering these rich forms of source material.

e. *Private Consulting Services* No area of expert consulting services is more dynamic than that provided by private entities. Expert consulting services are structured for two major rationales: first, to act as a resource directory, a referral network for attorneys searching for a specific expert, and a corresponding topic; and second, to provide evaluative and research services. As to the former, a fee of some type is usually charged, say between $50 and $200 for that referral. Two of the most often seen and well known of these private consulting services are:

- Technical Advisory Service for Attorneys (TASA), 1166 DeKalb Pike, Blue Bell, PA, 19422, 1-800-523-2319; and,
- Professional Safety, Inc. (PSI); 100 Euston, Royal Palm Beach, FL 33411, 1-800-562-7233.

Another influential player in providing references to experts and litigation support in general is the Association of Trial Lawyers of America (ATLA, 1050 31st Street N.W. Washington, DC, 20007).

In medical claims, the investigator could correctly depend upon any expert from these fields and subfields:

- Allergy
- Anesthesiology
- Cardiology
- Chest Surgery
- Chiropractics
- Dentistry
- Dermatology
- Endocrinology
- Gastroenterology
- Geriatrics
- Gerontology
- Gynecology
- Hematology
- Hospital Administration
- Immunology
- Industrial Medicine
- Internal Medicine
- Medical Laboratory Technology
- Medical Photography
- Neurology and Neurosurgery
- Nuclear Medicine Nursing
- Obstetrics
- Occupational Therapy
- Ophthalmology and Optometry
- Orthopedics
- Osteopathy
- Otolaryngology
- Pathology
- Pediatrics
- Pharmacy
- Physical Medicine/Physical Therapy
- Plastic Surgery
- Preventive Medicine
- Proctology
- Psychiatry and Psychoanalysis
- Psychology
- Radiology
- Surgery
- Urology
- Veterinary Medicine[41]

Experts also play a major role in case evaluation and screening for government agencies, attorneys, and investigators. There are a variety of private companies, both for profit and not for profit, whose purpose is the evaluation and assessment of case and claim. For example, in medical cases, such companies review the medical records and documentation and reach a conclusion on their validity and a projection on a patient's future condition. These same companies may also review fact patterns to determine whether a technical or structural deficiency exists in a product, service, or action due to a vendor, dealer, or manufacturer.

An investigator looking for expertise need not rely on private, for-profit firms. Experts can be located in other areas, including:

- Colleges and universities
- Professional associations
- Scholarly literature and reviews
- Trade schools
- Telephone books
- *Who's Who* books

Though the field of expert service companies is wide, investigators should not overlook local authorities, such as the family physician, an auto mechanic in a product liability case, the osteopathic specialist in rehabilitative back and neck medicine, and so forth.

Whether the investigator utilizes the expert witness in a testimonial fashion or as a quality control assessor, the expert must meet certain minimum criteria. "In general, credentials should show that the expert has devoted a substantial part of his or her professional life to the applicable subject area. Among the matters to investigate are education, licensure or board certification, if applicable, and practical experience. Experience should be evaluated in terms of quality as well as quantity.

Factors affecting quality include exposure to authorities in the field or recognition by peers through awards or honors or membership in professional societies. Authorship of articles in applicable trade or professional publications is also impressive, and any article should be reviewed for content to determine what positions the expert has gone on record as taking. The more education or practical experience the expert has, the better the expert is both from the standpoint of evaluating the case and the ultimate testimony that will be presented at trial."[42]

Finally, investigators must not be duped or overly impressed with expert credentials; for one expert who attests that a certain condition is causally tied or correlated to given circumstances, another will take the same circumstance and deny such a relationship. For one psychiatrist who claims that evidence of insanity exists, another may assert that the defendant is as lucid as the rest of the population. The testimony of experts cannot be viewed as infallible. Treat testimonial and evidentiary results of experts sensibly,[43] and remember that an expert, when paid for his or her consultation, will favor the payor, and in this sense, there is always a clear and present economic bias.

2. *Expert Service Contracts*

Expert consulting services charge litigation teams in various ways, including set fee, hourly rate, or in some circles, a fee based on whether the case is won or lost. Profit motive is the driving force of the private consulting firms. Expert service contracts are initiated either by the consulting firm or by documents authored by the law firm, an example of which is given in Figure 4.3. Be certain that the contract covers accurately the costs and fees of usage. Surprises are avoided by clear contracts. Experts can become an extraordinary liability.[44]

D. Character Witnesses

Investigators must be forever mindful of the credibility of the claim and the claimant. One cannot assume that an allegation is true.[45] Every investigative assignment should be adjudged as to its credibility and authenticity. Investigators must be wary of those making claims to outlandish victimization. Check the character of a story's source. Check the facts from a credibility perspective. Just as the criminal about to be sentenced will march his mother and brother before the tribunal to attest to his or her character, the alleged victim or injured party must be vetted. One must be sure, as sure can be, of character and veracity. Then check the character of the party attesting to character. Be wary of intimate witnesses, those too close to the party. Be cautious about accepting the word of those entangled by family or finance with the party entreating their reputational perspective. Character witnesses can be as flawed or righteous as those on whose behalf they speak. Finally, be skeptical of those who speak for a larger community when giving reputation evidence. It is difficult enough to know one's own view let alone the mass known as the community. In the final analysis it is a blend of both worlds—the character witness giving his or her own impression, in lay form, as to the community's perception and belief about the defendant's reputation.[46]

Character witnesses relay circumstantial insight and evidence about a particular party. The whole essence behind the character witness is not that he or she is an expert in the psychological or psychiatric sense, but instead is qualified to give a judgment of a community's perception of an individual's reputation.[47]

III. PROCESSING WITNESSES

As indicated in Chapter 3, the techniques of interviewing a witness call for effective interaction. "Interviewing witnesses is an art. Usually, if the witness is a friend or relative of the client, he or she will readily speak to the attorney or the investigator. When the witness is not such a person, the job of the interviewer will be not only to get a statement but to get the witness to speak at all."[48]

(Date)

(Name)
(Address)

RE: Matt Helms v. Christine White

_______ County Common Pleas Court Case No. ________________

Dear Dr.____________________:

This letter will confirm our conference of April 4, 2008, in connection with retaining your services as an accident reconstruction expert. As discussed, please evaluate this case to determine the following:

1. the pre-skid speed of the Helms vehicle;
2. the time comparison from Mr. Helms' first reaction to the White vehicle as a hazard to the interval of time that the White vehicle was on Route 79 before impact; and
3. whether the presence of a guardrail on the south edge of Route 79 could have lessened the severity of the impact and resulting injuries.

I am enclosing a check for $1,000.00 representing your retainer for work on this case. It is my understanding that, should the work be completed or stopped for any reason before using up the amount of the retainer, the balance will be refunded. It is my further understanding that your normal fee schedule for this type of work is as follows:

Preparation Time........................$75.00/hour
(Includes: background review, site visit, field work, engineering analysis, reports, meetings, depositions, travel time)

Court Time.....$500.00/eight-hour day or part thereof
All Expenses (Includes air fare, tolls, lodging, meals, mileage, film, prints, aerial photography, etc.)

Under separate cover, I am forwarding a packet of background materials on this case for your review. You may feel free to contact my client, Mr. Stephen Nemeth, at (216) 555-2432 if you need any information directly from him. I would ask that you not prepare a written report of your findings until I request it at a later date. Please note that the trial of this case has been scheduled for September 10, 2008.

Mr. Bart Brizee is the paralegal in my office who will be assisting me on this case. Please feel free to contact either of us if you have questions. If the terms outlined above comport your understanding of your engagement on this case, please so indicate by signing the enclosed copy of this letter and return it to me in the envelope provided.

Very truly yours,

____

Attorney

FIGURE 4.3 Expert service contract.

NAME/ADDRESS

IN RE: Witness Statement

Our Client:

Date of Accident:

Dear:

I am an investigator for the above-named client who has granted me full power of attorney to collect information regarding the above-reference accident. A copy of that power of attorney is enclosed. I am writing about my client whom I represent for recovery of economic loss and damages that resulted from an incident seen by you.

Would you please call me at your convenience to advise me of the facts you saw relative to this matter. I must stress that this matter may be unjustly resolved without your assistance. If you have any questions, Please feel free to call.

Sincerely,

____

(Investigator)

Enclosure

FIGURE 4.4 Sample witness correspondence.

Sample letters advising witnesses of your desire for them to cooperate and provide you with information as a witness appear in Figures 4.4 and 4.5. Notice that the letters are neither antagonistic nor overly legalistic in approach or design. Instead, they convey the intention to work amicably with the witness and show that his or her testimony is sufficiently urgent.

Figure 4.6 is the enclosure referenced in the letter above. Investigators should evaluate the quality of the witness by the statement he or she offers.

IV. CONCLUSION

The chapter provides a thumbnail sketch of witnesses—those parties who will deliver testimonial proof about a claim or assertion; corroborate a claim or fact; aid and assist the investigator by confirming events and condition; or expertly assess the validity of a case. Types of witnesses, from lay to expert, who lack character were analyzed as well as practical suggestions for working with witnesses.

IN RE: Witness Statement

Our Client:

Date of Accident:

Dear:

I am an investigator for the above-named client who has granted me full power of attorney to collect information regarding the above-referenced accident. A copy of that power of attorney is enclosed. I am writing to request your assistance in representing my client who was injured in an accident that you witnessed. I am attempting to recovery my client's economic losses and damages as a result of this incident.

I have enclosed a form for information concerning the facts you observed on the day of the accident. I also have enclosed a self-addressed envelope for your use. If, for any reason, filling out this form will be difficult or inconvenient, please feel free to call me, and my office will be glad to take your statement over the phone.

Thank you for taking the time to tell us the facts of this incident. Without your information, this matter may not be resolved justly. If I can be of any assistance, please feel free to call.

Sincerely,

____

(Investigator)

Enclosure

FIGURE 4.5 Sample witness correspondence.

Request for Witness Statement

Your Name: ____

Date of Birth: ____

Where were you when you saw the facts concerning this incident?

____

____

____

____

What did you see?

____

____

____

Did you hear anyone, including the people involved in the incident, say anything?

____

____

____

____

____

____

____

Do you know of any other witnesses? ( ) YES ( ) NO

If yes, do you know the names of the witnesses or can you describe them?

____

____

____

____

____

____

____

Additional comments:

____

____

____

____

____

____

____

FIGURE 4.6 Request for witness statement.

NOTES

1. Bennett L. Gershman, "The Eyewitness Conundrum," *N.Y. St. B. J.* 81 (2009), 24; Law witnesses cannot always be trusted or be deemed reliable. See "Police, Prosecutors Still Rely On Unreliable Eyewitness Accounts," *Courts Today*. (October–November 2008), 12.
2. Ralph F. Brislin, *The Effective Security Officer's Training Manual* (Butterworth-Heineman, 1995), 89.
3. See Charles P. Nemeth, *Law and Evidence* (Prentice Hall, 2001).
4. Patricia W. Kittredge, "Guideposts for the Investigation of a Negligence Case," *Prac. Law*. 90 (1973), 55; J. Stannar Baker, "Reconstruction of Accidents," *Traffic Dig. Rev*. 17 (1969), 9; P. Magarick, "Investigating the Civil Case: General Principles," *Am. Jur. Trials* 1 (1987), 361.
5. *Am. Jur. Trials*. 2(1987), 229, 235.
6. Someone Is Missing, at http://www.someoneismissing.com/noreport.htm, visited August 28, 2009.
7. Federal Rule of Evidence (Fed. R. Evid.) 601.
8. Fed. R. Evid. 701.
9. "Evidence: Lay Opinion Testimony—Sound of Car Running over Body," *Crim. L. Rep*. (January 7, 2009), 353.
10. Nemeth, *Law and Evidence*, 151 et seq., with text in second edition to be published in 2010.
11. Fed. R. Evid. 701.
12. Timothy J Perfect et al., "How Can We Help Witnesses to Remember More? It's an (Eyes) Open and Shut Case," *L. Human Behavior*. 32 (2008), 314.
13. Charles P. Nemeth, *Litigation, Pleadings, and Arbitration* (Anderson, 1990), 421; for an excellent analysis of historic distrust of lay opinion, see D. Garrison "'Gary' Hill, Lay Witness Opinions,: *S. Carolina Law*. (September 2007), 34.
14. Fed. R. Evid. 702.
15. Chris Vail, "Presenting Winning Testimony in Court," in *The Security Supervisor Training Manual*, Sandi J. Davies and Ronald R. Minion, eds. (Butterworth-Heinemann, 1995).
16. Fed. R. Evid 702.
17. See Nemeth, *supra* note 12, at 421; see also John Tarantino, *Trial Evidence Foundations* (James Publishing, 1987), 4–5.
18. 647 F. Supp. 544, 547 (S. D. Ga. 1986).
19. Beverly Hutson, *Paralegal Trial Handbook* (Wiley, 1991), 3–15.
20. Mark Dombroff, *Dombroff on Unfair Tactics* (Wiley, 1988), 415.
21. Lawrence S. Charfoos and David W. Christensen, *Personal Injury Practice: Technique and Technology* (Lawyer's Co-Operative, 1986).
22. Dombroff, *supra* note 19, at 417.
23. For more complete coverage of the use of experts, see Andre Moenssens, "The Impartial Medical Expert: A New Look at an Old Issue," *Med. Trial Technique Q*. 25 (1978), 63; Robert Porro, "Expert Witnesses: Crossroads of Law, Science and Technology," *Am. Trial Advoc*. 2 (1979), 291; Michael T. Smith and Walter R. Lancaster, "Impeaching a 'National Expert' in a Catastrophic Collision Case," *For the Defense* 23 (1981), 8.
24. *Frye v. United States*, 293 F. 1013 (1923).
25. Fritz Jekel, "When an Expert Isn't an Expert," *Trial*. (July 2008), at 50.
26. *Daubert v. Merrell Dow Pharmaceuticals*, 509 U.S. 579 (1993).
27. *Kumho Tire Co. v. Carmichael*, 526 U.S. 137 (1999).
28. *Supra* at 25.
29. Ellen Moskkowitz, "Junk Science," *Hastings Center Rep*. 48 (1996); see also Lewis H. LaRue and David S. Caudill, "A Non-Romantic View of Expert Testimony," *Seton Hall L. Rev*. 35 (2004), 1; Gary Edmond, "Expertise in the Courtroom: Scientists and Wizards: Panel Three: Science, Scientists and Ethics: Article: Supersizing Daubert Science for Litigation and Its Implications for Legal Practice and Scientific Research," *Vill. L. Rev*. 52 (2007), 857.
30. Michael H. Gottesman, "Should State Courts Impose a 'Reliability' Threshold?" *Trial*. (September 1997), 20–23.
31. Edward R. Cavanagh, "Decision Extends Daubert Approach to All Expert Testimony," *N.Y. St. B.J.* (July/August 1999), 9; see also Edward J. Imwinkelried, "The Next Step After Daubert: Developing a Similarly Epistemological Approach to Ensuring the Reliability of Nonscientific Expert Testimony," *Cardozo L. Rev*. 15 (1994), 2271.
32. Paul Reidinger, "They Blinded Me with Science," *ABA J.* (September 1996), 58–62.

33. In fact, the Federal Judicial Center has formally recognized the need for judicial involvement by increasing science training for district court judges and by publishing a handbook on scientific evidence, which includes detailed "reference guides" on scientific and technical specialties frequently encountered in the courtroom. Paul S. Miller and Bert W. Rein, "Whither Daubert? Reliable Resolution of Scientifically-Based Causality Issues In Toxic Tort Cases," *Rutgers L. Rev*. 501 (1998), 563; see also Victor E. Schwartz and Cary Silverman, "The Draining of Daubert and the Recidivism of Junk Science in Federal and State Courts," *Hofstra L. Rev*. 35 (2006), 217.
34. 119 S.Ct. 1167 (1999).
35. Robert W. Littleton, "Supreme Court Dramatically Changes the Rules on Experts," *N.Y. St. B.J.* (July/August 1999), 8, 12.
36. *Id.*
37. *Id.*
38. For example, it is very unlikely that *Frye* would have permitted *Palm Crease* evidence as recently occurred. See "Palm Crease Expert Was Properly Allowed to Identify Sex Abuser's Hand in Photograph," *Crim. L. Rep.* (February 11, 2009), 525.
39. Paul C. Giannelli, "Daubert 'Factors'," *Criminal Justice* (Winter 2009), 42; Mara L. Merlino et al., "Judicial Gatekeeping and the Social Construction of the Admissibility of Expert Testimony," *Behavioral Sci. Law*. 26 (2008), 187; Edward J Imwinkelried, "Law for the Expert Witness," *Jurimetrics*. (Winter 2008), 241.
40. Paul L. Kirk, "Locating Scientific and Technical Experts," *Am. Jur. Trials*. 2 (1987), 293, 302–356.
41. *Lawyer's Desk Reference Manual*, (Thomas-West, 2008).
42. See D. Rubsamen, "Locating Medical Experts," *Am. Jur. Trials*. 2 (1987), 112–133.
43. Charfoos and Christensen, 493.
44. *Id.* at 502.
45. Michael Wagner in his keenly authored work, "Expert Problems," manifests a brilliant recognition of expert fees out of control. "Perhaps no more than any other professionals, lawyers know what hourly rate billing can mean. Hours are deposited on billing sheets, bit by bit, day by day. They do not look like much while they accrete, but before long the bill is a mountain. The gradual deposits of time are continuous; with hourly billing there is less incentive not to do something. If you are paid for every hour, you think less about the need for what fills up that hour's time. If you want to be stuck by your expert like some clients are stuck by their attorneys, insist on an hourly billing." Michael J. Wagner, "Expert Problems," *Litig*. 15 (1989), 35, 36.
46. "Asking Character Witnesses Hypotheticals that Assume Guilt Generally Is Permissible," *Crim. L. Rep.* (December 19, 2007), 320.
47. "Evidence-Character Witnesses—Impeachment with Evidence of Defendant's Prior Convictions—Preservation of Issue," *Crim. L. Rep.* (March 4, 2009), 609.
48. See J. McCord, *Litigation Paralegal* (West Publishing, 1988).
49. Mark Weinstein, *Introduction to Civil Litigation* (West Publishing, 1986), 54.

5 Collection of Information

I. THE NATURE OF INFORMATION AND THE RULES OF COLLECTION

Records, files, documentary evidence, and other written and oral forms of information are the "stock in trade" of the good investigator. In order to track clues in a typical investigative pattern, some form of documentary, testimonial, or physical evidence is necessary. The investigator must depend upon facts more than opinion or rumor. Critical to the success of any investigation are the integrity and substantiality of information gathered. For example, a security firm that is hired to determine the character of a potential employee may attach any or all of the following to its written report:

- Past character references
- Offense reports
- Military reports
- Litigation documents
- Credit history reports
- Deeds, titles, or insurance documents
- Arrest reports

The mere assertion that a person's character is flawed will not cut it. The documents posed here flesh out the claim of bad character and corroborate the conclusion.

The scope of this chapter involves information and its collection. Professional investigators need to master the art of information gathering as well as its analysis. What to look for and whom to ask are perennial issues for the investigator. Information is everywhere. The trick is how to get it and be assured of its meaningfulness. Acquiring information largely depends upon accessibility to either persons or institutions. In the process of acquiring information, the investigator must respect the law and the fundamental tenets of privacy. As the American Society for Industrial Security remarks:

> Many organizations, notably some credit agencies, operated with little legal restraint. Inaccurate and often irrelevant records were maintained, and flagrant misuse of information was common. Until recent years, investigators—whether public or private, for ill or good—had almost open access to many kinds of data banks. Subsequent laws and regulations have placed restrictions on what information can be gathered, how it can be obtained, and what use can be made of it. To violate these restrictions exposes all parties involved, including the investigator, to certain risks.[1]

Attention to privacy and the constitutional rights of others should be an ongoing ethical and professional concern of the security investigator.

> Under current circumstances the investigator must, by and large, identify for himself what is permissible in the way of gathering information. He must find out what restraints apply to him as well as what rights he is entitled to exercise in the course of an investigation. On occasion, the investigator should re-verify these rights and limitations when a new investigation is undertaken. Every investigator should stay abreast of the changes resulting from legislative or regulatory action, as well as from court decisions, in each jurisdiction where he conducts investigations.[2]

Both federal and state statutes address the issue of information-gathering and the perennial issue of individual privacy. A short list of federal legislation includes:

- Privacy Act of 1974[3]
- Financial Privacy Act of 1978[4]
- Privacy Protection Act of 1980[5]
- Fair Financial Information Practices Act of 1981[6]
- Privacy of Electronic Fund Transfers Act of 1981[7]
- Fair Credit Reporting Act of 1970[8]
- Omnibus and Crime Control Bill of 1968[9]
- Freedom of Information Act (FOIA)[10]

At every level of the investigative process, security operatives need to exercise the type of demeanor and professional courtesy consistent with these enactments. The U.S. Department of Justice, through its Bureau of Justice Statistics, authored *Privacy and Security of Criminal History Information: An Analysis of Privacy Issues*, stating:

> "Privacy" has gained attention of late in every area of personal affairs. Of singular importance has been the subject of "privacy and security" of criminal justice information. Often the desires for anonymity by those who have confronted the criminal justice system clash with society's inquiries pursuant to a "right to know."[11]

In the same vein, the *National Advisory Commission on Criminal Justice Standards and Goals* calls upon state governments to adopt legislation that provides for:

> the protection of security and privacy in criminal justice information systems. The enabling statute should establish the minimum standards for protection of security and privacy and civil and criminal sanctions for violation of the rules and regulations adopted under it.[12]

The Hallcrest Report: Private Security and Police in America issues similar cautions about privacy concerns, although its picture manifests the preeminence of the security industry when compared to its public counterpart. Here private sector justice operates without the onerous constitutional restraints so evident in public policing. *Hallcrest* concludes:

> The information sources used by private investigators are much the same as those used by law enforcement officers. However, the private investigator is not subject to as many limitations as the police officer on collecting information since the admissibility of evidence in court is frequently not a concern. In the private sector, an investigator can pursue a case to the level of detail and expenditure set by the client. On the other hand, the police detective may be hampered by large caseload and internal case management criteria that limit the time and resources which can be devoted to a single case. The main constraint upon private investigators is the Privacy of Information Act, which restricts access to many credit, banking, and government records, and also most police information. Telephone company records, credit information, employer information, and criminal record information are frequently off limits to private investigators.[13]

In the age of virtual access, increasing concerns involving privacy are evident. Various state and federal efforts to protect privacy rights are just touching upon the dilemma.[14] For example, in the area of criminal histories, much is a stake. Review the Request for Criminal History Record Information issued by the Commonwealth of Pennsylvania (Figure 5.1). Requesters are either criminal justice agencies, individuals, or noncriminal justice agencies. In the instructions, which appear on the reverse side of the form, individuals are advised that a full criminal report will not be made available, only a "rap sheet."

SP 4-164 (12-99)

PENNSYLVANIA STATE POLICE

REQUEST FOR CRIMINAL RECORD CHECK

FOR CENTRAL REPOSITORY USE ONLY (LEAVE BLANK)

PART I: TO BE COMPLETED BY REQUESTER (INFORMATION WILL BE MAILED TO REQUESTER ONLY)

DATE OF REQUEST

*** TYPE OR PRINT LEGIBLY WITH INK ***

NOTE: IF THIS FORM IS NOT LEGIBLE OR NOT PROPERLY COMPLETED, IT WILL BE RETURNED UNPROCESSED TO THE REQUESTER. A RESPONSE MAY TAKE THREE WEEKS OR LONGER TO PROCESS.

WARNING: A PERSON COMMITS A MISDEMEANOR OF THE THIRD DEGREE IF HE/SHE MAKES A WRITTEN FALSE STATEMENT, WHICH HE/SHE DOES NOT BELIEVE TO BE TRUE.

REQUESTER NAME	
ADDRESS	
CITY	STATE ZIP

CONTACT TELEPHONE NUMBER (INCLUDING AREA CODE)

☐☐☐ - ☐☐☐ - ☐☐☐☐

REQUESTER IDENTIFICATION (ONLY CHECK ONE BLOCK)

☐ INDIVIDUAL/NONCRIMINAL JUSTICE AGENCY – ENCLOSE A CERTIFIED CHECK/MONEY ORDER IN THE AMOUNT OF $10.00 PAYABLE TO: "*COMMONWEALTH OF PENNSYLVANIA*." THE FEE IS NONREFUNDABLE.

☐ FEE EXEMPT NONCRIMINAL JUSTICE AGENCY

*** DO NOT SEND CASH OR PERSONAL CHECK ***

NAME/SUBJECT OF RECORD CHECK (LAST)	(FIRST)	(MIDDLE)

MAIDEN NAME AND/OR ALIASES	SOCIAL SECURITY NUMBER (SOC)	DATE OF BIRTH (DOB)	SEX	RACE

REASON FOR REQUEST (CHECK ONE BLOCK)

☐ EMPLOYMENT (IF APPLICABLE, CHECK ONE OF THE FOLLOWING) ☐ ELDER CARE ☐ CHILD CARE ☐ SCHOOL DISTRICT

☐ ADOPTION/FOSTER CARE

☐ OTHER (SPECIFY) ____________

ONLY CHECK THIS BLOCK IF YOU WANT TO REVIEW *YOUR ENTIRE* CRIMINAL HISTORY

☐ INDIVIDUAL ACCESS AND REVIEW OR FIREARMS CHALLENGE–ENTIRE CRIMINAL HISTORY (AVAILABLE ONLY TO SUBJECT OF RECORD CHECK OR LEGAL REPRESENTATIVE WITH LEGAL AFFIDAVIT OF LEGAL REPRESENTATIVE ATTACHED)

REQUESTER CHECKLIST

DID YOU ENTER THE FULL NAME, DOB, AND SOC?

DID YOU ENCLOSE THE $10.00 FEE (CERTIFIED CHECK/MONEY ORDER)?

*** DO NOT SEND CASH OR PERSONAL CHECK ***

DID YOU ENTER YOUR COMPLETE ADDRESS INCLUDING ZIP CODE AND TELEPHONE NUMBER IN THE BLOCKS PROVIDED?

AFTER COMPLETION MAIL TO

PENNSYLVANIA STATE POLICE
CENTRAL REPOSITORY – 164
1800 ELMERTON AVENUE
HARRISBURG, PA 17110-9758
717-783-9973
BUSINESS HOURS 8:15 am - 4:15 pm (Monday – Friday)

PART II: CENTRAL REPOSITORY RESPONSE ONLY ****DO NOT WRITE BELOW THIS LINE****

INFORMATION DISSEMINATED

☐ NO RECORD ☐ CRIMINAL RECORD ATTACHED

INQUIRY DISSEMINATED BY | SID NUMBER

THE INFORMATION DISSEMINATED BY THE CENTRAL REPOSITORY IS BASED ON THE FOLLOWING IDENTIFIERS THAT MATCH THOSE FURNISHED BY THE REQUESTER.

☐ NAME ☐ SOCIAL SECURITY NUMBER
☐ DATE OF BIRTH ☐ RACE
☐ SEX ☐ MAIDEN/ALIAS NAME

CERTIFIED BY

(DIRECTOR, CENTRAL REPOSITORY)

This response is based on a comparison of data provided by the requester in Part I against the information contained in the files of the Pennsylvania State Police Central Repository only, and does not preclude the existence of criminal records which might be contained in the repositories of other local, state, or federal criminal justice agencies.

FIGURE 5.1 Request for criminal record check form.

Many of the alleged restrictions on public record access for private security operatives are alleviated by the interplay between public and private police. With record numbers of public police moonlighting as private security officers, access to records becomes an academic argument.

The Hallcrest Report stresses profitability of the relationships between private investigators and public law enforcement. "Private security firms trade heavily upon personal relationships;

personalities rather than legitimacy or legality of need determine the amount of information and level of cooperation received from law enforcement."[15] In its national survey of private investigative firms, the practice of lending information is pervasive.

> Private investigative firms reported frequent contact with detectives in law enforcement agencies; in fact, 58% reported daily or weekly contact. Little contact was reported with law enforcement supervisors and managers. Law enforcement administrators in the national survey, however, reported less frequent contact of their detectives with private security personnel; only 44% reported daily or weekly contact with their detectives. Cities above 100,000 population reported twice as much daily contact. …
>
> Thus, private investigators report frequent contact with law enforcement detectives, but purportedly do not seek law enforcement information or provide information from their investigations on a regular basis. … Four out of ten firms reported that they employ off-duty law enforcement officers. Officers employed in this capacity could be in a position to obtain police information to gain favor with their secondary employer in private security.[16]

The underground network of sharing information does not cease here. Private security investigators hone relationships with numerous other parties, including:

- Court clerks
- Correctional personnel
- Deed and title personnel
- Notaries public
- Bankers
- Insurance representatives
- Telephone company employees
- Personnel agencies

By forging complementary and tactful relationships with information sources such as those listed above, the investigator has access to an unlimited supply of information. Despite bureaucratic and regulatory obstructions, an inquisitive person will eventually gain access to the desired information, even though the practice is legally suspect.

In order to ensure fairness, government and its guardians of records balance the interests of both the subject of the file or document and the public's need, desire, and right to examine the data and information contained therein. Dual-edged by nature, privacy protects the individual from excessive scrutiny and review, and in doing so, stifles the flow of and access to information, thereby thwarting public understanding. In balancing these competing interests, access and dissemination must adhere to these principles:

1. No personal information systems should be maintained whose very existence is secret.
2. A data subject should have access to information about himself and know the purposes for which it is maintained.
3. A data subject should be permitted to challenge and seek corrections of information about himself.
4. Data should be used only for the purposes for which they were intended, unless the data subject consents.
5. Information used should be accurate, timely, relevant, and complete.
6. Information should be protected against unauthorized access, alteration, or destruction.[17]

II. LEADS AND CONTACTS FOR THE PRIVATE INVESTIGATOR

Any good investigator develops contacts and sources for information, and security professionals have come to rely on both public and private sources. The more predictable contacts are:

- Government employees
- Code enforcement officers

- Credit office employees
- Tow truck operators
- Bank officers and personnel
- Body shop and auto repair specialists
- Department and retail store employee
- Tax agents
- Telephone employees
- County clerks
- Private security employees
- Recorders of deeds
- Police officers
- Registers of wills
- Newspaper reporters and editors
- Neighborhood snitches
- Insurance company personnel
- Neighborhood busybodies
- School and educational personnel
- Social club heads and board members
- Hospital and medical personnel
- Tag, title, and inspection employees
- Emergency medical services personnel
- Corporation registration and licensing employees[18]

The investigator should maintain a list of information sources, which references information by topical concern, similar to that shown at Figure 5.2. The investigator identifies a topic, such as a deed or death certificate, and then refers to the source chart.

Contacts, for the most part, are preexisting sources. There is nothing very original here in some settings. Institutions of government, by way of example, have always existed and provide information sources. Even so, there are many information sources that need to be developed and honed. The *Security Investigator's Handbook* notes that contacts do not happen overnight. "If the experienced investigator wants to be successful, he would do well to find out where his sources of information are. Developing contacts is a lengthy process, but knowing where to find public information is only a matter of careful preliminary research."[19]

Web Exercise: Visit HowToInvestigate.com. It is a rich web location that instructs on how to gain access to public records. http://howtoinvestigate.com/public_records.htm

Thus, access to information depends upon creativity and innovation. The investigator needs to push the right buttons yet do so in an efficient and effective way. Even if it assumed that information is available for public review and inspection, the task of finding it and knowing the steps and processes to gain access to it are just as critical to a successful investigation. "The well-prepared investigator knows where information in general is kept, and what kinds of information are kept where. If he knows this, he will have a head start on finding something in particular. If he does not, he will be like a man looking for a needle and not even knowing which haystack to search."[20]

Information may be retrievable from either public or private sources, some governmental, others private in design. Cultivate relationships with those whose access to information is worth mining. Understand that most occupations are grounded in some sort of information base that is useful to the investigative process. Contacts come in many shapes and sizes:

- Airline clerks, attendants
- Barbers
- Bartenders
- Bell hops

Information Sources

The investigator may wish to expand this database depending on local issues and resources.

Address	City Directory; Telephone Directory; Voters Registration.
Attorneys	Martindale-Hubble Lawyers Directory; State Lawyers Manual; State Bar Registries.
Automobiles	State Dept. of Motor Vehicles.
Owners	State Dept. of Motor Vehicles.
Liens	State Dept. of Motor Vehicles.
Autopsy Report	County/City Clerk, County/City Court House; Bureau of Vital Statistics; City Health Department.
Business Reputation	Local Better Business Bureau; Trade Associations.
Civil Litigation	U.S. District Court House; Justice of the Peace (townships) (credit bureaus).
Corporations	Articles of Incorporation; County Court House (home office); Dun & Bradstreet; Poors' Directory of Director.
Deaths	County/City Clerk, County Court House; City Health Department; Coroner's Office; Bureau of Vital Statistics; Medical Examiner, County.
Deeds	City/County Clerk, County Court House; Recorder of Deeds.
Criminal Records	U.S. District Court, Local/State Police Dept.; Sheriff's or Marshal's Office.
Doctors	American Medical Association Directory; County Medical Association Directory; State Medical Association Directory.
Financial	Mortgages, County Court House; Dun & Bradstreet (credit bureaus).
Fires	Fire Marshal, Fire Department.
Liens	County Court House, Recorder of Deeds.
Location—Persons	Probate Court; Credit Companies (credit card leads); Banks (checks); Dept. of Motor Vehicles (license change).
Manufacturers	Thomas Buyers Guide & McRaes' Registry of Manufacturers.
Maps, Townships	County Surveyor's Office.
Marriage Licenses	County Clerk's Office, County Court House; Vital Statistics, State Board of Health. County Judge, Circuit Court, Court of Common Pleas, Municipal Archives & Record Retention Center. (Note: County Court House is usual place. Various cities and counties have different locations.)
Military Discharges	If public, County Court House.
Misdemeanor	Municipal Criminal Court; Local Police Department.
Mortgages	County Court House (See excise stamps for real value).
Names—Trade	Thomas Buyers Guide & McRaes' Registry of Manufacturers.
Officers of Corporations	Poors' Directory of Directors;
Co-partnerships & corporations	Moody Directory.
Probation	Municipal [or other] Criminal Court.
Property (Personal)	County Court House.
Real Estate	County Court House; County, City, or State Tax Bureau.
Trademarks	Thomas Buyers Guide & McRaes' Registry of Manufacturers.
Taxes	County or City Clerk.
Personal	City—Treasurer's License Record.
Property	City, County & State Tax Bureau.

FIGURE 5.2 List of useful information sources.

- Building managers
- Bus drivers
- Cab drivers (trip sheets)
- Car hops (drive-ins, etc.)
- Custodians
- Dance hall operators
- Dentists
- Doormen
- Elevator operators
- Garagemen
- Gas station attendants
- Hairdressers
- Hat check girls
- Hostesses
- Hotel clerks
- Janitors or maids (bars, hotels, motels)
- Mail carriers
- Neighborhood children
- News vendors
- Night watchmen
- Operators of street businesses
- Paper delivery boys
- Parking lot attendants
- Parolees and probationers
- Physicians
- Pool hall operators
- Public utility servicemen
- Railroad agents, conductors
- Shoe shine operators
- Switchboard operators
- Street vendors (all-night stands)
- Tradesmen (delivery services)
- Waitresses and waiters

Exactly who and what those sources will be depends upon the subject matter of the investigation. For example, the Federal Bureau of Investigation's Economic and Financial Crimes Training Unit publishes the *Guide to Sources of Information*, a reference authority essential to an investigator working in these particular fields.[21] The guide is a fundamental tool for the field investigator and is loaded with practical suggestions pertaining to information access, particularly the importance of developing community contacts and discerning the informal "community power structure." Known in some circles as a "reputational study," the investigator looks for and identifies the political players more capable than any other of providing critical information. The reputational study affords the investigator a feel for the power structure, whether economic, judicial, or social in nature. The investigator then concentrates on these players to gain access to information.

III. PUBLIC SOURCES OF INFORMATION

Public access to information is partially guaranteed under statutory and common law principles. However, that access is not without restriction, as in the case of privacy, and it is subject to certain

Social Security Numbers—State Codes

001–003	New Hampshire	505–508	Nebraska
004–007	Maine	509–515	Kansas
008–009	Vermont	516–517	Montana
010–034	Massachusetts	518–519	Idaho
035–039	Rhode Island	520	Wyoming
040–049	Connecticut	521–524	Colorado
050–134	New York	525	New Mexico
135–158	New Jersey	526–527	Arizona
159–211	Pennsylvania	528–529	Utah
212–220	Maryland	530	Nevada
221–222	Delaware	531–539	Washington
223–231	Virginia	540–544	Oregon
232–236	West Virginia	545–573	California
237–246	North Carolina	574	Alaska
247–251	South Carolina	575–576	Hawaii
252–260	Georgia	577–579	District of Columbia
261–267	Florida	580	Virgin Islands, Puerto Rico
268–302	Ohio	581–584	Puerto Rico
303–317	Indiana	585	New Mexico
318–361	Illinois	586	Guam, American Somoa, Philippine Islands
362–386	Michigan	587	Mississippi
387–399	Wisconsin	589–595	Florida
400–407	Kentucky	596–599	Puerto Rico
408–415	Tennessee	600–601	Arizona
416–424	Alabama	602–625	California
425–428	Mississippi	627–645	Texas
429–432	Arkansas	646–647	Utah
433–439	Louisiana	648–649	New Mexico
440–443	Oklahoma	654–658	South Carolina
449–467	Texas	667–675	Georgia
468–477	Minnesota	680	Nevada
478–485	Iowa	700–728	RR Reitrement Board
486–500	Missouri		(All States—until July, 1963)
501–502	North Dakota	764–765	Arizona
503–504	South Dakota	716–717	Pennsylvania Railroad

FIGURE 5.3 State codes for Social Security numbers.

regulatory processes. More common public requests include judgments, birth records, marriage records, filings for incorporation and other business entities, tax records, voter registrations, and motor vehicle and auto licensing documentation.

Records involving government benefits, such as Social Security, Medicaid, or disability or veterans' benefits are regularly reviewed requests for the investigator. To determine previous residence or locality through the use of the Social Security number, look at the first three digits, since number represents residence at time of application and issuance (Figure 5.3).

A. Federal Agencies

A wealth of information exists in the public domain; the following agencies can provide valuable data and information:

- Federal Aviation Administration
- Department of Justice
- Department of Transportation
- Civil Rights Commission
- Internal Revenue Service
- Federal Trade Commission
- National Oceanic and Atmospheric Administration
- Census Bureau
- Occupational Safety and Health Administration
- Veterans' Administration
- Department of Agriculture
- Transportation Safety Board
- Department of the Interior
- Civil Aeronautics Board
- Department of Commerce
- Department of Energy
- Consumer Product Safety Commission
- Department of Education
- Employment Standards Commission
- Department of Homeland Security

At the federal level, the investigator needs to identify both subject matter and corresponding agency to make an inquiry. The chart in Figure 5.4 will be helpful if you become familiar with it.

Web Exercise: Visit the FBI's web site. It is an excellent research resource for anyone working in the justice system. http://www.fbi.gov/publications.htm

Investigative Practice	Federal Agency
Banking	Office of the Controller of the Currency, U.S. Treasury Department; Board of Governors of the Federal Reserve System; Federal Deposit Insurance Corporation (FDIC); Federal Home Loan Bank Board; Farm Credit Administration; Resolution Trust Corporation (FTC).
Criminal Matters and Records	Federal Bureau of Investigation; U.S. Department of Justice; National Crime Information Center (NCIC); Department of the Treasury; Department of Drug Enforcement Administration; Central Intelligence Agency; Bureau of Alcohol, Tobacco, and Firearms.
Labor	National Labor Relations Board; Department of Labor; Occupational and Safety Health Administration (OSHA).
Forensic Matters	U.S. Department of Defense; U.S. Army: Pathology; U.S. Air Force: Pathology; Forensic Laboratories of the Federal Bureau of Investigation.
Political Conduct	Congressional Record Index; Congressional Quarterly; Office of the Public Record; Code of Federal Regulations; Federal Elections Commission.
Securities	Securities and Exchange Commission; Department of the Treasury; Federal Bureau of Investigation.

FIGURE 5.4 Federal agency and their investigative areas.

B. State and Local Agencies

Although state and local governments amass sweeping levels of information and data, there is no uniform method to accessing such information. There are usually directories that list agencies that can be useful for accessing information (e.g., *National Directory of State Agencies, The Pennsylvania Manual, Illinois Blue Book*). Entries often include phone numbers, addresses, functions, agencies, and major personalities of government. For example, review the sample entry from *The Pennsylvania Manual* given in Figure 5.5.[22]

Automobile accident report forms, authored by state police authorities, as well as local and municipal entities, are a staple of private security investigators who work for either a plaintiff or a defendant (see Chapter 3, Figures 3.5–3.7). While the legal admissibility of accident reports is a contested arena, there are few restrictions on access to accident reports as a pure public record.

Every state sets policy on records access, and every state designates various offices or officers to handle the record processing. Typical agencies that amass source material for the investigator include, but are not limited to:

- Department of Motor Vehicles
- Tax Assessors
- Department of Transportation/Streets and Highways
- Voter Registration Offices
- Bureau of Vital Statistics
- Department of Labor and Industry
- State Revenue Commissions
- Department of Corrections
- Department of Insurance
- Department of Corporations and Business
- Department of Business
- Secretary of State
- Professions and Licensing
- Department of Vocational Rehabilitation
- District Attorney's Office
- Medical Examiner's Office
- Office of the County Coroner
- County Recorder of Deeds
- Traffic Department
- Registrar of Wills
- Department of Public Works
- County Clerks
- County and Local Courthouses

Record availability is increasingly online. Copies of wills, tax records, traffic infractions, and reports of the medical examiner are just a few of the legions of public documents now accessible in the virtual world.[23]

IV. PRIVATE SOURCES OF INFORMATION

While government agencies at the federal, state, and local levels may provide the bulk of information needed by the investigator, private sources of information should not be neglected. Private firms and entities are now in the information business, and security professional take full advantage of these services. See Figure 5.6.[24]

RONALD L. SODER **Member, Board of Claims**

Ronald L. Soder, born June 23, 1936, in Philipsburg, son of Lydia Soder Anderson and the late Carl H. Soder; Cooper Twp. H.S., 1954; Penn State Univ. (B.S.C.E.), 1958; frmr. commissioned officer: U.S. Air Force; consulting eng.; mem.: Amer. Soc. of Civil Eng., Amer. Soc. of Highway Eng., Aviation Cncl. of Pa.; registered prof. eng.; registered prof. land surveyor; apptd. Engineer Member, Board of Claims Nov. 2002; married Ann E.; 3 children.

The Board of Claims is both a judicial and an independent administrative agency. The Board was created October 5, 1978, according to Legislative Act 260 and supercedes the former Board of Arbitration of Claims. By statute, the administrative services for the Board of Claims shall be provided by the Department of Auditor General. (See "Powers and Duties" of the Auditor General.) An executive secretary, counsel, and supporting staff are appointed by the Board.

Administration – The Board is composed of three members: an attorney, who serves as Chief Administrative Judge and chair; a civil engineer; and a citizen of the Commonwealth. Appointments to the Board are made by the Governor with the advice and consent of the Senate. Each member shall be appointed for a term of eight years.

The powers and duties of the Board, originally set forth in the Act of May 20, 1937, were restated and revised by Act 142 of 2002, as amended. Act 142 provides, among other things, that the Board of Claims has exclusive jurisdiction to hear and determine claims against the Commonwealth arising from contracts to which the Commonwealth is a party (other than claims arising out of the medical assistance program administered by the Department of Public Welfare). Act 142 also provides the Board with concurrent jurisdiction to hear and determine claims arising from Commonwealth contracts in which the Commonwealth is the claimant. Appeals from decisions of the Board are to the Pennsylvania Commonwealth Court.

PENNSYLVANIA COMMISSION ON CRIME AND DELINQUENCY

3101 North Front Street
Harrisburg, PA 17110

WALTER M. PHILLIPS JR. **Chair, Pennsylvania Commission on Crime and Delinquency**

Walter M. Phillips Jr., born Dec. 28, 1938, in Philadelphia, son of the late Walter M. and Mary B. Phillips; Andover Acad., Andover, Mass., 1957; Princeton Univ. (A.B.), econ., 1961; Univ. of Calif. Hastings Law Sch. (J.D.), 1966; frmr. asst. dist. atty.: Phila.; frmr. asst. atty./chief: Narcotics Unit, U.S. Atty. Office for the S. Dist. of N.Y.; frmr. state dep. atty. gen./spec. prosecutor for official & police corruption; frmrly. priv. pract.; frmr. instr.: trial advocacy, Rutgers Law Sch.; frmr. partner: Phillips & Phela, Hoyle Law Firm; of cnsl. to: Obermayer Rebmann Maxwell & Hippel; frmr. chair: Phila. Bd. of Ethics; trustee: Del. Valley Citizens Crime Comm.; mem.: Pennsylvanians for Modern Cts. Adv. Bd.; frmr. mem.: Police Commissioner Search Comm., Police Corruption Task Force; awds.: N.Y. Police Dept. Cert. of Commendation-1973, Bur. of Narcotics & Dangerous Drugs Cert. of Apprec.-1973; apptd. Chair, Pennsylvania Commission on Crime and Delinquency Mar. 2004; married Valerie O.; 2 children.

MICHAEL JOSEPH KANE **Executive Director, Pennsylvania Commission on Crime and Delinquency**

Michael Joseph Kane, born Dec. 20, 1951, in Philadelphia, son of the late Michael J. and Claire A. Kane; Bishop Eustace Prep. Sch., Pennsauken, NJ, 1970; St. Joseph's Univ. (B.S.), accounting, cum laude, 1975; Univ. of Colo. Sch. of Law (J.D.), 1979; frmr. chief dep. dist. atty.: Denver, Colo.; frmr. sr. dep. dist. atty.: Pa. Office of Atty. Gen.; frmr. asst. U.S. atty.: Middle Dist. of Pa.; frmr. Dep. Sec. for Enforcement: Pa. Dept. of Rev.; frmr. spec. dep. dist. atty.: Boulder, Colo.; frmrly. priv. prac.; frmr. dir.: Bur. of Corp. Taxes; mem.: Hampden Twp. Zoning Hearing Bd.; awds.: U.S. Treas. IRS Director's Awd.-1998, U.S. Dept. of Justice Spec. Achiev. Awd.-1994, U.S. Dept. of Labor, Office of Labor Racketeering Outst. Performance Awd.-1991; apptd. Executive Director, Pennsylvania Commission on Crime and Delinquency June 2005; married Cathleen; 2 children.

Chair: Walter M. Phillips Jr. **Members:** James Anderson, Jeffrey Beard, Lisa Bennington, Gilbert M. Branche, Susan Burt-Collins, Esther Bush, William T. Cannon, Ralph Cappy, Thomas W. Corbett Jr., Dominick DiPaolo, Jonathan Encarnacion, Jack Godlesky, Kate Harper, Renée Cardwell Hughes, Calvin B. Johnson, Errika F. Jones, Susan Kelly-Dreiss, Jeffrey Kolansky, Carol

FIGURE 5.5 Entry from The Pennsylvania Manual.

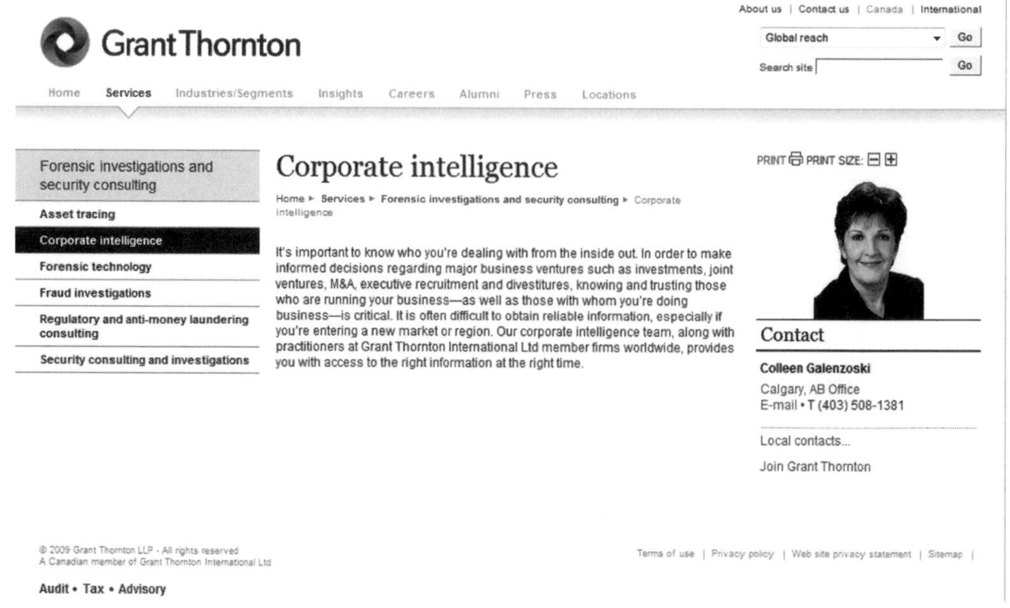

FIGURE 5.6 Grant Thornton website. www.grantthornton.ca/services/forensic/forensic_investigations/corporate_intelligence. With permission.

A. Directories, Databases, and Atlases

Directories, atlases, and databases are essential tools when seeking information. Although the areas covered by these resources tend to be rather global, more particularized information on trademarks, congressional record announcements, corporate operation and value, affirmative action programs, labor and employment statistics, and other mundane business record keeping can be discovered within these sources. With the advent of electronic data transmission and Internet capacity, increasing amounts of this type of information can be discovered online.

> **Web Exercise:** Visit Ebsco, one of the world's largest providers of online databases and research sources. http://www.ebscohost.com

1. Business Databases

There are a multitude of databases with information regarding business and industry. The leading ones are:

Moody's/Value Line: Corporate schematic of ownership and value.
Dow Jones Spectrum Profiles: Security Exchange Commission (SEC) extracts on institutional holdings, tender offers, and insider trading.
Dow Jones News Service: Stock, commodity, futures and options trading information, and other news services.

The following national business databases are also available:

- Standard & Poor's News
- Dunn's Financial Records
- Standard & Poor's
- Disclosure Data Base

- Register of Corporations
- Trade & Industry ASAP
- Moody's Corporate News
- Dow Jones News/Retrieval Database
- Moody's Corporate Profiles
- Mergers and Acquisitions
- Investext
- Corporate Affiliations
- PTS Annual Reports Abstracts
- Insider Trading Monitor
- Trade and Industry Index
- Business Wire
- Business Dateline
- Trinet Company Data Base
- Wall Street Journal
- Dunn's Electronic Yellow Pages
- Thomas Register Online
- Dunn's Market Identifiers
- Publishers, Distributors and Wholesalers
- Dunn's Million Dollar Directory

2. Miscellaneous Databases

Other databases covering nonbusiness information include:

Congressional Record Abstracts: Abstracts of the congressional record, congressional information service, abstracts of congressional publications.
Lexis and *Westlaw*: Case law, statutory, and administrative decision-making through electronic transmission.
Medical Indexes: The indexes and abstracts of articles from major medical journals.
Infotrac: A directory of legal articles and citations.
Labor Law: Summaries on labor relations decisions.
Nexis: Electronic news service.
Congressional Statistics Index: Thorough index of statistical publications of U.S. government agencies.
Federal Register: Publication of notices, rules, and regulations of government offices.
City Directories: Addresses based on name and street number.
Directory Listings of Professions: ATLA, ABA, and state and local bar association lists.
Who's Who Publications: Notably in law, engineering, medicine, and other scientific fields.
Telephone Directories: Available at most local libraries.

These databases may provide both specialized, narrow information necessary for the investigation, or the type of global background needed to comprehend fully the case at hand.

B. Libraries

Federal, state, county, and municipal libraries are often forgotten as sources of investigative information. Many local and state libraries have significant law collections, directories of all kinds, telephone books, and other source materials. Research librarians can assist on historical and contemporary questions that may influence law and legislation. University and college libraries are another resource, generally stocked with an array of scholarly journals and periodicals and other

OVERVIEW

The Keystone Library Network (KLN) provides the 14 State System universities and library partners with abstracts and access to 7,634 academic journals, 1,712 magazines, conference proceedings for 44 associations and 40,568 business reports including country reports, industry reports, market research reports and SWOT analyses. The KLN maintains catalogs (PILOT) of its members' holdings.

FIGURE 5.7 Keystone Library network overview.

information necessary to research any technical or sophisticated question. State college and university libraries are generally participants in interlibrary loan programs, affording access to every major library in the continental United States. University libraries also have access to literally every other library imaginable through its database systems and electronic software for full text journals. See Figure 5.7.[25]

> **Web Exercise:** Visit the web site for the Louis L. Manderino Library at the California University of Pennsylvania, a regional state college with extraordinary access to electronic collections, which lists its subject matter holdings. http://www.library.cup.edu/l2.cfm?Parent=33

C. Newspapers

Most major city newspapers have a library or holding acquisition center, usually referred to as a *morgue*, for all previous editions of the newspaper. Stories of topical concern are arranged chronologically or in some other order for appropriate indexing and cataloging.

Access to information in a newspaper is only limited by the scope of the paper's coverage. Figure 5.8 lists the possibilities. As a rule, newspapers are placed onto microfilm, microfiche, or other electronic medium for storage or research purposes. When looking for back issues of particular publications, consult the reference librarian, the index to the particular newspaper, or the text newspapers on microfilm. There are also abstract databases now available through online computer systems. They are:

- AP News
- Newswire ASAP
- Businesswire

Department	Lead
Obituaries	Family, previous residence, previous occupation, other background information, photograph or likeness.
Advertising	Credit records, business relationships.
Editorial	Major stories, corporate and business activities, urban crime, numerous other leads.
Local columnist	Personal information, political information.

FIGURE 5.8 Newspaper research topics.

- PR Newswire
- Chicago Tribune
- Reuters
- Financial Times Fulltext
- UPI News
- Japan Economic Newswire
- USA Today Decisionline
- McGraw-Hill News
- Washington Presstext

D. The Internet

A plethora of information is at the investigators disposal when using the Internet and its search engines. The most commonly employed search engines are:

- All the Web
- AltaVista
- ArchiePlex
- Ask Jeeves
- Bing
- Dogpile
- Excite
- Go.com
- Google
- HotBot
- LookSmart
- Lycos
- MetaCrawler
- MSN Search
- Northern Light
- Teoma
- Web Crawler
- Wise Nut

Internet subject directories include:

- About.com
- Big Hub
- Invisible Web
- Links2Go
- Open Directory Project
- Qango
- Yahoo

E. Professional Associations and Groups

Many quasi-private and not-for-profit associations, groups, and foundations can provide access to relevant information. Consult the *Encyclopedia of Associations*, a reference tool found in most libraries, which comprises more than 12,500 associations and includes the following categories:

1. Trade, business, and commercial organizations.
2. Agricultural organizations and commodity exchanges.
3. Governmental, public administration, military, and legal organizations.
4. Scientific, engineering, and technical organizations.
5. Educational and cultural organizations.
6. Social welfare organizations.
7. Health and medical organizations.
8. Public affairs organizations.
9. Internal foreign interests, nationality, and ethnic organizations.
10. Religious organizations.

Some of the more influential bodies and groups the investigator should keep in mind are:

The Better Business Bureau: The bureau receives hundreds of thousands of complaints nationwide each year. It also maintains extensive files on con artists and other unsavory characters. Their main office is: Better Business Bureau, 230 Park Avenue, New York, NY, 10017.

U.S. Department of Commerce: A provider of background information on companies in other countries, financial references, and general reputation in trade and financial circles. The U.S. Department of Commerce also has regional and district offices throughout the United States. U.S. Department of Commerce, Washington, DC, 20230.

F. Auto Records

The investigator will find other sources, whether government, quasi-public, or private in nature, whose complete or partial function is to compile information on motor vehicles and their operators. For example, the U.S. Department of Commerce keeps records on individuals whose driver's licenses or permits have been revoked for driving while intoxicated or for causing a vehicular death in violation of the Highway Safety Code. The American Association of Motor Vehicle Administrators and the American Trucking Association have informational pamphlets and booklets that assist investigators in checking certain motor vehicle records. The National Automobile Dealers Association issues a publication that lists the licensing requirements for motor vehicle dealers, salespeople, and others in related fields.[26]

> **Web Exercise:** Visit www.einvestigator.com for an excellent resource on auto records. Policies, addresses, and general requirements for all fifty jurisdictions are available at this location.

Of enormous assistance in cases of motor vehicle theft, fraud, and collusive insurance claims, is the work of the National Automobile Theft Bureau (NATB), which maintains offices in Atlanta, Chicago, Dallas, New York, San Francisco, Boston, Detroit, Los Angeles, and Houston. The NATB maintains a data bank of 2.5 million active online records and employs full-time agents whose sole purpose is to assist public and private law enforcement officers as they combat motor vehicle crime. The data bank includes information on:

- Passenger vehicles
- Semitrailers
- Trucks
- Marine equipment
- Truck tractors
- Off-road equipment
- Trailers

The NATB also has 350 million manufacturers' records of assembly and shipping, including these motor vehicle companies:

- American Motors
- International
- Audi
- Kawasaki
- British Leyland
- Mack
- Chrysler
- Mercedes-Benz
- Ford
- Porsche
- General Motors
- Toyota
- Harley-Davidson
- Volkswagen
- Honda

Vehicle identification numbers (VINs) are also held within the databank of the NATB, as well as information relating to salvaged and stolen parts. The private investigator may also wish to purchase commercial manuals that highlight the skills of auto theft prevention and detection.

Whether using public or private sources, the security investigator must collect, collate, and interpret sufficient data to support, refute, or establish his or her investigative direction. The evidentiary sources are only limited by the scope of the facts and the imagination, creativity, perseverance, logic, and deductive reasoning of the investigator.

V. THE BACKGROUND INVESTIGATION

Security firms conduct a wide array of background investigations for a host of clientele. Whether the corporation about to hire an executive wishes to confirm his or her background or the federal prospective employee is being scrutinized by security independent contractors, background investigation is a staple of the security industry. As in other forms of investigation, the public record, in most circumstances the information within federal, state, and local agencies, is of public record: "Held at city hall, courthouses, and county offices, this information includes property deeds and titles, records of lawsuits, marriages, births, deaths, probated wills, financial statements, transfers of property, tax liens, mechanic's liens, property taxes, military discharges, divorces, criminal convictions, records of lunacy hearings, and other matters."[27]

In most county courthouses, information involving property, voter registration, mortgages and deeds, tax liens and liability, divorce, marriage, adoption, and criminal records are easily accessible. Security firms usually provide the investigator with standardized forms to complete these searches.

No other exercise better tests the investigators capacity to collect information than the background investigation. To conduct this type of investigation properly the investigator must consider and evaluate the following:

- Personal life and information
- Criminal background
- Motor vehicle record
- Educational background
- Employment history
- Reputation and character
- Economic interests (e.g., real property, assets)
- Financial conduct

Background investigations are summarized in Figure 5.9.

Background Check Worksheet

Case name: ______________________________

Case File Number: ______________________________

Investigator: ______________________________

Personal Information:

Social Security #: ______________________________

Date of Birth: ______________________________

Height: ______________________________

Weight: ______________________________

Eye Color: ______________________________

Hair: ______________________________

Sex: ______________________________

Race: ______________________________

Additional Information: ______________________________

Department of Motor Vehicle Record:

Name: ______________________________

Address: ______________________________

Date of Birth: ______________________________

OLN #: ______________________________

Expiration Date: ______________________________

Class: ______________________________

Restrictions: ______________________________

Suspension/revocations: ______________________________

Statewide Criminal Check: ______________________________

Organized Crime Check: ______________________________

Additional Information: ______________________________

FIGURE 5.9 Background check worksheet.

Computer Services Request Form

Case Name:	Subject Name:
Case File Number:	Subject Address:
Date:	
Requested by:	Subject Birthdate:
Search Performed:	Subject Social Security #:
Search Retrieved:	County:
IRSC Search Case Number:	Additional Subject Information:
Cost of Search: Billed:	

☐ Credit Check	☐ Drivers Record
☐ Preliminary Asset Search	☐ Motor Vehicle Registration
☐ National Locate	☐ Automated Name Index
☐ Pre-Employment Check	☐ National Drivers Record
☐ Preliminary Background Search	☐ National Automated Number Index
☐ National Pre-Employment Check	☐ National Fictitious Business Filings
☐ Sleuth SID	☐ Business Public Filings
☐ National Identifier Search	☐ Business Credit Report
☐ Interstate Public Filings	☐ National Business Report
☐ National Movers Index	☐ Business Factual Data Report
☐ On-Line Property Search	☐ Special Request
☐ National Statewide Property Search	☐ Newspaper Magazine Index
☐ National Real Property	☐ National Aircraft Title Search
☐ Statewide UCC	☐ National UCC
☐ Statewide Marriage & Death	☐ Criminal Convictions History
☐ Superior & Municipal Criminal Index	☐ National Civil Court Index
☐ Voter Registration	☐ Workers Compensation Claim Filings
☐ Federal Court Records	☐ Multistate Corporate Filings

FIGURE 5.10 Computer services request form.

Some of the information sought may be accessed through databases that are computer ready. See Figure 5.10. Many security firms are now subscribing to databases and online services, examples of which have been referred to in previous sections of this chapter. A Computer Services Request Form, such as the one shown in Figure 5.10, organizes and categorizes the many options of database subscription services.

VI. REAL PROPERTY TITLE SEARCH

The permanency of real estate records provides a dependable data source for investigators. Rich in historical and personal information, title searches display a good deal of information about a specified client. The chain of title lists a great deal of useful information, such as:

- Partners and co-venturers in the transfer of grantor/grantee
- Mortgages
- Credit history
- Relatives and other personal information

- Marriages and divorces
- Previous residences and addresses
- Civil actions
- Level of financial worth
- Building permits
- Tax liens or previous obligations not met
- Satisfaction pieces
- Partnerships and other joint ventures
- Criminal conduct/fraud
- Existence of trusts
- Legal owner versus equitable owner
- Liens and other secured interests

Although there are diverse ways in which the varied jurisdictions record and catalog real estate transactions, there are some uniform practices.[28] Titles can be searched and analyzed by and through:

- Grantor (seller) index
- Grantee (buyer) index
- Tax parcel numbers
- Plot plans
- Date of transaction
- Street addresses
- Deed numbers
- Deed books

If these standard methods of tracking ownership result in a dead end, the investigator has alternative methods and means by evaluating title abstracts, tax reports and records, Universal Commercial Code (UCC) lien filings, second and third mortgage filings (look at the mortgage books), judgments, and promissory notes with security. A helpful tool to the investigator who is searching land records is given in Figure 5.11.[29]

TITLE SEARCH

1. Client: ______ File No.: ______
2. Current Owners (As title is vested): ______
______
3. Brief Property Description: ______
______
4. ______ County taxes paid through: ______
City or Town of ______ taxes paid through: ______
See attached tax sheet for listing information.
5. Res. Cov.: Book ______ Page ______ Date of Recording ______
Amended.: Book ______ Page ______ Date of Recording ______
Amended: Book ______ Page ______ Date of Recording ______
Set back:
Front: ______
Side: ______
Rear: ______
Utility Easements: ______
______
6. Map Information:
Book/Cabinet: ______ Page/Slide: ______
Set Backs: Front: ______ Rear: ______
Side: ______
Easements ______
Does Survey Match Plat? ______
7. Means of Access: ______
8. U.C.C.'s: (only HHG or fixture filings) - None
File No.: ______
Grantor: ______
Grantee: ______
Date: ______
Collateral: ______
9. DT's:

Book/Page	Grantor	Trustee	Beneficiary	Inst. Date	Date Rec.	Face Amt.

10. Judgments: ______
______
11. Suits Pending: ______
12. Special Proceedings: ______
13. If Corporate Party, Name of Record: ______
14. Home Owner's or Property Owner's Assessments: ______
15. Are there any grantors in chain not joined by spouses?
Name: ______
Book/Page: ______
Marital Status: ______
16. Are there any estates in chain?
Decedent: ______
Date of Death: ______
Administration Info.: ______
Tax Certificate: ______
17. Utility Easements:

Instrument	Book/Page	Grantor	Grantee	Inst. Date	Date Rec.

18. Are there any other defects or caveats?
______
______
______
19. Search period was from:
Date and Time of Recording: ______
of ______ (deed, will, DT)
from: ______ to: ______
(Trustee) for: ______ (Beneficiary)
face amount (if DT): ______
to: ______, ______ .m., ______ day of ______, 19 ______.
20. SD Memo: ______ attached
Title Policy: ______ attached
Title Opinion: ______ attached

Last out in current Owners Outs: ______
Have you drawn out metes and bounds calls or have a copy of a survey? ______
Abstractor:

FIGURE 5.11 Title search form.

NOTES

1. American Society for Industrial Security, *Basic Guidelines for Security Investigations* (1981), 5.
2. *Id.* at 5, 6.
3. 5 U.S.C. § 552a.
4. 12 U.S.C. § 3401 *et seq.*
5. 42 U.S.C. § 2000aa-6.
6. See U.S. Code.
7. See U.S. Code.
8. 15 U.S.C. § 1681 *et seq.*
9. 5 U.S.C. § 5315-5316, 7313.
10. 5 U.S.C. § 552.
11. U.S. Department of Justice, Bureau of Justice Statistics, *Privacy and Security of Criminal History Information: An Analysis of Privacy Issues* (U.S. Government Printing Office, 1980), 1.
12. U.S. Department of Justice, *Report of the National Advisory Commission on Criminal Justice Standards and Goals* (U.S. Government Printing Office, 1973), 9.
13. W. Cunningham and T. Taylor, *The Hallcrest Report: Private Security and Police in America* (Chancellor Press, 1985), 57.
14. Laura Spadanuta, "Protecting Personal Information," *Sec. Mgmt.* (October 2008), 24.
15. *The Hallcrest Report, supra* note 13, at 57.
16. *Id.*
17. U.S. Department of Justice, Bureau of Justice Statistics, *supra* note 11, at 9.
18. P. Fuqua and J. Wilson, *Security Investigator's Handbook* (Gulf Publishing, 1979), 21–22.
19. Fuqua, *supra* note 18, at 22.
20. *Id.* at 17.
21. Federal Bureau of Investigation, Training Division, Economic and Financial Crimes Training Unit, *Guide to Sources of Information* (U.S. Government Printing Office, 1980).
22. Commonwealth of Pennsylvania, *The Pennsylvania Manual*, Vol. 118 (2007), 469.
23. Robert McCrie, "Manual to Online Public Records and Public Record Research Tips Book," *Sec. Letter.* (January 2009), 4.
24. Grant Thornton web site. Corporate intelligence page, http://www.grantthornton.ca/services/forensic_investigations/corporate_intelligence, visited August 26, 2009.
25. Pennsylvania State System of Higher Education, Keystone Library Network Page, http://www.passhe.edu/executive/academic/kln/Pages/default.aspx, visited August 26, 2009.
26. Federal Bureau of Investigation, *supra* note 21, 65–68.
27. Fuqua and Wilson, *supra* note 18, at 18.
28. See Charles P. Nemeth, *Reality of Real Estate* (Prentice Hall, 2007).
29. North Carolina Bar Foundation, *II Practical Skills Course* (1988), 57–58.

6 Collection of Evidence and Preservation of the Scene

I. INTRODUCTION

Standard investigative practice calls for the security officer to attentively protect the crime scene and preserve the evidence. "Collection, preservation and the assurance of evidentiary integrity"[1] are central to the investigative regimen. This is true in any type of case consisting of criminal conduct or civil injuries; insurance investigations for arson, fraud, and vehicular accidents; terrorist acts; bomb threats; executive protection threats; intrusions into hotels, motels, colleges, and universities; violent labor disputes; workers' compensation, as well as suspected retail theft. The skills and competencies required of a public police officer apply equally to the private security officer. This chapter presents a comprehensive analysis of methods and techniques employed by security investigators who must ensure the integrity of evidence and preserve the scene.

The security investigator requires certain "tools" in order to accomplish a thorough and useful collection of evidence at a scene. Some of these are:

- Binoculars
- Blankets
- Brushes
- Bullhorns
- Cables
- Chains
- Chalk and chalkline
- Checklists
- Cutters
- First aid kits
- Flares or fuses
- Floodlamps
- Plaster of Paris
- Screwdriver
- Scribes
- Sketching supplies
- Spatula
- Sponges
- Sprays
- Stamps
- Steel measuring tape
- Swabs
- Syringes
- Tags
- Tape recorder
- Templates
- Thermometer
- Tinsnips
- Towels
- Transceivers
- Tubes
- Tweezers
- Vacuums
- Wax
- Wire
- Wrenches[2]

II. PRELIMINARY STRATEGIES AND RESPONSES

If the investigator is fortunate enough to have early access to the civil or criminal scene, securing the scene's physical integrity—the conditions surrounding the occurrence and the preservation of its evidence—whether evidence of personal injury, or damage to property, or contraband, is a critical responsibility. This initial scene search should be a planned, coordinated, and competent action that is legally permissible and does not interfere with or obstruct the function of public justice. To elucidate, investigators for insurance companies should be cautious upon approach and announce to public law enforcement their status and intentions. Without exception, private investigators must give way to official action, function, or activity. Only persons who have a legitimate investigative interest should be permitted into the scene, and the number of such persons should be minimal. As a rule, the larger the number of persons on the scene, the greater the potential for scene contamination.

Two fundamental priorities govern investigative conduct upon initial visitation:

1. The acquisition and preservation of physical, real, documentary, and tangible evidence.
2. The notation of mental impressions regarding motive and *modus operandi* (MO).

Upon entry, the investigator must make every effort to capture events and conditions and to preserve them for immortality. The U.S. Department of Justice, through its National Institute of Justice, has published a reference work for private and public law enforcement titled *Crime Scene Search and Physical Evidence Handbook*.[3] It emphasizes the urgency of the preliminary review:

> Aside from any other consideration, the investigator should consider the crime scene as highly dynamic, that is, undergoing change; and fragile, in the sense that the evidence value of items it contains can be easily downgraded. Usually, there is only one opportunity to search the scene properly. Making a good preliminary survey of the layout helps to use that opportunity to best advantage.[4]

Preservation of the scene is a hallmark responsibility for the investigator since the scene will change by the mere passage of time. "The investigator should first take into account all the information and opinions that have been accumulated by persons preceding him on the scene. The apparent physical focal point or points of the crime are of particular interest in this information exchange, as are the perceptions of other officers as to items or material having potential evidentiary value."[5] The maintenance of crime scene integrity begins with the observations of the first officer on the scene. The steps for that responding officer are:

a. Note or log dispatch information (e.g., address/location, time, date, type of call, parties involved).
b. Be aware of any persons or vehicles leaving the crime scene.
c. Approach the scene cautiously, scan the entire area to thoroughly assess the scene, and note any possible secondary crime scenes. Be aware of any persons and vehicles in the vicinity that may be related to the crime.
d. Make initial observations (look, listen, smell) to assess the scene and ensure officer safety before proceeding.
e. Remain alert and attentive. Assume the crime is ongoing until determined to be otherwise.
f. Treat the location as a crime scene until assessed and determined to be otherwise.[6]

The Pennsylvania State Police, in its *Crime Laboratory Operations Manual*, corroborates the importance of this early stage in the investigative process by noting:

- Form objectives of the search and deciding what to look for.
- Take special note of evidence that may be easily destroyed such as shoeprints in dust, footprints, etc.
- Organize the search by making assignments for photographs, fingerprints, and evidence handling.
- Decide on a search pattern and issuing instructions to assist personnel.[7]

Web Exercise: Review the recommended procedures for crime scene preservation at: http://www.ncjrs.gov/pdffiles1/nij/200160.pdf

The need to preserve physical evidence requires a resolute attempt to cordon off and secure the scene and physical conditions at the scene in order to prevent—or at least minimize—any distortions or aberrations of the original scene. A few prototype forms for physical evidence collection are outlined in the forms that follow.[8] The checklist for physical evidence (see Figure 6.1[9]) is usable in both criminal and civil litigation.[10]

In Figure 6.2,[11] Physical Scene Investigation Checklist, the investigator is provided with step-by-step instructions on how to perform a preliminary review and examination. Note that the checklist

Checklist for Physical Evidence

		Yes	No	Does Not Apply
1.	Were fingerprints located and photographed?			
2.	Were latent fingerprints found, developed, and lifted?			
3.	Did you call for a firearms examiner to help extract bullets from walls, ceilings, etc.?			
4.	In homicide or woundings, did you obtain bullets removed by the medical examiner?			
5.	Did you search for all possible types of physical evidence?			
6.	Have you collected items of evidence that make jigsaw matches?			
7.	In case of vehicular accident, did you recover paint, window glass, or headlight glass from victim's body or vehicle?			
8.	Have you properly packed and marked evidence to go to the laboratory?			
9.	Have you located footprints of shoes or bare feet in the out-of-doors scene and taken photographs and made casts?			
10.	If there is an apprehended suspect, have you examined the inside of their shoes, the soles, and the welt for fine sand, clay or mud?			
11.	Have you collected trace evidence by vacuum cleaning from suspect's clothing?			
12.	Have you collected pieces of bed sheets, pillow slips, and other bedding involved in rape or homicide?			
13.	Have you had someone in the family or close to the family look at the scene of indoor crimes to find out what has been disturbed?			
14.	Has a list of missing objects been made?			
15.	Have you checked for tools marks and broken glass that are signs of breaking and entering?			
16.	Have you checked windows for broken glass or for bullet holes?			

FIGURE 6.1 Checklist for physical evidence.

includes reporting weather and lighting conditions; establishing a perimeter to secure the scene by keeping out foreign parties; observations regarding odors and the sensible policy of calling in additional help, if necessary.

Another important form is the Protection of the Scene Checklist in Figure 6.3.[12] By adhering to the standards and policies presented in this document, the private investigator will be ensured of evidence integrity. Pay particular attention to the materials and supplies (such as signs, lighting, flags, rope, chalk or crayon, barricades, and other security personnel) needed to prevent intrusion.

When examining particular activities, such as bombs and explosives in executive protection situations, the focus on physical evidence becomes more refined. Some clues for the recognition of concealed explosive devices include:

- Recently disturbed ground
- Sawdust
- Brickdust
- Wood chips
- Electrical wire
- String

PHYSICAL SCENE INVESTIGATION CHECKLIST

A. General:
   1. If the investigator is weak in his knowledge of scene investigation he can do great harm to the investigation by inadvertently destroying the evidence.
   2. An apparent suicide is always investigated as though it is a homicide.
   3. A body should not be removed until all required investigation steps have been taken.
   4. If the body must be moved (advancing fire, etc.), record in all ways possible the location and position of the body.

B. Approaching the Scene:
   The investigation should begin as soon as the investigator becomes aware of the incident. All senses should be put to work—and most of all common sense must be used. BE ALERT! BE CURIOUS! Be complete in recording what you observe.
   1. Observe vehicles (moving or parked)
   2. Observe persons
   3. Observe unusual conditions

C. Arrival at the Scene:
   1. The first duty is always to the injured person. If the victim(s) shows any sign of life, he should be afforded all possible lifesaving measures.
   2. Notation should be made regarding:
      a. Date
      b. Time of arrival
      c. Weather conditions
      d. Lighting conditions
   3. The next duty is to establish a perimeter and secure the scene. Be observant for:
      a. Suspicious vehicles and persons at or around the immediate scene.
      b. Possible witnesses near or around the immediate scene (Be able to identify them for subsequent investigation—name, address, business and home phone numbers).
      c. Open doors, windows, unattached objects which could be associated with the offense.
      d. Points of entry and exit.
   4. If the incident occurred within a closed area such as a house, be careful that your path of entry and exit does not destroy evidence. As examples, look for:
      a. Footprints in oil/tar/paint/snow/etc.
      b. Dusty prints on shiny floors
      c. Empty cartridges—projectiles
      d. Broken glass that could have latent fingerprints
      e. Cigarette/cigar butts, other smoking paraphernalia
   5. Try to enter and exit by the same path, carefully keeping in mind all conditions as they existed upon your arrival.
   6. Observe odors which may be lingering at the scene of the incident. The odor may be present upon arrival only, and may dissipate rapidly depending upon its chemical makeup. Examples include:
      a. Perfume—which could be a link between male and female suspects.
      b. Cooking gas—which could be an attempt to cover up a possible homicide.
      c. Gasoline—indicative of arson or possible cover-up of homicide.
      d. Any other unusual odors which would not otherwise be normally associated with the existing surroundings.

D. Calling for additional help:
   Evaluate the condition at the scene and call for whatever additional help is indicated, such as:
   1. Extra personnel (This would depend upon the nature of the incident, the layout of the buildings, or terrain to be protected.)
   2. Ambulance
   3. Fire Department (In some jurisdictions, fire departments handle rescue and ambulance services.)
   4. Other Agencies (e.g., Medical Examiner/Coroner)

FIGURE 6.2 Physical scene investigation checklist. Reprinted from *Death Investigation and Examination: Medicolegal Guidelines and Checklists* with permission. Copyright 1986 The Forensic Sciences Foundation, Inc.

PROTECTION OF THE SCENE CHECKLIST

A. Protection—Preservation—Control of the Scene:
   1. Protective measures are required:
      a. To record all persons at the scene.
      b. To prevent removal, destruction, rearrangement, or concealment of physical evidence.
      c. To preserve the scene in its natural state until such time as photographs have been taken and measurements, sketches, and notes are made.
      d. To keep out unauthorized persons who may unwittingly or purposely do some act which may interfere with the successful conclusion of the investigation and prevent the identification and apprehension of the perpetrator(s).
   2. Protection of areas adjoining or surrounding the exact spot where an incident occurred is vital.
      a. In buildings, evidence may be present that shows how the victim/perpetrator entered or left the premises.
      b. In an open area, evidence may be present that shows the route of travel.
      c. Physical evidence may have been dropped accidentally or hidden in adjacent areas.
      d. Fences, gates, bushes, or other shrubbery may contain fibers accidentally torn from clothing.
      e. Soft ground may contain foot, heel, or tire marks.
   3. The following is suggested scene protection equipment—to be carried as standard equipment in all investigative vehicles.
      a. 300 feet of rope or suitable material to rope off the scene.
      b. Emergency lighting (when practical).
      c. Flags easily visible at night to mark specific points of interest for overall pictures of out-of-door crime scene.
      d. 100-foot tape measure
      e. Chalk or crayon
      f. "Keep Out" signs
      g. Street closure barricade

B. Protection of the Scene:
   1. Open Scene—an area that is generally in open terrain and could be affected by the elements. Methods include:
      a. Roping off
      b. Barricading
      c. Use of existing barriers—fences, ditches, roads
      d. Use of natural barriers, such as hills, woods, and streams
   2. Closed Scene—an area that is generally not affected by the elements, e.g., buildings, houses. Methods include:
      a. Roping off
      b. Closing doors, windows
      c. Posting security measures (for lengthy crime scene operations)
      d. Security personnel

FIGURE 6.3 Protection of the scene checklist. Reprinted from *Death Investigation and Examination: Medicolegal Guidelines and Checklists* with permission. Copyright 1986 The Forensic Sciences Foundation, Inc.

- Fishing line
- Dirty rope (fuses)
- Aluminum foil
- Partly opened drawers
- Fresh plaster or cement
- Loose floorboards
- Disturbed carpeting
- Loose electrical fittings
- Out-of-place objects
- Greasy paper wrapping, etc.[13]

If security personnel are conscious of the risks of explosive devices and can recognize their components, camouflage, or disguises, then they will easily detect clues to their presence. Unfortunately, clues may not be present. A neat and tidy bomber will leave no trace of his or her work unless it is a "lure" to draw personnel into a kill zone. However, an untidy or ill-trained bomber may leave external visible clues, which include:

- Abandoned vehicles
- Abandoned vehicles on routes
- Accidents/crashes on routes
- Disturbed ground, small hollows after rain
- Military containers of ammunition/explosives
- Footprints or vehicle tracks for no apparent reason
- Vegetation camouflage, cut, bent, or withered
- Cut vegetation
- Heaps of leaves or scrub
- Marks on trees (indicating traps to the enemy)

They may also leave internal clues:

- Obviously out of place or "lure" objects
- Explosive wrappings, ammunition, or explosive containers
- Sawdust, brickdust, or metal filings
- Dusty footprints
- Scratched or new paint and timber
- Clothes pegs, nails, electric leads, tin foil, string, wire, mousetraps, watch, and clock parts
- Marks on walls (indicating traps to the enemy)
- Loose floorboards or raised carpeting, tiles, etc.
- New brickwork, plastering, or concrete[14]

Private security personnel involved in investigating bomb threats will find the Bomb Search Report outlined in Chapter 8 (see Figure 8.10) very useful.

> **Web Exercise:** Crime scenes have come to depend upon a the crime scene technician. Read about the usual expectations for this position at http://www3.sc.maricopa.edu/ajs/crime_scene_technician.htm

III. SCENE SKETCHES AND OTHER GRAPHIC PORTRAYALS

The investigator should make a representative sketch of the scene as a standard addition to the written report. Scene survey sketches are considered mandatory in most criminal and civil investigations. A scene sketch is a handmade pictorial representation of conditions at a scene. Some typical uses of sketches are:

- To refresh the memory of the investigator.
- To record the exact location of evidence found in relationship to pieces of furniture or fixed objects.
- To provide a permanent record.
- To assist all persons concerned in understanding facts.
- To supplement photographs and notes.

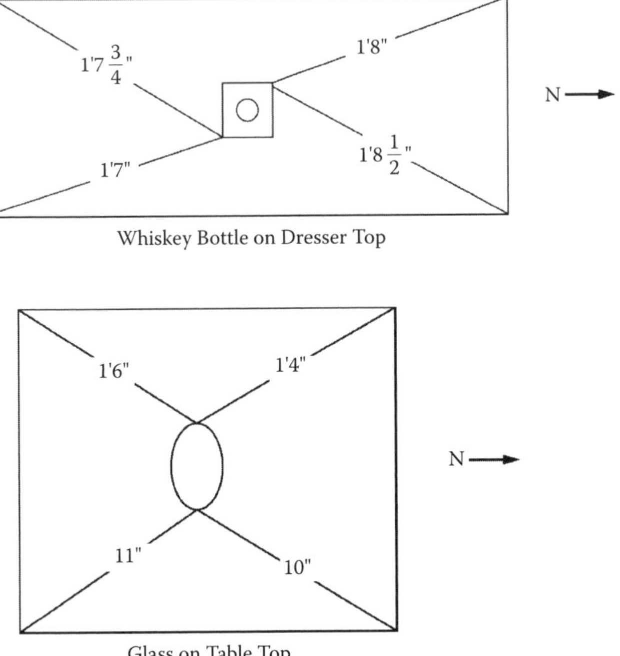

FIGURE 6.4 Triangulation sketching method.

> **Web Exercise:** New and innovative approaches using cutting edge technology are now available to justice professionals when sketching the scene. Visit: http://www.crime-scene-vr.com/_Crime_scene_sketch.html

Although there is no absolute sketch method to follow, all sketches must be accurate, made to scale, and recorded uniformly.[15] If one aspect of a sketch is accurate, such as the dimensions of a field in which a body was found, and the position of an object within the field is only roughly estimated, the distortion thus introduced renders the sketch relatively useless. It is important that the coordinate distances of an item in the sketch be measured in the same manner."[16]

Sketching methods fall into these basic categorizations:

1. Triangulation (Figure 6.4[17])
2. Baseline or coordinate (Figure 6.5[18])
3. Cross projection (Figure 6.6[19])
4. Rough and smooth (finished) sketches (Figures 6.7[20] and 6.8[21])

A. Rules for Sketching

Regardless of the sketching method chosen,[22] the following rules apply:

- Decide what is to be sketched—the key features.
- Indicate North on the sketch. (Use a compass if necessary.)
- Control all measurements by using measuring tape or ruler.
- Have someone else verify all measurements. (Do not estimate distance by pacing.)
- Take two separate sets of measurements when noting the position of a body; one set from the head and another from the feet.

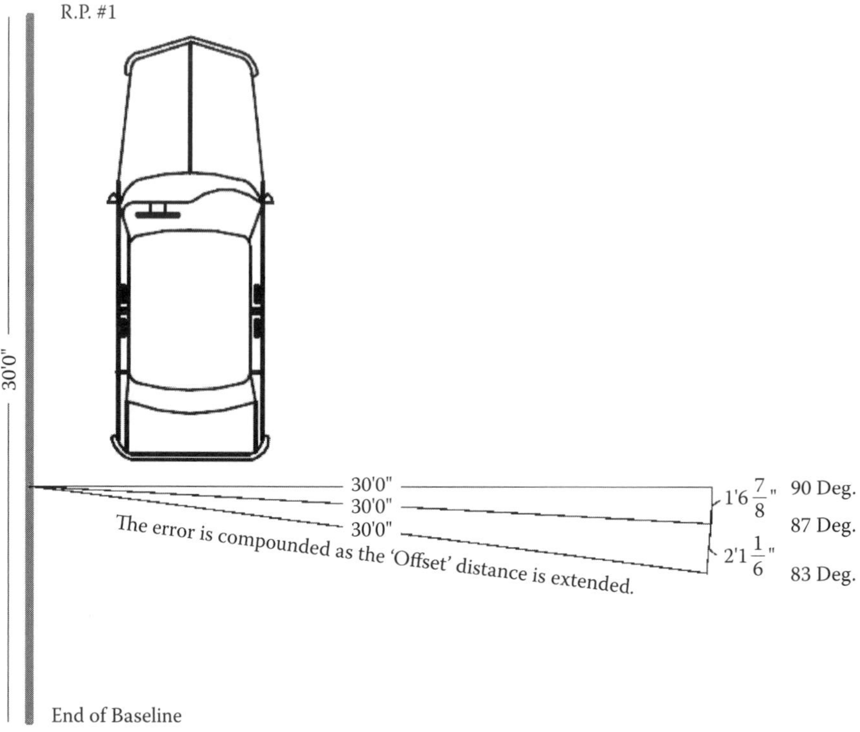

FIGURE 6.5 Baseline (coordinate) sketching method.

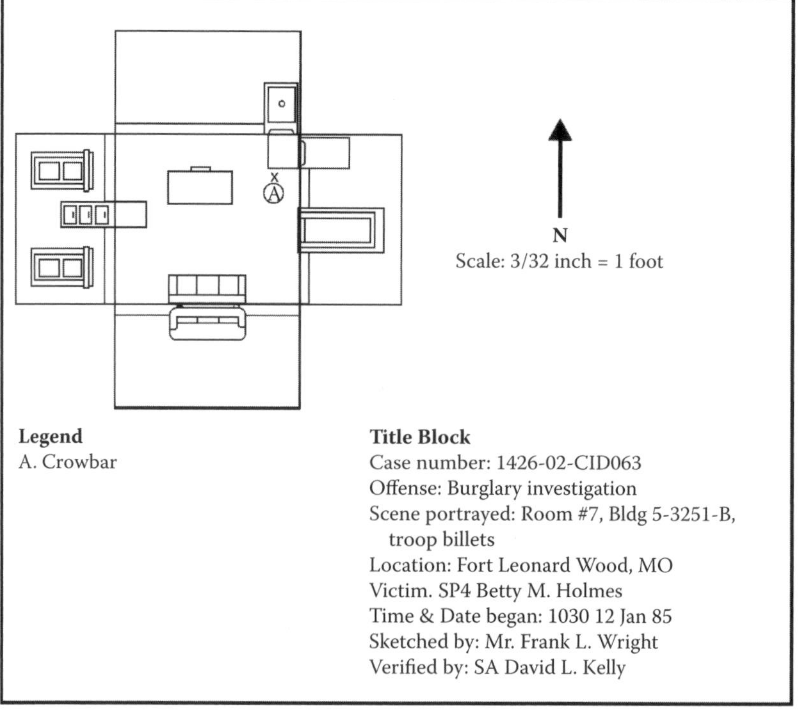

FIGURE 6.6 Cross projection sketching method.

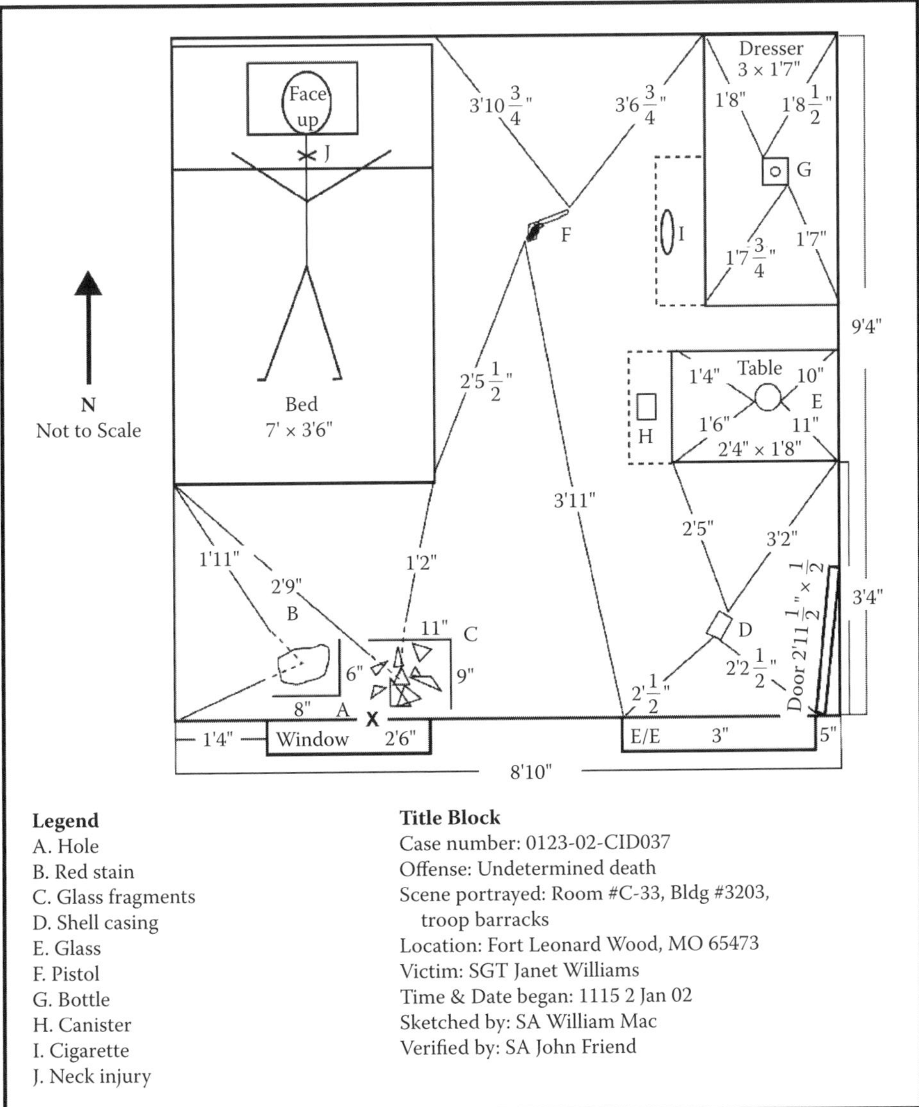

FIGURE 6.7 Rough sketch of possible crime scene.

- Locate all objects accurately and identify all objects drawn in sketch either by numerals or letters. Draw "stick" figures to represent bodies.
- Include all essential items in the drawing.
- Make all sketch corrections at the scene.
- Record date, time, by whom drawn, case number and names of persons who assisted with measurements.
- Use legend (drawing and charting symbols).

B. Rules for Measuring

All measurements should be taken from fixed objects.[23] Some locations for taking indoor measurements are:

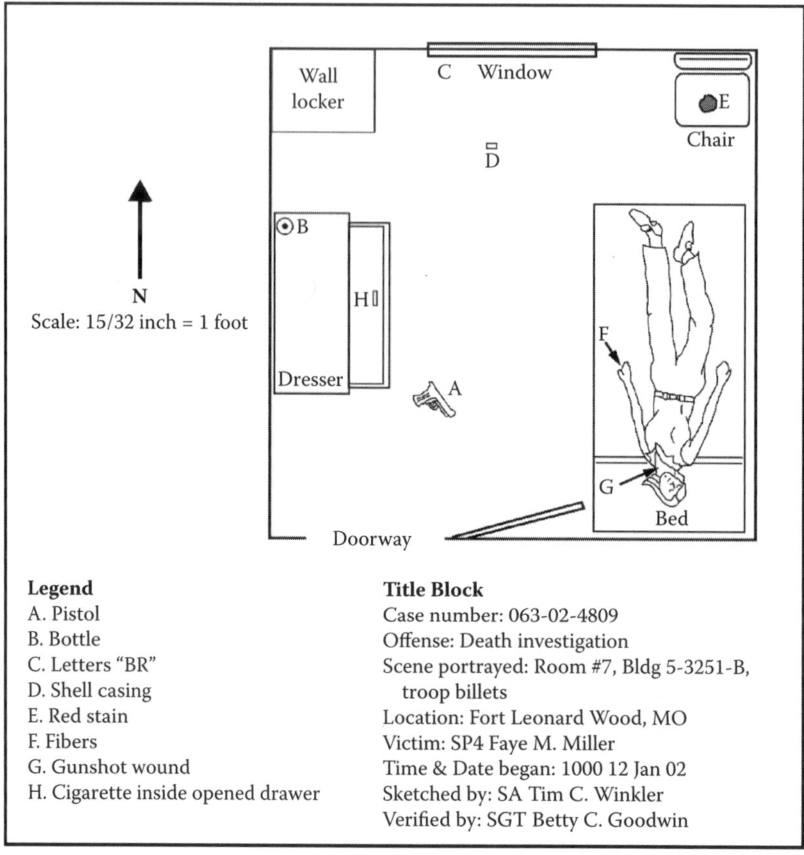

FIGURE 6.8 Smooth or finished sketch.

- Walls
- Room corners
- Door and window frames
- Bathroom fixtures

Outdoor measurements should also be taken from fixed objects:

- Corners of buildings (record address)
- Light poles (record pole number)

Graphic portrayals are not limited to scene sketches. External injury and wound charts serve the investigator in cases of workers' compensation, personal injury, and disability cases. See Figure 6.9.

IV. PHOTOGRAPHIC EVIDENCE

Photographic evidence, whether by traditional film or digital means, also plays a key role in the development of an investigator's case. The scene shown in Figure 6.10 would be difficult to present accurately with a sketch or description alone. Evidence such as this must be depicted as accurately as possible in photographs since the scene will be altered after objects such as vehicles and bodies are moved.

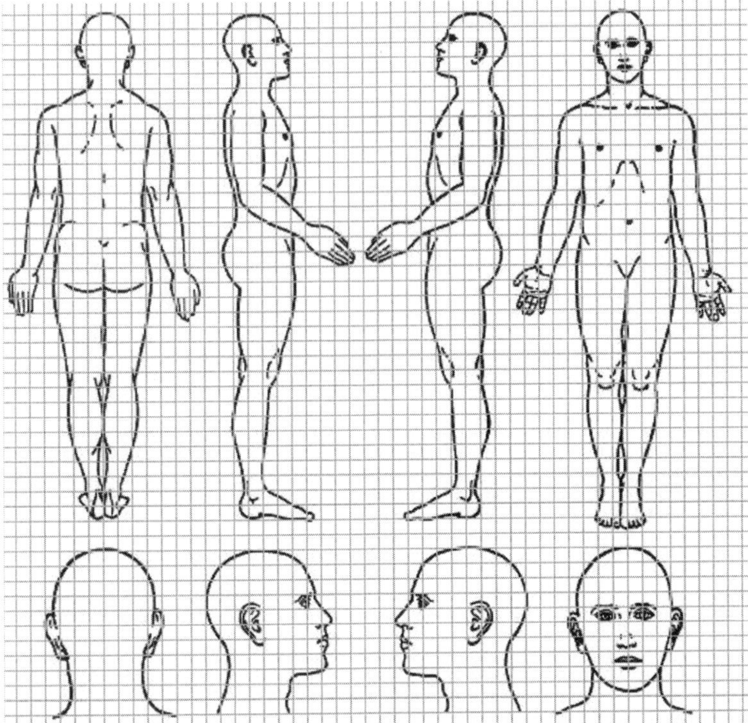

FIGURE 6.9 Blank wound chart.

FIGURE 6.10 Evidence of skid marks.

Private investigators working in civil or criminal matters usually become adept photographers. However, since they frequently are not on the scene as early as public law enforcement investigators, cooperative arrangements and relationships with public police are mandatory. "Probably more pictures for use in court are obtained from police photographers than any other source. Almost every police department is equipped with some photographic equipment, a camera or two at least, and in a city of any size, you will find a police photographic laboratory. Patrol cars are often equipped with cameras. In special accident investigations, cars are more elaborately equipped as are the station wagons or trucks used as field crime investigation laboratories."[24]

> **Web Exercise:** Find out how digital photography is changing the landscape of photography at the crime scene, accident or other event at: http://www.fletc.gov/training/programs/technical-operations-division/digital-photography-for-law-enforcement-dple

Photography is also regularly employed by coroners, medical examiners, forensic experts, scientific experts, attorneys, claims adjusters, and government agencies. "Today law enforcement officials and attorneys everywhere realize the importance of photographing the scene of the crime. Good crime scene photographs are useful even though the case never reaches trial. They give police officials and attorneys the best possible pictorial record of the scene of the crime. Pictures also are useful when questioning witnesses and suspects. Often a guilty party will confess when confronted with indisputable photographic evidence. ... Throughout the world, the standard police practice is to make photographs of all scenes of serious crimes as soon as possible after discovery, before anything is moved or even touched. This rule is so well known now that there is little excuse for anyone ignoring it."[25]

In order for photography to reach its primary evidentiary quality, it must precisely depict the scene, persons, or objects as found. It must also avoid being inflammatory or too gruesome for subsequent admission.[26] Thus, the investigator performing photographic functions is concerned about two fundamental queries:

1. What is the time relationship between the event or condition in question and the photographic action?
2. What photographic perspective, angle, or plan was employed during the photographic action?

A true and reliable representation is a photographer's seminal obligation, since significant distortions reduce or destroy the evidentiary value of the photographs. Taking pictures from various angles and directions aids in the development of a reliable perspective. A professional photographic portfolio accounts for:

- Approaches to the scene
- Surrounding areas
- Close-ups of entrances and exits
- General scenario shots
- Differing angle shots
- Differing height shots
- Shots of location before and after removal of evidence
- Color *and* black-and-white shots taken in cases where defense challenges gruesomeness of photos

A. Location of Crime Scene

The following suggestions for recording exterior and interior crime scene locations are from the *Crime Laboratory Operations Manual*:[27]

Exterior Locations:

1. Establish the location of the scene by photographs from a distance to include a landmark.
2. Take medium-distance photographs to show the relative position of closely related items of evidence.
3. Take close-up photographs of individual items of evidence.

Interior Locations:

1. Establish the location of the building by photograph.
2. Photograph from eye level, rooms and other interior areas from typical observation points to show relative positions of all items within the area.
3. Take medium-distance photographs to show the relative positions of closely related items of evidence.
4. Take close-up photographs of individual items of evidence.

The Photographer's Photo List in Figure 6.11 aids in recording significant information.

A diversity of photographs gives a permanent, accurate perspective to a case that the limitations of memory do not permit. Pictures taken from various angles and directions ensure a comprehensive and trustworthy record.

Photographer's Photo List

Date of Complaint__________ Time__________
D# __________ Date Pictures Taken __________ Time__________
Victim's Name __________
Location __________
Type of Complaint __________
Investigating Officers __________
Photographer__________

Camera __________ Focal Length __________
Lens Type – 1 __________ Diaphragm __________ Shutter__________
2__________ Diaphragm __________ Shutter__________
Filter __________ Type of Lighting__________
Method of Printing __________ Enlarger Lens__________
Paper __________ Contrast __________

Exposure No.

Remarks:

FIGURE 6.11 Record of photographs taken of evidence and/or crime scene.

FIGURE 6.12 Wide angle aerial view.

FIGURE 6.13 Close-up view.

Look at the photos of an automobile accident (see Figures 6.12–6.15) from several different perspectives, including wide-angle, close-up, posterior, anterior, and aerial views. Can you make any conclusions or deductions regarding the condition of the vehicle? Consider why these pictures would be important in an investigation of an auto accident case.

B. Photography and Special Applications

1. Vehicular Accidents and Related Auto Claims

Timeliness, always a pressing concern of the investigator, takes on added meaning in a case involving autos. Because of the need to get traffic moving again, officials must intrude at the scene and

FIGURE 6.14 Posterior view.

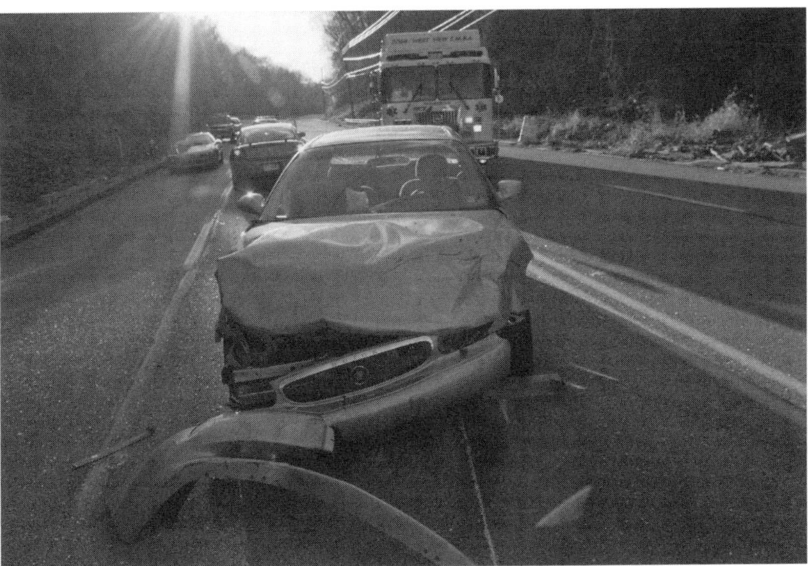

FIGURE 6.15 Anterior view.

move evidence to prevent further accidents. The scene should be recorded promptly and accurately before removal of evidence. When photographing a vehicular accident scene, standard practice comprises pictures or notations of:

- The overall scene of the accident—from both approaches to the point of impact.
- The exact positions of the vehicles, injured persons, and objects directly connected to the accident.
- All points of impact, marks of impact, and damage to real property.
- All pavement obstructions and defects in the roadways.
- Close-ups of damage to vehicles. One photograph should show the front and one side, and another [photograph] should show the rear and other side of the vehicle.

- Skid marks. If possible, photographs should be taken before the vehicle has been removed and again after it has been moved.
- Tire tracks, glass, and other associated debris.[28]

A visual aid or checklist will assist the investigator who is required to photograph the scene. Pictures should reflect some of the issues included within Figure 6.16.[29]

An investigator whose practice is geared toward personal injury, insurance defense, or motor vehicle property damage claims must develop photographic skills. The photographer in this area of expertise should, at a minimum, consider these questions when photographing evidence:

1. What is the extent of damages to the vehicle?
2. What is the extent of personal or bodily injury to the victim, driver, pedestrian, or other interested parties?
3. Have any parts or components of the vehicle been identified as or suspected of being defective and, if so, have they been properly photographed?
4. Has the automobile been photographed from various angles and directions?

Guideline Checklist—Auto Accident Scene

A. Scene
   1. Description/State of Repair of Road
   2. Road/Weather/Lighting/Visibility, etc.
   3. Description of Collision (abutment, other car(s), etc.)

B. Vehicles (Victim's and Others)
   1. Make/Model, etc.
   2. Speed (comparison with speed limit)
   3. Direction Traveling
   4. Safety Devices
      a. Lap Belts
      b. Shoulder Belts
      c. Other Restraints
      d. Locked Doors
      e. Cushioned Dash
      f. Pushout Windows
   5. Vehicle Defects
   6. Evidence of Alcohol/Drugs

C. Other than Vehicular Collision (single vehicle, explosion, avalanche, etc.)
   1. Description of Events
   2. Evidence of Alcohol or Drugs

D. Victim
   1. Location at Moment of Accident
      a. Driver/Passenger (seat location)
      b. Body Location (post accident)
   2. Clothing (description/condition)
   3. Alcohol or Drugs Present (where, form)
   4. Consistency of Injuries w/Accident

E. Other
   1. Possibility of Homicide
   2. Possibility of Suicide

FIGURE 6.16 Reprinted from *Death Investigation and Examination: Medicolegal Guidelines and Checklists* with permission. Copyright 1986 The Forensic Sciences Foundation, Inc.

5. Has the scene of the accident been photographed and fully identified?
6. Have injuries of victims, passengers, pedestrians, or other parties been photographed at various stages (e.g., at time of incident, during treatment, and at intervals thereafter)?

Various examples of photographic evidence pertaining to auto cases are assembled in Figures 6.17–6.19. Answer the questions that accompany each photo.

FIGURE 6.17 Overturned vehicle in high-speed collision: Can you pinpoint any evidence, within the confines of this picture that leads to a conclusion or deduction about how the accident may have occurred?

FIGURE 6.18 Evidence of skid marks: Can deductions be made relative to the speed of the vehicle in question?

FIGURE 6.19 Vehicle from high-speed collision: Can a deduction be made regarding the degree or angle of impact?

2. Bodily Injuries and Photographic Method

Depending on the time at which the pictures of bodily injuries are taken, conditions can either improve or worsen; however, injuries tend to worsen during the first two to three weeks in a bodily injury case. Fresh injuries tend to minimize the range and extent of damages. Take photographs at regular intervals in order to show bruised areas as they become more visible.

In the majority of cases, a good investigator should photograph actual injuries and complement the photos with solid demonstrative evidence.

3. Arson/Insurance Fraud

Private investigators are often hired to investigate claims of insurance fraud involving the burning of the insured's vehicle. "When photographing the arson scene, complete coverage of the damage is important. But perhaps of even greater importance are objects or areas that are suspected to have been the point or points of initiation of fire. Close-up photographs should be made of all such objects or areas."[30]

Chapter 10 provides photographs and checklists pertaining to arson investigation.

4. Burglary/Criminal Trespass/Forcible Theft

In the protection of assets, the security investigator confronts cases of burglary and varied forms of larceny and theft. In cases of burglary, photographic proof of illegal breaking and entering assists the prosecution in meeting this elemental burden. See Figure 6.20 for a representation of photographic proof of forced entry.

When investigating property offenses, the photographer focuses on:

- The interior and exterior of the building.
- Damaged areas, particularly those around the points of entry and exit used by the criminal.
- Close-ups of damaged containers that were the targets of the burglar—safes, jewelry boxes, strong boxes, etc.

FIGURE 6.20 A case of burglary—points of forced entry: Can you identify points or evidence of forced entry?

- Tool marks, both up close and from a perspective that will allow the position of the mark with respect to the general scene to be noted.
- Fingerprints. Although fingerprints are of major interest to all types of investigations, they are of particular value in a burglary investigation. Fingerprints are photographed only when they are visible without development and when they cannot be lifted after they have been developed.[31]

5. Comparative Micrography

The comparative analysis of tool marks and fragments, the reconstruction of parts to a whole, ballistics comparisons, or other forms of microanalytical study are readily admitted forms of evidence. In cases where a product is alleged to be defective, comparative micrography plays an indispensable function. Stress points and fractures in materials often show defective design and manufacture. If it is alleged that alteration to product design, misuse, or a failure to follow instructions is an affirmative defense, comparative micrography can, at least in some cases, demonstrate the credibility of this type of argumentation. Investigators must scrutinize and evaluate the quality of this form of judgment, making sure that the comparison of a test plate and the actual sample is fair—that the test was performed under similar facts and circumstances. Remember that this type of sophisticated microanalysis can be performed by the FBI laboratory in Washington, DC, or by criminalistics laboratories located in most major American cities.

See Figure 6.21[32] for a helpful flow chart on how to ensure the integrity of digital images.

V. DRUG AND ALCOHOL ABUSE EVIDENCE

The war against illegal drug use has resulted in a significant increase in the use of security forces and enterprises. As the American Society for Industrial Security (ASIS) reminds its membership:

> No segment of society is immune to the pressing problems associated with drug and alcohol abuse. These problems cost industry millions of dollars each year in lost work hours, accidents, and theft. For the sake of safety and job performance alone, management must form clear policies stating that no

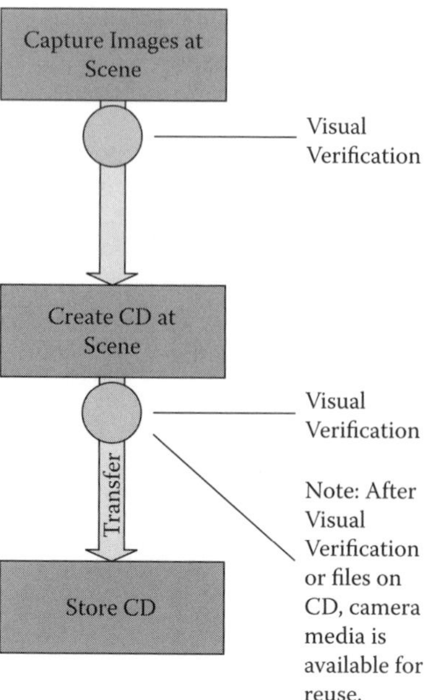

FIGURE 6.21 Ensuring the integrity of digital images.

> one under the influence of alcohol or illegal drugs will be permitted to work. The company must also decide whether violators will be rehabilitated or discharged. The likely spread of these habits from one employee to another is an insidious side effect.[33]

American corporations are relying heavily upon the expertise of private security, not just from the perspective of identifying prospective employees' habits, but also in monitoring their employees who might be using substances in the workplace. Surveillance photography is an effective means of gathering evidence in order to prosecute a drug case. See Figure 6.22[34] for an all-encompassing list of the required information.

VI. DOCUMENTARY EVIDENCE

Proficient investigators know the ins and outs of collecting information, documents, and reports. Invariably, extensive time is spent collecting documents and creating standard correspondence files. Be creative; think hard about those persons who can provide leads and other matters of evidentiary value.

A. Police Records

Police regularly complain that the majority of the time expended in their job relates primarily to paperwork and secondarily to social work. Investigators will quickly discern the magnitude of documentation. Discovery of police documentation, from field notes to a final report, should be of professional interest to an investigator working on a particular case. Investigators fill out many standardized forms and documents during the typical criminal or civil case. Some of the more common examples are described below.

1. Alcohol or Chemical Reports

There has been an increased emphasis on the defense and prosecution of driving while intoxicated or driving under the influence cases. Forms or documentation relative to states of intoxication are

Guideline Checklist—Drug Overdose

A. Report
  1. Date/Time/Reporting Means
  2. Who Reported/Relationship to Victim
  3. Time Delay between Crime and Report
  4. Reported Circumstances of Crime

B. Scene
  1. Description/Condition/Relationship to Victim (home, etc.)
  2. Location of Medicine, Drugs, Alcohol, and Containers
  3. Location of Paint, Glue, Solvents, and Containers
  4. Location of Paraphernalia
  5. Location of Soot or Pill Residue/Blood Tinged Swabs or Tissue
  6. Suicide Note
  7. Evidence of Struggle/Illness, etc.

C. Medicine/Drugs/Alcohol (product and container)
  1. Medicine Prescribed for Victim
     a. Type/Amount Prescribed/Amount on Hand
     b. Location (table, floor, bathroom, etc.)
     c. Victim's History of Normal Ingestion
     d. Same Medication Prescribed by more than one M.D.
     e. "Stockpiling"
     f. Recent use Indicators
     g. Evidence of Accidental Ingestion
  2. Medication Prescribed to Another Person
     a. Type/To Whom Prescribed/Relationship to Victim
     b. Location
     c. Amount Prescribed/Amount on Hand
     d. Same Medication Prescribed by More Than One M.D.
     e. "Stockpiling" Another Person's Medications
     f. Recent Use of Another Person's Medication
     g. Evidence of Accidental Ingestion
  3. Illicit Drugs and Narcotics/Alcohol/Paint, Glue, Solvent
     a. Types/Quantities/Form (powder, pill, etc.)
     b. Evidence of Use or Accidental Ingestion

D. Paraphernalia
  1. Smoking
  2. Drinking
  3. Injecting
  4. Ingesting
  5. Inhaling

E. Residue (soot, powder, etc.)
  1. Types
  2. Quantity

F. Victim
  1. Clothing Condition/Appropriateness/Contents
  2. Tattoos, Rings, Pins, etc. (suggesting drug cult)
  3. Needle Injection Sites (old and new)
  4. Paraphernalia Still on/in Body
  5. Pills and Capsules in Hands or Mouth/on Face
  6. Soot or Pill/Capsule Residue on Body
  7. Drug History
  8. Rigor and Livor Mortis Consistent with Body Location and Position
  9. Resuscitation Efforts (when/kind/by whom)
  10. Hospital/Emergency Room/M.D. administered drugs (when/type/quantity/means)

FIGURE 6.22 Drug overdose investigation checklist. Reprinted from *Death Investigation and Examination: Medicolegal Guidelines and Checklists* with permission. Copyright 1986 The Forensic Sciences Foundation, Inc.

helpful. One such form, Psycho-Physiological Test Results (Figure 6.23), records a person's ability to do specific functions such as walking, placing a finger to the nose, bending, and standing erect. Another is an Alcohol Influence Report, which reports breathalyzer results measuring alcohol vapor in the respiratory system.

2. Accident Reports

Police accident reports are relied upon heavily because they are fresh impressions of liability. Because they are usually at the scene of an accident before any other investigative party, police will transcribe the facts; however, they also may make judgments regarding conduct probative of either civil or criminal liability. Police reports are thoroughly examined in other portions of this text.

3. Domestic Relations Documentation

In the area of domestic relations, police departments expend considerable resources protecting spouses and children from abuse. More and more police departments are being expected to file and keep paperwork regarding these matters, and public outcry increases when police do not take an activist role in these matters. A Domestic Violence Offense Report typically is filled out by a police agency. This type of document is quite effective in corroborating or supporting any claim for abuse as grounds for divorce or may serve as evidence in custody or visitation contests.

4. Radio Logs

Another example of police documentation is the Radio Log document. Recent 911 controversies alleging a slower than usual response time emphasize the crucial nature of radio logs.

5. Arrest Reports—Narcotics

Another form regularly used is an Arrest Report for a Narcotics Division. With the plague of drugs affecting our entire society, police departments have set up narcotics units whose individuals are solely dedicated to the investigation and prosecution of narcotics matters.

6. Violence in the Workplace

An unfortunate reality for commercial entities is the increase in violence in the workplace. The costs of violence are reason enough to adopt documentation policies. There are various reasons:

- Businesses are beginning to realize the high costs of just one violent incident. These costs can include medical and psychiatric care as well as potential liability suits, lost business and productivity, repairs and clean-up, higher insurance rates, consultants' fees, increased security measures and—most important of all—the death or injury of valued employees and coworkers.
- Threats and other violent, abusive behaviors are no longer tolerated in the workplace.
- Executives, professionals, and administrative personnel are no longer immune to acts of violence in the workplace.
- Layoffs, increased workload, having to do more with less, and other unpopular changes in the work environment have been associated with increased risk for violence.
- Recent reports and surveys suggest that workplace violence impacts large numbers of employers and employees.
- It's the right thing to do. Employers have both a moral and a legal obligation to provide a safe workplace for their employees, clients, and visitors.[35]

If violence occurs prepare a Threat Report like the one shown in Figure 6.24.

7. Missing Person Reports

A missing person report is useful to investigators who are working on cases of insurance fraud, escape from prison, violation of probation and parole, change of identity, or other forms of subterfuge. See Figure 6.25[36] for a sample Report of Person form.

Psycho-Physiological Test Results

CD#____________________ Subject____________________

Date____________________

1. Walking Heel-to-Toe
7 steps forward, turn to right/left, 4 steps back

__________ Staggering
__________ Unable to perform
__________ Other

__________ Performed correctly
__________ Falling off balance
__________ Did not follow instructions
__________ Off white line

2. Finger to nose
Right hand _____ times

__________ Missed nose ____ times
__________ Touched nose _____ times
__________ Did not follow instructions
__________ Performed correctly

Left hand _____ times

__________ Missed nose ____ times
__________ Touched nose _____ times
__________ Did not follow instructions
__________ Performed correctly

3. Bending forward
Eyes closed, feet together, tuck in chin, bend for 30 seconds

__________ Falling
__________ Other

__________ Swaying side to side
__________ Swaying front to back
__________ Little/no motion
__________ Did not follow instructions

4. Standing Erect
Eyes closed, feet together, arms alongside

__________ Falling
__________ Other

__________ Swaying side to side
__________ Swaying front to back
__________ Little/no motion
__________ Did not follow instructions

5. Alphabet
Ask subject to recite the alphabet

__________ Yes
__________ No

__________ Recited correctly
__________ Unable to recite correctly

6. Counting
Ask subject to count to ten

__________ Yes

__________ Forward 1-10
__________ Able to perform correctly
__________ Missed numbers

__________ No

__________ Backwards 1-10
__________ Able to perform correctly
__________ Missed numbers

Other optional tests: Explain test and note observations

Officer's Signature ____________________

FIGURE 6.23 Psycho-physiological test results summary.

Threat Report

Name of person(s) making threat ______________________________

Relationship to company ______________________________

Relationship to recipient of threat, if any______________________________

Name(s) of the recipients or victims______________________________

____

Date and location of incident ______________________________

What happened immediately prior to the incident______________________________

____

____

____

The specific language of the threat ______________________________

____

____

Any physical conduct that would substantiate an intention to follow through with the threat______________

____

How the threat-maker appeared, both physically and emotionally______________________________

____

____

Names of others who were directly involved, and any actions they took ______________________________

____

____

____

How the incident ended ______________________________

____

____

Names of witnesses ______________________________

____

____

What happened to the treat-maker after the incident______________________________

____

____

What happened to other employees directly involved in the incident, if any ______________________________

____

____

Names of any supervisory staff involved and how they responded______________________________

____

____

What event(s) triggered the incident______________________________

____

Any history leading up to the incident______________________________

____

The steps that have been taken to assure the threat will not be carried out ______________________________

____

____

Suggestions for preventing this type of incident from occurring again ______________________________

____

____

FIGURE 6.24 Threat report.

REPORT OF PERSON

Serial No. ______ ☐ MISSING ☐ DEAD ☐ SUSPICIOUS ☐ WANTED Case No. ______

NAME	ADDRESS	AGE	RACE	SEX	F.P. CLASS

HEIGHT	WEIGHT	BUILD	COLOR OF HAIR	COMPLEXION

DATE OF BIRTH	PLACE OF BIRTH	OCCUPATION	NEXT OF KIN

SOCIAL SECURITY NO.	DRIVER'S LICENSE NO.	SERVICE RECORD & SERIAL NO.

SCHOOL ATTENDED	GRADE	LODGE OR UNION AFFILIATIONS

JEWELRY WORN	MONEY CARRIED

PERSON REPORTING	ADDRESS	PHONE NO.	RELATION, IF ANY

REPORTED TO	HOW REPORTED	DATE & TIME REPORTED

MISSING PERSON (USE GUIDE ON BACK SIDE FOR DETAILED INFORMATION.)

DATE AND TIME LAST SEEN	WHERE LAST SEEN	BY WHOM

PREVIOUS DISAPPEARANCES	MAY HAVE GONE TO

DESCRIPTION BROADCAST BY	DATE & TIME	WILL FAMILY PAY FOR DISTRIBUTION OF CIRCULAR?

DATE AND TIME LOCATED	WHERE LOCATED	BY WHOM

DEAD PERSON

FOUND BY	ADDRESS	PHONE NO.

DATE AND TIME FOUND	LOCATION	CONDITION WHEN FOUND

EVIDENCE OF FOUL PLAY	CORONER	VERDICT

AUTOPSY	PERFORMED BY	WHERE

RELATIVE OR FRIENDS NAME	RESIDENCE	PHONE NO.

NOTIFIED BY	DATE & TIME	FINAL DISPOSITION

SUSPICIOUS PERSON

CAUSE OF SUSPICION	SEEN LOITERING
DATE AND TIME	PLACE
RESULTS OF INVESTIGATION	FINAL DISPOSITION

WANTED PERSON

WANTED BY	WANTED FOR
DATE & TIME	PLACE

REMARKS

INVESTIGATING OFFICER(S)	REPORT MADE BY	DATE & TIME

FIGURE 6.25 Report of person. Reprinted from Report of Person, Form No. 114 with permission. Copyright 2009 G. A. Thompson Co

Describe the Suspect.

The primary or most useful information to obtain when describing a suspect is:

Sex ________ Race ________________ Age _______ Height _________ Weight ________

If a weapon is used it is very helpful to know if the weapon is a:

❑ Revolver

❑ Automatic

Other useful information is:

____
Hair

____
Color of eyes

____
Glasses

____
Moustache/Beard, Sideburns

____
Complexion

____
Tattoos, Amputations, Scars, or Marks

____
Speech impediments or accents

____
Distinguishable gait or limp

____
Hat

____
Shirt

____
Coat

____
Tie

____
Pants and Shoes

FIGURE 6.26 Form used to describe suspect and suspect's vehicle.

8. Disposition Sheets

In final record-keeping, the police department maintains a Disposition Sheet, which confirms the arrest and selected charges.

9. Suspect Descriptions

Two forms of suspect descriptions are outlined below. Abbreviated suspect descriptions can prove helpful during the initial investigation (Figure 6.26), but the suspect description forms shown in Figures 6.27 and 6.28 are much more comprehensive and will result in more accurate information.

Vehicle Description.

The primary or most useful information to obtain when identifying a motor vehicle is the *license number*, with state of issue or identifying colors. ______________________
Otheruseful information is:

What make? ______ Body Style? (2 dr., 4 dr., conv., etc.) ______ What year? ______

What color? Two color (two tone)? ______ Identifying dents, scratches? ______

The police can use answers to as many of these questions as possible. Please remember that wrong information is worse than no information at all. Answer only those questions that you're sure of.

1. How many suspects were there? ______
2. What did they do? ______
3. What did they say? ______
4. What did they take? ______
5. Which way did they go? ______
6. Were there any other witnesses? ______
   Names and addresses? ______
   Phone numbers? ______
7. Is there any other information you feel is important? ______

COMMUNITY CRIME PREVENTION

MINNEAPOLIS SAFE POLICE

Vision
The City of Minneapolis is the safest place to live, work and visit.

For individuals with disabilities:
If you need this material in Braille, large print, computer disk, or cassette tape, call 612-673-2912. Sign language interpreters available—call 612-673-3220 or 612-673-2626 (TTY). Please allow two weeks for accommodation.

DESCSUSP.P656/03

FIGURE 6.26 (continued).

B. Medical Records

Standard medical records are indispensable in the investigation of any medical, personal injury, or related claim. Medical releases authorizing the transferral of information from a hospital, physician, consultant, emergency room, or employer should be signed. A general medical release, granted by the client, is shown in Figure 6.29.[37]

Being attentive to privacy considerations and the emerging or existing legislation that guides the personal integrity of medical records is an ongoing security concern. Medical records prompt a host of ethical and practical dilemmas. The Electronic Privacy Information Center warns not only consumers but the investigators:

Details Description

1. SEX (Male, Female)
2. RACE (Caucasian, African American, Native American, Pacific Islander, Asian, etc.)
3. AGE ________
4. HEIGHT (Compare with person with whom you work) ____ ft. ____ in.
5. WEIGHT (Compare with person with whom you work) _____lbs.
6. PROBABLE NATIONALITY (American, English, Latin, Scandinavian, Japanese, etc.)
7. BUILD (slender, medium, heavy, stocky, athletic, very heavy, very thin, etc.)
8. POSTURE (erect, stooped, slumped, etc.)
9. COMPLEXION (fair, dark, red, tanned, pale, freckly, pimply, rough, smooth, etc.)
10. HEAD (large, medium, small, round, square, oblong, broad, inclined forward, backward, sideways)
11. HAIR (color ______; color at temples _____; baldness: frontal, top, receding at hairline, totally bald; texture: thick, thin, coarse, straight, wavy, kinky, curled, bushy; parted on right, left, middle, no part)
12. EYES (brown, blue, green, grey, hazel; clear, bloodshot; large, small, deep-set, protruding, straight, slanted, cross-eyed, narrow, squinting, close-set, wide apart; eyelashes: long, short; glass eye. If glasses worn: type, color of rims, etc.)
13. FOREHEAD (broad, narrow, high, low, receding, vertical, bulging)
14. EYEBROWS (thin, bushy, penciled, natural, arched, horizontal, slanting up or down, meeting)
15. NOSE (long, medium, short; thin, thick, straight, concave, convex, pointed, flat, turned up, turned down, pointed to right or left; nostrils: large, small, high, low, flared)
16. MUSTACHE OR BEARD (short, medium, long, pointed, ends turned up or down; thick, thin; type of beard or sideburns) Compare with color of hair
17. CHEEKS (full, fleshy, sunken, etc.)
18. CHEEKBONES (high, low, prominent, not prominent)
19. MOUTH (turned up or down at corners, held open or closed, distorted by speech or laughter)
20. LIPS (with reference to either upper or lower: thick, thin, puffy, overhanging, compressed, protruding, retracted over teeth; cracked, scarred; red, pale, blue)
21. TEETH (white, yellow, stained, loose, decayed, broken, filled, braced, capped, receding or projecting, false, prominent bridgework, etc.)
22. CHIN (small, large, normal, square, curved, pointed, flat, double, dimpled, protruding, receding, etc.)
23. JAW (long, short, wide, narrow, thin, fleshy, square, heavy, etc.)
24. EARS (small, medium, large, close to or projecting from head; oval, round, rectangular, triangular; pierced, cauliflowered, hairy; contour of the lobe, lower portion)
25. NECK (small, medium, long, straight, curved, thin, flat, goiterous, crooked; Adams' apple: flat, prominent, medium, absent)
26. SHOULDERS (small, heavy, narrow, broad, square, round, stooped, not equal, etc.)
27. HANDS (long, short, broad, narrow, thin, fleshy, rough, bony, soft, smooth, hairy, square, tapered, etc.)
28. FINGERS (short, long, slim, thick, tapered, square, stained, mutilated, etc.)
29. FINGERNAILS (length, description, foreign matter under nails; painted)
30. VOICE (pleasant, well-modulated, low, high, lisp or other impediment of speech, gruff, polite, regional or foreign accent)

REMEMBER EXACT LANGUAGE USED ____________________

____

____

____

____

FIGURE 6.27 More detailed suspect description form.

31. WALK (long or short stride, energetic, slow, fast, springy step, limp)
32. APPEARANCE (loud, conservative, neat, sloppy)
33. CLOTHING: (list color, pattern, type, material, condition, how worn)

Hat or cap __________

Overcoat __________

Pants __________

Suit __________

Dress __________

Shirt __________

Tie __________

Shoes __________

Socks __________

Belt __________

Mask __________

34. JEWELRY (rings, watches, chains, earrings, tie pins, lapel pins, bracelets, cuff links, etc.)

Describe __________

35. PECULIARITIES (most important of all) (scars, marks, tattoos, moles, birthmarks)

Describe __________

36. TYPE OF WEAPON USED:

Name __________

Address __________

Date __________

FIGURE 6.27 (continued).

Besides information about physical health, these records may include information about family relationships, sexual behavior, substance abuse, and even the private thoughts and feelings that come with psychotherapy. This information is often keyed to a Social Security number. Because of a lack of consistent privacy protection in the use of Social Security numbers, the information may be easily accessible.

Information from your medical records may influence your credit, admission to educational institutions, and employment. It may also affect your ability to get health insurance, or the rates you pay for coverage (OTA report). More importantly, having others know intimate details about your life may mean a loss of dignity and autonomy.[38]

Federal efforts to control access to medical records are often seen in legislative initiatives. During the 104th U.S. Congress (1996), Congress posed the language of privacy protection and medical records in the Medical Privacy in the Age of New Technologies Act of 1996.[39] Sanctions for privacy violations are also authorized:

SEC. 311. WRONGFUL DISCLOSURE OF PROTECTED HEALTH INFORMATION.
(a) Offense.—Whoever knowingly—
(1) obtains protected health information relating to an individual in violation of this Act;
(2) discloses protected health information to another person in violation of this Act;
(3) coerces or attempts to coerce a health information trustee to disclose protected health information in violation of this title; or

The Stanford University Safety & Security Report

Describing a Suspect and Vehicle

Reporting a Crime | Suspect / Vehicle Description

Reporting Crime & Suspicious Activity

All students, faculty, staff and visitors at Stanford are encouraged to report all crimes and public safety related incidents to the Stanford Department of Public Safety in a timely manner.

Anytime you need **immediate** police, fire, or medical response, **dial 9-9-1-1** from University phones (all Stanford prefixes). From non-university phones, dial 9-1-1. Remember that 9-1-1 is a **free** call from pay phones and any cell phone. In addition, emergency phones with blue lights are located in many areas on campus. These phones are either blue emergency towers or pay phones with blue lights on top. For a **non-emergency** police response on campus, dial 723-9633.

Call 911 if you think a crime is in progress, which might be indicated by:

- A whistle, scream or call for help.
- A strange car repeatedly driving up and down the street.
- Seeing someone you don't know or recognize enter your neighbor's room or home, enter an office or lab with no apparent business or transaction, or loiter in a parking area or at a bike rack near your home, dorm, or work.

Remember that the police cannot be everywhere at once, and they depend on individuals in the community to assist them in crime prevention by reporting suspicious activities.

How to Describe a Suspect and Vehicle

INSTRUCTIONS: This form is to aid you describing a suspect or a suspect's vehicle. This does not take the place of phoning 9-911 or 911.
In an emergency, do not take the time to fill in this form.
Call 9-911 from a campus phone, or 911 from a non-campus phone or cell phone.

Date ____________________________
Time ____________________________
Location ____________________________
Direction of Travel ____________________________
Weapon ____________________________

Suspect Information

FIGURE 6.28 Stanford University form for describing suspect and vehicle.

Male _____ Female _____
Adult _____ Juvenile _____ Approximate Age _____
Race ______________________________
Height __________ Weight __________
Hair Color ______________________________
Eye Color ______________________________
Mustache, bear, sideburns or other facial hair ______________________________
Tattoos, scars or other identifying marks ______________________________
Gait, limp or amputations ______________________________

Suspect's Clothing

Hat ______________________________
Glasses ______________________________
Shirt type and color ______________________________
Pants type and color ______________________________
Shoes ______________________________

Automobile Information

Make ______________________________
Model ______________________________
Color ______________________________
Year ______________________________
Body style (2-door, 4-door, convertible, truck, etc.) ______________________________
License plate number ______________________________
Distinguishing features (spoiler, racing stripes, tinting, damage, etc.) __________________

FIGURE 6.28 (continued).

MEDICAL RELEASE

You are hereby authorized to release to the investigator any and all information, without limitation, that you possess. This release includes, but is not limited to, billing information, admission records, X-ray reports, lab reports, nurses' notes, progress reports, and discharge summaries.

This authorization shall not expire until expressly canceled. A copy of this release shall be as effective as an original.

Name: ______________ NAME OF CLIENT ______________

Dated: ______________________________

Signature: ______________________________

FIGURE 6.29 Medical release authorization form. Reprinted from Lawyer's Guide to Medical Proof with permission. Copy 1984 Matthew Bender & Company, Inc., a member of LexisNexis Group. All rights reserved.

(4) without authorization pursuant to this Act, identifies or attempt to identify an individual who is the subject of protected health information that a health information trustee has converted into coded health information, shall be punished as provided in subsection (b).

(b) Penalties.—A person referred to in subsection (a) shall be fined under title 18, United States Code, imprisoned not more than 1 year, or both, except that—

(1) if the offense is committed under false pretenses, the person shall be fined under title 18, United States Code, imprisoned not more than 5 years, or excluded from participation in the program under title XVIII of the Social Security Act, the program under title XIX of such Act, or any other federally funded health care program, or any combination of such penalties;[40]

INFORMATION SECURITY POLICY

1) Purpose

To provide guidelines for ensuring that only authorized persons have appropriate access to computerized information, while safeguarding the information's confidentiality, security and integrity.

2) Policy

a) *Definitions*

i) Security

Protection of information resources from unauthorized change, destruction, or disclosure, whether intentional or accidental.

ii) Information Resources

These include, but are not limited to: hardware, software, storage media, computer signon codes, and information transmitted stored, printed, and/or processed by a computer system.

iii) Confidential Information

Information that requires special safeguards due to its private nature, including: patient care and treatment information, including patient's identity and diagnosis; and, personnel information regarding salaries, benefits, performance reviews and disciplinary action.

b) *Development and support of information security process*

1. The Hospital will implement processes to ensure sufficient security and confidentiality for its information.
2. The Hospital will address security issues during the purchase and implementation of new information systems.
3. Management staff in each department will develop and maintain information security policies specific to their department, if appropriate, which are consistent with this policy.
4. The orientation program for new employees will address the Hospital's information security policies. At the time of orientation, each new employee will sign a confidentiality agreement that summarizes the Hospital's information security policies and the individual's responsibilities regarding these policies. This agreement will be filed in the employee's records in the Personnel Department.
5. Management staff in each department will inform their staff of institutional and departmental information security policies. Management will ensure that these policies are addressed at departmental staff meetings annually.

c) *Authorization to Access information resources*

1. Only persons who have valid business reasons for accessing the Hospital's information resources will be granted access. Individuals will be given access to information resources in keeping with their job requirements.
2. No one may access the Hospital's information resources or applications without prior written authorization and approval. It is illegal to use a Hospital computer or access information stored or maintained by the Hospital without the Hospital's consent.
3. All passwords to the Hospital's computer systems are confidential and are the property of the Hospital. These include, but are not limited to, passwords to network systems, mainframe systems, PCs, voice mail, and long distance telephone codes.

d) *Computer equipment security*

1. Terminals, network devices, and personal computers in unsecured areas will be secured against theft and use by unauthorized persons.
2. Personal computers in unsecured areas will be set up to use power-on passwords and keyboard passwords, to prevent unauthorized persons from using the device without providing the appropriate password.
3. Anyone who signs on to a computer system must sign off and/or physically secure the terminal or PC when leaving it unattended.
4. Where possible, computer systems will be set up to automatically sign off or password-protect terminals and PCs after a specified period of inactivity.
5. Access to data centers will be secured by means of locked entryways, Only persons authorized to operate or maintain the computer systems will be issued keys, passcards, or other means for unlocking the entryway. Authorized visitors to the Data Center will be escorted by authorized staff.

FIGURE 6.30 Information form outlining security policy.

A policy statement or draft laying out the several parameters of information disclosure, release, and protection is an essential security function. Every office entrusted with the protection of records should implement a policy similar to that shown in Figure 6.30.

Requesting hospital records from emergency rooms, consultants, or other medical professionals working for hospitals is standard investigative practice. A client authorization request for hospital records is shown in Figure 6.31.

e) *Security of computer-related media*

1. Printed reports containing confidential or sensitive information will be stored in a secure area, inaccessible to unauthorized persons. Confidential reports will be rendered unreadable before being discarded.

2. Diskettes, tapes, and other media containing confidential information will be labeled "confidential" and will be protected appropriately.

3. Diskettes, tapes and other medial containing computer files will be stored in areas accessible only to authorized persons.

f) *Protection of computerized files*

1. Departments and individuals must establish regular schedules for making backup copies of data files stored on personal computers, network file servers, and other computer systems.

2. Backup copies will be stored in a safe location (not exposes to heat or magnetic fields). Backup copies for network file servers and mainframe computer systems will not be stored in the same room as the servers or data storage devices.

3. Virus protection programs will be installed and executed regularly on each PC and computer system.

4. Software will not be copied from public access bulletin boards or other non-Hospital computer systems without first being scanned by a virus protection program.

g) *Dial up access to information sources*

1. Authorized employees, physicians, and other authorized parties will be permitted to use telephone lines to access Hospital information resources, with proper safeguards.

2. All dial-up connections to Hospital computer systems will be routed through devices that provide for password verification, call-back security, or other similar features.

3. Modems or personal computers that do not have dial-up access security features will not be connected to direct-inward-dial telephone lines.

h) *Violations of Information Security Policy*

1. Failure to comply with these information security policies and procedures may result in disciplinary action, termination of access privileges to Hospital information systems, and civil or criminal actions, at the discretion of Hospital management.

2. Management staff in each department will monitor and counsel their staff in matters of information security.

3) Procedure

a) *Security Administration*

i) A system security administrator will be designated for each network system and each mainframe application.

(1) System security administrators will be responsible for issuing signon codes for the system(s) for which they are responsible. System security administrators are responsible for ensuring that all persons who receive signon codes have proper authorization to access the system.

(2) The Information Systems Department will maintain a list of all designated system security administrators and their backups.

b) *Obtaining authorization to access information resources*

i) Requests for access to the Hospital's information resources must be submitted in writing to the appropriate system security administrator.

ii) Requests for access to information sources must be approved by the appropriate Hospital management.

iii) All persons who request access to computer systems will be required to sign a Confidentiality Agreement that summarizes the Hospital's information security policies and the individual's responsibilities regarding these policies.

c) *Issuance of computer signon codes*

i) Each person authorized to access a Hospital computer system will be issues a unique, individual identification code and password. The person must supply this identification immediately after initial contact with the computer, or further access will be denied.

ii) Each authorized user is responsible for changing his or her password periodically (at least every 90 days) on systems where this can be done.

FIGURE 6.30 (continued).

Another example of a medical information request document that complements an investigative file is a request for a copy of an office record. In this case, the correspondence is usually directed to the treating physician's clerk or other paraprofessional who handles the records. This should not be confused with a direct request for a medical evaluation or report, which is usually in the form of a standardized document, such as a tabulated bill. See Figure 6.32.

Date:

To:

RE:

Our File No.:

Dear ______________________:

I have retained this firm to represent me in injuries sustained as a result of an accident that occurred on ____________________. Please send to this firm's address the medical records for this accident as well as a complete billing summary for services rendered to date. Please bill ____________________ for this report.

Sincerely,

____

Patient Account #: ______________________________

FIGURE 6.31 Client authorization for hospital records.

Date:

Name:
Address:

IN RE: Request for Copy of Office Record
Name of Patient:
Date of Injury:

Dear Dr. ____________________:

Please be advised that I am an investigator in the above-referenced case and have been given full power of attorney to seek information and records. Attached is a copy of the power of attorney. I am writing at this time to request a copy of the medical record that has been prepared by your office for this patient. Please send me a copy of this record as soon as possible.

I have enclosed a copy of a medical release which authorizes me to acquire this information. If there is any charge for copying or printing the requested material, please send a statement together with the requested information.

Sincerely,

Name of Investigator

Enclosure

FIGURE 6.32 Request for copy of medical office record.

Access requests for every type of record, whether it is an admission and discharge record, emergency room record, x-ray report, medical expense record, billing statement, payroll information, life squad report, or death certificate, follow a similar format.

VII. RECORDS INVOLVING ECONOMIC DAMAGES

Customarily, investigators involved in cases of workers' compensation, disability, social security, or personal injury collect not only evidence of actual medical injuries, but also records concerning economic losses. Economic losses can take many forms, from losing the value of a certain property to the loss of past, present, and future earnings capacity. Because of these factors, the investigator needs to gain access to employment and payroll records.

An example of an authorization and request for employment records in shown in Figure 6.33, which inquires about the client's payroll history, as well as the period of employment and the extent of weekly and overtime pay.

Often, employers compile and maintain records dealing with medical benefits because of a medical insurance, workers' compensation, or disability plan. A release or authorization for this information directed to the employer is shown in Figure 6.34. A wage release authorization is shown in Figure 6.35.

AUTHORIZATION AND REQUEST FOR EMPLOYMENT RECORDS

To: ______________________ Re: ______________________
Name of Employee

______________________ ______________________
Address

______________________ ______________________

______________________ ______________________

S.S.#: ______________________

You are hereby requested and authorized to furnish to my Attorney whose name and address is:

or my attorney's authorized representative, any information you may have regarding my past or present employment. Please provide copies of any records along with any other requested information. I would appreciate your full cooperation.

Dated: ______________________ ______________________
Employee

Additional Remarks: ______________________

____

____

____

____

____

____

Dated: ______________________ ______________________
Title

FIGURE 6.33 Authorization and request for employment records.

Information regarding tax returns can be secured by Internal Revenue Service (IRS) Authorization Form 2848-D, and an example of this form is shown in Figure 6.36.

MEDICAL BENEFIT RELEASE FORM

This employee's records release authorizes you to furnish to the investigator named any record, information, or knowledge which is in your possession. This release includes, but is not limited to, information concerning my rates of pay, sick records, overtime records, vacation records, personnel records, injury and health records, tax and social security records, and insurance benefits records. The release shall remain valid until it is expressly canceled. A copy of this release shall be as effective as an original.

Name: NAME-OF-CLIENT

Social Security Number: ______________________

Date of Birth: ______________________

Name of Investigator: ______________________

Dated: __________ Signature ______________________

FIGURE 6.34 Authorization to release medical benefit information.

WAGE RELEASE

This wage release authorizes you to furnish to the investigator named any record or information that you possess concerning my wage and earning records. This release includes, but is not limited to, information concerning my rate of pay, number of hours worked, gross pay, net pay, or weekly check amounts.

This release shall remain valid until it is expressly canceled. A copy of this release shall be as effective as an original.

Name: NAME-OF-CLIENT

Social Security Number: ______________________

Date of Birth: ______________________

Name of Investigator: ______________________

Dated: __________ Signature ______________________

FIGURE 6.35 Authorization to release wage ifnormation.

VIII. PRESERVATION OF EVIDENCE

Collection and preservation of evidence and the assurance of its integrity during the investigative process are undeniable responsibilities of the public and private police system. Investigators are continually concerned with whether the chain of custody of the evidence has been distorted, broken, contaminated, abused, reformulated, recast, or changed in any significant way. Evidence such as tools, guns, glass fragments, hairs, fibers, body parts—any real, physical evidence—should be stored in an environment that maintains, as scientifically as possible, its original status.[41] "The investigator himself should bear in mind the possibility that he himself may destroy or contaminate

Form **8821** (Rev. August 2008) Department of the Treasury Internal Revenue Service

Tax Information Authorization

► **Do not sign this form unless all applicable lines have been completed.**

► **Do not use this form to request a copy or transcript of your tax return. Instead, use Form 4506 or Form 4506-T.**

OMB No. 1545-1165

For IRS Use Only

Received by:

Name

Telephone ( )

Function

Date / /

1 Taxpayer information. Taxpayer(s) must sign and date this form on line 7.

Taxpayer name(s) and address (type or print)	**Social security number(s)**	**Employer identification number**
	Daytime telephone number ( )	Plan number (if applicable)

2 Appointee. If you wish to name more than one appointee, attach a list to this form.

Name and address

CAF No. ....

Telephone No. ....

Fax No. ....

Check if new: Address ☐ Telephone No. ☐ Fax No. ☐

3 Tax matters. The appointee is authorized to inspect and/or receive confidential tax information in any office of the IRS for the tax matters listed on this line. Do not use Form 8821 to request copies of tax returns.

(a) Type of Tax (Income, Employment, Excise, etc.) or Civil Penalty	**(b)** Tax Form Number (1040, 941, 720, etc.)	**(c)** Year(s) or Period(s) (see the instructions for line 3)	**(d)** Specific Tax Matters (see instr.)

4 Specific use not recorded on Centralized Authorization File (CAF). If the tax information authorization is for a specific use not recorded on CAF, check this box. See the instructions on page 4. If you check this box, skip lines 5 and 6 . ► ☐

5 Disclosure of tax information (you **must** check a box on line 5a or 5b unless the box on line 4 is checked):

a If you want copies of tax information, notices, and other written communications sent to the appointee on an ongoing basis, check this box . . . . . ► ☐

b If you do not want any copies of notices or communications sent to your appointee, check this box . . . . ► ☐

6 Retention/revocation of tax information authorizations. This tax information authorization automatically revokes all prior authorizations for the same tax matters you listed on line 3 above unless you checked the box on line 4. If you do not want to revoke a prior tax information authorization, you **must** attach a copy of any authorizations you want to remain in effect **and** check this box . . . . . ► ☐

To revoke this tax information authorization, see the instructions on page 4.

7 Signature of taxpayer(s). If a tax matter applies to a joint return, **either** husband or wife must sign. If signed by a corporate officer, partner, guardian, executor, receiver, administrator, trustee, or party other than the taxpayer, I certify that I have the authority to execute this form with respect to the tax matters/periods on line 3 above.

► **IF NOT SIGNED AND DATED, THIS TAX INFORMATION AUTHORIZATION WILL BE RETURNED.**

► **DO NOT SIGN THIS FORM IF IT IS BLANK OR INCOMPLETE.**

Signature Date | Signature Date

Print Name Title (if applicable) | Print Name Title (if applicable)

☐☐☐☐☐ PIN number for electronic signature | ☐☐☐☐☐ PIN number for electronic signature

For Privacy Act and Paperwork Reduction Act Notice, see page 4. Cat. No. 11596P Form **8821** (Rev. 8-2008)

FIGURE 6.36 Form authorizing release of tax information.

evidence before it is noticed or recognized. Minute spurts of blood, particles of dust, dirt, and debris are not always obvious to the naked eye and can be destroyed or rendered worthless as evidence if the investigator is not sufficiently observant during his investigation. Defense counsel should recognize the possibility or probability of contamination having occurred and conduct his cross-examination accordingly.'"[42]

The entire concept of chain of custody governs the conduct and tactics of an investigator:

> Chain of custody is the description of the identification and control of evidence from the time it is collected at the scene until it is entered into evidence in court. The legal "chain of custody" must be maintained at all times.[43]

The Pennsylvania State Police, in their *Crime Laboratory Operations Manual*, offer timeless advice on the preservation of evidence.

> Each item of evidence should be placed in a suitable container, and this container should be properly identified and sealed. The laboratory can only aid in the investigation if evidence has been preserved. … As a general rule, to guarantee the value of the evidence collected, evidence should be packaged to:
>
> 1. Prevent loss: Package all evidence in such a manner that small items will not be lost from the container or in the seams or folds of a container. Envelopes are poor containers for small items such as paint chips, since they can leak out at the corners or become lodged in the folds and be difficult to remove without loss or damage. Pill boxes or plastic vials should be used for this type of evidence.
> 2. Prevent contamination: Separate items so that there is no mixing of items from various locations. NEVER place items from the scene and from the suspect in the same container. Each article of clothing from a victim or suspect of a crime should also be individually packaged and identified so that no trace evidence is transferred from one item to the next.
> 3. Prevent alteration: Handle and package the evidence in such a manner that it reaches the laboratory in the same condition as collected. Use common sense.[44]

The FBI, in its *Handbook for Forensic Science*,[45] has published guidelines on how evidence should be packaged, processed, and mailed for any analysis. See Figure 6.37[46] for a summary version of those packaging and safety standards.

The integrity of evidence can also be protected by the use of tags, tapes, and various forms of labels.[47] Calling for a hands-off approach, evidence tamper tapes warn prospective individuals to keep out unless authorized. Property evidence tags are usually tied to the bag, box, or other packaging; they account for the exact chain of possession—from whom, to where, and what date and time is recorded. See Figures 6.38[48] and 6.39.[49]

In this age of communicable diseases, the investigator must exercise caution in handling materials and in the storage of fluids and other perishable evidence. The use of gloves when handling syringe needles, plastic vials, eyedroppers, and other devices ensures not only the unchallengeable quality of the evidence, but also the safety of the person performing the investigative function.

> **Web Exercise:** For packaging and preservation requirements for the many of types of evidence, see the FBI's *Handbook of Forensic Services* at: http://www.fbi.gov/hq/lab/handbook/forensics.pdf

Title 49 - U.S. Department of Transportation
400 7th Street, Southwest, Washington, D.C. 20590, telephone: (202) 366-4000

CFR Title 49, Section(s) and/or Subpart(s) for D-Marking specify that the person who offers hazardous material(s) for transportation must mark each package in the manner required by this title, a telephone number is provided to obtain specific directions.

97

FIGURE 6.37 FBI packaging and safety standards.

Collection, Shipment, Identification and Packaging Charts			
	Amount Desired		
Specimen	Standard	Evidence	Send By
Abrasives	Not less than one ounce.	All	Registered mail or equivalent
Acids	10 ml.	All to 100 ml.	Call Chemistry-Toxicology Unit at (202) 324-4318 for instructions.
Alkalies: Caustic Soda, Potash, Ammonia, etc.	10 ml. of liquids. 10 g. of solids.	All to 100 ml. All to 100 g.	Call Chemistry-Toxicology Unit at (202) 324-4318 for instructions.
Ammunition (Live Cartridges)			Call Firearms-Toolmarks Unit at (202) 324-4378 for instructions.
Anonymous Letters, Extortion Letters, and Bank Robbery Notes		All original documents.	Registered mail or equivalent

98

FIGURE 6.37 (continued).

Identification	Wrapping and Packing	Remarks
Outside container: type of material, date obtained, investigator's name or initials.	Use film cannister or plastic vial. Seal to prevent any loss.	Avoid use of envelopes.
Same as above.	Use plastic/glass bottle. Pack in sawdust, glass, or rock wool. Use bakelite or paraffin-lined bottle for hydrofluoric acid.	Label acid, corrosive, etc.
Same as above.	Use plastic or glass bottle with rubber stopper held with adhesive tape.	Label alkali, corrosive, etc.
Same as above.	Call Firearms-Toolmarks Unit at (202) 324-4378 for instructions.	Unless specific examination of the cartridge is essential, do not submit.
Initial and date each document, if advisable.	Use proper enclosure. Place in envelope and seal with "Evidence" tape or transparent cellophane tape. Flap side of envelope should show: (1) wording "Enclosure(s) to FBIHQ from (name of submitting office)," (2) title of case, (3) brief description of contents, (4) file number, if known. Staple to original letter of transmittal.	Do not handle with bare hands. Advise if evidence should be treated for latent fingerprints.

99

FIGURE 6.37 (continued).

Collection, Shipment, Identification and Packaging Charts			
	Amount Desired		
Specimen	Standard	Evidence	Send By
Blood:			
1. Liquid Known Samples	One tube each (sterile) 5cc-10cc blood only. No preservatives.	All	Registered mail or equivalent
2. Small quantities:			
a. Liquid Questioned Samples		All	Registered mail or equivalent
b. Dry stains Not on fabrics		As much as possible.	Registered mail or equivalent
c. For toxicological use		20 cc of blood and preservative mixture.	Registered mail or equivalent
3. Stained clothing, fabric, etc.		As found.	Registered mail or equivalent
Bullets (projector without cartridge)		All found.	Registered mail or equivalent
Cartridges (live ammunition)		All found.	Call Firearms-Toolmarks Unit at (202) 324-4378 for instructions.
Cartridge Cases (shells only)		All	Registered mail or equivalent

100

FIGURE 6.37 (continued).

Identification	Wrapping and Packing	Remarks
Outside test tube: use adhesive tape. Name of donor, date taken, doctor's name, investigator's name or initials.	Wrap in cotton/soft paper. Place in mailing tube or suitable strong mailing carton.	Submit immediately. Don't hold awaiting additional items for comparison. Do not freeze, keep refrigerated until mailing. Do not add refrigerants and/or dry ice to sample during transit. Label "Fragile."
Same as above.	Same as above.	If unable to expeditiously furnish sample: Dry on nonporous surface, scrape off or collect (use eye droppers or clean spoon), transfer to nonporous surface or absorb in sterile gauze and let it dry.
Outside pillbox or plastic vial: label with type of specimen, date secured, investigator's name or initials.	Seal to prevent leakage.	Keep it dry. Do not use envelopes.
Same as liquid samples.	Medical examiner should use a standard blood collection kit.	Preservative desired (identify preservation used). Refrigerate. Can freeze.
Use tag or mark directly on clothes: type of specimens, date secured, investigator's name or initials.	Wrap each article separately. Label outside package as to contents. Place in strong box to prevent shifting of contents.	If wet when found, dry by hanging. DO NOT USE HEAT TO DRY. Avoid direct sunlight while drying. Do not use preservatives.
Initials on base, nose or mutilated area.	Pack tightly in cotton or soft paper in pill, match, or powder box. Place in box. Label outside of box as to contents.	Unnecessary handling obliterates marks.
Initials on outside of case near bullet end.	Same as above.	Live ammunition is dangerous. Handle with care.
Initials preferably on inside near open end and/or on outside near open end.	Same as above.	Spent cartridge cases.

101

FIGURE 6.37 (continued).

Collection, Shipment, Identification and Packaging Charts			
	Amount Desired		
Specimen	**Standard**	**Evidence**	**Send By**
Casts (Dental or Die Stone Casts of Tire Treads and Shoe Prints)	Send in suspect's shoes and tires. Photographs and sample impressions are usually not suitable for comparison.	All shoe prints and entire circumference of tires.	Registered mail or equivalent
Checks (fraudulent)		All	Registered mail or equivalent
Check Protector, Rubber Stamp, and/ or Date Stamp Known Standards (if possible, send actual device)	Obtain several copies in full word-for-word order of each questioned check-writer impression. If unable to forward rubber stamps, prepare numerous samples with different degrees of pressure.		Registered mail or equivalent
Clothing		All	Registered mail or equivalent
Codes and Ciphers (found on items of racketeering cases)		All	Registered mail or equivalent
Documents (charred or burned)		All	Registered mail or equivalent
Drugs: 1. Liquids		All	Registered mail or equivalent
2. Powders, Pills, and Solids		All to 30 g.	Registered mail or equivalent

102

FIGURE 6.37 (continued).

Identification	Wrapping and Packing	Remarks
On back of cast before it hardens, write location and date taken, and investigator's name or initials.	Wrap in paper and cover with suitable packing material to prevent breakage.	Label "Fragile." Plaster of Paris is no longer recommended, see page 30 for more information.
See Anonymous Letters on pages 98/99.	See Anonymous Letters on pages 98/99.	Advise what parts are questioned or known. Furnish physical description of subject.
Place name or initials, date, name of make and model, etc., on sample impressions.	See Anonymous Letters on pages 98/99.	Do not disturb inking mechanisms on printing devices.
Mark directly on garment or use string tag indicating type of evidence, date obtained, investigator's name or initials.	Wrap each article individually. Place in strong container with identification written on outside of package.	Do not cut out stains, leave clothing whole. If wet, hang in room to dry before packing.
See Anonymous Letters on pages 98/99.	See Anonymous Letters on pages 98/99.	Furnish to Racketeering Records Analysis Unit.
Outside container: indicate if fragile, date obtained, investigator's name or initials.	Pack in rigid container between layers of cotton.	If moisture is added use atomizer, otherwise, not recommended.
Affix label to bottle in which found, including date it was found and investigator's name or initials.	Make sure container does not leak. Seal with tape to prevent any loss.	Mark "Fragile." If possible, use heat-seal plastic bags.
Outside of pillbox: affix label with date found and investigator's name or initials.	Seal with tape to prevent any loss.	If powders, pills, or solids are found in paper bags, place them in plastic bags to prevent any loss.

103

FIGURE 6.37 (continued).

Collection, Shipment, Identification and Packaging Charts			
	Amount Desired		
Specimen	Standard	Evidence	Send By
Drug Records/ Wire Taps	All original documents, tapes, and transcripts.		Registered mail or equivalent
Money Laundering Records	See Drug Records on page 33.		
Racketeering Records/Wire Taps	All original documents, tapes, and transcripts.		Registered mail or equivalent
1. Prostitution Records	See Racketeering Records on page 33.		
2. Loan sharking Records	See Racketeering Records on page 33.		
3. Video Gaming Devices	See Racketeering Records on page 33.		Call Racketeering Records Analysis Unit (RRAU) at (202) 324-2500 for instructions.

EXPLOSIVES: Detonators, Blasting Caps, Detonating Cord, Black Powder, Smokeless Power, (202) 324-2696, for shipping instructions. (For an emergency after regular hours,

Fibers	Entire garment or other cloth item.	All	Registered mail or equivalent
Firearms (unloaded weapons)		All	Registered mail or equivalent

.04

FIGURE 6.37 (continued).

Identification	Wrapping and Packing	Remarks
Initial and date each document. If too voluminous, initial and date the box containing the documents.	Documents: follow the instructions for Anonymous Letters. Wire tap tapes: label each tape. Mark packages: "MAGNETIC TAPES, DO NOT X-RAY."	Indicate kind of examination(s) requested: Latents, Handwriting, Chemistry-Toxicology, All of the above.
Same as drug records on page 33.	Same as drug records.	
Same as drug records on page 33.	Same as drug records.	
Same as drug records on page 33.	Same as drug records.	
Same as drug records on page 33. Record serial numbers on each machine. Include date and investigator's name or initials.	Call Racketeering Records Analysis Unit (RRAU) at (202) 324-2500 for instructions.	Field examinations may be more feasible, particularly on multiple machines.

High Explosives and Explosive Accessories, call the Explosives Unit, FBI Laboratory, call (202) 324-3000.)

Outside container or on the object fibers are adhering, include date and investigator's name or initials.	Use folder paper or pillbox. Seal edges and openings with tape.	Do not place loose in an envelope.
Identify gun with a string tag bearing complete description. Mark inconspicuously and have investigative notes reflecting how and where gun is marked.	Wrap in paper and identify contents of packages. Place in cardboard box or wooden box.	Unload all weapons before shipping. Keep from rusting. See Ammunition on pages 98/99, if applicable.

105

FIGURE 6.37 (continued).

Specimen	Amount Desired: Standard	Amount Desired: Evidence	Send By
Flash Paper	One sheet.	All to 5 sheets.	Call Racketeering Records Analysis Unit (RRAU) at (202) 324-2500 for instructions.
Gasoline	10 ml.	All to 10 ml.	Call Chemistry-Toxicology Unit at (202) 324-4318 for instructions.
Gems		All	Insured registered mail or equivalent
General Unknown:			
1. Solids (non-hazardous)	10 gms.	All to 10 g.	Registered mail or equivalent
2. Liquids (non-hazardous)	10 ml.	All to 10 ml.	Registered mail or equivalent
Glass Fractures		All	Registered mail or equivalent
Glass Particles	All of bottle or headlight. Small piece of each broken pane.	All	Registered mail or equivalent

106

FIGURE 6.37 (continued).

Identification	Wrapping and Packing	Remarks
Outside container: label indicating date and investigator's name or initials.	Place in individual polyethylene envelopes, double-wrap in manila envelopes, and seal with paper tape the inner wrapper.	Fireproof, place in vented location away from any other combustible materials and, if feasible, place in watertight container immersed in water. Mark inner wrapper "Flash Paper," "Flammable."
Outside container: label indicating type of material, date, and investigator's name or initials.	Use an all-metal container packed in wooden box.	An all-metal container should be used for its fireproof qualities.
Outside container: label indicating date and investigator's name or initials.	Use jeweler's box or place in cotton in pillbox.	
Outside container: label indicating date and investigator's name or initials.	Same as Drugs, see pages 102/103.	Call Chemistry-Toxicology Unit at (202) 324-4318 for instructions.
Same as Liquid Drugs, see pages 102/103.	Same as Liquid Drugs. see pages 102/103.	Same as above.
Separate questioned from known. Mark which is the interior or exterior of glass removed from frame.	Wrap each piece separately in cotton. Pack in sturdy container to prevent shifting and breakage. Identify contents.	Avoid chipping. Mark "Fragile."
Outside container: Label indicating date and investigator's name or initials.	Place in film cannister or plastic vial. Seal and protect against breakage.	Do not use envelopes, paper, or plastic bags.

107

FIGURE 6.37 (continued).

Specimen	Amount Desired: Standard	Amount Desired: Evidence	Send By
Gunshot Residues			
1. Cotton applicator swabs with plastic shafts. (Do **not use wood shafts**).		All	Registered mail or equivalent
2. On cloth Only to determine weapon to target distance.		All	Registered mail or equivalent
Hair	Twenty-five full-length hairs from different parts of head and/or pubic region.	All	Registered mail or equivalent
Handwriting and Hand Printing Known Standards			Registered mail or equivalent
Insulation			
1. Glass Wool	1" mass from each suspect area.	All	Registered mail or equivalent
2. Safe	Sample all damaged areas.	All	Registered mail or equivalent
Latent Fingerprints (see Latent Fingerprint Section page 35).			
Matches	One to two books of paper. One full box of wood.	All	Federal Express, UPS, or equivalent
Medicines	**See Drugs on pages 102/103.**		
Metal	1 lb.	All to 1 lb.	Registered mail or equivalent

Collection, Shipment, Identification and Packaging Charts

108

FIGURE 6.37 (continued).

Identification	Wrapping and Packing	Remarks
Outside container: Date and name or initial. Label as to name of person and which hand (left/right).	Place swabs in plastic containers.	Do not use glass containers.
Outside container: Indicate date, obtained from whom, description, name or initials.	Dry and package individually in **unused** brown wrapping paper or brown grocery bag.	Do not mix items. Use more than one bag, or wrap different items separately.
Outside container: Type of material, date, and investigator's name or initials.	Folded paper or pillbox. Seal edges and openings with tape.	Do not place loose in envelope.
Indicate from whom obtained, voluntary statement included in appropriate place, date obtained, and investigator's name or initials.	Same as Anonymous Letters, see pages 98/99.	Same as Anonymous Letters, see pages 98/99.
Outside container: type of material, date, name or initials.	Use pillbox or plastic vial. Seal to prevent any loss.	Avoid use of glass containers and envelopes.
Same as above.	Same as above.	Same as above.
Outside container: label indicating type of material, date, and investigator's name or initials.	Pack in metal container and in larger package to prevent shifting. Pack matches in box or metal container to prevent friction between matches.	Keep and label: "Keep away from fire."
Outside container: label indicating type of material, date, and investigator's name or initials.	Use paper boxes or containers. Seal and use strong paper or wooden box.	Melt number, heat treatment, and other specifications of foundry if available. Keep from rusting.

109

FIGURE 6.37 (continued).

Specimen	Amount Desired: Standard	Amount Desired: Evidence	Send By
Oil	10 ml. together with specifications.	All to 10 ml.	Federal Express, UPS, or equivalent
Obliterated, Eradicated, or Indented Writing		All	Registered mail or equivalent
Organs of the Body		200 g. of each organ.	Call Chemistry-Toxicology Unit at (202) 324-4318 for instructions.
Paint: 1. Liquid	Original unopened container up to 1/4 pint, if possible.	All to 1/4 pint.	Registered mail or equivalent
2. Solid (paint chips or scrapings)	At least 1/2 sq. in. of solid, with all layers represented.	All. If on small object, send object.	Registered mail or equivalent
Plaster Casts - Tire Treads and Shoe Prints (see pages 102/103).			
Plastic Replica Casts of Stamped Impressions (see page 63).			
Powder Patterns (see pages 102/103). (For Gunshot Residues see pages 108/109.)			
Rope, Twine, and Cordage	One yard or amount available.	All	Registered mail or equivalent

110

FIGURE 6.37 (continued).

Identification	Wrapping and Packing	Remarks
Same as above.	Use metal container with tight screw top. Seal to prevent leakage.	DO NOT USE DIRT OR SAND FOR PACKING MATERIAL. Keep away from fire.
Same as Anonymous Letters, see pages 98/99.	Same as Anonymous Letters, see pages 98/99.	Advise whether bleaching or staining methods may be used. Avoid folding.
Outside container: Victim's name, date of death, date of autopsy, name of doctor, investigator's name or initials.	Plastic or glass containers. Metal lids must have liners.	Call Chemistry-Toxicology Unit at (202) 324-4318 for instructions.
Outside container: Type of material, origin if known, date, investigator's name or initials.	Use friction-top paint can or large-mouth, screw-top jar. If glass, pack to prevent breakage. Use heavy corrugated paper or wooden box.	Protect spray can nozzles to keep them from going off. Avoid contact w/adhesive materials. Wrap to protect paint smears. Do not use envelopes, paper/plastic bags, or glass vials.
Same as above.	If small amount, use round pillbox or small glass vial with screw top. Seal to prevent leakage. Do not use envelopes. Do not pack in cotton.	Avoid contact with adhesive materials. Wrap so as to protect smear. If small amount: seal round pillbox, film canister, or plastic vial to protect against leakage/breakage.
On tag or container: Type of material, date, investigator's name or initials.	Wrap securely.	

111

FIGURE 6.37 (continued).

Collection, Shipment, Identification and Packaging Charts			
	Amount Desired		
Specimen	Standard	Evidence	Send By
Safe Insulation, readily transferred to tools and clothing, is found between walls of fire-resistant safes, in vaults, and in safe cabinets (pages 108/109).			
Saliva Samples	1.5" diameter stain in center of filter paper.	All	Registered mail or equivalent
Shoe Print Lifts (impressions on hard surfaces)	Photograph before making of dust impression.	All	Registered mail or equivalent
Soils and Minerals	Samples from areas near pertinent spot.	All	Registered mail
Tape (Adhesive Tape)	Recovered roll.	All	Registered mail or equivalent
Tools/Toolmarks	Send in the tool. If impractical, make several impressions on similar materials as evidence using entire marking area of tool.	All	Registered mail or equivalent

112

FIGURE 6.37 (continued).

Identification	Wrapping and Packing	Remarks
Outside envelope and on filter paper: Type of sample, name of donor, date of collection, and collector's initials or name.	Seal in envelope.	Stain should be circled in pencil for identification. Filter paper available from hospitals and drugstores. Allow to dry.
On lifting tape or paper attached to tape: date, investigator's name or initials.	Prints in dust are easily damaged. Fasten print or lift to bottom of box so that nothing will rub against it.	Always secure crime scene area until shoe prints or tire treads are located and preserved.
Outside container: type of material, date, investigator's name or initials.	Use pillbox or plastic vial.	Avoid glass containers and envelope.
Same as above.	Place on waxed paper, cellophane, or plastic.	Do not cut, wad, distort, or separate tapes that are stuck together.
On object or on tag attached to an opposite end from where toolmarks appear: date recovered and investigator's name or initials.	After marks have been protected with soft paper, wrap in strong wrapping paper, place in strong box, and pack to prevent shifting.	If necessary to remove item from its source by cutting, indicate where item was cut.

113

FIGURE 6.37 (continued).

Collection, Shipment, Identification and Packaging Charts			
	Amount Desired		
Specimen	Standard	Evidence	Send By
Typewriting, known standards	For instructions on known standards: see Documents page 27.		Registered mail or equivalent
Urine	Preferably all urine voided over a period of 24 hours.	All	Registered mail or equivalent
Vaginal Samples			
1. Slides (microscope)	Minimum of two slides.	Minimum of two swabs.	Registered mail or equivalent
2. Swabs	Two unstained swabs from same package as stained.		Registered mail or equivalent
Water	100 ml.	100 ml.	Registered mail or equivalent
Wire	3 ft. (Do not kink).	All (Do not kink).	Registered mail or equivalent
Wood	One foot or amount available.	All	Registered mail or equivalent

114

FIGURE 6.37 (continued).

Identification	Wrapping and Packing	Remarks
On specimens: serial number, brand, model, etc., date recovered, and investigator's name or initials.	Same as Anonymous Letters on pages 98/99.	Examine ribbon for evidence of questioned message.
Outside container: name of liquid, date taken, investigator's name or initials.	Use plastic specimen container. Seal tight with lid.	Make sure that package does not leak.
Outside envelope and on filter paper: type of sample, name of donor, date of collection, and collector's name or initials.	Use commercial slide box.	Slide box available at hospitals. Doctor should not fix slides. No cover slips. Air-dry.
Same as above.	Seal in envelope.	Allow swabs to dry before packaging.
Same as Urine.	Same as Urine.	Same as Urine.
On label or tab: describe type of material, date, investigator's name or initials.	Wrap securely.	Do not kink wire. (See also tool/toolmarks on pages 112/113.)
Same as above.	Wrap securely.	

115

FIGURE 6.37 (continued).

EVIDENCE

Case No. ____

- [ ] TO BE TESTED FOR DNA
- [ ] TO BE TESTED FOR FINGERPRINTS
- [ ] HANDLE WITH CARE
- [ ] UNPROCESSED EVIDENCE
- [ ] DO NOT HANDLE
- [ ] OTHER ____

Place evidence found ____

____ date & time ____

Victim ____

Complainant ____

Department — Signature Rank

SAMPLE

CHAIN OF POSSESSION

	DATE/TIME	SIGNATURE
FROM		
TO		
FROM		
TO		
FROM		
TO		
FROM		
TO		

SAMPLE

FIGURE 6.38 Evidence tag. Form E-TAG. Reproduced with permission. Copyright 2009 G. A. Thompson Co.

ALERT SECURITY BAG™

EVIDENCE

Station/Section/Unit/Dept ____________________
Case Number __________ Item# __________
Type of Offense ____________________
Description of Evidence ____________________
Suspect ____________________
Victim ____________________
Date and Time of Recovery ____________________
Location of Recovery ____________________
Recovered By ____________________

CHAIN OF CUSTODY

Received From __________ By __________
Date __________ Time __________ AM / PM
Received From __________ By __________
Date __________ Time __________ AM / PM
Received From __________ By __________
Date __________ Time __________ AM / PM
Received From __________ By __________
Date __________ Time __________ AM / PM

Warning: THIS IS A TAMPER EVIDENT SECURITY PACKAGE. ONCE SEALED, ANY ATTEMPT TO OPEN WILL RESULT IN OBVIOUS SIGNS OF TAMPERING.

MANUFACTURED IN USA BY PACKAGING HORIZONS CORPORATION
www.SecurityBag.com
1-888-467-1916

FIGURE 6.39 Chain of custody form used on evidence bags.

Numerous commercial companies provide compact kits for the investigation of blood, collection of evidence in rape cases, ballistics analysis, gunshot residue tests, and other matter. Whatever the investigator chooses, if he or she is unsure of his or her skill or expertise in handling complicated evidence packages, he or she should defer to the expert. The American Society for Industrial Security affirms this position.

> Collection and preservation of evidence are only a part of any professional investigation, but they frequently prove to be the most important part in solving a crime and prosecuting a suspect. An otherwise efficient investigation can be ruined by careless evidence handling or inadequate knowledge of this vital aspect of the work.[50]

From a forensic perspective, the investigator should acquire a rudimentary understanding of fingerprints; trace materials; biological fluids; rocks, soil, and other geological materials; fibers; hair; rope; string; thread; firearms; tools and tool mark evidence; questioned documents; and explosive materials. As a final admonition, professionalism is an essential part of the investigative process. Without adherence to legal and ethical principles; without the inferential and deductive thinking conducive to productive investigation; and without common sense, persistence, and perseverance, the investigative method will be flawed.

NOTES

1. Charles P. Nemeth, *The Paralegal Resource Manual*, 3rd edition (McGraw-Hill, New York, 2008), 338.
2. W. Bennett and K. Hess, *Criminal Investigation* (West Publishing, 1981), 42–43.
3. U.S. Department of Justice, National Institute of Justice, *Crime Scene Search and Physical Evidence Handbook* (U.S. Government Printing Office, 1973).
4. *Id.* at 15.
5. *Id.*
6. U.S. Department of Justice, *Crime Scene Investigation: A Guide for Law Enforcement* (2000), 11.
7. Pennsylvania State Police, *Crime Laboratory Operations Manual* (1985), 2.1.
8. For a fascinating look at the new world of electronic crime scenes, such as computer hard drives, and the need for first responders to exercise the same caution on approach to a crime scene, see National Institute of Justice, *Electronic Crime Scene Investigation: A Guide for First Responders* 2nd edition (2008).
9. A. Joseph and H. Allison, *Handbook of Crime Scene Investigation* (Allyn & Bacon, 1989), 29–31; see also A. Moenssens and F. Inbau, *Scientific Evidence in Criminal Cases* (Foundation, 1987).
10. See also National Institute of Justice, *Crime Scene Investigation: A Reference for Law Enforcement Training* (2004).
11. The Forensic Sciences Foundation, Inc., *Death Investigation and Examination: Medicolegal Guidelines and Checklists* (1986), 9.
12. *Id.* at 11.
13. G. Knowles, *Bomb Security Guide* (Butterworth-Heinemann, 1976), 69.
14. *Id.* at 115–116.
15. Al Lohner, "Crime Scene Diagramming Software Steadily Gains Converts," NCJ 194850, *Law Enforcement Technology* (April 2002), 58, 60–62, 63.
16. U.S. Department of Justice, *supra* note 3, at 36.
17. Headquarters, Department of the Army, Law Enforcement Investigations 125 (2005), https://rdl.train.army.mil/soldierPortal/atia/adlsc/view/public/12038-1/FM/3-19.13/FM3_19X13.PDF, visited August 26, 2009.
18. Tacoma Police Department, *Forensic Services Policy and Procedure Manual* (2004), 4.
19. U.S. Department of the Army, *supra* note 17, at 123.
20. *Id.* at 121.
21. *Id.* at 122.
22. Tim Dees, "Crime Scene Drawing Programs," *Law and Order.* (August 2001), 12.
23. The Forensic Sciences Foundation, *supra* note 11, at 13.
24. C. Scott, 1 Photographic Evidence § 13 (1980), 19.
25. *Id.* at 344–345.

26. David A. Bright and Jane Goodman-Delahunty, "Gruesome Evidence and Emotion: Anger, Blame, and Jury Decision-Making," *L. Human Behav.* 30 (2006), 183.
27. Pennsylvania State Police, *supra* note 7, at 2.2.
28. U.S. Department of Justice, *supra* note 3, at 44–45.
29. The Forensic Sciences Foundation, *supra* note 11, at 77.
30. U.S. Department of Justice, *supra* note 3, at 43.
31. *Id.* at 44.
32. "Standards and Guidelines Best Practices for Maintaining the Integrity of Digital Images and Digital Video," *For. Sci. Comm.* (April 2008), Figure 2.
33. American Society for Industrial Security, *Basic Guidelines for Security Investigations* (1981), 79.
34. The Forensic Sciences Foundation, *supra* note 11, at 55.
35. The International Association of Chiefs of Police (IACP), *Combating Workplace Violence*, (2002), 1–2.
36. Report of Person, Form No. 114, G. A. Thompson Co., P.O. Box 64681, Dallas, TX 75206.
37. M. Houts, *Lawyer's Guide to Medical Proof* (Matthew Bender, New York, 1984).
38. Electronic Privacy Information Center, Medical Record Privacy, http://www.epic.org/privacy/medical, visited August 26, 2009.
39. H.R. 3482, 104th Cong. 2nd Sess. 1996.
40. H.R. 3482 Sec. 301.
41. The compelling nature of DNA evidence has surely heightened chain of custody concerns for both the public and private sector. See William P. Kiley, "The Effects of DNA Advances on Police Property Rooms," *FBI Law Enforcement Bulletin* (March 2009), 20.
42. Harry A. Gair, "Sketching and Preparing Expert Witnesses, *Am. Jur. Trials*. (2, 1987), 585, 587.
43. Pennsylvania State Police, *supra* note 7, at 2.5.
44. *Id.* at 2.5.
45. FBI *Handbook for Forensic Services* (U.S. Government Printing Office, 2007).
46. U.S. Department of Justice, *Handbook of Forensic Science* (1994), 97–123.
47. FBI, *supra* note 45.
48. G. A. Thompson, *supra* note 36.
49. Packaging Horizons, www.securitybag.com, One Danforth Drive, Easton, PA 18045.
50. American Society for Industrial Security, *supra* note 33, at 28.

7 Surveillance Techniques

I. PURPOSES AND FUNCTIONS

To surveil is to watch another, whether by personal observation or technological means. Surveillance is an integral component for any security practice, but its object, that is the person surveilled, and the activities under scrutiny, are unknowing subjects. To have any effectiveness, surveillance needs to take place without notice or public awareness. The use of surveillance should be a blend of the aggressive and the cautious. Aggressive in the sense that it is one of the more remarkable tools in the security professional's toolbox, while simultaneously recognizing the privacy implications of its usage.

Surveillance complements traditional methods of investigative tracking. The techniques complement direct observation. Surveillance or covert observation is not only risky but also difficult. Its purposes are multifaceted:

- To protect undercover officers or to corroborate their testimony.
- To obtain evidence of a crime.
- To obtain evidence of a civil wrong.
- To locate persons.
- To check on the reliability of informants, witnesses, and other parties.
- To locate hidden property or contraband.
- To obtain probable cause for search warrant processes.
- To prevent the commission of an act or to apprehend a suspect in the commission of an act.
- To obtain information for later use in interrogation.
- To develop leads and information received from other sources.
- To know at all times the whereabouts of an individual.
- To obtain admissible legal evidence for use in court.

The American Society for Industrial Security (ASIS) defines surveillance practice as:

> Broadly stated, a surveillance may serve to detect or prevent questionable or illicit acts, to obtain evidence of such acts, to help in identifying persons, or to collect general intelligence information. Often a surveillance may be conducted only in the hope of developing leads in a case if other efforts have been unproductive.[1]

The uses of surveillance for private security specialist are myriad.[2] Many private security firms stress the fraud discovery capability of surveillance, whether corporate or governmental.

Surveillance could also be classified according to its function. For example, surveillance could be strictly for the purposes of gathering intelligence about a specific person, crime, or activity. Second, surveillance may be a preparatory step, setting the stage for an eventual drug sweep or apprehension of retail thieves. Similarly, surveillance may serve as a backup for an undercover investigator's activities. This type of surveillance serves two primary purposes: first, the observation corroborates the undercover agent's activity and testimony; and second, if trouble erupts, the surveillance team assists the undercover operative. Finally, surveillance is an effective tool in postpurchase activity, especially in drug cases, receipt of stolen property or other fencing operations, internal corporate fraud, and other business and industrial theft. Post-purchase surveillance has many applications in criminal settings including:

- Determine where the money or goods go after the sale or transaction.
- Identify subsequent buyers or purchasers of stolen goods, drugs, or other materials.
- Keep the suspect under observation in case the undercover officer was duped in a previous transaction.

Web Exercise: Surveillance practice is not without its critics. Indeed many argue constitutional dimensions. Others claim more effective tools exist. Check out a Canadian study at: http://www.library.ca.gov/CRB/97/05/crb97-005.html

II. TACTICS AND STRATEGY IN SURVEILLANCE

Planning and preparation are key elements in surveillance practice. This portion of the chapter gauges the various procedural steps essential to intelligent surveillance policy and practice.

A. What Are the Steps of Surveillance?

Successful surveillance requires—as do all aspects of criminal and civil investigation—four basic steps:

1. Planning
2. Organizing
3. Directing
4. Controlling[3]

Preparation is key to efficient surveillance practice. Planning and organization are fundamental to best practices in surveillance.[4] Preliminary assessment of the case or question under investigation will lead to intelligent decision making regarding the use of surveillance. Consider these issues:

- Is there any alternative to surveillance?
- Do you know what information is needed from the surveillance?
- Have you decided what type of surveillance is needed?
- Do you know enough about the area of surveillance to determine equipment and manpower needs?
- Do you have the required equipment and manpower?
- Are proper forms available to record necessary information during the surveillance?
- Are all signals pre-established?[5]

Be attuned to the legal and ethical dynamics of surveillance. Perennially tied to the constitutional protection of privacy and heavily regulated by legislation, the surveillance must not commence without legal inquiry. John Dale Hartman prompts the practitioner to gauge the ethics and legality of surveillance before embarking.

- Were the agents in a place in which they had a right to be?
- Were the documentations limited to the view available to any other member of the general public?
- Did the agents do anything to enhance the secured view that exceeds the view available to the general public?

- Was the view secured from a position where the employee could reasonably expect someone in the general public or another coworker to be at any given time?
- Was the area in which the documentations were made one in which the employee could reasonably expect privacy from an outside view?
- Was the area one in which the agent was statutorily prohibited from making clandestine observations?
- Was the area one over which the employee maintains exclusive control or was access available to others?
- If the surveillance involved a "private area," was the employee warned that activities were subject to observation and documentation?
- Were the efforts used by the agent limited to those objectively considered reasonable and unobtrusive or did the agent conduct an operation that can only be described as offensive, unreasonable, and blatant?
- Were the documentations limited to those related to the issue at hand?
- Could the documented activities be considered embarrassing to the subject?
- Was the reason for the surveillance related to legitimate business purposes and conducted for a legitimate cause or was an unlawful motive involved?
- Was the operation one that could violate an existing contract or intrude on an employee's right to collective bargaining?[6]

Always keep in mind the "Who-What-When-Where-How-Why" analysis. Because surveillance is a costly undertaking, the client, as well as the firm, must justify this form of expenditure. Does the client's problem lend itself to surveillance tactics? Is there no alternative mechanism for discerning the same information? Will the surveillance activities place the client or agents of the firm in jeopardy?

B. What Is the Exact Objective of Surveillance?

Effective surveillance sets goals and parameters. Solid surveillance practice keeps the endgame in view by laying out specific objectives for the action. While these objectives may change due to a change of circumstance or facts discovered, surveillance must not be a freewheeling discovery exercise. It must have an initial purpose in mind with full awareness that the purpose may be subject to change. At a minimum, the objective should correlate to the purpose of the surveillance. The ends of the surveillance will be as varied as the subject matter of that surveillance. More typical examples might be:

- Is the subject acting in accordance with a complete or partial disability claim?
- Is the subject faking or feigning injuries alleged in a workers' compensation or personal injury case?
- Is the subject operating a stolen property ring?
- Is the subject suspected of raiding cash registers?
- Is the subject suspected of shoplifting?
- Is the subject, in a retail establishment, suspected of passing goods and merchandise to friends through nonsecure exit points?
- Is the subject taking alcohol or narcotic substances into the workplace?
- Is the subject sexually harassing workers at his or her place of employment?

C. Where Is the Location of Surveillance?

Professional surveillance requires a full understanding of not only the subject but also his or her surrounding environment. In a phrase, know your territory. Become familiar with the geographic, cultural, and environmental qualities in which the target lives and works.[7] More specifically, be aware of entry and exit points at enclosed locations. Trace and track streets and byways. Precisely pinpoint the location of public law enforcement relative to the place of surveillance. Other relevant questions involving locale are:

- What is the character and quality of the neighborhood in which you are conducting surveillance?
- Can you easily be disguised, or are outsiders quickly labeled and identified? Which type of surveillance will work best depends on freedom of movement.
- Is auto surveillance possible or is stationary or foot surveillance more likely?
- What areas of cover might you adopt, such as rooming houses, hotels, or apartments?
- What public transportation is readily available?
- Given the density of the area, is it preferable to have multiple investigators at the location?
- Do you have maps, charts, or diagrams of the area in question?
- Have you made sketches of possible ways to avoid observation or apprehension?

Be on the safe side before any surveillance in a specific location takes place. Visit and inspect the locality and familiarize yourself with the neighborhood's style of dress, language, and other cultural nuances.

D. When Will Surveillance Occur?

The decision to commence surveillance activities is both organizational and tactical. The surveillance decision should also be based on tactical considerations, such as the following:

- Is surveillance likely to be more effective at night or in the daytime?
- Which time of the day will result in less of an opportunity to be "burned" or found out?
- Will the time of day, such as rush hour, evening, or dusk, affect the amount of surveillance employed for the task?
- Are there difficulties with visibility, angle of observation, or clarity of direction at certain times of the day?
- Can auto surveillance be used more effectively at certain times rather than other types of surveillance?
- Will specialized equipment be needed to conduct surveillance?
- How does the location of surveillance affect the chosen time?

Also consider how long the surveillance is supposed to last. This can depend on a number of things, including:

- Budgetary considerations of the client.
- The complexity or simplicity of the case in question.
- The nature of the surveillance, whether it calls for more underground activities.
- The sophistication of the subject being surveilled, requiring greater sensitivity and patience in the surveillance process.

E. Who or What Will Be Surveilled?

The surveillance subject can be either a person or a nonhuman entity, such as a plant, business, industry, or other installation. No matter who or what is under surveillance, that person or entity is labeled the "subject." "It can be a person, place, property, vehicle, group of persons, organization, or object."[8] Within this broad categorization fall the following:

- Persons suspected of criminal activity.
- Persons suspected of fraud in a civil context.
- Persons in need of evaluation in personal injury or workers' compensation cases.
- Persons suspected of labor violations.
- Persons involved in public riot or other disorder activities.

On the other hand, the surveillance subject that is a place or a location could be any of these:

- The residence of a suspected felon.
- Fencing locations for stolen goods.
- Locations for terrorists in executive protection cases.
- Houses of prostitution.
- Houses of gambling.
- Drug dens.
- Illegal alien hideouts.
- Illegal medical operations.
- Auto body chop shops.

The target of surveillance will impact the comprehensiveness of that surveillance. In other words, the drug dealer selling on a neighborhood street has less of an expectation of privacy than a citizen praying at the local church. The level of intrusion will depend on many factors, although the extent of the intrusion will be guided by constitutional expectations of privacy. A highly intrusive, technologically entranced surveillance of a home is a trickier proposition than the criminal on the street. The home or domicile affords the highest expectation of privacy.

Factors considered by the courts in addressing the permissibility of a view into the home include

- the time at which the view is secured
- the duration of the surveillance
- the distance to the target under surveillance
- the positioning of the investigator
- the use of the area under surveillance
- the distance between the activity and the residence
- the efforts taken by the subjects to ensure their privacy
- whether the portal used to view the activity has curtains or blinds and whether they were drawn at the time
- whether the activities in question were visible to the general public
- whether the enhancement efforts were effected to confirm observations visible with unaided vision or whether the view would not be visible without an enhancement device
- the sophistication of the equipment used by the agents to secure the view
- whether the view can be considered to violate the reasonable expectation of privacy maintained by the subject
- whether the efforts made by the officers were to conceal themselves and not to enhance an otherwise unavailable view.[9]

III. SURVEILLANCE: PREPARATORY STEPS

As already noted, effective surveillance requires advanced planning and preparation. Many issues need to be considered before launching into surveillance. Although most competent investigators are capable of conducting reasonably good surveillance, the results and effectiveness will markedly grow when smaller details have been considered.

> **Web Exercise:** Being prepared and understanding the goal of a surveillance program go hand and hand. Visit EMC corporation for an inside look at the planning process in surveillance at: http://www.emc.com/collateral/hardware/solution-overview/h1115-3-sams-sb-ldv.pdf

A. Personal Behavior and Attire

The surveillance officer should have an ordinary appearance that blends into the territory. Any exceptional physical characteristics attract the subject's attention. The surveillance officer must be a natural player under all circumstances, acclimating into the environment subject to the surveillance. The agent must exhibit uncanny attentiveness and resourcefulness since unpredictability is a constant of the surveillance process. No matter how well it is planned and adopted, many events and conditions are unanticipated. The agent should have superior skills of observation and high memory retention. The agent needs absolute patience and mental endurance. Surveillance is not, at least in the majority of cases, a quick fix, as is depicted on television. Instead, the agent must be a painstaking, perseverant, and dogged observer of the subject.

In addition, investigators must always be mindful of their appearance and demeanor. A surveillant's clothing should not stand out from others in the environment, and it is highly recommended that the clothing selected be reversible. The agent must not be unnecessarily noticeable. The overall approach of the agent must be subdued, not attracting attention—not running, darting, or hiding, nor acting in a mysterious fashion.[10] In the same light, if auto surveillance is employed, the vehicle should be completely inconspicuous. Bright colors, loud exhaust systems, blatant antenna systems, and siren devices have no place in surveillance activities.

At times, agents will work undercover, requiring additional emphasis on intelligent planning. Before commencing undercover, the investigator must be trained in these principles:

- Undercover investigators should never become emotionally or sexually involved with any of the subjects of the investigation. More than one case on record has been compromised this way.
- The undercover operator should not consume alcohol. Even though it may serve the purpose to have the subject do so, the undercover operator should not.
- The undercover investigator should never, under any circumstances, steal anything—even to become part of the group and even though the item may be returned to the client. The agent can help the subjects of the investigation take merchandise from a security room, and bring it to the edge of the receiving dock, but that's about it. The agent must never aid in actual removal of the item from the premises, or even load the merchandise in a vehicle. This has, and it will continue to have, a boomerang effect. The thief may suggest that the agent had been behind the whole thing, and management may believe it.
- The operative should not take security identification or other investigative identification on assignment.
- The undercover operator should leave nothing in the car that can reveal the identity of the operative. Do not leave notes in the glove compartment; one never knows when the subject or other person involved in the investigation will have access to the agent's car.

B. Surveillance Equipment

The agent must consider his or her technological needs before embarking. Having the right equipment for the task at hand is critical to success. Equipment check is central to the planner. Review the checklist.

- Is there any need for radio or electronic monitoring equipment, cameras, or remote receivers?
- What types of specialized equipment could be of use to the surveillant?
- Are radio communications protected or subject to breaches in integrity?
- What type of photographic equipment is necessary?
- If electronic surveillance techniques are employed, what are the legal restrictions within your jurisdiction?

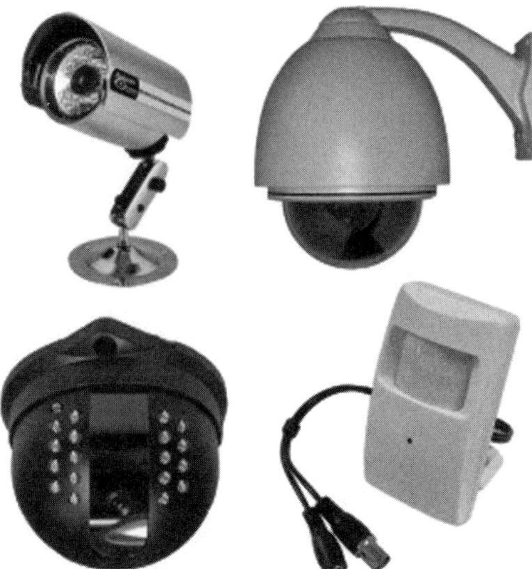

FIGURE 7.1 Enhanced surveillance equipment.

The complexity of the surveillance process has triggered a multimillion dollar industry that produces surveillance materials and equipment. This reliance on equipment is sometimes labeled "enhanced surveillance." See Figure 7.1.

For further research, Ross Engineering of Adamstown, Maryland, has recently begun publication of a journal titled *Surveillance*.[11] *Physical Security: Practices and Technology* by Charles Schnabolk provides a comprehensive examination of technology employed in security practice with excellent insight into the electronic aspect of surveillance.[12]

1. Closed-Circuit Television Equipment

A number of manufacturers produce high-resolution, high-sensitivity closed-circuit television (CCTV) systems for the purposes of ongoing surveillance. With CCTV systems, each camera is wired directly into individual monitors. In situations where the CCTV is connected into a conventional home unit, the CCTV camera has to "'feed' the picture image through a device called a modulator into the master antenna, where it is tuned along with the channels that transmit radio frequency signals."[13] Figure 7.2[14] depicts the CCTV system.

Although CCTV is touted as an indispensable tool in security technology, overreliance may be unwise. C. A. Roper points out the specific disadvantages:

1. The monitoring screen does not provide as faithful a reproduction of the scene as does direct vision. For this reason, small details are not discernible or are vague to the eye.
2. Dividing the guard's attention between several monitoring screens may not provide the continuity of coverage desired.
3. The resulting eye strain and the boredom of watching a monitor may cause a lack of attention on the part of the security guard.
4. The area viewed may contain so may obstructions that even several CCTV cameras could not give proper coverage; a roving guard or guard patrol would be a better choice in this case.
5. The camera is incapable of taking corrective actions in response to an event that is taking place. The time required to move a security guard or guards to the area may be too great.[15]

Many security companies have an impressive array of surveillance cameras, many of which are creatively disguised in such components as:

- Garbage cans
- Mailboxes

- Fence posts
- Car antennae
- Clocks
- Cigarette packs
- Exit signs
- Tie clips
- Cameras
- Pocketbooks

One effective strategy is to hide the camera's eye within an unassuming sprinkler system (see Figure 7.3).

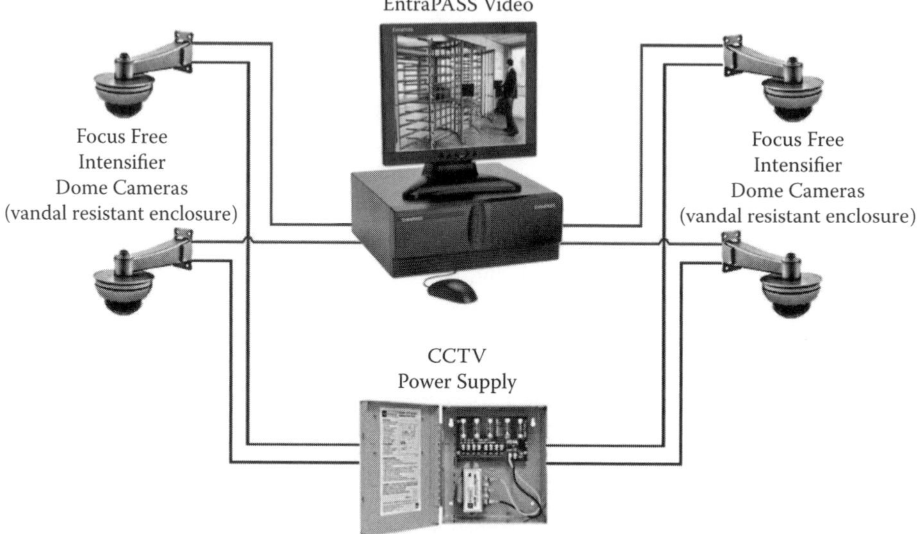

FIGURE 7.2 CCTV diagram.

FIGURE 7.3 Camera disguised as a sprinkler

2. Photographic/Video Equipment

Employing the photograph as an aid is wise; however, the agent will have the added pressure of operating photographic equipment correctly. "Good surveillance photographs require good police work plus good photographic techniques. Such techniques include the use of telephoto lenses, the use of infrared flashes or lamps, the processing of film for maximum film speed, and the use of motion picture and time lapse cameras."[16]

Photographic surveillance can either be active or passive in nature. In the active category, the investigator is making a conscious decision to be on the scene with the correct equipment. The investigator must be attuned to the difficulties of normal light photography, taking into consideration distances, light, exposure, and climatic factors, and whether or not telephoto shutter speeds, depth of field, and other accessories are needed to take acceptable pictures. Telephoto lenses are also a necessity. It is becoming even more common for the private security industry to employ video recording devices as they become more economical for firms to own and operate.

Passive surveillance is mechanically commenced by the suspect him- or herself. Video technology has obviously impacted the industry's surveillance practices in a positive way. See Figure 7.4. Many devices can sense the presence of an intruder and trigger the operation of a camera.

Photoelectric detectors: Relies on a beam of light falling upon a photosensitive detector. If the beam is broken, the camera operates.

Audio detectors: Relies on a microphone detector which triggers the camera when noises are made.

Vibration detectors: Triggers camera operation with any sensitive detection of movement.

Capacitance detectors: A capacitance field is established surrounding an area. A person who breaks the field triggers the camera.

Ultrasonic detectors: Sound wave patterns which generate camera operation.

FIGURE 7.4 Motion sensitive camera.

Surveillance Checklist

Client: ______________________ Investigator: ______________________

Subject: ______________________ Location: ______________________

To be checked by investigator: (1) When planning a surveillance; (2) Immediately prior to departing en route to surveillance; (3) When returning rental vehicle (to ensure all equipment has been removed); (4) When returning equipment to office (to ensure all equipment is accounted for).

___ 1. Dress appropriately (warmly, casually, dress clothes, etc.). Also, should you have alternative change of clothes with you?
___ 2. Binoculars
___ 3. Video camera—extra cartridges and/or video cards; fully charged batteries; outlet adapter
___ 4. Digital camera—extra cards; fully charged and extra batteries
___ 5. Wrist watch
___ 6. Pen and paper
___ 7. MP3 player
___ 8. Appropriate forms and signs (pretext interview book, traffic count forms, hand counter, magnetic signs for doors, traffic survey signs, etc.
___ 9. Food and drink
___10. Proper vehicle as indicated by area and cover with a full tank of gas
___11. Cellular phone fully charged with adapter
___12. Proper identification—company and personal ID; business cards, etc.
___13. Expense advances
___14. Reservations/lodging secured for out of town assignments
___15. Handcuffs (when appropriate)
___16. Handgun (when appropriate)
___17. Flashlight

Date(s) of Surveillance: ______________________

Commence: ______________________ Discontinue: ______________________

Remarks/Precautions: ______________________

____

____

FIGURE 7.5 Surveillance checklist.

The ASIS concurs in the importance of photography in surveillance methods:

> Photographic equipment of every sort should be considered. Concealed cameras or videotape equipment may be adroitly placed, not requiring the presence of an investigator except to check on its operation periodically. Time lapse cameras, which can shoot scenes over a long period of time, are often helpful to develop evidence; arrangements should be made for quick film development if information is needed for subsequent surveillance. Hand-held cameras can be disguised in various ways (by being placed inside a briefcase or by being made to resemble a book).[18]

With all these preparatory steps in mind, and before starting any surveillance process, complete the surveillance checklist as outlined at Figure 7.5.

Surveillance evidence needs to be attentive to claims regarding its integrity and chain of custody. See Figure 7.6.

Daily Photography Record

Investigator ______________________ Date of Report ______________________

Subject______________________ Claim #______________________

Alleged Impairment ______________________ Address______________________

Camera Information

Owner ______________________ Make ______________________

Serial Number______________________ Model ______________________

Shutter speed______________________ Exposure program ______________________

F stop______________________ Aperture value ______________________

ISO speed rating ______________________ Focal length ______________________

Pixel dimension X & Y ______________________ Resolution ______________________

Orientation X & Y______________________ Lens ______________________

Memory Card Information

Make ______________________ Capacity ______________________

Type

Photo Record				
File Name	**Time**	**Description of Activities**	**No. Feet Exposed**	**Subject Distance**

State exactly where photos were taken: Home ( ) Business ( ) Other Location ( )

Provide exact street address:______________________

From what vantage point were pictures taken; i.e., across the street, adjacent building, etc.

____

____

____

____

____

____

FIGURE 7.6 Daily record of photographs taken during surveillance.

IV. TYPES OF SURVEILLANCE

Surveillance techniques and methods fall into two major categories:

Stationary: The agent is either in a fixed location planted within or on a stake-out.
Moving: Moving either by foot or by vehicle in tight, close, loose, or rough proximity to the subject.

Moving surveillance can be either loose or close:

Loose Surveillance is when caution must be exercised—when the subject must not become aware or even suspicious [that] he is being followed.
Close Surveillance means simply to stay close to him because of contacts he may make, something he might pass to another person, or simply because of prevailing congested conditions.[19]

A. Stationary Surveillance

Although dramatized as the exciting police stake-out in the movies, stationary surveillance is usually a long and tedious process. The situation usually involves the security officer who hopes to observe something "go down" such as a theft, robbery, drug deal, sexual assault, or other activities that are not easily detected or observed. Stationary surveillance requires substantial patience while waiting and watching, sometimes without any result over extended periods of time. One of the continuing frustrations of the security professional is in meeting the challenge that surveillance boredom causes. Protracted periods of stationary surveillance can result in extreme occupational burnout.

In stationary surveillance, a stake-out position is selected to observe the target. Typical stake-outs are:

- Adjacent or parallel rooms, apartments, or other locations in the field of vision.
- Dummy vehicles
- Nondescript or inconspicuous vehicles.

Aside from waiting and watching and watching and waiting, the rewards eventually come. In surveillance patience is a virtue! Do not prematurely disengage. The temptation to so do is often referred to as the "burned" complex, that is, a belief and assumption that the lack of activity means the subject is on to the agent or aware of his or her surveillance. The agent then believes that his or her hard work is a complete waste of time and becomes discouraged. When the agent acts in haste, the case is often lost. Be patient, take your time, and realize that a person who has adequately prepared the surveillance plan rarely gets caught.

B. Moving Surveillance

1. Foot Surveillance

Foot surveillance is either individual or by team composition. Most experts believe that the team number should be no more than three. However, for economic and tactical reasons, a one-man surveillance operation is sometimes the only acceptable method. Some companies recognize that one-man surveillance may be the cheaper option, and it may produce disappointing results, though acceptable given the expenditure.

a. *Two-Man Technique*

Two-man foot surveillance teams increase the chances for a positive finding. Two agents give greater flexibility to a plan of operation; two agents also afford greater security against detection and reduce the risk of being spotted. If one comes under suspicion, he or she can duck out while the other takes over.

b. *Three-Man Technique—The ABC Method*

In some security circles, the three-man foot surveillance, referred to as the ABC method, is the most desirable strategy. By using three agents the risk of losing the subject or being detected and identified is minimized. Personal and strategic flexibility in dealing with unanticipated events is the ABC method's strongest asset. Two typical ABC scenarios are described below and illustrated in Figures 7.7 and 7.8.

1. Basic ABC Procedure—Normal Pedestrian Traffic (Figure 7.7)
   - Agent A is to the rear of the subject and with a reasonable distance between them. What is reasonable depends on the number of people on the street between Agent A and the subject. The fewer the people, the greater the distance should be. A common mistake of the new agent is to have too much distance between him- or herself and the subject.
   - Agent B follows Agent A. Agent B's responsibility is the keep Agent A in sight and to detect associates of the subject. The distance between Agents A and B is slightly more than the distance between Agent A and the subject.
   - Agent C is on the opposite side of the street and slightly to the rear of the subject. Agent C's responsibility is to keep both the subject and Agent A in sight.

2. ABC Procedure on Very Crowded Street (Figure 7.8)
   - All three agents are on the same side of the street as the subject.
   - Agent A should follow very close to the subject.
   - Agent B concentrates on keeping Agent A in view.
   - Agent C concentrates on keeping Agent B in view.

The ABC method works better than a one- or two-man surveillance because the subject is less likely to feel that he or she is being followed. Suspicions are aroused more easily with a one-man foot patrol. With the three-man method, if any of the agents is noticed, one of the three agents can easily drop out without causing the surveillance to end.

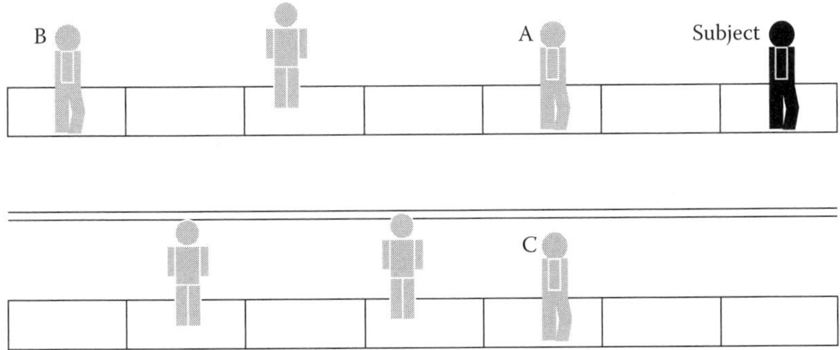

FIGURE 7.7 Basic ABC surveillance.

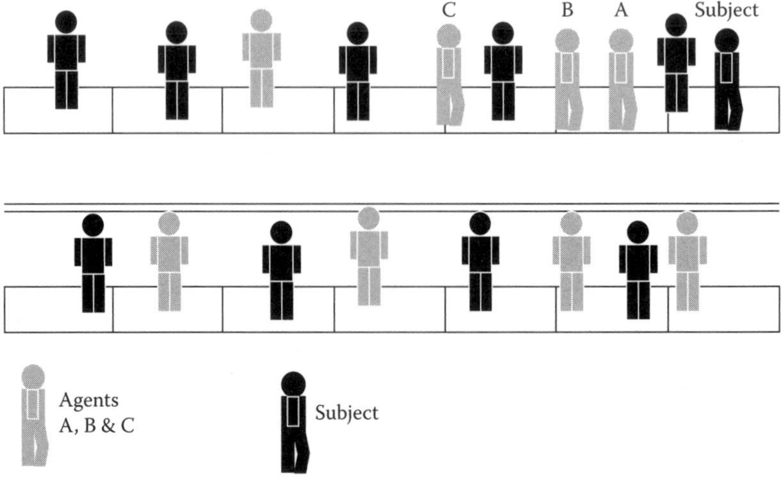

FIGURE 7.8 ABC procedure on a crowded street.

Certain conduct might indicate the subject's suspicion of being followed. According to Pinkerton's *Investigations Department Training Manual*,[20] the suspect may:

- Reverse his direction.
- Watch for your reflection.
- Drop a piece of paper to see who picks it up.
- Board a conveyance, then get off just before it leaves.
- Walk around a corner and stop.
- Use someone else to help him.
- Use multiexit buildings to escape you.

The suspect may also use a decoy, escape down an alley, take the last taxi, or even change his or her appearance, disguise him- or herself, or lose him- or herself in a crowd. In some circumstances, the subject may confront the investigator. If this occurs:

- Act in a natural manner.
- Act indignant and walk away from subject in the same direction the investigator/agent had been going before approached.
- Determine if subject is following you by looking at a plate-glass window and using it as a mirror.
- Be sure the subject is not the investigator/agent's supervisor conducting a field investigation.
- If the subject is tailing the investigator/agent, the agent can lose the subject in an office building, subway, crowd, bus, taxi, and so forth.
- The investigator/agent must drop the suspicious subject in a natural manner to create doubt in the subject's mind as to whether or not he or she was being followed.

2. Auto Surveillance

Auto surveillance is a regular and reliable method of general intelligence gathering. Though it may be used to surveil premises and individuals on occasion, the primary function is in the surveillance of other vehicles. Naturally, the appearance of the vehicle should be subdued. It is strongly recommended that two agents be in the vehicle since driving restricts full and uninterrupted observational capacity. "The driver must have exceptional car handling ability; the second must be constantly alert and ready to assist the driver in maintaining surveillance."[21]

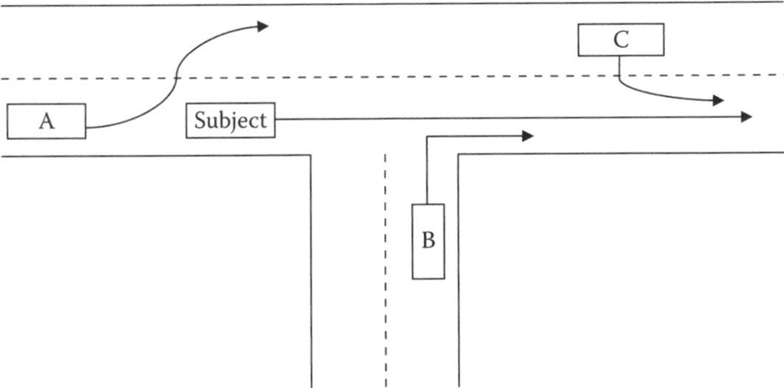

FIGURE 7.9 Basic auto surveillance.

Except in rare and exceptional circumstances, the auto agents should not violate traffic laws and should fully cooperate if police intervene or seek identification. Public law enforcement officers are skilled in detecting vehicles on a contrived and steady tail of another vehicle.

Distance from the surveilled target is also a recurring concern in planning moving auto surveillance. Distance will largely depend on traffic conditions, topography, and the ability of the agent and the subject to move. Once behind the subject, the agent must use every means possible to avoid any prolonged viewing of his or her vehicle by the subject in his or her rearview mirror. By using other surveillance groups and vehicles (these vehicles being described as *cover vehicles*), the image projected in the rearview mirror can be confused (Figure 7.9).

Auto surveillance technique and procedure is guided by the geographic or topographic area where surveillance is taking place. For example, compare and contrast the surveillance technique employed on an open highway versus city traffic. Predictably, dense city traffic can cause immense frustrations for the surveillant, such as when the subject vehicle makes abrupt traffic adjustments. The pattern of traffic lights, stop signs, and the number of cars between the surveillant's vehicle and the subject have much to do with keeping position, not getting burned or identified, and witnessing events and activities in the subject's vehicle. On the open highway, such as an interstate or other four-lane road, using multiple surveillance vehicles is a generally wise practice since the subject of surveillance has a wider plane of view, thereby enabling him or her to identify or become accustomed to one particular automobile. In highway situations, it is more advantageous to have multiple surveillance vehicles. In the multiple-vehicle surveillance scheme, the *lead vehicle*—the actual pursuit car—is referred to as the "eyeball." Sound policy dictates that the other vehicles, depending on conditions, switch and give up their various positions to minimize the potential for detection. The laws of traffic etiquette and habit such as passing, moving to other lanes, acceleration or deceleration of the vehicle, or temporary pullover make a switch of position or control relatively easy.

a. *Auto Surveillance Techniques*

Obviously, a surveillance method that is easily detected is of little value to the private security specialist. Persons engaged in illegal, illicit, or questionable conduct tend to act defensively and with a suspicious body language. In auto situations, the subject driver is generally on the lookout for persons who tail. The situations described below include tactical plans to minimize detection and carry out successful auto surveillance. However, these suggestions are general; events, conditions, circumstances, and territories may make these strategies inappropriate.

(1) Open Highway/Interstate Highway In individual situations, keep your distance, consider a change of hat, coat, or sunglasses, even changing license plates. A temporary pull-off onto the shoulder or at a rest stop may be appropriate (Figure 7.10).

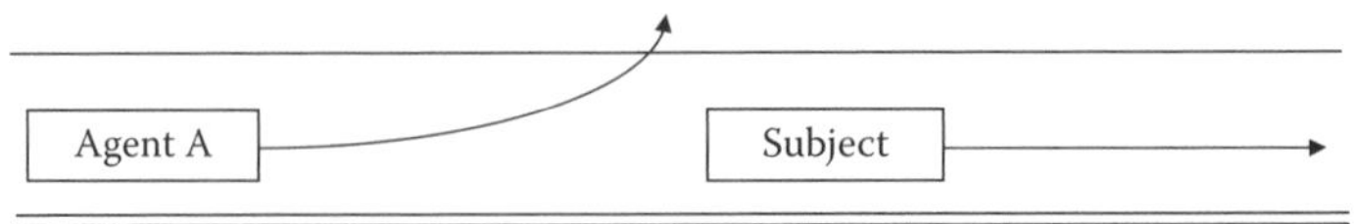

FIGURE 7.10 Highway pull-off method.

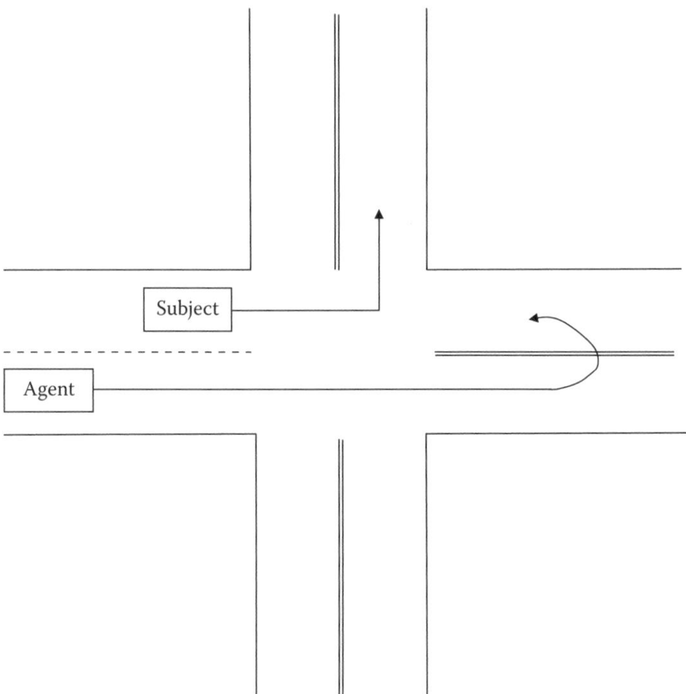

FIGURE 7.11 Surveillance left turn procedure #1.

(2) Left Turn (Subject Left Lane; Agent Right Lane) A switch of lanes may be obvious. Go through the intersection and make a U-turn. If a switch of lane is not likely to be detected, do so (Figure 7.11).

(3) Left Turn (Subject in Lane without Traffic Signal) If the agent mimics the subject, detection is probable. Go through the intersection and make the first feasible U-turn to get back into position behind the subject (Figure 7.12).

In the left-turn situations described above, the agent has to proceed through the intersection, which heightens the risk of losing the subject. For this reason, one-man auto surveillance is often unsuccessful. With the use of multiple surveillance vehicles, the lead car can pass through the intersection, and the second or third vehicle can follow the subject through the left turn.

(4) Left Turn (Subject Passes through Green; Agent Stuck at Red) In multiple-vehicle situations, the lead vehicle, after proceeding through the intersection and making contact with the other agents, must make an aggressive U-turn and attempt to reestablish surveillance (Figure 7.14).

(5) Illegal or Improper Turn by Subject When the subject makes illegal turns, mimicry by the lead vehicle results in absolute and automatic detection. The lead vehicle should continue straight and make a U-turn (Figure 7.12).

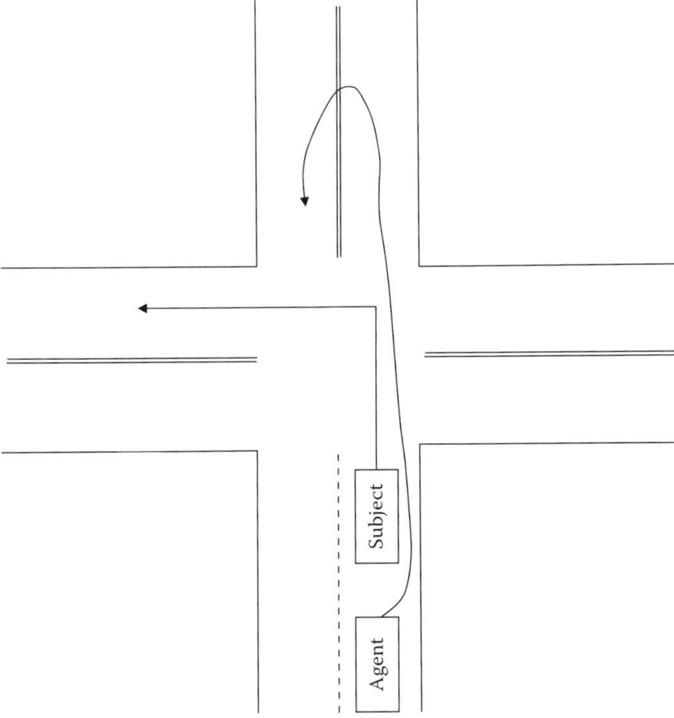

FIGURE 7.12 Left turn procedure #2.

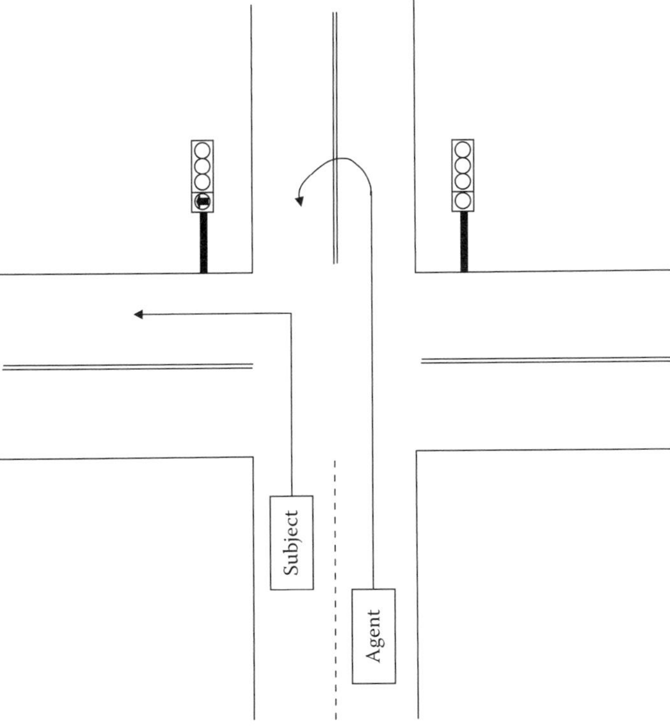

FIGURE 7.13 Left turn procedure #3.

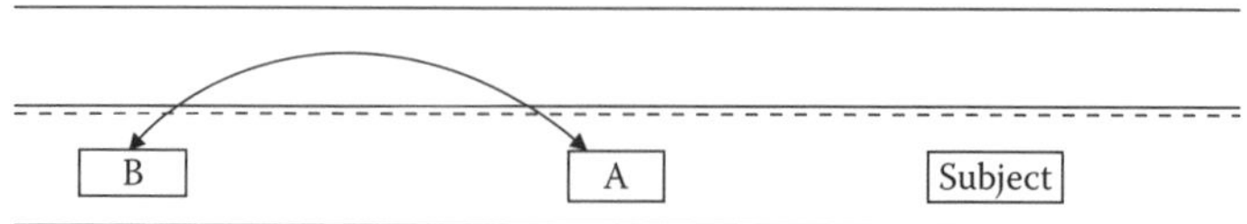

FIGURE 7.14 Vehicle position change.

(6) Multiple Surveillance (Changing Position of Vehicles) To avoid detection, alternate the positions of the lead and other surveillance vehicles. Do not change lead vehicle position until another agent is ready to, and capable of, assuming the lead position (Figure 7.14).

(7) Traffic Light (Subject Runs through Red) Subjects often run traffic lights. The agent should wait at the intersection and hope that the light will change quickly or that the subject vehicle will be caught at the next light (Figure 7.15).

(8) U-Turn by Subject In cases of multiple auto surveillance, the lead team can notify the other surveillance vehicles, then continue straight, turn around, and try to reestablish the tail (Figure 7.16).

(9) Stopping Beyond a Corner or on the Crest of a Hill by Subject To avoid detection, the lead vehicle must drive past the curb. In cases using multiple vehicle surveillance, the lead vehicle agent should relay the position and location of the subject to other surveillance agents (Figure 7.17).

(10) Right or Left Turn into an Alley by Subject Because an alley is not a normal intersection, do not turn into the alley. Lead vehicle should stop before the alley. Meanwhile, the secondary passenger in the lead vehicle can observe the subject and advise the other surveillance vehicle what the subject is doing (Figure 7.18).

(11) Leading Surveillance Leading surveillance requires several drivers and vehicles. This technique is a boxing-in strategy to keep the subject between a lead vehicle and other surveillance vehicles. Although it is not always an acceptable method, this technique works best in situations in which the subject's direction and eventual destination is known. By enclosing the subject vehicle in this manner, the surveillance vehicles following have more leeway in distance (Figure 7.19).

(12) Progressive Surveillance Progressive surveillance is not a continuous, ongoing, or predictable method of watching the subject's vehicle. When one is tracking or surveilling highly attuned, tail-conscious subjects, progressive surveillance is particularly effective. Progressive surveillance avoids the possibility of a subject identifying or witnessing routine practices by the surveillance vehicle. The method involves stationing surveillance vehicles at various points along a known or suspected route of travel, especially at intersections. The vehicles are hidden at these intersections or agents are stationed on foot. If the subject fails to reach a particular intersection, progressive surveillance makes it possible to determine where he or she turned off. An example of progressive surveillance is:

First Day: One investigator follows the subject to the bus stop and drops him or her.
Second Day: A different investigator is waiting for the subject at the bus stop and rides on the bus with him or her to his or her destination. The investigator remains on the bus when the subject alights.
Third Day: Another investigator is waiting when the subject gets off the bus and follows him or her either to his or her first stop or for a short distance and drops him or her, and so forth.

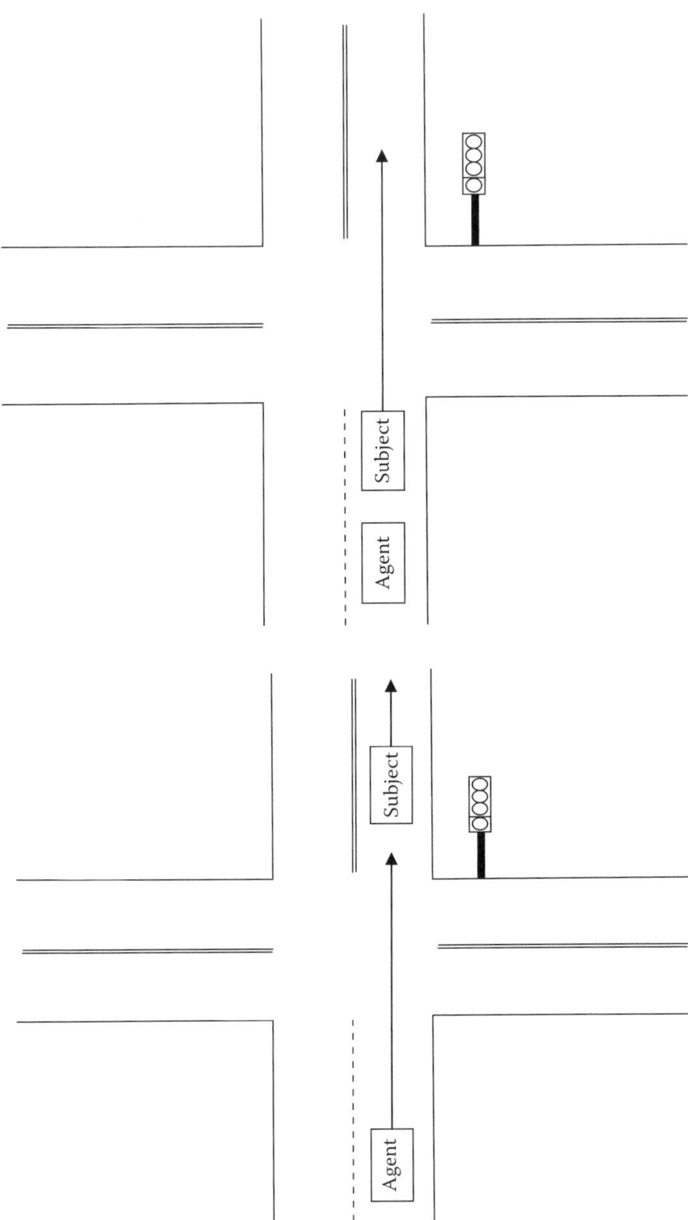

FIGURE 7.15 Procedure at a traffic light.

Progressive surveillance is costly, but in cases where detection is likely or the subject catches on to surveillance quickly, it is strongly recommended.

(13) Parallel Surveillance Figure 7.20 is a depiction of vehicles operating on parallel streets. The technique is remarkably useful in removing multiple surveillance vehicles from the subject's view on a street with little or no traffic and gives greater flexibility to agents when turns occur. Multiple surveillance vehicles must adapt and adjust their positions as turns are made or acceleration or deceleration takes place. Constant contact is mandatory.

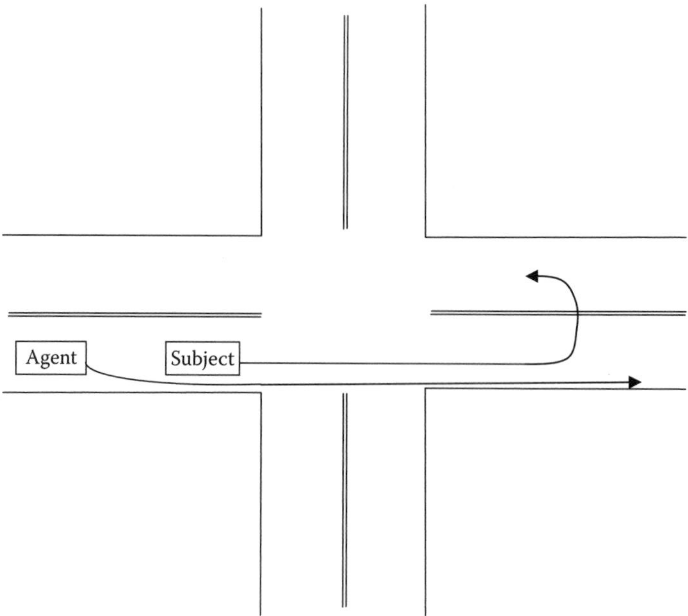

FIGURE 7.16 Subject U-turn procedure.

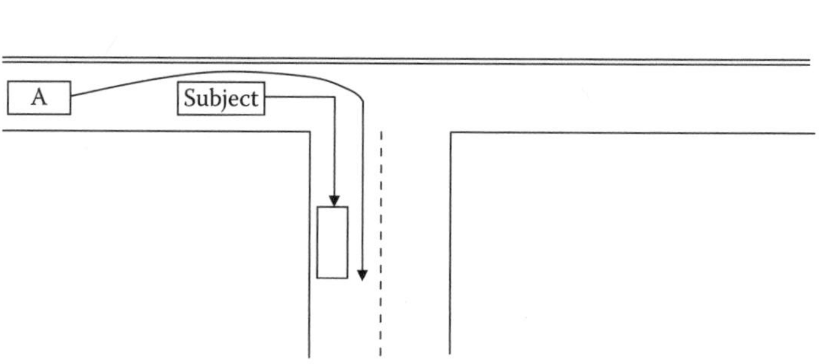

FIGURE 7.17 Stopping on a hill.

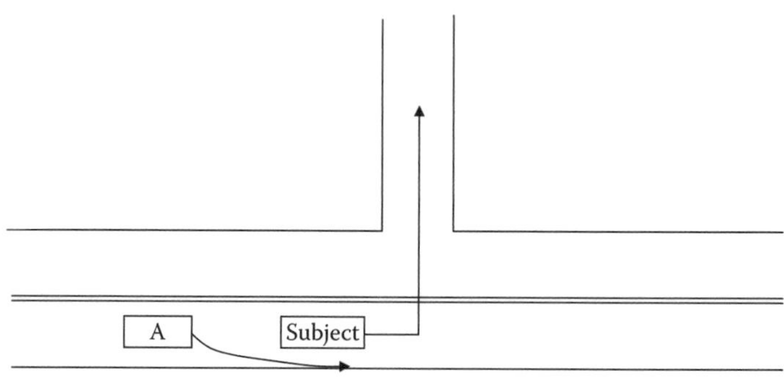

FIGURE 7.18 Turn into alley by subject.

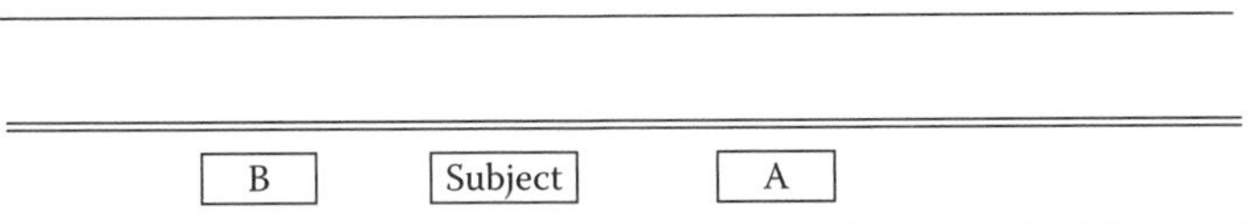

FIGURE 7.19 Leading surveillance.

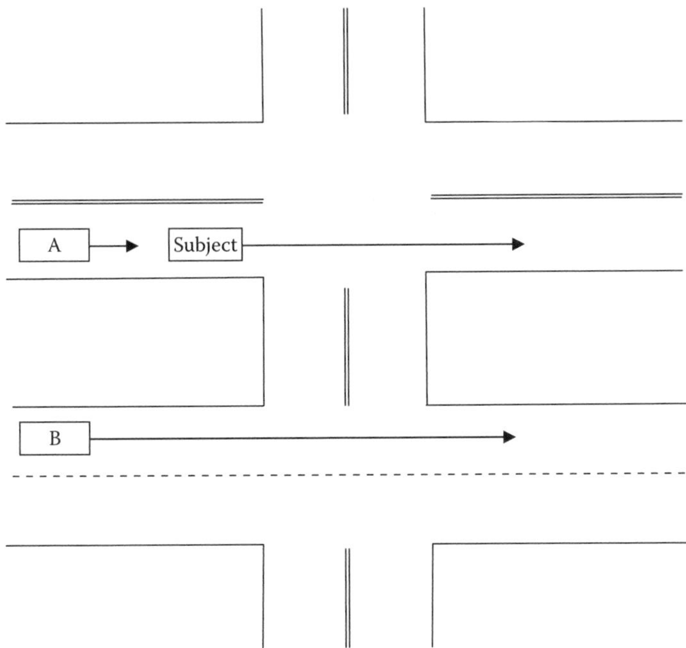

FIGURE 7.20 Parallel surveillance.

C. Hybrid and Other Special Surveillance Techniques

1. Foot and Auto Surveillance

Some combination between foot and auto surveillance is often advisable, particularly in congested urban areas. Figure 7.21 shows a subject vehicle being tailed by a surveillance vehicle on a suspected or known route. Note that, one block up, a foot surveillance agent awaits the subject vehicle's arrival.

As mentioned earlier, no surveillance vehicle should have only one agent, the driver. The demands of auto operation are a major distraction to an agent's observational skills. The second party in the vehicle, often referred to as the footman, has the following occupational responsibilities:

1. Watch the subject's car; keep the driver advised of its movement.
2. Place the subject under surveillance immediately if the subject should get out of his car. The driver will park the car and join the other agent when he or she can (Figure 7.22).
3. If the surveillance car is stopped by a light, the footman must keep the subject's car in sight. If the subject turns right or left at an intersection when the surveillance car is stopped, the footman should get out of the surveillance car and get to the corner in case the subject makes another turn. If necessary, the footman is to run to that corner. If the subject's car proceeds straight ahead and surveillance car is stopped at a light, the footman should alight so that he or she can watch the movements of the subject's vehicle, particularly if the subject turns right or left at the following intersection (Figure 7.23.)

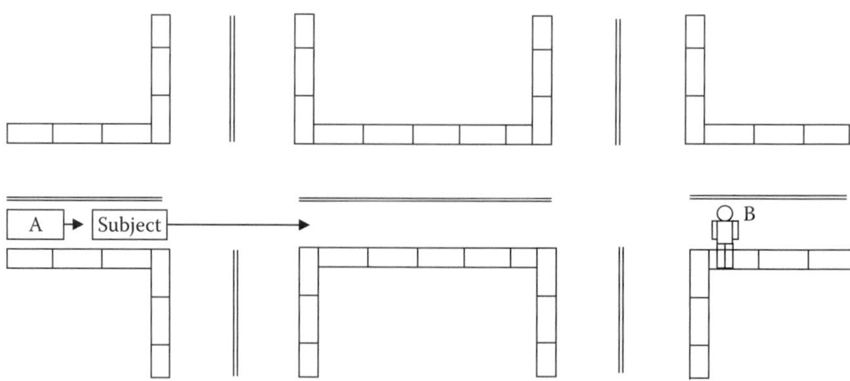

FIGURE 7.21 Foot and auto surveillance.

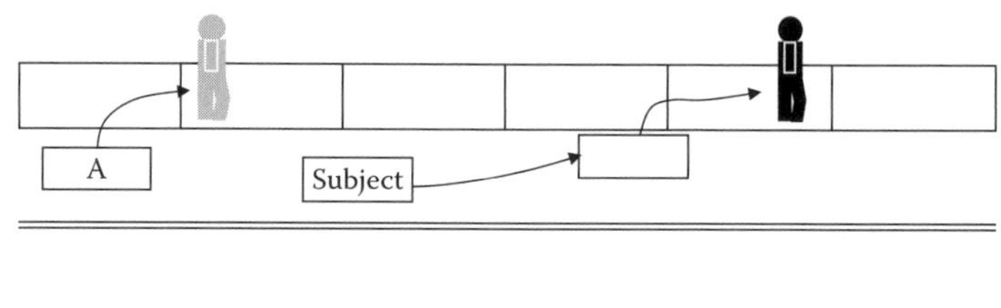

FIGURE 7.22 Step #2 Foot and auto surveillance.

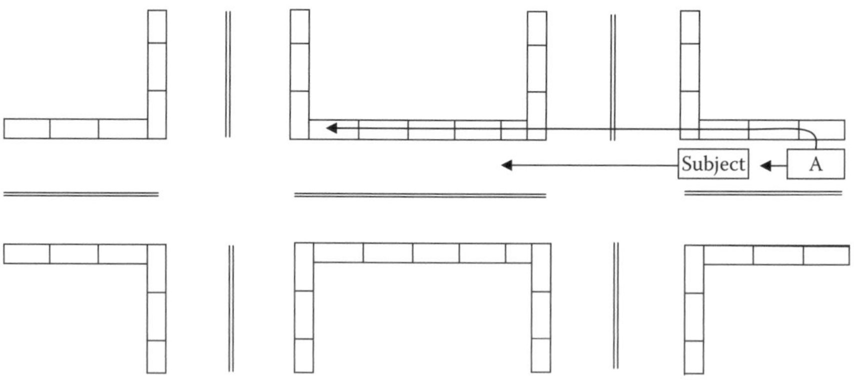

FIGURE 7.23 Step #3 Foot and auto surveillance.

2. Surveillance at Bus Stops

Surveillance of a subject at a bus stop requires special attention. The following methods are suggested:

1. As the subject approaches the bus, get close rapidly so that you are as close to the subject as possible when the bus stops.
2. Enter the bus directly behind subject in order to be able to walk by him or her unseen when he or she takes a seat.
3. Always take a position to the rear of the bus and behind the subject.

4. Sit on the same side of the bus as the subject. We tend to look at those persons across from us.
5. If possible, remain seated when the subject stands to leave the bus. Wait until the subject is alighting, then leave the bus with him or her. Subjects who are surveillance conscious will walk to the door of the bus and then return to their seats, thereby catching the investigator off guard.

3. Use of Pretext

A pretext is an alleged, assumed, or feigned representation or introduction that conceals the real intention and purpose of the surveillance. A pretext is an acting job and is not to be confused with the technique of "roping," which refers to the investigator's capacity to draw out or obtain information without an individual realizing it. People are reluctant to give information to law enforcement officials (either public or private in nature); thus, pretexts are often necessary in performing the functions of investigation. A pretext is not a direct or affirmative misrepresentation, nor is it an affirmative allegation or impression of false authority or control. The investigator merely conceals his or her true purpose and affords the respondent an opportunity to talk and relay information. However, caution must be exercised because the operation of a pretext skims dangerously near the legal issues of privacy, obstruction of justice, and official misrepresentation. Pretexts should be adopted with these reservations:

- Only thoroughly experienced and trained investigators are assigned to surveillance and/or pretext work, especially in those instances where the subject has a suit pending for personal injuries alleged to have resulted from an accident of some nature.
- The pretext interview with the claimant should be limited to an identification of the subject and an observation of any apparent condition that would indicate that the claim is misrepresented.
- The pretext investigator is not to enter the claimant's residence if it can be avoided.
- The pretext investigator should never be on the surveillance team, for this would likely give away the surveillants. If manpower restraints make it necessary for the same person to be involved in pretext and surveillance, special care must be exercised to ensure that the surveillance investigator and the designated investigator are not identified as the same person. The use of a hat, sunglasses, false mustache, change of clothes, and so forth can be used to disguise the investigator. The designated investigator must never allow his or her automobile to be seen by the subject.
- A surveillance will not be continued after the pretext investigator is assured the subject is aware of the surveillance.
- The investigators will not tell neighbors or other persons having no legitimate interest therein of the personal business or intimate activities of the subject under surveillance nor tell false stories about the subject.
- The investigators will not spy upon the subject in the privacy of the subject's home or take pictures of the subject under such circumstances.
- The investigators will strictly limit their picture-taking to activities that are inconsistent with the subject's claim.
- The investigators must not falsely represent themselves to be a federal, state, county, or city law enforcement officer, nor a newspaper reporter, nor an employee of or representative of a bona fide concern or organization.
- The investigators will not furnish a company's address or telephone number.
- The investigators will not furnish any information through which their identity might be established, nor permit anyone to obtain the license number of the automobile they are using.

a. *Examples of Pretext*

There are several different types of pretext that security investigators might use to obtain information. Some examples are:

Personal Injury Accident: The security investigator represents that he or she is an agent of the National Accident Prevention Association, which acquires and studies data on reported accidents.

Bank Account: The security investigator calls a bank indicating that he or she is a merchant checking whether there are sufficient funds to honor a check.

Character and Community Reputation: The security investigator indicates to neighbors that he or she is considering relocation to the area but is concerned about the character, reputation, and the manner of living of a perspective next-door neighbor.

Claim Settlement Verification: The investigator acts as if he or she is a representative of the National Claims Bureau, which is a nonprofit entity created by the insurance industry to calculate and report on the amount of settlement reached in insurance cases.

Disability Case: The following pretexts may provide the investigator with information:

- The security investigator tells the subject that one of his or her relatives suffered a similar injury or illness and that the investigator has heard that the subject's therapeutic regimen and treatment had been most effective. The investigator asks if the subject could advise him or her of doctors' names and results and whether results were positive.
- The investigator says that he or she is conducting a survey to determine the rate of unemployment in a particular trade occupation.
- The investigator indicates that he or she is a contractor and had heard that the person being surveyed was a skilled carpenter or tradesman. The investigator asks whether the individual has any interest in doing work on the side.

Acquiring a Handwriting Sample: The following pretexts may allow the investigator to acquire a writing sample:

- The investigator advises the subject that he or she is conducting a survey for a consumer group, Manufacturer's Trade Association, and that he or she needs to obtain certain data. The investigator then asks for a signature after the survey has been completed.
- The investigator asks the subject to sign a petition for a worthwhile (but fictitious) cause.

Location of Persons: The following pretexts may help locate a suspect:

- The investigator indicates to a neighbor of the subject that he or she was once a roommate or close friend of the subject and that he or she is trying to retrieve goods that were borrowed by the subject.
- The investigator indicates that he or she was once a coemployee with the subject and that he or she had shared tools and other belongings and is seeking the return of the items.

Video Surveillance Pictures: The following pretexts may allow the investigator to take pictures of the suspect:

- One investigator walks up to the subject and says that his or her car has broken down (or needs directions, etc.) while the other agent in a vehicle operates a camera in a discreet manner.
- The investigator gives the impression that he or she is a freelance writer, photographer, and filmmaker and that he or she is engaged in the collection of information for a national magazine or in the preparation of a film for educational purposes.

Occupation or Employment of Subject: The following pretexts may ascertain the subject's occupation:

- The investigator calls the subject's residence acting as if he or she is employed by a private nongovernment employment agency. The investigator preferably talks with someone other than the subject asking if the subject has acquired a position and what that position is.

- The investigator says that he or she is conducting a national survey for a business and industrial concern that is seeking qualified employees in the area in which the company will be located.

Stockholder or Shareholder Suit: The investigator indicates that he or she represents a firm (located in a distant city) that plans to contract with the subject's firm, but has heard rumors and innuendo regarding legal problems and difficulties.

Suicide/Murder of Business Owner: The investigator makes clear that he or she represents a principal who is interested in purchasing the business once owned by the deceased but who needs information regarding total assets and liabilities. During the course of the discussion, the investigator indicates that the deceased should have done much more business and inquires if he or she knew if the deceased had any personal difficulties such as domestic squabbling, financial troubles, or ongoing illnesses.

The above pretexts are merely introductory suggestions regarding circumstances and events that arise in private investigation. Always be attentive to the ethical and legal boundaries these activities encompass. Investigators must be on their guard not to violate accepted standards of conduct.

V. SURVEILLANCE FORMS AND REPORTS

As in all facets of private investigation, report writing, note taking, and accurate documentation are essential for a professional practice. The daily grind of surveillance needs to be reported and recorded for later reference and compared with accumulated data and evidence. Most firms regularly keep a surveillance log, which will serve as a cover sheet to a more substantial report. An example of this is given in Figure 7.24.

Field notes are of the utmost importance in the eventual construction and drafting of a surveillance report. "Complete notes are invaluable later for developing leads and for carrying out the substantive work of the investigation."[22] The surveillance officer must always remember that note taking serves as the foundational support for whatever eventual documentation is submitted to the client. The surveillance report probably makes the biggest impression on a client. Keep in mind these points regarding notes:

1. Surveillance reports are compiled from investigator's notes.
2. Notes must be accurate, exact and thorough—investigator may have to testify from them.
3. Notes should show investigator's initials and dates.
4. Notes should reflect events listed opposite a time caption in chronological order, to the nearest minute.
5. Notes must be handed in with the investigator's report.
6. The supervisor must check investigator's notes with his report to determine:
   (a) if time captions are correct, and
   (b) if any pertinent information was left out of the report.[23]

The culmination of surveillance activities results in either a daily, weekly, or summary surveillance report. Review Figure 7.25, titled Daily Surveillance Report, written in a memorandum in chronological date, time, and activity format. Note the sequential and conceptual order of presentation. Paragraph 1 calls for a summary or debriefing of the activities undertaken. Paragraph 2 requests a discussion on the proposed method of surveillance. Paragraph 3 seeks an explanation for a deviation from said plan. In paragraph 4, the activity log commences.

Another proposed format of construction for a surveillance report is shown in Figure 7.26. Some differences in style are apparent. First, this example uses a synopsis format, as seen on the first

Surveillance Log Cover Sheet

Subject ______________________ Conducted by (Investigators) ______________
Address ______________________ ______________________
Telephone ______________________ Case No. ______________________
Social Security # ______________________ Case Name ______________________
Date of Birth ______________________
Description ______________________
____
Type of Injury ______________________
____
Vehicles ______________________
______________________ Date ______________________

Persons Observed	**Times Observed**						

Synopsis:

☐ Subject Observed ☐ Contact Observed ☐ Photos Attempted
☐ Subject not observed ☐ Unusual activity ☐ Assessment data obtained

________ Hours ________ Minutes = Total time on subject

Administrative Data:

Equipment:

Van: ____________ Starting Mileage: ________ Finish Mileage: ________
Photos Yes _____ No _____
Video Yes _____ No _____

____
____
____

FIGURE 7.24 Cover sheet of surveillance log.

page of the report. Second, this report places more emphasis on factual and comprehensive writing (e.g., see the 8:15 a.m. designation). This type of detailed authorship is most commendable. Other specific points include:

- The investigator is required to print all proper names.
- The investigator must indent all descriptions of cars and people.
- The investigator must always describe the person being followed and what he is wearing the first time he is observed, at the beginning of each day, and any changes of clothing thereafter.
- The surveillance report must note photographic or video exhibitions taken on the assignment and file appropriate forms and documentation.

Daily Surveillance Report

To:

From:

RE: Surveillance of

On: [Date]

(Paragraph 1)

Summary of debriefing to include date, time, information received from supervisor

(Paragraph 2)

Proposed method of surveillance.

(Paragraph 3)

Any deviation from plan and reason for such.

(Paragraph 4)

Activity Log

Example:

6/22/09

8:00 a.m. Smith exits residence and enters car. (Include color, make, model, year if known, and registration.)

8:03 a.m. Smith drives to CoGo's convenience store via Main Street and enters the store.

8:06 a.m. Smith exits the store, carrying two medium-sized bags. (photograph taken)

FIGURE 7.25 Sample daily surveillance report form.

XYZ Insurance
Claimant: Jim Smith
Worker's Compensation Claim Investigation
Claim No. 1234A BCD
Wednesday, June, 17, 2009

Synopsis:

Jim Smith was observed on this date working under the hood of his pickup truck. It was a particularly hot day, with temperatures up to 96 degrees.

In the early afternoon he was observed walking briskly with a sure stride; then he was observed pulling weeds in his garden, bending over at the waist to do so, and hanging clothes onto a clothesline in his backyard.

Smith was also observed bending forward to raise the door of his garage with his right hand grasping a small piece of rope. After placing several objects into the back seat of an automobile, he reached upward over his head with his right hand to grasp the rope attached to the garage door handle. He yanked the cord downward, pulling the garage door shut in one easy motion. He returned to the driver's seat of the automobile and drove away.

At no time did Smith's face reflect signs of pain or discomfort, and he did not exhibit any signs of strain or difficulty.

Reading of this entire report is recommended.

COMPANY: XYZ Insurance
CLAIMANT: Jim Smith
INVESTIGATION TYPE: Worker's Compensation Claim Investigation

OFFICE: Wilmington
CLAIM NO.: 1234A BCD

CONFIDENTIAL

City	Day of Week	Date
________	________	________

COMMENCED: 5:30 am DISCONTINUED: 7:00 pm

Received details and commenced surveillance of Jim Smith, known to reside at 67 Oak Street, Anytown, DE, 00000.

5:30 am This investigator, after receiving details of this assignment, departed Wilmington en route to Anytown, DE.

8:02 am Arrived in Anytown and proceeded to Anytown Post Office, 100 W. Main Street.

8:15 am Contacted the Anytown Post Office, who provided directions to the Smith residence. These directions are as follows:

Take Main Street going east through town 2.2 miles. At the intersection of E. Main Street and Oak Street turn right onto Oak Street. The Smith residence is the third house on the left. A mail box with the house number, 67, is at the end of the driveway.

8:32 am Proceeded to the vicinity of the subject's residence and found it to be a suburban, middle-class residential area, consisting of mostly wood-frame, one and two story structures. The estimated value of these homes is between $75,000 and $85,000.

9:00 am Located the Smith house. The subject's residence is described as a red sided two story home with an enclosed front porch. There is a paved driveway to the right of the residence leading to a small-frame garage located to the right rear of the home. The garage stands apart from the home and is sided red.

The residence appears to be well maintained. The lawn and shrubbery show signs of regular care; there is a small flower garden and vegetable garden, also showing signs of care. The vegetable garden is located at the rear of the property.

The Smith residence, consisting of .75 acres, is estimated to be valued at $75,000.

Parked in the driveway, heading toward the garage is a:

1999 Chevrolet Silverado pickup truck, Silver in color, current Delaware license number 000 XXXX.

FIGURE 7.26 Surveillance report form sent to client.

9:01 am	While initially driving by the Smith residence, I observed that the hood of the above-described pickup truck was raised. Sitting on the edge of the truck's left front fender, bending slightly over the engine, was an individual described as: Male, white, age 44, 5'8" tall, 178 lbs., muscular build with pot belly, deeply tanned, close-cropped light brown hair, wearing no shirt and faded blue jeans Believed to be Jim Smith, and hereafter referred to as Smith. It should be noted that the weather is clear and sunny, the temperature averaging 96 degrees Fahrenheit, and humidity high.
9:42 am	I have established surveillance of the Smith residence. Smith is not in sight at this time. The hood of the pickup truck is now down, Smith apparently having returned to his house. Noted at this time, parked in the driveway to the left of the silver pickup truck is a: Shiny, red 2005 Chevrolet Cobalt, current Delaware license number 111 ZZZZ.
10:11 am	I observed a female described as: White, age 25, 5'4" tall, 155 lbs, chunky build, pale complected, dark, shoulder-length wavy hair, wearing light colored, short sleeved top with dark colored slacks This female left Smith's residence with several, small, active children. They entered the above described Cobalt and she drove away.
11:17 am	Activity at the Smith residence observed since the departure of the Cobalt. A moderate, continuing flow of local traffic, pickup trucks and automobiles, passed the Smith residence.
12:00 pm	Still no activity observed at the Smith residence since the Cobalt's departure at 10:11 am.
12:35 pm	Smith, now wearing a white, sweat-stained T-shirt, walked briskly from the rear of the house across the yard to the flower garden on the right side of the house. Smith walked with a sure stride, his upper torso appeared to be slightly stiff as he walked, his arms swinging mechanically, close to his body.
12:36 pm	Smith was observed for 8 minutes pulling weeds from the flower garden. This physical movement involved his bending forward at the waist, knees slightly crooked, his arms extended forward toward the ground, using both hands to pull and discard weeds. Smith, in the bent-over position, moving very slowly forward along the edge of the garden, raised upright only twice during this 8 minute period, apparently to arch his back and stretch. During this period, Smith was observed weeding his garden, he slowly inched forward a total of 3 feet along the garden's edge.
12:43 pm	At this time, Smith raised upright and immediately proceeded to walk from the garden to the tool shed (approximately 17 feet), with no obvious hesitation or difficulty.
12:45 pm	Smith, after leaving the tool shed, was briefly observed hanging several pieces of clothing on the outside clothesline on the left, rear side of the house. When observed, he was using both arms to hang the clothes, his hands raised to head level in front of his body. This activity lasted approximately 2 minutes.
12:54 pm	I observed an automobile, described as: Blue, 2008 Ford Mustang, current Delaware license number 123 ZYXW Drive into the paved driveway and park next to the silver pickup truck. A man described as: White, age 72, 5'3" tall, 148 lbs., bony build with hunchback, pale complected, short white hair, wearing dark colored hat, white long-sleeved shirt and overalls, alighted from this automobile and walked slowly into the Smith house.
12:58 pm	Smith and the elderly man described above left the house, the older man returning to the blue automobile, and Smith walking toward the garage door. Again, Smith walked in a confident manner, a grin on his face, showing no apparent distress.
12:59 pm	Smith, at the closed garage door, bent forward to the ground and gripped a small piece of rope attached to the door handle in his right hand. Smith then, in one, smooth, unbroken motion, swiftly raised upright, raising the garage door completely open.
1:00 pm	Smith entered the garage (empty of cars) and picked up in his right hand a large plastic container the size of a clothes basket and an unidentified object in his left hand. With these objects in his hand, Smith walked swiftly, approximately 30 feet to the back of the blue car.

FIGURE 7.26 (continued).

1:01 pm	Smith opened the trunk and bent forward over the rear of the car at a 90 degree angle and placed the objects in the car. He then raised upright and closed the trunk and walked back to the garage in the above-described manner.
1:02 pm	Smith then reached upward over his head with his right hand to grasp the cord attached to the garage door handle. He yanked the cord downward, pulling the garage door shut in one easy motion.
1:03 pm	Smith returned to the blue car, climbing into the driver's seat with no apparent hesitation. Smith had a constant smile on his face, showing no signs of discomfort or strain while walking, opening and closing the garage door, or getting into the blue automobile.
1:04 pm	Smith, driving the blue automobile, backed into the driveway, then drove forward onto the road. He then drove the blue automobile out of my sight.
2:15 pm	Smith had not returned to the house.
3:00 pm	As no further activity was observed, I departed the area en route to Wilmington, discontinuing surveillance for this day.
5:20 pm	Arrived at the Wilmington office and began report preparation.
7:00 pm	Concluded this report and discontinued work for the day.

SUPERVISOR'S NOTE: The license plate of the silver Chevrolet pickup truck (DE 000 XXXX) and the red Chevrolet Cobalt (DE 111 ZZZZ) were found to be registered to Jim Smith at 67 Oak Street, Anytown, DE, 00000.

Additional surveillance is recommended to further document the activity of Jim Smith.

Final until further advised.

FIGURE 7.26 (continued).

NOTES

1. American Society for Industrial Security, *Basic Guidelines for Security Investigations* (1981), 41.
2. Michael A. Gips, "Image Is Everything in Stopping Crime," *Sec. Mgmt.* (February 2004), 12; "Public Cameras Yet to Be Real-Time Intelligence for Security," *Corporate Sec.* (January 31, 2007), 6.
3. Pinkerton's, Inc., *Surveillance Manual* (1990), 2.
4. K. C. Scott-Brown and P. D. J. Cronin, "Detect the Unexpected: A Science for Surveillance," *Policing* 31 (2008), 395.
5. W. Bennett and K. Hess, *Criminal Investigation* 235 (West Publishing, 1981), 235.
6. John Dale Hartman, *Legal Guidelines for Covert Surveillance Operations in the Private Sector* (Butterworth-Heinemann, 1993), 168–169.
7. National Institute of Justice, *Video Surveillance of Public Places*, COPS, February 2006.
8. Bennett and Hess, *supra* note 5, at 225.
9. Hartman, *supra* note 6, at 32-33.
10. Pinkerton's, Inc., *Investigations Department Training Manual* (1990), 114.
11. Jim Ross, Ross Engineering, Inc., 7906 Hope Valley Court, Adamstown, MD 21710.
12. C. Schnabolk, *Physical Security: Practices Plus Technology* (Butterworth, 1984), 324. For an interesting web location that features the intricacies of casino surveillance, see http://www.casinosurveillancenews.com, visited August 30, 2009.
13. *Id.* at 327.
14. See www.Biometric-CCTV.com, visited August 30, 2009, 8641 S. Warhawk Rd., Conifer, CO 80433.
15. Carl A. Roper, *Physical Security and the Inspection Process* (Butterworth-Heinemann, 1997), 165.
16. Eastman Kodak Co., *Photographic Surveillance Techniques for Law Enforcement Agencies* (1972).
17. *Id.* at 17.
18. American Society for Industrial Security, *supra* note 1, at 42.
19. Pinkerton's, Inc., *supra* note 3, at 11.
20. Pinkerton's, Inc., *supra* note 10, at 115.
21. Pinkerton's, Inc., *supra* note 3, at 1.
22. American Society for Industrial Security, *supra* note 1, at 44.
23. Pinkerton's, Inc., *supra* note 3, at 9.

8 Report Writing

I. INTRODUCTION

Despite its drudgery, report writing is a core and mandatory function throughout the investigative process. Report writing—that is, the compilation, drafting, and authorship of various reports and documents relating to an investigative case—serves as the formal record of investigative steps and practices. Reports are crucial to historical accuracy and ensure an objective appraisal of events and conditions surrounding the case at hand. Reports also promote professional best practices for the security industry. And yet the quality of report writing remains, as Tim Dees puts it, an "ill at the top of the list."[1]

A. Efficiency in the Investigative Process

Reports and record keeping promote productivity and efficiency in the typical security agency's operation. "There is a direct relationship between the efficiency of a security operation and the quality of its records and record procedures. The simple task of performing security in health care facilities only a few years ago is in sharp contrast to the exceedingly complex and difficult problems and demands of today's facilities. In meeting these demands, the security operation must function according to plans that provide for detailed records regarding each phase of its operational responsibility."[2] The value of reports are twofold: first, initial steps are memorialized; second, subsequent investigative actions are not a rehash of the first steps taken. As case investigations progress, it is difficult to remember it all, and report documents keep the investigator on an efficient path.

At a minimum, reports are shared and collaborative documents that allow all interested parties access to the plan of action chosen and the processes already completed. Bennett and Hess, longtime experts in the investigative realm, properly hold that "[y]our reports, like your notes, are a permanent record that communicates important information to many others. They are used, not simply filed away."[3] Without reports, the case and its personnel are likely to falter or at least proceed in a less efficient way. Police departments are increasingly reliant upon software programs to ensure efficiency in the draft and final reports, and such software programs go a long way toward assuring efficiency.[4]

> **Web Exercise:** Review and evaluate a popular report writing software program at http://www.policeone.com/police-products/traffic-enforcement/Electronic-Citations/tips/1656052-All-in-one-report-writing-software

B. Reports and Memory

Both short-term and long-term memory are subject to a variety of forces that can affect clarity and recall. Note taking at the scene and creation of the report as soon as possible after an event reduces the risk of inaccuracy. Case documentation, fully accepting the fallibility of human memory, provides a permanent locale for later reference. "The need to retrieve information contained in a report may occur within hours or days after it is written or perhaps even years later. A quick and effective technique for evaluating a security system is to determine how many questions concerning past activity are answered by personal memory as opposed to answers supplied according to documented facts."[5] The passage of time, the fading capacity to remember, and the diversity of external influences, such as varied opinions, all undermine the quality of memory alone and the urgent need for a documentary record.

C. Reports and Organizational Method during the Investigation

Reports force the investigator to evaluate a case in a formal sense rather than an exclusively extemporaneous method. Reports, by their very construction, force the investigator to memorialize events and circumstances surrounding a case. Inevitably, the reports themselves engender a stronger organizational method. While oral communication tends to be spontaneous, communicating thoughts in written form requires a more formal organizational approach. The investigator must keep in mind the who, what, when, where, and how of the case and author language that reflects these fundamental queries of the skilled investigator. From an administrative perspective, reports and documentation organize the functions of a security firm. R. Gallati, in *Introduction to Private Security*, emphasizes the importance of records:

> Basically, the security budget and security public relations are dependent upon records. Communications are not going to be up to standard unless they are based upon adequate files. Without proper records, you simply are not going to be able to tell where you have been, where you are, or where you are going.[6]

Consider some of the records that influence the structural operation of a private security firm.

- Incident reports
- Memorandum files
- Expenditure records
- Equipment files
- Personnel files
- Logs and other sequential documentation
- Intelligence files
- Investigative and evidentiary records
- Statistical files
- Arrest and other action reports

In essence, formal documentation mirrors the task and functions of the private investigator and gives a formal mechanism to track and trace a case's progress. In this way, the reports themselves breathe organizational life into the security firm and its employees.

D. Reports as Proof of Services Rendered

Security firms and investigators, like other service providers, must prove the delivery of security services or minimally need to provide evidence to a client of what has thus far been accomplished. The report demonstrates, to new and long-term clients, exactly what has been undertaken thus far. A report corroborates the assertions of the security provider that it did X or Y. Reports not only cover the professional tracks of the investigator but also provide clients with a formal proof of work done so far. Sophisticated clients, especially those with business and industrial concerns, are investing a sizable chunk of money in the world of security services and have a rightful expectation of a documentary record of those activities. Permanent records reflect the firm's efforts. Records and reports can secure a company's goodwill as well as educate the client on the nature of investigative results.

Thus, the report is not only a tool of investigation, but also a critical communicative aid between client and investigator. Pinkerton's, Inc., stresses this fact to its agents by its motto, "A Report Is Our Product."[7] The compelling need for professionally drafted reports is fully appreciated by Pinkerton's:

> We consider client reports to be the most important responsibility that an investigator and handling manager has. No matter how well or professionally an investigation is conducted, the report is what the client receives. They will use this report to hire, fire, suspend, discontinue compensation payments, settle a claim, go to court, continue an investigation, obtain peace of mind, prosecute, and to determine if they will pay our bill.[8]

Confirming this position regarding report writing, author Robert Gallati states:

> Security, as we have previously stated, must continually be "sold"; otherwise it may not receive the attention it warrants. In order to sell anything, one must communicate; in order to persuade, one must educate while communicating.[9]

Thus, the report serves as an important public relation's tool for the security professional and a defensive tool in the event a client alleges nonperformance of services.

II. CHARACTERISTICS OF SOLID REPORT WRITING

Report writing is as effective as its quality of content and structural format. Solid report writing depends on many factors, including proper grammar and usage, an historical record that has been accurately recorded, and other factors, as discussed below.

A. The Role of Note Taking

Reports should be fresh and reliable products but not solely the result of spontaneous thinking. Instead, the final draft of a report should reflect a logical process, careful review of collected information, and a combination of personal observation and memory. Field notes play a critical role in the draft of any report. The taking of field notes is a regular exercise in both public and private law enforcement. From first visitation to the last meeting at an investigative scene, the professional investigator writes down observations, questions, ideas, and thoughts that arise at scene. Field notes tend to be less formal than any subsequently filed document, but this does not minimize their importance. Field notes are preliminary observations that need to be visited at a later time when the investigator is ready to draft a more formal record of these observations. In fact, field notes are often a mishmash of ideas that will be formally organized when the investigator's report is written. Figure 8.1 is an example of a case report form.

As the terminology implies, note taking is less formal than a finalized report, it is a cryptic, abbreviated relation of facts and conditions relative to the case. Of usual importance are the standard lines of inquiry—the who, what, when, where, and how of the matter. An investigator's notes should record general details such as:

- Weather
- Lighting conditions
- Clothing of victims/suspects
- Description of roads
- Location of roads
- Emergency medical personnel on the scene
- Statements

CASE NAME	CASE NUMBER
DATE / /	TIME AM PM
1. EVIDENCE	
2. WITNESSES	
3. GENERAL OBSERVATIONS	
INVESTIGATING OFFICIAL	SIGNATURE

FIGURE 8.1 Case report form.

- Activities of other investigative personnel: forensic technicians, photographers, survey sketchers, police
- Important addresses and phone numbers
- Other relevant information

Notes corral the details, provide a basis for a report, supplement sketches and photographs, and are classified as documentary evidence for the investigator. Notes are gathered in chronological order corresponding to the investigator's steps or sequence of receipt of information. In addition to those items listed above, notes should specifically designate:

- Date and time call received
- Time of arrival
- Names of officers present
- Names and complete demographic information of witnesses present
- Anything touched, moved, or altered
- Any statements made by witnesses to officers present
- Exact geographic location of scene
- Overall scene conditions
- Photographs taken, including photographer's name, time photos were taken, scene depicted by photos, setting, speed film, and so forth
- Real and physical evidence, including description, identification marks, date, time, and exact location where found, by whom found, and custodian of evidence

Gallati stresses the importance of taking good notes:

> The investigator must acquire the habit of making complete, comprehensive notes. They must not trust their memory. They are to place their initials and the date on each page as well as number them. They should be in chronological order.[10]

This mental montage of information will be heavily relied upon by the investigator as the report document is finalized.

B. The Essential Qualities of a Solid Report: Accurate, Brief, and Complete

Accuracy is a perpetual concern to the security professional in two contexts: first, whether the information included in the report is factually and legally correct; and second, whether the information contained in the report is technically correct.

Notes that are filled with chronological or sequential gaps will provide little aid in recall and are dubious factually. In fact, if incomplete notes are relied upon to refresh memory during the testimonial phase of trial litigation, attorneys can easily poke holes in the accuracy and credibility of such notes; thus, thoroughness is imperative. The final report comprehensively portrays the major results of the investigation. Stylistic attention is just as wise for the author. Cox and Brown use common sense and a bit of humor to drive home the stylistic aspect of report writing:

> 1. *Accuracy is important in word use as well as in information.* Poor word choice will get you into trouble. One officer wound up in court on three occasions trying to explain what he meant when he said that the suspect "crowded" him. Was he pushed, shoved up against the wall, verbally intimidated, or what? *Value judgments must be avoided, and brief details should be given instead.* For example, don't say, "The child seemed afraid of his father." Instead, give the facts that led you to this assumption: "When the father came into the room, the boy stopped talking and began to cry. The father smiled and offered the boy candy, but the son backed up to his mother and clung to her, crying harder."
> 2. *Brevity is important, as long as it is not used at the cost of accuracy or completeness.* This applies to words, too. Never use a complicated word when a simple one will do. The active form is shorter and generally more accurate than the passive form.
> 3. *Completeness is essential.* One of the stories used recently on this point is that of the young lawyer Abraham Lincoln, who won a case because he proved that the moon was not shining on a night that the presumed suspect was supposedly identified by the full light of the moon. Do not assume anything, even the obvious. A recent case in Australia made the front page of a newspaper for its rather humorous point: A man was alleged to be drunk, and the report stated that the officer observed the man's eyes to be bloodshot. "Both of them?" asked the defense attorney. Looking at the now clear-eyed defendant the officer said firmly, "Yes, both of them." Whereupon the defendant removed his clear, artificial eye and rolled it on the table. Case dismissed.[11]

The investigator has the professional obligation to ensure that spelling is correct, that sentences are grammatically sound, and that the presentation provided is logical and comprehensive. Grammatical rigor is central to professional report writing. Conciseness, brevity of thought and idea, and an objective presentation do much to ensure the authenticity and usefulness of a report. Opinions and emotional responses without factual justification are to be avoided at all costs. The American Society for Industrial Security notes:

> Review the report carefully for typographical or other errors, testing to insure that the reader will understand all details, and that the need for information has been satisfied. Good grammar, carefully chosen words, appropriate punctuation, and all other considerations suggested previously should be kept in mind during the review. A well-conducted investigation followed by a well-planned report can all be spoiled by inattention to the final review.[12]

Before submitting a report to a client or supervisor, the investigator should take the time to read and review its contents thoroughly. In making the final assessment, the investigator should make sure the report is:

- Factual
- Clear
- Accurate
- Mechanically correct
- Objective
- Written in standard English
- Complete
- Legible
- Concise

C. Report Design or Format

Effective report writing also requires familiarity with the basic styles and formats of report design. The checklist format, the most abbreviated and least narrative of all report systems, simply calls upon the author to check by mark, asterisk, or initial the information requested. Numerous examples of the checklist format are included throughout this text.

The narrative format requires the greatest level of composition. A typical example of an arrest report, such as that shown in Figure 8.2,[13] has a substantial space provided for a narrative exposition of the facts.

Some reports are intentionally designed to call upon the investigator to make a deduction, a finding, or a conclusion regarding certain matters. Sometimes a list of alternative explanations or descriptions might be requested. Interpretative questionnaires can call for deductive or inferential conclusions regarding a suspect's description, motive, or *modus operandi* (method of operation or MO).

III. STANDARD REPORTS FOR THE PRIVATE INVESTIGATOR

What follows is a representative sample of forms, documents, and reports that are regularly filled out by security professionals. Some forms are presented elsewhere in this text (e.g., on surveillance, administration, and initial interview) and are not repeated here. Investigators should keep in mind that standardized forms and documents need to be tailored to the unique requirements of the investigator's practice and the clients served. Standardized forms are a starting point.

A. Activity Reports

Private investigators will be called upon to narrate the substance of their activities over specific periods of time and according to specific activities, as in these examples categorized by Brislin:

- Shift Logs or Daily Logs
- Vehicle Logs
- Visitor/Contractor Logs
- Material Control Passes/Logs
- Incident Reports[14]

1. Daily Reports

Some investigators are asked to fill out Daily Activity Reports, which relay the times arrival and departure at the scene, as well as investigative action taken throughout the course of the day. Some

NO. ____________ NO. ____________

NO. ____________ NO. ____________

ARREST REPORT

NAME OF PERSON ARRESTED | ALIAS OR NICKNAME(S) | ARREST DATE | RT. THUMB PRINT

ADDRESS OF SUSPECT | OCCUPATION | TIME ☐ AM ☐ PM

SOCIAL SECURITY NO. / / | DRIVER'S LICENSE INFORMATION: STATE | LICENSE NUMBER | TYPE | EXPIRES

AGE | RACE | SEX | EYES | HAIR | HEIGHT | WEIGHT | DATE OF BIRTH | PLACE OF BIRTH | TATTOOES OR ID. MARKS

WHERE ARRESTED | HOW ARREST MADE: ☐ ON VIEW ☐ CALL ☐ WARRANT | WARRANT NO. | WARRANT DATE

OFFENSE(S) SUSPECTED OR CHARGED

DATE OFFENSE COMMITTED | TIME ☐ A.M. ☐ P.M. | COURT

WHERE OFFENSE COMMITTED | TYPE PREMISES | BUSINESS TRADE NAME

ARMED ☐ YES ☐ NO | TYPE WEAPON | CHECK ALL ITEMS WHICH APPLY ☐ DRUNK ☐ DRINKING ☐ CURSED ☐ RESISTED ☐

PREVIOUS ARRESTS | OTHER PERSONS ARRESTED FOR SAME OFFENSE

VEHICLE INVOLVED | YEAR | MAKE | MODEL | STYLE | COLOR | LICENSE # | STATE | EXP. | IMPOUNDED ☐ YES ☐ NO | WHERE

PROPERTY PLACED IN PROPERTY ROOM

NAME OF COMPLAINANT | RELATION OF COMPLAINANT & SUSPECT - IF ANY?

ADDRESS OF COMPLAINANT | BEST PHONE | OTHER PHONE

WITNESSES NAME. | BEST CONTACT ADDRESS | AGE | BEST PHONE | OTHER PHONE | PARENT OR GUARDIAN?

1

2

NOTE FACTS OF ARREST NOT INCLUDED ABOVE.

ARRESTEE'S RIGHTS GIVEN BY | DATE | TIME | PLACE

RESULTS OF INVESTIGATION | NCIC #

ARRESTING OFFICERS | REPORT MADE BY | FINAL DISPOSITION

Use supplementary report for additional information not covered above.

SAMPLE

FIGURE 8.2 Sample of an arrest report. G. A. Thompson Form LE-7 reproduced with permission.

reports note the activity under investigation and request a description of the action taken. A Daily Report, filed by security departments, combines the checklist and narrative methods of report composition. See Figure 8.3.

2. Review Reports

It is customary practice in the security industry to compose weekly, monthly, and even yearly review documents regarding investigative activities. In both public and private law enforcement,

SECURITY DEPARTMENT OFFICER'S DAILY REPORT					
REPORT OF	SHIELD NO	SHIFT FROM AM PM	TO AM PM	S M T W T F S	DATE
RELIEVED OFFICER AT AM PM	RELIEVED BY OFFICER AT AM PM		RADIO NUMBER	TOTAL HRS.	

ITEMS NO. 1 THROUGH 13 MUST BE CHECKED YES OR NO. ITEMS CHECKED YES MUST BE EXPLAINED UNDER DETAILS.			DETAILS REPORT BELOW THE DETAILS OF EACH ITEM CHECKED YES AND ALL OTHER UNUSUAL OCCURRENCES OR MATTERS OF INTEREST. LIST LICENSE NUMBER OF ALL PARKING VIOLATORS
WERE THERE ANY	YES	NO	
1 FIRE HAZARDS			
2 SMOKING VIOLATIONS			
3 DOORS OR WINDOWS OPEN OR BROKEN			
4 VAULTS OR SAFES OPEN			
5 TRESSPASSER(S)			
6 SUSPICIOUS ACTIVITIES			
7 THEFTS-ATTEMPTED			
8 THEFTS-COMMITTED			
9 PROPERTY DAMAGE			
10 SECURITY LIGHTS OFF			
11 PARKING VIOLATIONS			
12 EXITS BLOCKED			
13 SAFETY HAZARDS			

EXAMINED BY	OPERATION INSPECTED BY	
INITIALS SGT. LT. CAPT. SEC. OFF.	SIGNED	
DATE		OFFICER SIGNATURE

FIGURE 8.3 Sample of security officer's daily report form.

this type of documentation serves to measure productivity and foster personal accountability in job performance. An annual summary of security department activities is presented in Figure 8.4.

3. Patrol and Observation Reports

Many of the security investigator's functions rely upon the skills and techniques of observation. Figure 8.5 contains those lines necessary to compose a brief description of time, date, and conduct observed.

SECURITY DEPARTMENT YEARLY ACTIVITIES REPORT		
DATE ______________	20	20
A THEFTS/MISSING		
1. COMPANY		
2. EMPLOYEE		
B MALICIOUS DAMAGE TO PROPERTY		
1. COMPANY		
2. EMPLOYEE		
C TAMPERING WITH EQUIPMENT		
D FOREIGN CAPS/TABS/OBJECTS		
E CONCEALED SHORTAGE		
F PRODUCT PROBLEMS		
1. DIVERSION		
2. OTHER		
G CRANK CALLS/LETTERS		
H MOTOR VEHICLE ACCIDENTS		
I EMPLOYEE PROBLEMS		
J ASSAULT & BATTERY		
K MEETINGS/CONFERENCES/COURT		
L NARCOTICS		
M CONFIDENTIAL		
N LARCENY FROM AUTO		
O WAREHOUSE/TRUCK CHECKS		
P CO-OPS		
1. COMPANY		
2. OUTSIDE AGENCIES		
Q CONTINUED INVESTIGATIONS		
R OTHER		

FIGURE 8.4 Sample of a security department's yearly activities report form.

4. Surveillance Reports

For a full discussion on surveillance reports, see Chapter 7.

5. Missing Person Reports

Missing persons are a concern for both public and private law enforcement personnel. The Missing Person Report, presented in Figure 8.6,[15] concentrates on information that could deliver leads to solve these cases.

Figure 8.7, Search for Current Whereabouts, should be of assistance to the private investigator on the hunt for a missing person or "skip witness." The report summarizes the extensive steps to be taken during the search.

Patrol and Observation Request

Date ______________________ Requesting Officer ______________________
Time ______________________ Termination Date ______________________
Location ____
Reason For Request ____

Officer's Observation

Officer ______________________ Observation ______________________
Time ______________________ Date ______________________
____

Officer ______________________ Observation ______________________
Time ______________________ Date ______________________
____

Officer ______________________ Observation ______________________
Time ______________________ Date ______________________
____

Officer ______________________ Observation ______________________
Time ______________________ Date ______________________
____

Officer ______________________ Observation ______________________
Time ______________________ Date ______________________
____

Officer ______________________ Observation ______________________
Time ______________________ Date ______________________
____

Officer ______________________ Observation ______________________
Time ______________________ Date ______________________
____

Officer ______________________ Observation ______________________
Time ______________________ Date ______________________
____

FIGURE 8.5 Sample of a patrol and observation report form.

6. Undercover Investigation Reports

The undercover investigative report calls for the most elaborate form of narrative. Review an excerpt from an undercover report in Figure 8.8.

7. Bomb Search Reports

Private security investigators involved in executive protection and prevention of terrorism are often assigned bomb search responsibilities. Explosive devices are a constant concern for those entrusted with the safety of others. See Figure 8.9.

8. Inspection Reports

Inspection reports are helpful tools in the assessment of civil liability. For example, the safety and security of a parking authority or public building, or a given product design, can be gleaned from inspection documentation. A failure to inspect gives rise to an inference of negligence in civil

MISSING PERSON REPORT

Date

Case No.

TYPE OF MISSING - PERSON
D = DISABILITY
I = INVOLUNTARY
E = ENDANGERED
J = JUVENILE
V = DISASTER VICTIM

Name: Last / First / Middle / Suffix

Sex: M = Male F = Female

Race: ☐ White ☐ Black ☐ Unknown ☐ Alaskan ☐ American Indian ☐ Asian/Pacific Islander

DOB: Month / Day / Year

State of Birth

Height: Ft. Inches

Weight: Pounds

Eyes: ☐ BLU = Blue ☐ BRO = Brown ☐ BLK = Black ☐ GRY = Gray ☐ GRN = Green ☐ HAZ = Hazel ☐ MAR = Maroon ☐ PNK = Pink ☐ XXX = Unknown

Hair: ☐ BLK = Black ☐ BRO = Brown ☐ BLN = Blond ☐ RED = Red ☐ WHI = White ☐ SDY = Sandy ☐ GRY = Gray ☐ XXX = Unknown

Scars, Mark, Tattoo

Social Security #

DRILICNO: State Yr. Exp.

NCIC FPCLASS: RT RI RM RR RL LT LI LM LR LL

Blood Type: ☐ A Pos ☐ A Neg ☐ B Pos ☐ B Neg ☐ AB Pos ☐ AB Neg ☐ O Pos ☐ O Neg

Circumcision ☐ Yes ☐ No

Footprints Available ☐ Yes ☐ No

Body X-rays Available ☐ Yes ☐ No

Build: ☐ Very thin ☐ Thin ☐ Medium ☐ Muscular ☐ Heavy/Stocky ☐ Obese

Date of Last Contact Month / Day / Year

Does the missing person have corrected vision ☐ Yes ☐ No
☐ Glasses? ☐ Contact lenses?

Corrective Vision RX

Type of contact lenses and color: ☐ Hard ☐ Soft ☐ Longwear ☐ Semi ☐ Blue ☐ Brown ☐ Gray ☐ Green ☐ Clear

Does the missing person have any broken or healed bones, artificial body parts, or missing body parts? ☐ Yes ☐ No If so, describe

LICENSE PLATE AND VEHICLE INFORMATION

License Plate Number / State / Yr. Exp. / Type

Vehicle Identification #

Year

Make | Model | Style | Color | Other

OTHER INFORMATION

Reporting Agency

Reporting Officer

Complainant's Name

Complainant's Address

Complainant's Telephone Number

Relationship of Complainant to Missing Person

Missing Person's Address

Missing Person's Aliases

Missing Person's Occupation

Miscellaneous Number(s)

Below is a list of clothing and personal effects. Please indicate those items that have been found with the person or body. Include style, type, size, color, condition, etc.

Item	Style/Type	Size	Color	Markings	Item	Style/Type	Size	Color	Markings
Head Gear					Shoes/Boots/Sneakers				
Scarf/Tie/Gloves					Underwear				
Coat/Jacket/Vest					Bra/Girdle/Slip				
Sweater					Stockings/Pantyhose				
Shirt/Blouse					Wallet/Purse				
Pants/Skirt					Money				
Belt/Suspenders					Jewelry	See Back			
Socks					Other				

FIGURE 8.6 Sample missing person report. G. A. Thompson Form MPR-1 reproduced with permission.

SEARCH FOR CURRENT WHEREABOUTS

NAME OF ACTOR__________________________ PLACE OF EMPLOYMENT ______________________
ADDRESS ____
TELEPHONE NO__________________________ CELLULAR ______________________________
DATES RESIDENCE CHECKED _____________ OFFICER ________________________________
PERSON CONTACTED____
ON ________ BY __________ TIME _____ HOW CONTACTED ___________________________
ON ________ BY __________ TIME _____ RESULT __________________________________
ON ________ BY __________ TIME _____
ON ________ BY __________ TIME _____

A RELATIVES____
B NEIGHBORS____
C TELEPHONE COMPANY ____
D BUREAU OF MOTOR VEHICLES ____
E POST OFFICE ____
F PROBATION OFFICE____
G PENITENTIARY ____
H CITY IDENTIFICATION BUREAU____
I BUREAU OF CRIMINAL IDENTIFICATION____
J COUNTY JAIL ____
K OTHER (Specify)____
1 ____________________________________
2 ____________________________________
3 ____________________________________
4 ____________________________________

DATE ____________________	DATE ____________________
OFFICER ____________________	OFFICER ____________________
PERSON CONTACTED____________	PERSON CONTACTED____________
HOW CONTACTED ______________	HOW CONTACTED ______________
RESULT ____________________	RESULT ____________________
DATE ____________________	DATE ____________________
OFFICER ____________________	OFFICER ____________________
PERSON CONTACTED____________	PERSON CONTACTED____________
HOW CONTACTED ______________	HOW CONTACTED ______________
RESULT ____________________	RESULT ____________________
DATE ____________________	DATE ____________________
OFFICER ____________________	OFFICER ____________________
PERSON CONTACTED____________	PERSON CONTACTED____________
HOW CONTACTED ______________	HOW CONTACTED ______________
RESULT ____________________	RESULT ____________________

(If more than six contacts, use separate sheet)

Sworn to and subscribed before me this ________ day of ______________, 20___.
The above is a true and correct summary of the search I conducted on the above-named Actor.

SEAL MAGISTRATE OR NOTARY POLICE OFFICER

FIGURE 8.7 Search for current whereabouts form.

#219
Saturday, June 27, 2009

PROGRESS REPORT: Verbal report of these finding was given to the client on Monday, June 29, 2009. Marvin openly admitted to having stolen several watches and said a female supplied him with these watches. Strong admitted to having stolen PlayStation 3 game disks, which he sold for half (1/2) price on the street to purchase himself some drugs. After lunch, Jones stated that last Saturday, right after work, he observed Keeney drive from the back side of the parking lot to the shipping dock doors, where unusual activity involving Keeney and Griswald occurred. According to Jones, he thinks that Griswald and Keeney worked together to commit a theft. Dalton, who was aided by Don Sheridan, removed two (2) half barrel bar-b-que pits from the pit area of the shipping dock and proceeded to carry them outside the facility by way of the shipping dock garage doors. Dalton indicated that he had been given two grills by Griswald to keep.

Reading of the entire report is recommended.

At the start of today's shift, Gram, Strong, Jones, Dalton, Sheridan, Christine and John were all present for Saturday work. Roger, Nelson and Walker reported to the workplace late. Griswald, the Plant Manager, was noted to be present at the warehouse today. A new employee was also observed briefly on the dock at the start of the shift. He is described as:

> Male, black, age 22, 5'11" tall, 170 lbs., medium build, dark complexion, short curly black hair, thin mustache, wearing a white t-shirt, blue jeans and tennis shoes.

Although not all of the departments throughout receiving were working this date, all of the shipping dock employees observed worked diligently in their efforts to get processed merchandise loaded into trailers, as well as handling two (2) truckloads of Fort Worth merchandise that were unloaded, sorted and tagged for shipment.

At approximately 8:53 am, Merril and Jones discontinued their work efforts and proceeded to the cafeteria on the lower level of the facility where doughnuts were being served for employees who worked today. Employees from other work areas were also noted arriving in the cafeteria prior to the hour of 9:00 am. During this break, Marvin openly stated to a group of employees that he had committed a theft of several watches. Marvin contended that a female employee

FIGURE 8.8 Excerpt from a progress report.

actions. Inspection reports can be as uncomplicated as the Safety Inspection Checklist presented in Figure 8.10, to a slightly more demanding version of a building inspection report, which calls upon the investigator to make remarks or to note corrective action taken. See Figure 8.11.

9. Security Incident Reports

When a wrongdoing is discovered, most security firms compose what is known as an Incident Report (Figure 8.12). The security investigator's first contact with a case often involves a review of this document. A much more simplified checklist version of an incident report is given in Figure 8.13.

10. Investigative Reports

Investigative report forms portray many scenarios. In cases of missing property, a report addressing the circumstances and events surrounding the loss would be completed. Some reports summarize the client's complaint. See Figure 8.14.

Drafted with a checklist design, the Accident Investigation Checklist in Figure 8.15 ensures that the initial as well as subsequent parties assigned have full and complete access to information. A more complete document titled Investigation Report is quite similar to a public police offense report, as shown in Figure 8.16.

11. Traffic Reports

Traffic control violations, for those firms entrusted and empowered in this area, should be catalogued. See Figure 8.17.

BOMB SEARCH REPORT

REMEMBER: Keep well spaced apart
Do not search in adjacent areas.
DO NOT TOUCH SUSPICIOUS OR OUT-OF-PLACE OJECTS.

Area Searched: ______________________________
Suspicious object found at ______________________________
Description of object

____

Sketch of Object

Did the object have a visible or ticking clock timer? Yes/No
Did you see or smell a burning fuse? Yes/No
Did you see trip wires or booby traps? Yes/No
At exactly what time did you find the object? ______________
Sketch of object's position

Is the object easily accessible? Yes/No
DRAW YOUR EXACT ROUTE TO AND FROM THE OBJECT

Did you continue searching the area for other devices? Yes/No
Did you see other suspicious objects? Yes/No
Has area around the object (above/below) been evacuated? Yes/No
Are there people near the object? Yes/No
If yes, how many people are there?______________
Are all evacuees accounted for? Yes/No
Is the suspicious object near fuel/explosives, valuable equipment? Yes/No

HAND THIS FORM TO THE BOMB SQUAD WHEN THEY ARRIVE.

Name: ______________________ Rank: ______________________

FIGURE 8.9 Bomb search report form to be handed to bomb squad when they arrive.

12. Property Reports

In both retail and insurance settings, the private investigator is concerned about the internal and external effects of pilferage. The field investigator must catalog and accurately describe the stolen property in question. The Stolen Property Report requires not only an itemization but also detailed characteristics such as model, size, serial number, age, and value. See Figure 8.18.

Evidence that is found, seized, and secured in the field needs to be itemized for the purposes of ensuring proper chain of custody and acceptable identification. Report forms that itemize property track the journey of the evidence after it is seized. A record or receipt system is most advisable in order to ensure that there is no break in the chain of custody and that the evidence taken by private security operatives has not substantially changed in condition or form. The entry and exit of the

SAFETY INSPECTION CHECKLIST

Plant or department ____________________ Date ____________

This list is intended as only a reminder. Look for other unsafe acts and conditions, and then report them so that corrective action can be taken. Not particularly whether unsafe acts or conditions that have caused accidents have been corrected. Note also whether potential accident causes, marked "X" on previous inspection, have been corrected.

(✓) Indicates Satisfactory **(X) Indicates Unsatisfactory**

1. Fire Protection
- Extinguishing equipment ☐
- Standpipes, hoses, sprinkler heads, and valves ☐
- Exits, stairs, and signs ☐
- Storage of flammable material ☐

2. Housekeeping
- Aisles, stairs and floors ☐
- Storage and piling of material ☐
- Wash and locker rooms ☐
- Light and ventilation ☐
- Disposal of waste ☐
- Yards and parking lots ☐

3. Tools
- Power tools, wiring ☐
- Hand tools ☐
- Use and storage of tools ☐

4. Personal Protective Equipment
- Goggles or face shields ☐
- Safety shoes ☐
- Gloves ☐
- Respirators or gas masks ☐
- Protective clothing ☐

5. Material Handling Equipment
- Power trucks, hand trucks ☐
- Elevators ☐
- Cranes and hoists ☐
- Conveyors ☐
- Cables, ropes, chains, slings ☐

6. Bulletin Boards
- Neat and attractive ☐
- Display changed regularly ☐
- Well illuminated ☐

7. Machinery
- Point of operation guards ☐
- Belts, pulleys, gears, shafts, etc. ☐
- Oiling, cleaning, and adjusting ☐
- Maintenance and oil leakage ☐

8. Pressure equipment
- Steam Equipment ☐
- Air receivers and compressors ☐
- Gas cylinders and hose ☐

9. Unsafe Practices
- Excessive speed of vehicles ☐
- Improper Lifting ☐
- Smoking in danger areas ☐
- Horseplay ☐
- Running in aisles or on stairs ☐
- Improper use of air hoses ☐
- Removing machine or other guards ☐
- Work on unguarded moving machinery ☐

10. First Aid
- First aid kits and rooms ☐
- Stretchers and fire blankets ☐
- Emergency showers ☐
- All injuries reported ☐

11. Miscellaneous
- Acids and caustics ☐
- New processes, chemicals, and solvents ☐
- Dusts, vapors, or fumes ☐
- Ladders and scaffolds ☐

Signed

Use reverse side for detailed comments or recommendations

FIGURE 8.10 Safety inspection checklist/reminder form.

BUILDING SECURITY INSPECTION REPORT

A Security Inspection was made at ____________________________ on date and at the time shown below. Conditions, if any, having a bearing on the protection of Company property are also noted below.

Security Representative__________________________________

District ____ Date__________________________ 20____

Complete address of property inspected — Time From ___________ -AM

Central Office ( ) District ( ) Garage ( ) Locker ( ) Work Center ( ) — ___________ -PM

Carrier Hut ( ) Vehicle ( ) Acctg. Bldg. ( ) Commercial Bldg. ( ) — To ___________ -AM

___________ -PM

Regular Means of Admittance: Guard ( ) Locked doors or gate ( ) Door Tele. ( )

Code key set ( ) Cable box lock ( ) Sesame lock ( )

No.	Item		Satisfactory	Unsatisfactory	Remarks-Briefly describe conditions that prompted "unsatisfactory" classification and corrective action taken	
1.	Appropriate illumination					
2.	Condition of locks					
3.	Condition of fences					
4.	Condition of gates					
5.	Basement entrances					
6.	Outside doors					
7.	Windows					
8.	Guard services					
9.	Storage – Cable					
10.	Material storage, Cages					
11.	Tool storage					
12.	Talking set storage, Cages					
13.	Car or bin doors unlocked					
14.	Fire hazards					
15.	Identification & accountability of others found on premises	Employees				
		Non-employees				
16.	Responsible department advised:		Date:	Title:	Name	
17.	Repeated Condition:		Number ( ) above			

Use other side if necessary

FIGURE 8.11 Report form used during a building inspection.

SECURITY DEPARTMENT INCIDENT REPORT					
OFFENSE CATEGORY	DATE-TIME RECEIVED	DAY OF WEEK	DATE MO DAY YR	TIME AM. PM.	INVESTIGATION NO.

FORCED ENTRY		COMPLAINANT'S NAME	HOME PHONE
THEFT	PERS. PROP.		
	COMPANY PROP.	ADDRESS	BUSINESS PHONE
	COIN MACHINE		
	AUTO	STATUS ☐ VISITOR ☐ EMPLOYEE ☐ OTHER (SPECIFY)	
ROBBERY			

ASSAULT	DATE-TIME OF OFFENSE	DAY OF WEEK	DATE MO DAY YR	TIME AM. PM.
RAPE				
MANSLAUGHTER	PLACE	WEAPON USED		
DISTURBANCE				
VANDALISM				
TRAFFIC	TRADEMARK			
OTHER (SPECIFY)				

VICTIM'S NAME	ADDRESS		
SEX ☐ M ☐ F	AGE	RACE	STATUS ☐ VISITOR ☐ EMPLOYEE ☐ OTHER (SPECIFY)

MEDICAL TREATMENT ☐ YES (EXPLAIN) ☐ NO	DESCRIPTION OF LOST PROPERTY	VALUE

DESCRIPTION OF OFFENDERS								
NO. 1	SEX ☐ M ☐ F	RACE	HEIGHT	BUILD	EYES	HAIR	GLASSES ☐ Y ☐ N	COMPLEXION
	MARKS				AGE	HAT	COAT	SHIRT
NO. 2	SEX ☐ M ☐ F	RACE	HEIGHT	BUILD	EYES	HAIR	GLASSES ☐ Y ☐ N	COMPLEXION
	MARKS				AGE	HAT	COAT	SHIRT

WITNESS NAME 1.	ADDRESS	TELEPHONE
WITNESS NAME 2.	ADDRESS	TELEPHONE

LAW ENFORCEMENT AGENCY NOTIFIED	TIME	PERSON
1.	☐ AM ☐ PM	
2.	☐ AM ☐ PM	

NAME OF PERSON ARRESTED 1.	ADDRESS
NAME OF PERSON ARRESTED 2.	ADDRESS

CHARGES	
1.	2.

WAS PHYSICAL FORCE USED? ☐ YES ☐ NO	
SIGNATURE OF REPORTING OFFICER DATE	FOR SECURITY OFFICE USE ONLY APPROVED ____________ DATE NAME CARD COMPLETED ____________

FIGURE 8.12 Security department incident report form.

NARRATIVE – BE SPECIFIC IN WRITING OF THIS REPORT. BE SURE TO USE THE GUIDELINES: WHO, WHAT, WHEN, WHY, WHERE AND HOW. DESCRIPBE OFFENSE IN DETAIL, INCLUDE INITIAL STATEMENTS UTTERED BY VICTIM, WITNESSES AND SUSPECTS. EXAMPLE: IN CAR THEFT, WHAT WAS VICTIM'S RESPONSE TO DIRECT QUESTION, "WAS CAR LOCKED?" DESCRIBE SCENE OF OFFENSE AND CONTRIBUTORY CONDITIONS SUCH AS POOR LIGHTING, EXTREME ISOLATION, ETC. LIST EVIDENCE FOUND AT SCENE AND ALL OTHER RELEVANT INFORMATION SUCH AS SOBRIETY OF VICTIM, WITNESSES AND SUSPECTS. SAFEGUARD REPORT FOR REFERENCE.

FOR SECURITY DEPARTMENT USE ONLY

THIS OFFENSE IS DECLARED:

- UNFOUNDED ☐
- CLEARED BY ARREST ☐
- EXCEPTIONALLY CLEARED ☐
- INACTIVE (NOT CLEARED) ☐

SIGNED____________________ DATE ________
SECURITY DIRECTOR

FIGURE 8.12 (continued).

evidence from storage, a lab, or other protected facility should be tracked by log and chronological time frame.

13. Basic Security Survey

If called upon to determine a breach of security in a government installation, business, or industrial concern, investigators frequently compile a security survey. The security survey document, such as that in Figure 8.19, forms a permanent impression of a company's current security status. It is relied upon by policymakers and business officers in strategic decision making. The survey of the facility, place, or location is a comprehensive analysis of the entire physical plant, the perimeter, and the level of security or lack thereof.

SECURITY DEPARTMENT
INCIDENT REPORT

NATURE OF INCIDENT REPORT NO.

☐ Theft Of Property ☐ Liquor Violation
☐ Vandalism ☐ Other ______________________ ______________________

Date And Time Of Report

☐ Trespassing ______________________ ______________________

Date And Time Of Incident

☐ Time Card Violation ______________________ ______________________

Location Of Incident

☐ Unauthorized Entry/Exit ______________________

REPORT IN DETAIL: WHO WHAT WHEN WHERE HOW WHY

Complainant	Clock Or Social Security No	Department Or Address
Offender	Clock Or Social Security No	Department Or Address
Witness	Clock Or Social Security No	Department Or Address

DESCRIPTION OF INCIDENT: ______________________

Estimate of Theft or Damage $__________ Reported by: ______________________

Continued on Reverse side? ☐ Yes ☐ No ______________________

Security Officer Badge No.

FIGURE 8.13 Another sample security department incident report.

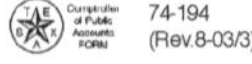
74-194
(Rev.8-03/3)

CLEAR FORM

MISSING, DAMAGED OR STOLEN PROPERTY REPORT

NOTE: If property has been stolen or is lost, destroyed or damaged as a result of negligence, this form should be completed and sent to the Office of the Attorney General within 72 hours of the occurrance.

Name of agency / institution	Agency no.

Place of occurrence	City	County

Police agency notified	Police report number	Disposal code	Estimated value at date of loss

SERIAL NUMBER(S)	PURCHASE DATE	PURCHASE VALUE

STATE PROPERTY NUMBER	COMPONENT NUMBER	DESCRIPTION	LOCATION

Person(s) responsible for asset(s)	Property Manager name	Property Manager phone

Report in detail (including what security measures were in place at the time.)

Please check one box.

☐ Our investigation of the circumstances surrounding the state property listed herein indicates reasonable cause to believe that the loss, destruction, or damage to this property **was** through the negligence of the person(s) charged with the care and custody of this property.

☐ Our investigation of the circumstances surrounding the state property listed herein indicates reasonable cause to believe that the loss, destruction, or damage to this property **was not** through the negligence of the person(s) charged with the care and custody of this property.

This form should be signed and dated by the agency/institution head or designated representative. If a designated representative completes this form, the rank of that individual should be greater than that of the property manager.

sign here ▶	Date
Printed name and title	

Retain this form for your files. If the property was missing, damaged, or stolen due to employee negligence, submit a copy of this form and a copy of the police report, if applicable, to the Office of the Attorney General. If your agency is in Austin, a copy may be sent via interagency mail. Otherwise, fax a copy to the Attorney General at (512) 479-8067.

FIGURE 8.14 Form used to record missing, stolen or damaged property.

ACCIDENT INVESTIGATION CHECKLIST		
	1. Driver #1	Name, address, and telephone number
		Driver's license number and state
		Date of birth
	2. Vehicle #1	Owner's name, address and telephone number
		Year, make, model, and color of vehicle
		Registration number and state
		Insured by: Name and address of Insurance Company
	3. Driver #2 Vehicle #2	If more than one vehicle, follow procedures 1 and 2. If more than one vehicle, follow procedures 1 and 2.
	4. Passengers	Name, address, telephone number, and date of birth.
		Position in vehicle (Left front #1, Right rear #2, etc.)
	5. Statements	Was vehicle moving (forward, backward), stopped in traffic lane, parked, etc.?
		If moving, in what direction? (North, South, etc.)
		What was the driver doing? (Turning right/left, going straight ahead, slowing down, backing from parked position, avoiding animal or pedestrian, etc.)
		Statements, in the report, should start by saying, Driver #1, (their name) stated in effect ....DO NOT USE QUOTES OR OPINIONS!
		Was vision obscured? (Other vehicles, trees, shrubs, etc.)
		Was any mechanical defect stated? If so, check.
	6. Witnesses	Name, address, telephone number, age
		How far they were from the scene (50 ft. North, etc.)
		What they actually saw or heard.
		DO NOT USE QUOTES OR OPINIONS!
	7. Injured	Name, address, telephone number, age
		Driver or passenger in what vehicle?
		List only apparent or known injuries. DON'T GUESS!
		Where injured were taken, how, and by whom.

FIGURE 8.15 Accident investigation checklist.

B. Major Criminal Documentation

1. The Offense Report

The offense report, often referred to as the *general crime report*, is the first major document completed in the examination and investigation of a *criminal* case. An offense report, such as that provided in Figure 8.20, calls for a fairly comprehensive examination of the *actus reus*—the illegal conduct under review. For example, Item 28, the narrative column, calls upon the report writer to fill in details of the criminal conduct. In order to corroborate this position, suspects, contacts, and other personnel involved in the case are catalogued. If the report document does not have sufficient space, most security firms have a continuation sheet or a supplemental report form. The supplemental report can be used to update the status of an investigation.

INVESTIGATION REPORT

1 Referral/Connecting/Property Slip #	2 Code	3 UCR Code	4 Trans Disc No	5 Case Number

6 Crime ☐ Accident ☐	7 Patrol District	8 NJS	9 Victim's Name		
			10 Race	11 Sex	12 Age

13 Date/Time Between At	14 hr.	15 Wk.	16 Mo.	17 Day	18 Year	19 Home address – City – State Phone

20 Location	21 Employer-School	22 Business Phone

23 Time Unit Notified	24 Person Reporting Crime	25 Age	26 Date and Time

27 Type of Premises	28 Code	29 Weapons-Tools	30 Code	31 Address	32 Phone

	33 Vehicle	34 Year	35 Make	36 Body Type	37 Color	38 Reg. Number & State	39 Serial Number

Value Stolen Prop	40 Currency	41 Jewelry	42 Furs	43 Clothing	44 Auto	45 Misc.

46 Total Value Stolen	47 Total Value Recovered	48 Teletype Yes ☐ No ☐	49 Alarm No.	50 Weather	51 Status Crime	52 Status Case

53 Cleared by Arrest

	Adult ☐	Juvenile ☐	Adult and Juvenile ☐	Narcotics Involved ☐

LIST INVOLVED—LIST AND IDENTIFY ADDITIONAL VICTIMS—DESCRIBE PERPETRATORS OR SUSPECTS—ACTION TAKEN INCLUDES FINDINGS AND OBSERVATIONS OF INVESTIGATOR—PHYSICAL EVIDENCE FOUND—WHERE—BY WHOM—DISPOSITION AND TECHNICAL SERVICES PERFORMED—INTERVIEW OF VICTIMS—WITNESSES—PERSONS CONTACTED—SUSPECTS—LIST—DESCRIBE STOLEN PROPERTY—VALUE—COURT ACTION—ATTACH STATEMENTS

54 Person Involved Address	Phone No.	Race	Sex	DOB	Arrest Suspect Witness
					☐
					☐
					☐
					☐
					☐

NARRATIVE:

55 Type Name	56 Badge Number	57 Page__ of __ Pages	58 Date of Report	61 Case No.
Signature________________	59 Typist		60 Desk Supervisor	

FIGURE 8.16 Sample investigation report form.

TRAFFIC VIOLATION LOG	Period:	Date:
Operation:	Designation:	Page: of:

TIME/DATE	VEHICLE DESCRIPTION	LICENSE/PERMIT	TYPE	COUNT	LOCATION

FIGURE 8.17 Sample of traffic violation log.

STOLEN PROPERTY REPORT

1. Victim's Name (Last, First, Middle)		2. Complaint No.
3. Victim's Address	4. Phone	5. Cell Phone
6. Address of Crime	7. Date of Crime	8. Date of Report

DESCRIPTION OF LOST/STOLEN PROPERTY

Quantity	Complete Item Description (Make, Model, Shape, Identifying Marks)	Color	Men'sor Women's	Size	Serial No.	Model No.	Age	Value

I understand that copies of this form may be distributed as necessary to requesting insurance agencies and further that all items listed have, to the best of my knowledge, been stolen.

Signature ____________________ Date ____________________

10. Victim Remarks

OFFICE USE ONLY

Date Received by

11. Instructions for completing form:
   a. Complete items 1–10 (except Complaint No.) neatly and accurately
   b. Complete include a detailed description, including photographs or drawings.
   c. Each item must include an approximately age and value.
   d. Please request aditional forms for additional listings.
   e. Return this form as soon as possible to: ____________________

Unit Referred to:

Reproduced by

Reviewer:

12. Reporting Officer No.	13. NCIC Entry by	14. Department Entry by	Page of

FIGURE 8.18 Sample of stolen property report.

BUSINESS SECURITY SURVEY

Business Name ______________________ Phone______________________

Address ____

______________________ Date______________________

	YES	NO	N/A
DOORS			
Do you have dead bolt on all exterior doors?	YES	NO	N/A
Have you taken care of side and rear door security? (solid steel doors, reinforcing bars, no outside handles)	YES	NO	N/A
Do outside doors have hinges on outside? (Install non-removable hinge pins)	YES	NO	N/A
Do you check all doors before leaving?	YES	NO	N/A
WINDOWS			
Have you taken care of side and rear window security? (Bars or grating on windows)	YES	NO	N/A
Do you check all windows before leaving?	YES	NO	N/A
KEY SECURITY			
Are all issued keys signed for employees?	YES	NO	N/A
Are all keys turned in when employees end employment?	YES	NO	N/A
Do you change locks if not?	YES	NO	N/A
Are keys labeled with their use? (If yes, discontinue and use coding system if needed)	YES	NO	N/A
LIGHTS			
Are all entrances/exits well-lit?	YES	NO	N/A
Are all sides of building well-lit?	YES	NO	N/A
Are there any dark areas around building?	YES	NO	N/A
Do you use motion detector lights?	YES	NO	N/A
Do you keep outside/inside lights on after closing?	YES	NO	N/A
ALARMS			
Do you use an alarm system that covers all points of entry? (Doors, windows, roof opening, loading dock, vents)	YES	NO	N/A
Do you have a current permit for the alarm from municipality?	YES	NO	N/A
Is the alarm monitored by an alarm company?	YES	NO	N/A
Is the alarm monitored by a police department?	YES	NO	N/A
Do you change the alarm code when employees leave?	YES	NO	N/A
CASH CONTROL			
Do you keep as little cash as possible on hand?	YES	NO	N/A
Do you make frequent bank deposits?	YES	NO	N/A
Do you make those deposits at different times?	YES	NO	N/A
Do you have a safe?	YES	NO	N/A
Is the safe anchored securely to the floor?	YES	NO	N/A
Is the safe in a well-lit, visible location?	YES	NO	N/A
Do you empty cash drawers at closing?	YES	NO	N/A
Do you keep bait money in the cash drawer that is traceable?	YES	NO	N/A

FIGURE 8.19 Sample business security survey form.

PHYSICAL ARRANGEMENT			
Do you keep front windows clear of signs/displays?	YES	NO	N/A
Do you put displays in full view of employees?	YES	NO	N/A
Do you keep expensive items away from entrances/exits?	YES	NO	N/A
Do you keep small items in counter cases?	YES	NO	N/A
Do you lock up small items at closing?	YES	NO	N/A
Do you keep front of premises visible from street?	YES	NO	N/A
TRAINING			
Are your employees trained in security?	YES	NO	N/A
ADDITIONAL CONCERNS			
Have you checked every exterior/interior opening? (Fire escapes, skylights, air ducts, suspended ceiling, etc.)	YES	NO	N/A
Do you check all potential hiding places at closing?	YES	NO	N/A
Do you keep tools/ladders lying outside?	YES	NO	N/A
Do you have more than one employee working at all times? (If not, play radio in back room to give idea of other worker)	YES	NO	N/A
Are you concerned about employee theft?	YES	NO	N/A
Do you thoroughly check references?	YES	NO	N/A
Do you tempt employees by being careless about security?	YES	NO	N/A
Do you tempt employees by overlooking losses?	YES	NO	N/A

FIGURE 8.19 (continued).

2. Arrest Report

Private security investigators have the same powers of arrest as any citizen and in most jurisdictions are held to a reasonable suspicion standard. Individuals are required to document all arrests for liability and record-keeping purposes. Police simply take over after a suspect has been arrested. Despite this looser legal standard governing arrest, search, and seizure activities for private police, the individual agents and the industry itself must be vigilant and regular about its activities. Documentation not only prompts regularity in due process but also cuts down on abuse. For security, the lawsuit is the deterrent to abuse of policing. The National Center for Policy Analysis reminds the investigator of its sharp teeth:

> Lawsuits are more potent against private enforcers than public enforcers. Victims of erroneous arrests and prosecutions can successfully sue private agents for damages. Although a wrongfully arrested person may have little status or money, lawyers are available on a contingency basis and the arrestor's employer usually would be a suable (insured) "deep pocket." The employer is responsible for the on-the-job damages of his or her employees under the doctrine of respondent superior. Nor will abusive firms receive many contracts for enforcement services. Competition and the common law promote quality protective services at prices customers are willing to pay.[16]

An example of an arrest document that a private security investigator would complete is given in Figure 8.21.

3. Defendant's Statement

As a precautionary measure, even though not legally required of all private security companies, before eliciting information or interrogating witnesses, the interviewee should be advised of his or her legal rights. There has been some challenge to the nonapplicability of constitutional (Miranda)

OFFENSE REPORT		17 Rep Area	1 Victim's Name (Last, First, Middle)	1A M.O. No.	2 Complaint No.
18 Attachments ☐ Supplemental ☐ Property ☐ Arrest ☐ Vehicle ☐ Other________	19 Time Disp 20 Time Clear	3 Victim's Address City 5 Victim's Place of Employment or School			4 Res. Phone 6 Bus. Phone
21 Weather		7 Victim's Sex – Race- Age	8 Location of Crime (Address)		
22 Describe Location of Offense		9 Reporting Person Sex – Race- Age			10 Res. Phone
23 Requested ☐ Crim. Inv. ☐ Traffic ☐ Juvenile ☐ Request to patrol ☐ Other________		11 Reporting Person's Address City			12 Bus. Phone
		13 Day, Date and Time Occurred		14 Date and Time reported	
		15 Crime or Incident	15A Crime Compensation ☐ YES ☐ NO		16 UCR

Parent Guardian Witness	24 Name	Age	Best Contact Address	Best Phone	Other Phone
	(1)				
	(2)				

Missing Persons Suspects	25 Name - Address	Sex	Race	DOB	Ht	Wt	Hair	Eyes	Other	Clothing
	(1)									
	(2)									
	(3)									

Vehicle Involved	26 Year – Make - Model	Color(s)	Reg No. – State - Year	Identifying Characteristics

27 Property ☐ Lost ☐ Stolen ☐ Damaged ☐ Other	Quan.	Description – Size – Color – Model – Style – Material – Condition	Serial No	Where Located	Age	Total Value

Item No	28 NARRATIVE (1) CONTINUATION OF ABOVE ITEMS (INDICATE ITEM NUMBER CONTINUED AT LEFT), INCLUDE ADDITIONAL VICTIMS, WITNESSES AND SUSPECTS AS OUTLINED ABOVE (2) DESCRIBE DETAILS OF INCIDENT (3) DESCRIBE EVIDENCE AND PROPERTY AND INDICATE DISPOSITION (4) M.O. – HOW DONE – FORCE USED – AT WHAT POINT – WITH WHAT TOOL OR WEAPON – OTHER ACTS
	OFFICE USE ONLY 34 Date · 35 Reproduced by

29 Reporting Officer No	30 Status ☐ UNFOUNDED ☐ CLEARED & CLOSED ☐ OPEN ☐ SUSPENDED		36 Unit Referred to	
31 2nd Officer No	32 Supervisor Approving	33 Daily Bulletin ☐ YES ☐ NO	37 Reviewer	Page of

FIGURE 8.20 Sample offense report form.

protections in the private sector. When police/private police work closely on a particular case, the potential for entanglement exists. These relationships, whereby private security, not bound by constitutional principles, provide public officers with evidence they could have not secured otherwise, is known as the "platinum platter doctrine."[17] Mutual cooperation or assistance on a case may provide a constitutional defense for a defendant at a later date.

Arrest Report	14 Rep Area	1 Suspect's Name (Last, First, Middle)	1A M.O. No.	2 Complaint No.
15 Location of Arrest		3 Suspect's Address City		4 Arrest No/Grade
16 Describe Type of Premises		5 Sex Race DOB Ht Wt Hair Eyes		6 ID No.
17 Day, Date/Time Arrested		7 NCIC Check Time		8 Social Security No.
18 Breathalyzer/Operator/ Time/ Reading	19 Parent/Guardian/Time Notified ☐YES ☐NO	9 Place of Birth	10 Weapon (Describe) Serial No.	
20 Resist? ☐YES ☐NO	21 Narcotic? ☐YES ☐NO 22 Armed? ☐YES ☐NO	11 Occupation	12 Res. Phone	13 Bus. Phone
23 Where suspect Employed or School		24 Day, Date/Time Occurred	25 Date/Time Reported	
26 Suspect Operators License No. State		27 Formal Charges		28 UCR
29 Hold Placed on Vehicle ☐YES ☐NO	Towed to	30 Charges Changed to		Date/Time

31 Vehicle Involved Year/Make/Model Color(s) Reg. No./State/Year 31A Vehicle Registered Owner Address

CODE: C-COMPLAINANT V-VICTIM W-WITNESS P-PARENT/GUARDIAN CO-SUSPECT

32 Name	Code	Residence	City	Res. Phone	Bus. Phone
(1)					
(2)					
(3)					
(4)					
(5)					

33 Arrest Procedure
(A) Arrested __Hrs. (B) Rights __ Hrs. (C) Transported __ Hrs. (D) Arrived __ Hrs.
(E) Processed & Rights __ Hrs. (F) Interviewed __ Hrs. (G) Arraigned __ Hrs. (H) Released/Committed __Hrs.
(I) Implied Consent Law __ Hrs.

Item. No.	34 Narrative (1) Continuation of above items (indicate "Item Number" at left) (2) Describe Details of incident not listed above (3) Identify additional witnesses, victims, etc. from Block No. 32.

35 Transporting Officer No	36 Arresting Officer No	37 Booking Officer No	
38 Transporting Officer No	39 Arresting Officer No	40 Searched by No	
41 Suspect's Money	42 Supervisor Approving	43 Daily Bulletin ☐YES ☐NO	Page of

FIGURE 8.21 Sample arrest report.

44 OFFICER'S OBSERVATIONS

ODOR OF ALCOHOL: Strong ☐ Moderate ☐ Faint ☐ Other ______

COMPLEXION: Flushed ☐ Mottled ☐ Pale ☐ Normal ☐ Other ______

EYES: Bloodshot ☐ Watery ☐ Glassy ☐ Contracted ☐ Dilated ☐ Other ______
Wearing Glasses ☐ Contact Lenses ☐

SPEECH: Incoherent ☐ Confused ☐ Jerky ☐ Profane ☐ Stuttering ☐ Good ☐ Other ______

BALANCE: Staggering ☐ Swaying ☐ Unable To Stand ☐ Needed Assistance To Walk ☐ Other ______

MENTAL ATTITUDE: Polite ☐ Excited ☐ Talkative ☐ Hilarious ☐ Combative ☐ Stupefied ☐
Other ______

CLOTHING CONDITION: Disorderly ☐ Orderly ☐ Soiled By Vomit ☐ Soiled By Urine ☐ Partly Dressed ☐
Other ______

CLOTHING (*Describe Clothing and Color of Garments*) ______
______

DEFENDANT INJURED? Yes ☐ No ☐ Retained in Hospital? Yes ☐ No ☐ Doctor ______

NATURE OF INJURIES ______
______

45 REASON FOR STOP

Driving Too Fast/Slow ☐ Accident ☐ Driving In Anappropriate Area ☐ Weaving/Drifting ☐
Nearly Striking Car Or Object ☐ Wide Radius Turn ☐ Stops Without Cause ☐ Looks Intoxicated ☐
Not In Marked Lane ☐ Equipment Violation ☐ Ran Stop Sign/Light ☐ Following Too Closely ☐
Bright/No Lights ☐
Other ______

46 FIELD TEST

1
WALK AND TURN
☐ Can't keep balance while listening to instructions
☐ Starts before instructions finished
☐ Stops while walking to steady
☐ Does not touch heel to toe
☐ Loses balance while walking
☐ Incorrect number of steps
☐ Cannot/refuses to do test

2
ONE LEG STAND
☐ Swaying while balancing
☐ Uses arms to balance
☐ Quite unsteady
☐ Puts foot down
☐ Cannot/refuses test

3
ALCOTEST
Mark level of discoloration

Instructions read per mtl form ______ ☐

47 CHEMICAL TESTING

Time of Test ______

CHEMICAL BREATH TEST: Administered by ______ Serial# ______

Device ______ Serial # ______

Results ______

URINE TEST SAMPLE: Obtained by ______

Sample Stored in ______

BLOOD SAMPLE: Taken by ______ At ______ Hospital

Sample Stored In ______ At ______ For Transportation

To ______ Lab ______

FIGURE 8.21 (continued).

WARNING

Before you are asked any question, you must understand your rights.

You have the right to remain silent.

Anything you say will be used against you in court.

You have the right to talk to a lawyer for advice before we ask you any questions and to have him or her with you during questioning.

If you cannot afford a lawyer, one will be appointed free of charge, at any time.

If you decide to answer questions now, without a lawyer present, you will still have the right to stop answering at any time. You also have the right to stop answering at any time until you talk to a lawyer.

This statement of my right has been read to me by the undersigned officer and I understand what my rights are.

Signed____________________________ Date__________ Time __________

Witness: ____

Witness: ____

FIGURE 8.22 Miranda warning.

To ensure testimonial admissibility, some private security investigators relay the Miranda warning (Figure 8.22). These rights may be waived, but the waiver must be made voluntarily, knowingly, and intelligently (Figure 8.23).

If a suspect's vehicle, personal effects, or other property are going to be searched, it is advisable, before commencing a search, to document and record the consent of the suspected party. The same constitutional challenge, as noted above, has been made, though unsuccessfully, in Fourth Amendment cases.[18] See Figure 8.24.

Once these constitutional issues have been addressed, acquire a statement from the suspect or witness. Witness statement documents come in many formats. Figure 8.25 provides one example.

WAIVER

This statement of my rights has been read to me by the undersigned officer, and I understand what my rights are. I am willing to make a statement and answer questions. I do not want a lawyer. I understand and know what I am doing. No promises or threats have been made to me, and no pressure or coercion of any kind has been used against me.

Signed__________________________ Date__________ Time__________

Witness: ____

Witness: ____

FIGURE 8.23 Waiver of rights form.

CONSENT TO SEARCH

[DATE]

STATE OF

COUNTY OF

I, ____________________, having been informed of my constitutional right not to have a search made of my automobile hereinafter mentioned without a search warrant and of my right to refuse to consent to such a search, hereby authorize ____________________ and ______________________________, Officers of the ____________________ Police Department, in ____________________, ____________________, to conduct a complete search of my automobile, a ______________________________, registration number ______________________. These officers are authorized by me to take from my automobile any letters, papers, materials or other property which may have been involved in an unlawful act. I realize that anything found by said officers that I cannot account for may be used as evidence against me in the event of a court trial.

This written permission is being given by me to the above-named Police Officers voluntarily and without threats or promises of any kind.

Signed__________________________ Date__________ Time__________

Witness: ____

Witness: ____

FIGURE 8.24 Consent to search form.

WITNESS STATEMENT

I, ______________________________, Age_______, Sex_______, Occupation ______________________ Address ______________________ ______________________, do hereby make the following statement of my own free will and accord concerning ______________________ ______________________, which occurred ______________________ ______________________ on the ______________________ day of ______________________, 20____.

Time:______________________

FIGURE 8.25 Sample witness statement form.

NOTES

1. Tim Dees, "Report Writing Aids," *Law and Order*. (December 2003), 18.
2. R. Colling, *Hospital Security*, 2nd edition (Butterworth: Heineman, 1982), 235. See how the rise of technology has influenced report writing in: Bryan Roberts, "The Keyboard Is Mightier than the Sword," *J. Calif. L. Enforcement*. 41 (2007), 14.
3. W. Bennett and K. Hess, *Criminal Investigation* (West Publishing, 1981), 79.
4. "Information Technology: More Police Departments Use Software Programs to Help Officers File Reports," *L. Enforcement Employment Bul.* (May 2007), 1.
5. Colling, *supra* note 2, at 234.
6. R. Gallati, *Introduction to Private Security* (Prentice Hall, 1983), 262.
7. Pinkerton's, Inc., *Investigator's Guide: Report Writing* (1990), 1.
8. *Id.* at 5.
9. Gallati, *supra* note 4, at 256.
10. *Id.* at 2.
11. C. Cox and J. Brown, *Report Writing for Criminal Justice Professionals* (Anderson, 1992), 14–15.
12. American Society for Industrial Security, *Basic Guidelines for Industrial Security* (1981), 63.
13. G. A. Thompson Co., P.O. Box 720254, Dallas, TX 75372, Form LE-7.
14. Ralph F. Brislin, *The Effective Security Officer's Training Manual* (Butterworth-Heinemann, 1995), 101–102.
15. G. A. Thompson Co., P.O. Box 720254, Dallas, TX 75372, Form MPR-1.
16. National Center for Policy Analysis, Potential Abuses under Private Law Enforcement, at http://www.mcpa.org; See also Charles P. Nemeth and K. C. Poulin, *Private Security and Public Safety: A Community-Based Approach* (Pearson Prentice Hall, 2005), 294.
17. Charles P. Nemeth, *Private Security and the Law*, 3rd edition (Butterworth-Heinemann, 2005), 88.
18. *Id.*

9 Investigative Method and Technique

Theft/Property Offenses

I. INTRODUCTION

Property offenses have a monumental impact on both personal and business environments. The impact of economic crime and its related costs are difficult to fully define and appreciate because criminal conduct takes on many forms and directions.[1]

> In an annual study of waste and abuse of on-the-job time, it was estimated that in 1981 employees cost the American economy "a staggering $120 billion" resulting from employee "time theft"—excessive socializing, conducting personal business on employer time, late arrivals, abuse of sick leave, etc. An interesting example of fraud is the estimated $73.2 million a year lost by the Bell Telephone operating companies through fraudulent billings, that is, telephone calls charged to a number that is not the caller's own. About $48 million of the loss is from pay phones.[2]

Those numbers have continued unabated until the present.[3]

Theft, retail shoplifting, corporate fraud, and other forms of white-collar crime attack not only profit potential in the commercial marketplace, but also undermine institutional and employer trust and, unfortunately, cause an indirect escalation of prices inevitably passed on to consumers. Economic crime impacts society in many indirect ways, such as:

1. BUSINESS Effects
   - increased costs of insurance and security protection;
   - costs of internal audit activities to detect crime;
   - cost of investigation and prosecution of suspects measured in terms of lost time of security and management personnel;
   - reduced profits;
   - increased selling prices and weakened competitive standing;
   - loss of productivity;
   - loss of business reputation;
   - deterioration in quality of service;
   - threats to the survival of small business.
2. LOCAL GOVERNMENT Effects
   - costs of investigation and prosecution of suspects;
   - increased costs of prosecuting sophisticated (e.g., embezzlement) and technology-related (e.g., computer) crime;
   - costs of correctional programs to deal with economic crime offenders;
   - cost of crime prevention programs;
   - cost of crime reporting and mandated security programs;
   - loss of tax revenue (e.g., loss of sales tax, untaxed income of perpetrator, and tax deductions allowed business for crime-related losses).

3. PUBLIC Effects
   - increased costs of consumer goods and services to offset crime losses;
   - loss of investor equity;
   - increased taxes;
   - reduced employment due to business failures.[4]

Although there may be considerable disagreement as to the exact amounts of economic losses due to theft and other property offenses, it is a certainty that "[c]rimes victimize all businesses, small or large, retail, wholesale, manufacturing, or service."[5] Cunningham and Taylor concur:

> Even using similar crime index and inflationary adjusting techniques, the direct cost of economic crime which was at least $67 billion in 1980, and other estimates, though not substantiated, would place economic crime at $200–300 billion. The cumulative direct and indirect costs are much greater, and valid estimates are necessary if public and private organizations are to allocate their resources cost-effectively.[6]

Case clearance rates—the rate at which cases are closed through a resolution and identification of the perpetrator—are low in property crime categorizations. Police resources and energies are more likely to be allotted for major personal crimes such as murder, rape, and robbery. Our culture has become so inundated with personal, felonious conduct that property offenses tend to take a back seat in the investigative scheme of things. There have even been efforts to "decriminalize" offenses such as shoplifting.[7]

Instead of referring to it as a traditional larceny, that is, the unlawful taking of another's property, legislators have constructed and designed a new statute for shoplifting that is less felonious than an actual larceny. Prosecution clearance rates, a measure of successful convictions, are even less impressive.

Private security operatives with residential contract responsibilities have a heavy burden in identifying and apprehending residential burglars. Aside from apprehension and identification, the security officer is also obliged to assist the client in the recovery of lost property. In an overwhelming number of cases, property lost in burglary cases (particularly those that involve little use of force) is rarely recovered.

From varied perspectives, the costs of crime from both personal and business viewpoints, are immeasurably negative.

> The impact of the many crimes against business cannot be ignored, since losses or shrinkages of the magnitude described cannot be tolerated. Crime against business has reached such proportions that it has been recognized as a major contributing factor in some business closings and corporate bankruptcies. The business community must begin to emphasize aggressive policies and procedures that anticipate and fight criminal opportunities that are particularly common to the business world.[8]

The focus of this chapter is the recurring criminal conduct that plagues private and public law enforcement—namely, retail theft and shoplifting, other forms of larceny, auto theft, and internal fraud. As a reminder, other portions of the text expound upon related principles.[9]

II. SHOPLIFTING

A plague of shoplifting occurs every day in the American economy. How has this plague come about? How do the thieves and actors rationalize the acts? What steps are being taken to minimize the damage?

A. Rationalizations and Justifications for Shoplifting

Business planners and other entrepreneurs take for granted a certain level of internal and external pilferage and shoplifting. Shoplifting has reached epidemic proportions due to a host of factors, including but not limited to cultural tolerance, sheer volume, a lack of remedy and corresponding consequence, and a legal system incapable of handling the rush of cases. In addition to these explanations, the perpetrators have rationalized away the criminality of shoplifting, urging a tolerant view that does not reach the traditional threshold of crime and punishment.[10] The act of shoplifting or retail theft has become so common that in many circles there is a cry for decriminalization.

> **Web Exercise:** The National Association of Shoplifting Prevention gives keen insight into the motivation of shoplifters at: http://www.shopliftingprevention.org/WhatNASPOffers/NRC/UnderstandingTheRootCauses.htm

The perpetrators of shoplifting are skilled at posing rationalizations that seek to excuse this illegal conduct. The rationalizations can be categorized as follows:

1. Shoplifting is not stealing but simply borrowing.
2. Shoplifting is a sign of the times.
3. Shoplifting is a correct, moral act.
4. Shoplifting is an indirect benefit or reward of the job.
5. Shoplifting is not a crime but instead a political act in a class struggle.

What is clear and irrefutable is that shoplifters have diverse motivations for the act and just as many rationalizations that explain it away as something more in the province of nuisance rather than crime. And some are more experienced than others. Robert O'Block, in his book *Security and Crime Prevention*, distinguishes between amateur and professional shoplifters:

> Shoplifting occurs for a variety of reasons, including desperation, impulse, peer pressure, revenge, or (rarely) kleptomania. Persons who shoplift for these reasons are generally amateurs and represent a majority over professional shoplifters, amateurs comprising about 85 percent of all shoplifters.[11]

Whatever rationalization is conveyed, the act of shoplifting or retail theft has become so common that in many circles it is synonymous with decriminalized conduct.

Aside from motivations, shoplifters can be classified according to type, as follows:

1. The amateur adult shoplifter
2. The juvenile shoplifter
3. The professional shoplifter
4. The kleptomaniac
5. The shoplifter-addict
6. Vagrant and the alcoholic shoplifter[12]

In *Corporate Fraud: The Basics of Prevention and Detection*, thieves and shoplifters are categorized according to motivation rather than personality. The standard rationalizations are referred to as "personal inducements," with the following synopsis indicating the motivations:

1. Economic—To fulfill actual or perceived economic needs.
2. Ideological—To take revenge against those with ideological differences.
3. Egocentric—To prove that they are clever and knowledgeable or because they have an extravagant sense of self-importance.
4. Psychotic—Out of a distorted sense of reality, e.g., delusions.[13]

Whatever the type or the motivation, it is a glaring difficulty for contemporary business.

B. Shoplifting Methods

Every investigator should become familiar with the techniques and methods of shoplifting and its related deceptions. As a rule, shoplifters must rely on their hands to commit acts of thievery. Shoplifters are keenly attuned and aware of their environment and, in scanning territory, they have a tendency to look quickly from side to side before committing the theft act. Because the shoplifter is performing an illegal act and is under the strain of trying to do so without getting caught, the physical movements and motions of the shoplifter tend to be less fluid and are instead quick, jerky, and sporadic. Body language speaks loudly. Shoplifters also use diversion, decoys, and disturbances that distract the eyes of salesclerks and other responsible personnel. Shoplifters engage in these deceptive tactics:

1. Palming is the simplest and most common method for theft. Palming is often aided by the use of a package, handkerchief, or glove. An accomplice may stand to screen the shoplifter.
2. Purses and pockets are common concealing places for shoplifted items. Look closely at shopping bags and boxes from other stores, umbrellas, school books, knitting bags, strollers, baby carriages, sample cases, briefcases, overnight bags, and lunch boxes.
3. A loose coat can conceal items.
4. A full skirt can conceal items. A proficient professional can "crotch carry" as much as a 25-lb. ham or eight cartons of cigarettes.
5. Rubber bands can be snapped around bundles of ties, stockings, or socks.
6. Hats, gloves, scarves, coats, sweaters, and purses can be worn out of the store.
7. Coats or sweaters may be thrown down over merchandise desired, and then picked up with the merchandise concealed inside.
8. Jewelry and other accessories can be dropped into clothing or inserted into the hair.
9. In fitting rooms, tight or closely fitting garments can be put on under street clothes. Packages and purses can be rearranged to conceal the addition of a dress or blouse.
10. Intentional confusion with merchandise: Handling so much clothing or products that sales personnel lose track; using accomplices or other party to distract sales personnel.
11. Price switching: Taking a price from one product with a higher price and relabeling with a lower price label.
12. Stepping around the end of the counter, using the excuse of wanting to see something, in order to steal expensive articles from the unlocked side of a showcase.
13. Distracting sales personnel by persistent bell ringing while accomplice steals merchandise.
14. Removing small items from a display case and hiding them in another portion of the store for later retrieval by an accomplice.[14]

The deception and the acts selected will vary by the establishment victimized. Store security personnel need to recognize the unique clues that signal impending shoplifting at a grocery store or any other mercantile operation. Watch out for:

1. Customer who enters the market with an empty paper bag in her purse, fills the bag with merchandise, and walks through an unused check-out line. If questioned, suspect assures the clerk that he or she has already been checked out.
2. Boxed items that are easily opened and reclosed may have more valuable items placed inside.
3. Produce bags are an easy mark for the shoplifter who brings his or her own crayon or stapler. This is called "price marking" and could occur on almost any product, but is very popular on meat items. [Today, many stores use computerized pricing.]
4. Supermarket shoplifters have been known to open an expensive package of tea and pour the contents into a pocketbook where it settles at the bottom.

5. A customer places an item in her purse and at the check-out counter asks for credit, explaining that another member of the family bought the item by mistake. If the clerk refuses the refund because of no receipt, the shoplifter wins. The shoplifter, of course, also wins if the store grants a refund.
6. Another variation of price switching is "cap switching." With prices frequently stamped on the caps, a shopper with a desire to steal will simply exchange the cap on a large size container for that on a small container.[15]

Security investigators will note differences in shoplifting not only by establishment but also by department. The attractiveness and expense of goods directly correlates to the level and intensity of shoplifting.

To identify and catch shoplifters, keen senses and developed skills of human observation are necessary.[16] By both direct and inferential conduct, the investigator can make reasonable, probable cause judgments relative as to suspected parties if he or she watches closely. Examples that tip off the observer are:

- Persons entering stores with heavy overcoats, out of season.
- Persons wearing baggy pants, full or pleated skirts (when current styles do not dictate the wearing of such apparel).
- Persons demonstrating darting eye movement and who conspicuously stretch their neck in all directions. Many professional shoplifters often do not give any clues other than eye movement.
- Persons who exit the store with undue hurriedness.
- Customers who do not seem interested in merchandise about which they have asked.
- Customers who do not seem to know what they want and change their mind frequently about merchandise.
- Individuals who leave the store with an unusual gait or who tie their shoes or pull up their socks frequently, or make any other unusual body movements that might assist them in concealing articles.
- Customers who walk behind or reach into display counters.
- A disinterested customer who waits for a friend or spouse to shop.
- Customers who constantly keep one hand in an outer coat pocket.
- Customers who make a scene to distract clerks, so that an accomplice can remove property without paying for it.[17]

In addition to the initial observations, security personnel should watch for other conditions, circumstances, and behavioral characteristics of suspects:

- Watching out for customers who ask to be shown more articles than a clerk can keep track of.
- Repeatedly sending a clerk away for more merchandise.
- Two or more customers shuffling articles at the same time and at the same counter.
- Two or three persons grouped together around a counter, thereby restricting the view of the sales clerk.
- Examining articles in corners and odd locations.
- Continuously dropping articles on the floor.
- Holding identical pieces of merchandise for comparison.
- Holding or crumbling merchandise.
- Hesitation or sudden decisions at elevators.
- Making exits via back stairways.
- Movement throughout the store but constantly reappearing at one counter.

- Large groups of teenagers entering and splitting into smaller groups.
- Removing tags from merchandise.
- Nervous actions such as moistening dry lips or perspiring excessively.
- Startled looks.[18]

The security firm or consultant should aggressively advise the merchant about ways to deter shoplifting. Merchants have many lines of defense:

- Train employees in the methods of shoplifting.
- Offer employees a reward for deterring shoplifting.
- All customers should be greeted immediately upon entering the store.
- Maximize visibility by raising cash register area, use convex mirrors, one-way mirrors are closed circuit television cameras.
- Use an electronic article surveillance system (EAS).
- Post signs in plain view stating that all shoplifters will be prosecuted.
- Keep cash registers locked and monitored at all times.
- Use cable tie-downs.
- Watch for price switching.
- Monitor all delivery men.
- Cashiers should check every item sold that might hide other merchandise.
- Have the cashier staple the customer's bag closed with the sales receipt attached.[19]

Even with initial, clearly dependable findings, the investigator should restrain in making an arrest. Watch until the evidence suffices for a successful prosecution and conviction.

J. Cleary, in *Prosecuting the Shoplifter: A Loss Prevention Strategy*, outlines elements for successfully investigating and prosecuting a shoplifting case:

1. *Logically and Systematically Gather Evidence.* When cases are lost in court, it is usually because of insufficient evidence. This means that the store manager or security person overlooked some facts in the store, facts now needed as evidence at trial. The ability to produce facts logically and systematically in the store that can be relied on at trial as evidence to prove the elements of the offense is a necessary skill.
2. *Make Decisions Based on Evidence Produced in the Store.* The essence of selective prosecution as authorized by the merchant's privilege is the ability to make decisions based on evidence found in the store. A retail employee must learn to see when the evidence supports the decision to prosecute a case. Sometimes the evidence will not be enough to support a decision to prosecute and support the decision to release the suspect.
3. *Produce the Two Types of Evidence Needed to Obtain Convictions.* Merchants must learn how to produce the two types of store prosecution evidence needed to obtain a conviction for shoplifting in any state. Eyewitness evidence is produced by watching the suspect on a sales floor conceal merchandise or switch a price tag or assist a companion who is concealing merchandise. The physical evidence is always produced after the suspect has first been detained on probable cause.
4. *Understand the Legal Meaning of the Suspect's Explanation.* Even veteran security people sometimes forget that the suspect's explanation is also evidence: defense evidence. Merchants must become good listeners. They will see that store managers and security people produce evidence with their ears, as well as with their eyes. As all those with even slight experience in dealing with shoplifting suspects know, very rarely will the person admit guilt. Most of the time people deny that they are shoplifting.
5. *Speak in Terms of Evidence.* In court, judges, prosecutors, and defense lawyers speak in terms of evidence. Thus, store managers and retail security persons must learn the language of evidence in their stores while they are handling the case and deciding whether to file a formal charge. Merchants will be shown how to discuss a shoplifting case in their stores in terms of what the evidence will prove in court. If the store manager or security person is speaking in terms of "suspicion" or "opinion," the chances of filing a clear case and losing it are much greater.[20]

The investigator must ensure and preserve the quality, content, and integrity of the evidence (see Chapter 6). The investigator must protect the chain of custody. J. Kirk Barefoot, in *Employee Theft Investigation*, offers sage advice on the chain of custody of evidence:

> The main point is to be able to show who had sole custody of the goods during any given time span, and to prove that no one else was in a position to tamper with or alter the evidence in any way. It is also suggested that the written report of the agent involved in the handling of the contraband should indicate the marking of such evidence for identification. If possible, the nature of the identifying marks and their location on the contraband should be included. In this way, the written report stands to corroborate the actual identification mark on the evidence and thus greatly bolsters the entire case.[21]

III. INTERNAL THEFT BY EMPLOYEES

Internal theft, waste, and fraud by employees account for the largest part of shrinkage in many companies. Within the retail setting, internal theft rates are astronomical. The National Institute of Justice's *Executive Summary, Theft by Employees in Work Organizations* reports:

> In each of the three industry sectors surveyed, roughly one-third of the employees reported some involvement in the taking of company property (e.g., merchandise, supplies, tools, and equipment) during the prior year. Additionally, over two-thirds of the sample reported counter-productive behavior such as long lunches and breaks, slow or sloppy workmanship, sick leave abuse, and the use of alcohol or drugs at work. ... The highest levels of property theft were reported by the younger (16 to mid-20s), unmarried, and male employees. In each type of industry those employees with the greatest unrestricted access to and knowledge about the property stolen (i.e., sales clerks in retail stores, engineers in manufacturing plants, and registered nurses and technicians in hospitals) were the occupational groups reporting the highest levels of theft. In addition, both property theft and particularly counterproductive behavior was more likely among those employees expressing dissatisfaction with their employment—especially dissatisfaction with their immediate supervisors and the company's attitude toward the workforce.[22]

Security firms must anticipate and plan for internal theft.[23]

A. Reasons for Theft

Considerable differences of opinion exist as to why internal pilferage and other forms of employee thievery have risen so markedly. Some theorists hold that employees and, for that matter, employers, have lost all sense of loyalty to one another and to the company. As Barefoot remarks:

> Unlike Japanese firms, which generally enjoy a high degree of loyalty on the part of their employees, the typical American employer has seen employee loyalty dwindle to a point where it can no longer be considered a viable factor in any well-balanced security program.[24]

How do employees rationalize their illegal conduct? A survey of one hundred certified public accountants and ninety data processing specialists revealed the following reasons that employees steal or embezzle from their employers:

1. they think stealing a little from a big company won't hurt;
2. most employees are caught by accident rather than by audit or design, thus fear of being caught is not a deterrent; and
3. employees steal for any reason the human mind and imagination can conjure up.[25]

Barefoot offers some other explanations:

- Population shifts
- Organized crime

- Limitation of reference checking
- Drugs
- Restrictions on screening
- Gambling
- Lack of security expertise[26]

Many public and private law enforcement officials note that the employee's rationale is often "Everybody does it. Why shouldn't I?" Private security investigators have to understand and contend with this type of reasoning since it permeates the thief's moral decision making.

B. Theft Strategies

How employee theft is consummated depends largely on positions, opportunities, and levels of access. In sum, people find a way to commit thievery and fraudulent acts depending on individual circumstances and conditions. Some of the crimes might involve:

- Merchandise swindles
- Embezzlement
- Organized crime schemes
- Commercial bribery and kickbacks
- Credit card fraud
- Receiving stolen goods
- Expense account fraud
- Price switching
- Medical and health care frauds
- Shoplifting
- Charitable and religious frauds
- Mortgage milking
- Insurance fraud
- Forgery and other document tampering
- False security fraud

Employee theft strategies and tactics are multidimensional, including:

- Passing merchandise across the counter to an accomplice.
- Putting merchandise in concealed places.
- Under-ringing cash registers.
- Overcharging a customer and pocketing the difference.
- Theft of merchandise through unsupervised exits.
- Failure to register sales.
- Writing false refunds.
- Collusion with delivery men and drivers.
- Stealing from the warehouse or stockroom.
- Stealing from returned goods and layaway.
- Voiding a sales check and then pocketing the money.
- Cashing fraudulent checks for accomplices.
- Giving fraudulent refunds to accomplices.
- Failing to record returned purchases and stealing an equal amount of cash.
- Falsifying sales records to take cash.
- Concealing thefts by falsifying store records.

- Taking money from cash registers.
- Giving employee discounts to unauthorized parties.
- Concealing stolen goods in trash or other containers.
- Shipping clerks mailing goods to their own address.
- Wearing store clothing and accessories home at the end of a shift.
- Intentionally damaging goods in order to buy them at discount.
- Buying damaged merchandise at discount prices and later substituting damaged goods for first quality merchandise.
- Stealing checks made payable to cash.
- Picking up receipts discarded by customers and using them for refunds.
- Stealing during early or late store hours.
- Stealing from the dock or other exit areas.
- Forging checks.
- Keeping collections on uncollectible accounts.
- Receiving kickbacks from suppliers.[27]

C. Investigating Theft

The American Society for Industrial Security warns investigators that even a company's most trusted employees must not be overlooked in the process of investigating an action:

> [T]he investigator must consider all possible suspects, not eliminating anyone because they seem honest. In a pre-employment interview, all the signs may indicate that an employee can be trusted. However, people change, and negative attitudes toward the company can develop for many reasons. An updated background investigation may reveal that the employee has become a victim of alcohol or drug abuse, is in a financial bind, or is being strongly influenced by unsavory associates.[28]

When conducting an investigation of internal theft among retail store clerks, one should consider the following questions:

1. Are the clerks waiting on the customers promptly and courteously?
2. Are all sales being rung up and the monies deposited in the cash register?
3. Is the cash register kept closed at all times other than when a transaction takes place?
4. Are the clerks giving the employee discount privileges to non-store employees?
5. Are the employee purchase procedures being followed?
6. Are employees taking extended breaks and lunch periods?
7. Is there an unusually close relationship between clerks in different departments, and do they handle each other's employee purchases?
8. Do certain customers insist on being serviced by a specific clerk even though other clerks are available?
9. Are the clerks following the store procedures on refunds and exchanges?
10. Are the clerks familiar with pricing within their department, thereby limiting the possibility of "price switching" by customers?
11. Are the proper taxes being charged?
12. Do clerks know where to find in-stock items that are not on display?
13. Are the clerks wearing store merchandise, such as jewelry, and "forgetting" to return it?
14. Are clerks placing store merchandise under the counter to be purchased by them at some later date?
15. Is there a specific clerk who is extremely proficient in her duties and adherence to store policies?[29]

Web Exercise: Read Charles Sennewald's reflection on why shoplifting rates have yet to meaningfully drop at: http://www.shoplifting.com/flawedstrategies.pdf

The investigator should also observe the conduct of the suspected employee. Look for behavior that sends up a red flag:

- Salesperson wears clothes with large, exterior pockets.
- Salesperson has a purse, bag, or other item behind the counter.
- Salesperson works alone at a register in a high volume, low cash sales department.
- Salesperson asks you if you want to put the item in another bag you are carrying.
- Salesperson writes figures on a scrap of paper near the register.
- Salesperson throws register receipts on the floor instead of giving them to you.[30]

Certain evidence may directly implicate a suspect.

- High shortage departments.
- Below-average cash sales.
- Consistent overages and shortages.
- Excessive "No Sales."
- Maladjusted employee.
- Store policy violators.
- Temporary personnel.
- Cash register consistently open.[31]

D. Obtaining Confessions or Statements

There is much to be concerned about when questioning suspects, both legally and personally. Case law and jury awards are replete with cases involving excessive force, sexual harassment, and the infliction of mental distress. Use common sense. Joseph Di Domenico, a longtime practitioner, notes the following regarding the investigator's conduct as he or she seeks a statement from a suspected thief.

1. The interview should be conducted in private.
2. Female store detectives should handle the interviews of shoplifting suspects who are children or female.
3. The store detective should ask the questions in a polite manner, without threats, force, or extending any promises to the suspect.
4. Store detectives should never make promises that they know they cannot or will not keep.
5. If the suspect requests to call a spouse, or even the police, either allow the suspect to make the call, or else put the call through for the person.
6. Do not treat the suspect like a "prisoner."
7. If a shoplifting suspect indicates to the store detective that certain medication is required because the suspect is under a doctor's care, the store detective should summon the store nurse, if there is a nurse on the staff. If the store has no nurse in attendance, the detective must exercise good judgment.
8. Do not lock the office door or post a guard in front of the door, which would give the impression that the subject is not free to leave at any time.
9. The completion of the case history form should be approached with some discretion.
10. When endeavoring to get the individual to sign the preprinted statement of admission form, explain to the subject that the form contains in print the oral admission made by the person.
11. The store detective should keep in mind that, in about 99 percent of the cases that will not be prosecuted by the store for some reason or other, one thing the shoplifter values more than any other factor is confidentiality.[32]

IV. BURGLARY

Of major interest to the security industry is the crime of burglary, a crime whose felonious intent may be oriented toward property, but always requires illegal entry into a domicile or other structure. Below is the traditional, common law definition of burglary—such crimes are now defined statutorily.

1. The premises must be the dwelling house of another.
2. There must be a breaking of some part of the house itself. The breaking can be constructive, as well as actual.
3. There must be an entry. The slightest entry of a hand or even an instrument suffices.
4. The breaking and entering must both be at night, but need not be on the same night.
5. There must be an intent to commit a felony in the house and such intent must accompany both the breaking and entry. The intended felony need not be committed.[33]

Statutory modifications of these elements have been quite common. A definition of "dwelling house" has been liberally construed and includes the following: chicken coop, cow stable, hog house, barn, smoke house, mill house, and any other area of any other building or occupied structure, including most commercial structures.[34] The term "breaking" does not require an actual destruction of property, merely the breaking of a plane or point of entrance in the occupied structure. Additionally, most jurisdictions have reassessed the nighttime determination and made the requirement nonmandatory. Many jurisdictions, however, make the time of the intrusion applicable to the gradation of the offense or the severity of possible punishment.[35] One must be aware, as well, that burglary is not necessarily a property offense. Appellate decisions have served to remind us of the requirement that the entry be spurred on by an intent to commit any felony within the dwelling.[36]

The investigation of burglary requires the same general investigative approach as all other offenses. Proof of the felony's elements are tied to the objective facts collected. Be concerned with these steps:

1. Carefully check the scene of the burglary for latent fingerprints.
2. If fingerprints are obtained, fingerprint all employees for the purpose of elimination.
3. Check polished floor surfaces or any papers on the floor, for any trace of footprints.
4. Check the area surrounding the burglarized building for tire marks or footprints that may be connected with the burglary.
5. Obtain an accurate, detailed description of all missing property or monies.
6. Check the loss-payable clauses of any insurance carried.
7. Interview all persons having access to the premises. This step should include the night watchman, the patrolman, or trooper working the area, the last person to leave the premises prior to the burglary, and the person who discovered and reported the burglary.
8. Attempt to trace any tools recovered.
9. If explosives are recovered, do not attempt to transport them. Contact the laboratory.
10. Take scale photographs of the attacked safe (if applicable).
11. If possible, obtain the make, serial number, size, and weight of the safe (if applicable).
12. If a suspect is arrested and charged with burglary at or near the scene of the crime, immediately obtain all the clothing he is wearing. ... Clothing may contain safe insulation, paint fragments, or metal particles.
13. If the suspect is in an automobile when apprehended, mark any recovered tools for identification and forward with all other evidence.[37]

In surveying the area subject to the burglary, be on the lookout for tools, instruments, and mechanical means and aids used to accomplish the breaking and entry. A list of common burglary tools includes the following:

- Wrecking bar or pry bar
- Diamond core bits
- Tapered punches
- Tire irons
- Core drills and bits
- Abrasive saws, chisels, wood bits
- Hammers and sledgehammers
- Pliers or wire cutters
- Pipe wrench
- Can opener or plate gripper
- Vise grip
- Bolt cutters
- Keyhole saw
- Oxygen-acetylene outfits
- Hacksaw and blade
- Crowbars
- Electric drills
- Screwdrivers

Private security plays a critical role in the reduction of business theft and burglary.[38] The former Law Enforcement Assistance Administration admonishes business, industry, and individuals, stating that their own negligence fosters an opportunity for burglary and other property offenses:

> Many experts also believe that no-force burglaries are frequently the work of individuals, many of them children, who simply cannot resist an easy opportunity to steal. If this is so, we could reduce the burglary rate and the size of the offender population by limiting the opportunities available to commit "easy" offenses. If failure to adequately protect personal and household property is directly related to the commission of the crime, can we say the victims are in some way responsible? This is a difficult question to answer.[39]

The best approach is to establish a theft/burglary deterrence program. In facility or perimeter protection, the security specialist takes on a wide array of responsibilities. Ralph F. Brislin's well-crafted text, *The Effective Security Officer's Training Manual*, suggests these preventive measures:

> [A] security officer must know what doors and windows are normally open/closed, locked and unlocked. … Often, while patrolling a security officer will notice that there are several other persons in the facility. … It is essential that prior to patrolling a security officer obtain as much information as possible as to what employees/visitors are in the facility. When are these persons scheduled to depart? Once all of this information has been obtained, a security officer should not be startled to find other persons in the facility. … Much of this information should be known by the security officer who is going off duty. A final part of theft prevention when patrolling will occasionally require a security officer to inspect equipment begin removed from the facility. The security officer must know what material can be removed from the facility with proper paperwork and authorization. … If no paperwork is required, the security officer should note in their shift log the identity and description of the person removing the material and what material is being removed.[40]

The checklist in Figure 9.1 will be of great utility to the security investigator.

BURGLARY PREVENTION CHECKLIST

Name:____________________________________Address:____

PREVENTION TIPS	OK	NEEDED	RECOMMEND REPLACEMENT
Doors:			
Strong Pintumbler locks:			
Front Door	______	______	______
Back Door	______	______	______
Side Door	______	______	______
Basement Door	______	______	______
Chain Latch:			
Front Door	______	______	______
Back Door	______	______	______
Side Door	______	______	______
Basement Door	______	______	______
Heavy-Duty Hinges:			
Front Door	______	______	______
Back Door	______	______	______
Side Door	______	______	______
Basement Door	______	______	______
Peephole:			
Front Door	______	______	______
Back Door	______	______	______
Doors with Windows:	______	______	______
Need Key to Open Inside and Out	______	______	______
Mailbox/Mail Slot in Door	______	______	______
Garage Door Pintumbler Lock	______	______	______
Windows:			
All Windows with Pintumblers	______	______	______
Bar or Strip of Wood (Patio Door)	______	______	______
Bars or Grillworks:	______	______	______
"Out-of-the-Way" Windows	______	______	______
Garage Windows	______	______	______
Basement Windows	______	______	______
Keys:			
Change Tumblers When You Move In or Out if Keys Are Lost	______	______	______
Don't Give Out Duplicate Keys	______	______	______
Keep Home and Automobile Keys Separate	______	______	______
Don't Put Name and Address on Keys	______	______	______
Keep House Key Hidden Outside	______	______	______

FIGURE 9.1 Burglary prevention checklist.

V. DEFENSIVE TECHNIQUES TO MINIMIZE AND IDENTIFY BURGLARY AND PROPERTY LOSSES

A. Tactics and Strategies

A highly skilled investigator possesses two fundamental traits: first, the investigator knows the territory to which he or she is assigned, its personalities, its geographic location, its layout, and its overall operation; and second, the investigator is able to apply theory in practical situations. Thus, a private security investigator enlisted by a retail establishment to determine how goods are being pilfered should have a comprehensive understanding of the establishment. Prospective suspects will be numerous; before proceeding on wild goose chases or professional conjecture, become familiar with the assigned area. As always, use common sense when formulating an investigative strategy and practices.

1. Site Security Surveys and Their Application

By evaluating the physical and procedural weaknesses of business establishments and then making recommendations on corrective action, the security survey makes a remarkable contribution to crime deterrence. Police departments, private security companies, and other consultants all engage in survey design and analysis. Upon completion of a field survey, a permanent record should be kept on file.

2. Determining Organizational Characteristics

Investigators, especially those working in institutional settings, should have a feel for the organizational and administrative makeup of their clients. Companies that are loosely organized and have administrative problems will be more likely to have serious problems with internal theft and pilferage. The National Institute of Justice urges:

> [T]he control of employee taking of property seems to be a problem that the business organization must keep visible on its list of priorities and objectives. It cannot be ignored or relegated to a topic of temporary or minimal importance, nor should it be assigned as a task for a specialized portion of the organization's management team. This research suggests that only by exhibiting a conspicuous and consistent climate of concern about the control of internal theft at all occupational levels can an organization hope to have a significant effect on the behavior of its employees.[41]

The entire corporate or institutional environment influences an investigator's judgment. To perform the job properly, the investigator must know how management operates, how it intends to pursue parties who are apprehended, and how it oversees the scheme of things. Companies that treat their employees poorly, that provide little or no feedback on performance, and that do not restrict or restrain conduct or behavior risk far greater losses due to employee misconduct. In essence, a lack of control results in an almost chaotic environment. As a rule of thumb, if employees feel the scrutiny of management, that there are repercussions to illegal and immoral conduct, and that the company has invested significant time and energy in ensuring the protection of its assets, it is less likely that criminal conduct will occur. There are many factors that enhance the potentiality for criminal conduct, especially internal theft, fraud, and embezzlement within the business entity, including:

- Inadequate pay, benefits, job security, and promotional opportunities
- Ambiguity in job roles, relationships, responsibilities, and areas of accountability
- Lack of recognition for good work, loyalty, longevity, and effort
- Lack of periodic audits and inspections
- Ambiguous corporate social values and ethical norms
- Tolerance or indifference toward antisocial behavior
- Bias or unfairness in selection, promotion, compensation, or appraisal

- A. Prevention measures
    1. Internal accounting controls
        a. Separation of duties
        b. Rotation of duties
        c. Periodic internal audits and surprise inspections
        d. Development and documentation of policies, procedures, systems, programs, and program modifications
        e. Establishment of dual signature authorities, dollar authorization limits per signatory, expiration date, and check amount limits
        f. Off-line entry controls and limits
        g. Batch totals, hash totals
    2. Computer access controls
        a. Identification defenses
            (1) Key or card inserts
            (2) Passwords and code numbers
            (3) Exclusion—repeated error lockout
            (4) Time activator/deactivator
            (5) Periodic code and password changes
        b. Authentication defenses
            (1) Random personal data
            (2) Voice, fingerprint, or palm geometry recognition
            (3) Callbacks
        c. Establishment of authorizations by levels of authority or levels of security (compartmentalization and "need to know")
- B. Detection measures
    1. Exceptions in logging systems
        a. Out of sequence, out of priority, and aborted runs and entries
        b. Out-of-pattern transactions: too high, too low, too many, too often, too few, unusual file access (odd times and places)
        c. Attempted access beyond authorization level
        d. Repeated attempts to gain access improperly—wrong password, entry code, etc.
        e. Parity and redundancy checks
    2. Management information system
        a. Monitoring operational performance levels for
            (1) The variations from plans and standards
            (2) Deviations from accepted or mandated policies, procedures, and practices
            (3) Deviations from past quantitative relationships, i.e., ratios, proportions, percentages, trends, past performance levels, indices, etc.
    3. Intelligence gathering
        a. Monitoring employee attitudes, values, and job satisfaction level
        b. Soliciting random feedback from or surveying customers, vendors, and suppliers for evidence of dissatisfaction, inefficiency, inconsistency with policies, corruption, or dishonesty by employees

FIGURE 9.2 Internal theft detection and prevention measures.

- Inadequate training on security matters and company policies with respect to sanctions for security breaches
- Failure to screen applicants thoroughly for sensitive positions before appointment
- General job-related stress or anxiety[42]

The company that invests resources in the detection and prevention of criminality will most likely be rewarded with lower internal theft rates. The measures listed in Figure 9.2 should provide obstacles to internal theft.

3. Theft Tests

Testing for internal and external shoplifting and pilferage falls into two major categories: honesty and service tests. When conducting an honesty test, the investigator determines whether employees are stealing cash during customer purchase transactions. In service testing, the investigator reports to management how he or she was treated during a specific transaction while observations were made.

> **Web Exercise:** Visit the web page for Jack Hayes International, a firm that specializes in assisting business with inventory shrinkage and retail theft controls at: http://www.hayesinternational.com/invntry_shrnk_cntrl_lss_prvntn.html

a. *Honesty Testing*

To detect theft, deception, fraud, pilferage, or other illegal conduct on the part of employees, investigators conduct honesty testing. In this type of test, the investigator simultaneously buys two of the same items. Prices can be the same or different. The investigator notes the register reading for the previous sale. The investigator then selects two of the same items and pays the employee the exact amount for the entire purchase. The investigator should then observe whether the cash register drawer was opened or closed before, after, or at the time of the purchase. In addition, the investigator should check whether the employee issued a receipt. The investigator should formally document these facts, the subsequent items purchased, and their related costs. Other notations worthy of mention:

- Was the purchase wrapped or was payment received from the investigator?
- Did the clerk call back the amount of the purchase or the amount of money tendered?
- Was the correct change given?
- Was the amount of the sale correctly recorded on the register?

Troubling or suspicious conduct should be reflected in the report. An example of a document recording honesty testing is shown in Figure 9.3.

Barefoot comments on arranging this type of testing:

> It is normally up to the agency supervisor or the retail security manager to make arrangements with the crew chief for storing the purchases while the target stores are being shopped. Ultimately, all merchandise is normally returned to the company for full credit, and this is usually handled through a high-ranking member of the store accounting staff. In this way, the rank-and-file sales personnel do not become aware that the merchandise has been returned for credit.[43]

(1) The Combination Buy In a combination buy, the investigator buys two or more different items at the same time and pays the employee the exact amount for the entire purchase. Observe and record whether the employee rings up all, part, or none of the transaction. The investigator records whether a receipt was received for the purchase. In a follow-up report, the investigator inserts findings regarding the exact time of the purchase and the reading on the register before the clerk rang up the transaction. (This is helpful if the employee fails to give you a receipt.) By knowing the amount on the register prior to your purchase, it will be easy to check the sale for which no receipt was received.

(2) The Double Buy In effecting a double buy, the investigator buys one or more items. The transaction should result in paying an uneven amount of money, larger than the price of the goods in total, resulting in change. Because an overage of funds exists, the cash register tabulates the difference, and a receipt is remitted to the investigator. In this scenario, the investigator receives a receipt to identify either the cash register used or reference to its employee operator. This serves the first purpose of the double-buy process, namely, identification.

SHOPPING INVESTIGATION REPORT

Firm__________ Store No.__________ Case No.__________

Address__________ City__________ State__________

Date__________ Time__________ Opr.__________ Report No.__________

NAME
NUMBER
LETTER __________
Sex__________ Age __________
Height __________ Weight __________
Build __________
Eyes__________ Nose __________
Teeth __________
Complexion__________
Hair Color __________
Style __________
Glasses __________
Jewelry __________
Other __________

SALESPERSON'S APPEARANCE
_____ Well Groomed
_____ Passable
_____ Average
_____ Unimpressive
_____ Unkempt
_____ Other

SALESPERSON'S ATTITUDE
_____ Enthusiastic
_____Pleasant
_____ Routine
_____Indifferent
_____Antagonistic
_____Served Promptly
_____Suggested other items
_____Offered a "thank you"
_____ Other

Reg loc.no: __________
Reg read: __________
Other cust/oprs/salespeople: __________

PAYMENT MADE

	$20	$10	$5	$1	50¢	25¢	10¢	5¢	1¢	
1. Pur										Trans #_____
2. Pur										Trans #_____

DESCRIPTION OF TRANSACTION

____

PURCHASES MADE

Total		

FIGURE 9.3 Sample shopping investigation report form.

The second phase of the double-buy investigation tests the honesty of the employee. After the employee has returned change, the investigator purchases an additional item. In buying the second item, the exact purchase price should be paid. The investigator should request that the employee put the second purchase in the same bag used for the first purchase. (The employee may even suggest this.) The investigator should be alert at this point to record whether a second receipt is received.

Pinkerton's, Inc., relates other sensible information regarding the double-buy process:

> Use common sense when making a double buy. It would not be normal, for example, to spend 39 cents on the first buy and ten dollars on your second buy. … Plan your approach and articles to be purchased prior to making your first buy. In this way you can control the type of goods in the first part so the bag will be large enough to hold the goods bought on the second part. … In picking items for your second

> buy in a double buy, try to locate goods as far away as possible from the register. ... It is also possible to wear out or take out an unwrapped item which you have purchased on the second part of a double-buy test. This could be the case when buying at a jewelry department.[44]

As one final caution, in a double-buy test, the second purchase must occur immediately after the first purchase so that the factual chain and monetary sequence are not interrupted by other purchasers. The investigator should not act in a contrived or awkward manner; he or she should appear completely disinterested and aloof. Upon the second buy, the investigator should immediately leave the retail area without waiting for a receipt (but if the employee harkens you to accept it, do so).

(3) The Exchange Buy When customers have difficulty in choosing between multiple products, dishonest employees succumb to temptation. In the exchange buy, the investigator has two or more items to consider. In the investigator's original decision, the choice is to purchase the less costly item. The investigator then pays the employee with an uneven amount of money. Upon receipt of change, package, and sales receipt, the investigator, acting as a bewildered customer, changes heart and decides to take the higher-priced item. The purchaser (investigator) then must pay the difference between the lower-priced item and the higher-priced item. At this juncture, the investigator should watch carefully to see whether the employee records, registers, or makes notation of the difference between the two prices or simply pockets the difference.

(4) The Refund Buy Investigators who perform the refund test return an item to the selling department. After receipt of the cash or credit refund, the money is then used to make an even money purchase. The objective of the refund buy is to test the store's system by attempting to get a refund without a receipt. If the employee will not grant the refund without the receipt, the investigator can then "discover" the receipt and complete the transaction.

b. Service Testing

In service testing, the scrutinized employee is assessed on diverse issues:

- Approach
- Suggested purchase
- Appearance
- Service effect
- Courtesy
- Product knowledge
- Salesmanship
- Closing of the sale

Service testing should take the following questions into account:

- How much of a product was purchased?
- What is the description of the merchandise?
- What is the price of the merchandise?
- What is the tax or other special assessment on the merchandise?
- What was the total amount paid?
- What money denominations were used as payment?
- Was the money handled at the register in compliance with the store's system?
- Was a receipt issued and what were its contents?
- Did the clerk charge the correct price and give the correct change?
- Was the clerk busy? Orderly? Clean?
- How did the employee act? Careless? Complaining? Professional?

Testing an employee's service level is a circumstantial tool for management, targeting employees who are weak in customer service or who are disgruntled, difficult, and likely to cause problems for the business enterprise.

VI. MISSING OR STOLEN PROPERTY

In cases of retail theft and business pilferage, the personal property document in Figure 9.4 is of considerable assistance. If a case of missing personal property leads to the allegation of theft or shoplifting, most security departments will have a Report of Theft document. Figure 9.5 contains space for comments not only about the theft, but it also solicits recommendations for response.

Tracking the location of property that was seized by private security operatives ensures a proper chain of custody. Figure 9.6 is a sample of a property control receipt used to trace the movement of property.

Security firms operating within larger corporations, educational institutions, hotels and motels, and transport companies generally have more than one incident to report in a typical workday.

<table>
<tr><th colspan="5">PERSONAL PROPERTY MISSING</th></tr>
<tr><td colspan="2">REPORTED BY BADGE</td><td>DEPT.</td><td>DATE REPORTED</td><td>TIME</td></tr>
<tr><td colspan="3">ADDRESS (IF NON-EMPLOYEE)</td><td colspan="2">REPORTED TO</td></tr>
<tr><td colspan="3"></td><td colspan="2">ESTIMATED VALUE OF ARTICLE</td></tr>
<tr><td colspan="5">LOCATION OF OCCURRENCE</td></tr>
<tr><td colspan="5">DESCRIBE ARTICLE IN DETAIL</td></tr>
<tr><td colspan="3">BY WHOM WAS LOSS DISCOVERED?</td><td>DATE</td><td>TIME</td></tr>
<tr><td colspan="3">BY WHOM WAS ARTICLE LAST SEEN?</td><td>DATE</td><td>TIME</td></tr>
<tr><td>WAS ARTICLE IN LOCKED CONTAINER?</td><td colspan="2">IN LOCKED ROOM?</td><td colspan="2">WERE LOCKS FORCED?</td></tr>
<tr><td colspan="5">HOW DID LOSS OCCUR?</td></tr>
<tr><td colspan="5"></td></tr>
<tr><td colspan="5">REMARKS</td></tr>
<tr><td colspan="5">DISPOSITION
☐ RETURNED TO OWNER ☐ OTHER, DESCRIBE________________________
☐ RETURNED TO FINDER</td></tr>
<tr><td colspan="3">RETURNED TO (SIGNATURE) DATE</td><td colspan="2">INVESTIGATED BY</td></tr>
<tr><td colspan="3"></td><td colspan="2">SECURITY OFFICE</td></tr>
</table>

FIGURE 9.4 Missing personal property chain of custody report form.

REPORT OF THEFT OR LOSS OF PROPERTY

Security Department

File # ____________

1. Complainant's Name	2 Location and Tele. Ext.	3 Date Reported	
4. Description of Item		Company Property ☐ Personal Property ☐	
5. Model #	6. Serial #	7. Company Inventory No.	8. Value
9. Estimated Time of Theft			
10. Last Known Location (Bldg., Floor, Office)		11. Property Assigned to or Owned by	
12. Describe Precautions Taken to Protect Property			
13. Furnish Additional Details			
14. Details Concerning Police Report			
		15. Report Prepared by	16. Date
17. Recommended Action			

FIGURE 9.5 Form used to report theft or loss of property.

Use of a special form to report losses is an outstanding way to track complicated and voluminous information. Figure 9.7 shows one style of this type of report.

Private security plays an integral role in the prevention, deterrence, and detection of theft and property offenses. The permissiveness of the legal system's reaction to property offenses; the rationalizations and justifications espoused by retail thieves and shoplifters and their diverse methods

PROPERTY CONTROL RECEIPT				
NAME		TITLE	SIGNATURE	
LOCATION			TELEPHONE EXTENSION	
PROPERTY SURRENDER AUTHORITY				
NAME		TITLE	SIGNATURE	
REMOVAL TYPE: ☐ PERMANENT ☐ TEMPORARY ☐ OTHER				
ITEM	COUNT	DESCRIPTION	ISSUE DATE	RECOVER DATE

FIGURE 9.6 Property control receipt form.

and techniques; and the increase in internal theft in the business environment, in an employer/employee context and in other corporate settings, are all indicative of the importance of having well-trained security officers and investigators. The specific recommendations, tactics, and strategies regarding the investigation of theft and property offenses covered here should help security professionals deal with these prolific, serious crimes.

REPORT OF LOSSES

SECURITY DEPARTMENT MONTH OF _____________ 20____

DATE OF REPORT	DATE OF LOSS	NAME	STATUS	NATURE OF LOSS	VALUE	LOSS OR THEFT	RECOVERED

FIGURE 9.7 Loss report form.

NOTES

1. Robert D. McCrie, "Shoplifting: Managing the Problem," *Security Letter*. (July 2006), 4; Read Hayes and King Rogers, "Catch Them if You Can," *Security Mgmt.* (October 2003), 80.
2. W. Cunningham and T. Taylor, *The Hallcrest Report: Private Security and Police in America* (Chancellor, 1985), 18.
3. Alan F. Greggo, "Attention Shoplifters," *Security Mgmt.* (December 2008), 56.
4. Cunningham and Taylor, *supra* note 2, at 19.
5. Robert O'Block, *Security and Crime Prevention* (Mosby, 1981), 156.
6. Cunningham and Taylor, *supra* note 2, at 25.
7. There has been a trend to decriminalization. See Charles P. Nemeth, *Criminal Law* (Prentice Hall, 2004).
8. O'Block, *supra* note 5, at 157.
9. "Loss Prevention: Portrait of Effective Anti-Shoplifting Programs," *Security Letter*. (October 15, 2008), 2.
10. Robert McCrie, "Retail Mgmt.: Center Helps Lp Dirs. & Aids Shoplifters To Break Habits," *Security Letter.* (November 3, 2008).
11. O'Block, *supra* note 5, at 158.
12. Pinkerton's, Inc., *Investigations Department Training Manual* (1990), 127.
13. J. Bologna, *Corporate Fraud: The Basics of Prevention and Detection* (Butterworth-Heinemann, 1984), 82.
14. Pinkerton's, Inc., *supra* note 12, at 131–132.
15. *Id.* at 134–135.
16. See Joseph Petrocelli, "Shoplifting," *Police*. (December 2008), 16.
17. O'Block, *supra* note 5, at 160–161.
18. Pinkerton's, Inc., *supra* note 12, at 136–137.
19. Mark Gleckman, "Crime Prevention/Community Relations," in *The Security Supervisor Training Manual*, Sandi J. Davies and Ronald R. Minion, eds. (Butterworth-Heinemann, 1995).
20. J. Cleary, *Prosecuting the Shoplifter: A Loss Prevention Strategy* (Butterworth-Heinemann, 1986), 19–21.
21. J. Kirk Barefoot, *Employee Theft Investigation* (Butterworth-Heinemann, 1979), 81.
22. U.S. Department of Justice, National Institute of Justice, *Theft by Employees in Work Organizations* (1983), iii.
23. See "Retailer Security Chief Pushes Proactive Approach," *Corporate Security*. (January 31, 2008), 8.
24. Barefoot, *supra* note 21, at 8.
25. Cunningham and Taylor, *supra* note 2, at 26.
26. Barefoot, *supra* note 21, at 7–9.
27. O'Block, *supra* note 7, at 184-185.
28. American Society for Industrial Security, *Basic Guidelines for Security Investigations* (1981), 91. See John H. Christman and Charles A. Sennewald, *Shoplifting: Managing the Problem* (ASIS International, 2006).
29. Pinkerton's, Inc., *supra* note 12, at 155–156
30. *Id.* at 161.
31. *Id.* at 160.
32. J. Di Domenico, *Investigative Technique for the Retail Security Investigator* (Lebhar-Friedman Books, 1979), 135.
33. W. L. Clark and W. L. Marshall, *A Treatise on the Law of Crimes* 984 (Callaghan, 1967).
34. *Id.* at 986–987.
35. *See* N.Y Crim. Law § 221.2 (McKinney, 1962).
36. *See* William Coates, "Criminal Intention of Burglary," *N.C.L. Rev.* 2 (1924), 110; see also *Champlin v. State*, 84 Wis. 2d 621, 267 N.W. 2d 295 (1978); *State v. Oritz*, 92 N.M. 166, 584 P. 2d 1306 (1978).
37. Pennsylvania State Police, Bureau of Training and Education, *Investigation of Safe Burglaries* (1972), 1–2.
38. See Charles P. Nemeth and K. C. Poulin, *Private Security and Public Safety: A Community Based Approach* (Pearson Prentice Hall, 2005), 71–72.
39. U.S. Department of Justice, Law Enforcement Assistance Administration, *The Costs of Negligence: Losses from Preventable Household Burglaries* (1979), 9.
40. Ralph F. Brislin, *The Effective Security Officer's Training Manual* (Butterworth-Heinemann, 1995), 59.
41. U.S. Department of Justice, National Institute of Justice, *Theft by Employees in Work Organizations* (1983), 2.
42. Bologna, *supra* note 13, at 98–99.
43. J. Kirk Barefoot, *Undercover Investigation*, 3rd ed. (Butterworth-Heinemann, 1995), 117.
44. Pinkerton's, Inc., *supra* note 12, at 165.

10 Investigative Method and Technique

Insurance Cases

I. INTRODUCTION

The insurance industry has an ongoing need for the services of private security professionals. Admirable performance records are prerequisites to a contractual relationship, because the insurance industry—in commercial, casualty, auto liability, and workers' compensation settings—can basically pick and choose in a competitive market. Private security's contribution to insurance practice and procedure is quite substantial and includes:

- Interviewing claimants and witnesses
- Record searches
- Securing statements
- Contacting credit bureaus
- Securing medical and autopsy reports
- Appearing in courts
- Subpoena service
- Obtaining motor vehicle records
- Locating witnesses
- Activity checks
- Establishing criminal histories
- Background investigations

Investigative practice in the insurance industry generally involves four basic types of insurance: life, fire, marine, and casualty. In general terms, investigators analyze tragedy (in insurance parlance, "casualty"). Insurance claims usually comprise these four areas of casualty coverage:

- Death
- Property damage
- Personal/bodily injury
- Illness and disability

An insured and insurer are contractual parties to an explicit, well-defined agreement, the *insurance policy*. As a result, when a claim occurs, the insurance company needs verification of the status, credibility, and authenticity of the claim in order to determine whether there is legal liability. Private security firms are frequently asked to perform these authoritative reviews.

Whatever the type of insurance claim, the underlying investigation determines the truth by obtaining the facts and recording the information. Insurance companies are primarily concerned with clear and accurate factual representations, which in turn permit their legal counsel to make judgments, develop tactical strategies, or formulate settlement positions. Traditional lines of inquiry in the insurance sector include, but are not limited to:

- Did the event (e.g., the accident causing the claim) actually occur?
- Is the insured liable?
- What is the extent of the injury or damage?
- Who was at fault?
- What is the claimant's medical history or prior injuries?
- Is the claimant truly disabled?
- What is the character, reputation, and credibility of witnesses for the claimant?
- Can surveillance produce results regarding the claimant's physical condition?
- In an uninsured motorist case, are there assets that can be attached?[1]

II. APPLICATION AND METHOD

The issues that the investigator faces are numerous. The investigator is advised to develop a series of forms, checklists, and other documentary tools that can assist in the performance of investigative work.

A. Property Claim for Cases of Arson

In fire casualty and property policies, a frequent inquiry involves whether damaged property, goods, or other collateral is a compensable claim. The crime of arson is often committed by the insured. Arson is a multimillion dollar drain on businesses, government entities, and individuals. When investigators review fire-damaged structures, the owners' names appear on the initial suspect list. Burning to defraud the insurer is particularly likely in economically depressed areas or when an owner is under extraordinary financial pressure. The investigator should consider these possible motives:

- Fraud
- Juvenile theft
- Effort to hide other crimes
- Riot
- Jealousy
- Vandalism
- Revenge
- Thrill (pyromania)
- Terrorism[2]

Establishing motive is a priority of the investigator.[3] The checklist in Figure 10.1 suggests motives or mitigating factors that might point to a fire set by the insured. A more comprehensive document regarding motivation and other issues relative to the proof of an arson insurance investigation case is shown in Figure 10.2.

1. Is there a need for cash?
2. Is there a reason to terminate the lease?
3. Is there cause to relocate a business?
4. Is there an unprofitable contract?
5. What is the profit picture?
6. What are people saying?
7. What type of neighborhood is the building located in?
8. Is the fire advantageous to anyone?
9. What other crimes might have been perpetrated?
10. Is there other trouble or difficulty in the neighborhood?
11. Is arson a common crime in the neighborhood?
12. Was insurance recently increased?

FIGURE 10.1 Motives for proof of arson.

Sources of Interview Information

The following is a list of some of the possible witnesses to acts committed in connection with an arson-for-profit scheme and the types of questions they should be asked:

I. Interview of Witnesses at Scene of Fire
   A. Possible Witnesses:
      - Tenants of building
      - Tenants of surrounding buildings
      - Businessmen in building
      - Businessmen in surrounding buildings
      - Customers in businesses in building
      - Customers in businesses in surrounding buildings
      - Passersby including: bus route drivers, taxi drivers, deliverymen, garbage collectors, police patrol, people waiting for buses and taxis
   B. Questions to Be Asked:
      - Did you observe the fire?
      - At what time did you first observe the fire?
      - In what part of building did you observe the fire?
      - What called your attention to the building?
      - Did you see anyone entering or leaving the building prior to the fire?
      - Did you recognize them?
      - Can you describe them?
      - Did you observe any vehicles in the area of the fire?
      - Can you describe them?
      - Can you describe the smoke and the color of the flame?
      - How quickly did the fire spread?
      - Was the building burning in more than one place?
      - Did you detect any unusual odors?
      - Did you observe anything else?
      - What else did you observe?

II. Interview of Fire Officers and/or Firefighters at Scene
   A. Questions to Be Asked:
      - What time was alarm received?
      - What time did you arrive at scene of fire?
      - Was your route to the scene blocked?
      - What was the extent of burning when you arrived?
      - Were doors and windows locked?
      - Was the entrance and/or passageways blocked?
      - What kind of fire was it?
      - What was the spread speed of the fire?
      - In what area(s) did the fire start?
      - What was the proximity of the fire to the roof?
      - Was there evidence of the use of an accelerant?
      - Was there any evidence of arson recovered?
      - Did the building have a fire alarm system?
      - Was it operating?
      - Was there any evidence of tampering with the alarm system?
      - Did the building have a sprinkler system?
      - Did it operate?
      - Was there any evidence of tampering with the sprinkler system?
      - Was there anyone present in the building when you arrived?
      - Who was that person in the building?
      - Did he or she say anything to you?
      - Were there any people present at the scene when you arrived?
      - Who were they?
      - Did you observe any vehicles at the scene or leaving when you arrived?
      - Can you describe them?
      - Were there contents in the building?
      - Was there evidence of contents removed?
      - Was the owner present?

FIGURE 10.2 Form for recording sources of interview information.

- Did the owner make a statement?
- What did the owner say?
- What is the prior fire history of the building?
- What is the prior fire history of the area?

III. Interview of Insurance Personnel

The profit in many arson-for-profit cases is the payment from an insurance policy or policies. There are three classes of people who may be interviewed in order to determine if the profit centers around an insurance claim. They are the insurance agent/broker, the insurance adjuster, and the insurance investigator.

A. Questions to Ask the Agent or Broker:
- Who is the insured?
- Is there more than one insured?
- Is the insured the beneficiary?
- What type of policy was issued?
- What is the amount of the policy?
- When was it issued?
- When does it expire?
- What is the premium cost?
- Are payments up to date?
- Have there been any increases in the amount of coverage?
- What amount?
- When did increase take effect?
- What was the reason for the increase?
- Are there any special provisions in the policy (e.g., interruption of business or rental income)?
- What are they, and when did they take effect?
- Has the insured ever received a cancellation notice on this property? If so, when? Why?
- Does the insured have any other policies?
- Were there previous losses at the location of the fire?
- Were there losses at other locations owned by the insured?

B. Questions to Ask the Insurance Claims Adjustor:
- Did you take a sworn statement from the insured?
- Did the insured submit documents regarding proof of loss, value of contents, bills of lading, value of building, etc.?
- Did you inspect the fire scene?
- Did you inspect the fire scene with a public insurance adjustor?
- Did you and the public adjuster agree on the cost figure in the loss?
- Have you dealt with this public adjuster before?
- Has the adjuster represented this owner before?
- Has the insured had any other losses with this company? If so, provide details.

C. Questions to Ask the Insurance Adjuster:
- Were you able to determine the cause of the fire?
- Did you collect any evidence?
- Who analyzed the evidence?
- What were the results of the analysis?
- Was the cause of the fire inconsistent with state of building as known through underwriting examination?
- Have you investigated past fires involving the location?
- Have you investigated past fires involving the insured?
- What were the results of the investigations?
- Have you had prior investigations involving the public adjuster?
- Have you had prior investigations involving buildings handled by the same insurance agent/broker?
- What were the results of these investigations?
- Does this fire fit into a pattern of fires of recent origin in the area?
- What are the similarities?
- What are the differences?
- Have you taken any statements in connection with this burning?
- Whose statements did you take?
- What do they reveal?

There may be restrictions on the amount of information insurance personnel can turn over without a subpoena, but the investigator should be able to determine enough to indicate whether the issuance of a subpoena or search warrant would prove fruitful.

FIGURE 10.2 (continued).

IV. Other Witnesses Concerning Finances of Insured

There are a number of other people who may have information relating to the finances of the owner which may indicate how they stood to profit from the burning. These witnesses would include business associates, creditors, and competitors. Following are the types of questions these witnesses may be able to answer:

- How long have you known the owner/insured?
- What is the nature of your relationship with the owner?
- Do you have any information on the financial position of the business?
- Is the owner competitive with similar businesses?
- Have there been recent technological advances that would threaten the business's position?
- Has there been a recent increase in competition that would affect the business's position?
- Have changes in the economy affected the business's position?
- Has the owner experienced recent difficulty in paying creditors?
- Has the owner's amount of debt increased recently?
- Has the business lost any key employees recently?
- Has the location of the business changed for the worse recently?
- Has the owner increased the mortgage or taken out a second or third mortgage?
- Has the owner had difficulty making mortgage payments?
- Do you have any other information about the owner's financial position?

FIGURE 10.2 (continued).

Proof of arson is difficult without credible, forensic physical evidence.[4] Investigators should use a checklist similar to that shown in Figure 10.3 when reviewing actual sites and locations. In sum, the investigator should look for anything at the scene that does not belong or the absence of anything that does belong.

Private investigators are often requested to perform a thorough fire inspection report on a burned vehicle. By answering questions such as those listed in Figure 10.4, the investigator can ensure he or she has made a comprehensive analysis.

B. Workers' Compensation

Workers' compensation is a legislative provision whereby injuries that occur in the workplace, within an employer/employee relationship, are litigated and resolved according to a predetermined compensation formula and remedial scheme. It is a legislative response that replaces the common law principles of negligence and intentional torts with a strict liability, no-fault, statutory remedy. Employees who are injured on the job must be able to demonstrate that their injuries were work related and were within the scope of employment. The problems with fraudulent claims are now legendary in investigative circles. As in disability cases, it is easy enough to feign injury, and the resulting costs for these frauds are higher employer premiums.[5] A worksheet to help collect information regarding the compensability of a claim is given in Figure 10.5.[6]

Prior to the enactment of workers' compensation legislation, American law was more concerned with assessing or analyzing the negligent or intentional conduct of the employer, such as an employer who provided unsafe tools or equipment, fostered a dangerous work environment, or failed to warn of dangers in the work environment. These lines of advocacy have been legislatively swept away, and injuries are now adjudged on a strict liability basis, that is, an injury in the workplace will be compensable regardless of who is at fault. The following examples taken from the Michigan State Code illustrate situations that indicate the basis of liability:

1. An employee who receives a personal injury arising out of and in the course of employment by an employer who is subject to this act at the time of the injury, shall be paid compensation as provided in the Act. In a case of death resulting from personal injury to the employee, compensation shall be paid to the employee's dependents as provided in this Act. Time of injury or date of injury as used in this act in the case of a disease or in the case of an injury not attributable to a single event shall be the last day of work in the employment of which the employee was last subjected to the conditions that resulted in the employee's disability or death.

2. Mental disabilities and conditions of the aging process, including but not limited to the heart and cardiovascular conditions, shall be compensable if contributed to or aggravated or accelerated by the employment in a significant manner.
3. An employee going to and from his work, while on the premises where the employee's work is to be performed, and within a reasonable time before and after his working hours is presumed to be in the course of his or her employment.[7]

Arson Investigation Questionnaire

1. Are there signs of accelerants of any kind?
2. Are there signs of explosives?
3. Are there signs of trailers (items that assist in the spreading of fire, like clothing, bedding, curtains) from one point to another?
4. Can a comparison be made between the normal course and conduct of a fire versus its most intense point? (Often signs of the origination point)
5. Are there any residues indicating incendiary devices?
6. What was the status of doors and windows?
7. Can a fire pattern be discerned?
8. What is the status and condition of closets?
9. Are hard floors like concrete, stone, or tile more intensely burned in some spots than others? (Look for spalling, which causes the cracking and flaking of cement.)
10. Was the location abandoned or lived in?
11. What was the thermostat setting?
12. What was the condition of the oil burner?
13. What is the wattage of light bulbs?
14. Were electrical conductors overloaded?
15. Were there significant amounts of extension cords?
16. Were items of value and significant expense recently removed from the building?
17. In a multifloored building, can you distinguish the pattern and trail of fire?
18. Are there any witnesses?
19. Is there any photographic evidence?
20. Has physical evidence been cared for to assure the chain of custody?

FIGURE 10.3 Arson investigation questionnaire.

As a result of this statutory construction, injuries on the job, from broken bones to lung disease, are subject to the provisions of the Workers' Compensation Act. In most jurisdictions a schedule of benefits is published (Figure 10.6[8]).

Upon initial interview and case assessment, the investigator's most pressing concern must be whether an injury exists and whether the injury is related to or arose from the work environment. To confirm the legitimacy of the claim, the investigator should consider using the techniques and tactics of surveillance—the most often used strategy to ensure the credibility of a claim. Workers' compensation, disability, and proof of contested injuries should rely heavily on the use of photographic or video surveillance. The end result of this type of surveillance should, by visual means, verify or refute the authenticity of the claimant's condition. The best approach is to consider the injury from the claimant's point of view to determine exactly how the injury affects the ability to function. The more extreme the claimant's movements are and the more they conflict with those of a truly disabled person, the more important it is to record the claimant's action visually. The investigator should also document whether the claimant is able to perform activities that bear on the alleged injury. Types of actions to look for include:

TOTAL FIRE INSPECTION REPORT

NAME OF INSURED ____________ INSPECTION DATE ____________

ADDRESS ____________ LOSS DATE ____________

INSURANCE COMPANY ____________ POLICY NUMBER ____________

SALVAGE EXAMINED AT (Location) ____________

YR. & MAKE OF VEHICLE ____________ VIN ____________

EXTERIOR

Body metal sagged or warped? ____________ Where? ____________

Glass melted or fused? ____________ Where? ____________

Any evidence of collision? ____________ Where? ____________

Have tires/wheels been changed? ____________ Which ones? ____________

Tires burned? ____________ Which ones? ____________

Condition ____________

Spare in trunk? ____________ Condition ____________

Exterior mirrors or other accessories missing? ____________

Which ones? ____________

Excessive wear in suspension linkage? ____________

Any additional observations? ____________

INTERIOR

Doors open? ____________ Which ones? ____________

Windows down? ____________ Which ones? ____________

Upholstery and trim burned? ____________ Extent? ____________

Floor mats burned? ____________ Extent? ____________

Any evidence of an accelerant? ____________

Any accelerant container? ____________

Any tension left in seat springs? ____________

Any evidence of personal property burning? ____________

What? ____________

Vehicle equipped with radio? ____________ Missing? ____________

Air conditioning? ____________ Missing? ____________

Any other accessories? ____________ Missing? ____________

Tools? ____________ Missing? ____________

Ignition key anywhere in evidence? ____________

Any additional observations? ____________

Hood up or down during the fire? ____________

Condition of drive belts? ____________

Wiring? ____________

Motor mounts? ____________

FIGURE 10.4 Fire inspection report form.

MECHANICAL CONDITION

Radiator melted? ____________ Full? ____________

Engine grease deposits? ____________ Evidence of burning? ____________

Start motor if possible. Run for 5 or 10 minutes.

Are there any cracks or breaks on block or head? ____________

Any unusual noises? ____________

If not possible to start motor, secure the services of a reliable mechanic. Remove oil pan and head. Check all parts for wear or breaks. When serious mechanical defects are discovered, obtain a brief statement from mechanic and have it witnessed, incorporating a description of defects and if, in the mechanic's opinion, they occurred prior to the fire.

Clutch, transmission, drive shaft, rear axle assembly: Jack up rear of car with motor running or, if not running, test running gear.

Evidence of wear or breakage? ____________ Clutch? Transmission? ____________

Drive shaft split or bent? ____________ Rear axle & housing worn? ____________

Broken? ____________

Any additional observations? ____________

FUEL SYSTEM

Where was gas cap during fire? ____________

Drain plug: Tampered with? ____________ If in tank, is it right? ____________

Gasoline: Burned from tank? ____________ If not, how much in tank? ____________

Fuel lines & connections: (trace to pump and carburetor)

Evidence of tampering? ____________ Where? ____________

How? ____________ Before or after fire? ____________

Fuel pump: Gasoline in sediment bowl? ____________ Bowl broken? ____________

Removed? ____________ Melted? ____________

Air filter in place? ____________ Missing? ____________

Any additional observations? ____________

ELECTRICAL SYSTEM

Battery: In place? ____________

If damaged, where burned? ____________ Clamp tight? ____________

Cable shorted out? ____________ How? ____________

Wiring: Any shorts? ____________ Disconnections? ____________

Switches: (on or off) Ignition? ____________ Lights? ____________

Spark plugs: Condition? ____________ Any wires disconnected? ____________

Distributor: In working condition? ____________ Burned or melted? ____________

Any additional observations? ____________

GENERAL REMARKS:

FIGURE 10.4 (continued).

CLIENT DATA SHEET: WORKERS' COMPENSATION CASE

IN RE: ______________________ Date Of Injury: ______________________

INS. CO: ______________________ Hearing Commissioner: ______________________

Hearing Date: ______________________

I.C. Docket No. ______________________

1. Full Name______________________S.S. No.______________________Age__________
2. Address______________________Telephone No ______________________
3. Name of Spouse or Nearest Kin and Address: ______________________

____

Number of children: ______________________

4. Employer and Address: ______________________

Job Held: ______________________

5. Hired In: ______________________Length of Employment: ______________________
6. Work Week: ______________ Hours per day: __________ Days per Week: ______________
7. Wage Rate: ______________ Per hour/day/week__________ For overtime: ______________
8. Average Weekly Wage: ______________________ Extras Furnished: ______________
9. Date of Accident: ______________________ Hour: ______________
10. Paid for Date of Injury? ______________________ Started Losing Time: ______________
11. Now receiving comp. ______________________ Weeks paid at__________per week
12. Place of accident______________________ County______________
13. Description of Accident and Injury: ______________________

____

____

Accident Details: ______________________

____

____

14. Any Part of Body Amputated?__________ Member and Point of Amputation: ______________

____

15. Notice of Accident: Who: ______________________ Title: ______________

When: ______________________

16. Witnesses: ______________________

____

17. Doctors: ______________________

Sent by: ______________________

18. Hospital: ______________________ From: ______________ To: ______________
19. Travel: ______________________
20. Returned to Work?______________- Date: ______________ Rate of Pay: ______________
21. Any statements or Recorded interviews given? ______________ To Whom: ______________
22. Other Attorneys Consulted? ______________________ Who: ______________
23. Third Party Liability: ______________________
24. All Other Injuries and Claims: ______________________

____

25. Prior Health: ______________________
26. Date of Contract: ______________________ Referred by: ______________________
27. Additional Information: ______________________

____

____

FIGURE 10.5 Client data sheet to be completed when working a worker's compensation case.

WORKER'S DISABILITY COMPENSATION ACT OF 1969 (EXCERPT)
Act 317 of 1969

418.361 Partial incapacity for work; amount and duration of compensation; effect of imprisonment or commission of crime; scheduled disabilities; meaning of total and permanent disability; limitations; payment for loss of second member.

Sec. 361. (1) While the incapacity for work resulting from a personal injury is partial, the employer shall pay, or cause to be paid to the injured employee weekly compensation equal to 80% of the difference between the injured employee's after-tax average weekly wage before the personal injury and the after-tax average weekly wage which the injured employee is able to earn after the personal injury, but not more than the maximum weekly rate of compensation, as determined under section 355. Compensation shall be paid for the duration of the disability. However, an employer shall not be liable for compensation under section 351, 371(1), or this subsection for such periods of time that the employee is unable to obtain or perform work because of imprisonment or commission of a crime.

(2) In cases included in the following schedule, the disability in each case shall be considered to continue for the period specified, and the compensation paid for the personal injury shall be 80% of the after-tax average weekly wage subject to the maximum and minimum rates of compensation under this act for the loss of the following:

(a) Thumb, 65 weeks.

(b) First finger, 38 weeks.

(c) Second finger, 33 weeks.

(d) Third finger, 22 weeks.

(e) Fourth finger, 16 weeks.

The loss of the first phalange of the thumb, or of any finger, shall be considered to be equal to the loss of 1/2 of that thumb or finger, and compensation shall be 1/2 of the amount above specified.

The loss of more than 1 phalange shall be considered as the loss of the entire finger or thumb. The amount received for more than 1 finger shall not exceed the amount provided in this schedule for the loss of a hand.

(f) Great toe, 33 weeks.

(g) A toe other than the great toe, 11 weeks.

The loss of the first phalange of any toe shall be considered to be equal to the loss of 1/2 of that toe, and compensation shall be 1/2 of the amount above specified.

The loss of more than 1 phalange shall be considered as the loss of the entire toe.

(h) Hand, 215 weeks.

(i) Arm, 269 weeks.

An amputation between the elbow and wrist that is 6 or more inches below the elbow shall be considered a hand, and an amputation above that point shall be considered an arm.

(j) Foot, 162 weeks.

(k) Leg, 215 weeks.

An amputation between the knee and foot 7 or more inches below the tibial table (plateau) shall be considered a foot, and an amputation above that point shall be considered a leg.

(l) Eye, 162 weeks.

Eighty percent loss of vision of 1 eye shall constitute the total loss of that eye.

(3) Total and permanent disability, compensation for which is provided in section 351 means:

(a) Total and permanent loss of sight of both eyes.

(b) Loss of both legs or both feet at or above the ankle.

(c) Loss of both arms or both hands at or above the ankle.

(d) Loss of any 2 of the members or faculties in subdivisions (a), (b), or (c).

(e) Permanent and complete paralysis of both legs or both arms or of 1 leg and 1 arm.

(f) Incurable insanity or imbecility.

(g) permanent and total loss of industrial use of both legs or both hands or both arms or 1 leg and 1 arm; for the purpose of this subdivision such permanency shall be determined not less than 30 days before the expiration of 500 weeks from the date of injury.

(4) The amounts specified in this clause are all subject to the same limitations as to maximum and minimum as above stated. In case of the loss of 1 member while compensation is being paid for the loss of another member, compensation shall be paid for the loss of the second member for the period provided in this section. Payments for the loss of a second member shall begin at the conclusion of the payments for the first member.

Rendered Thursday, June 11, 2009 **Page 1** **Michigan Compiled Laws Complete Through PA 37 of 2009**

© Legislative Council, Station of Michigan *Courtesy of www.legislature.mi.gov*

FIGURE 10.6 Excerpt from Worker's Disability Act of 1969.

History: 1969, Act 317, Eff. Dec. 31, 1969;—Am. 1980, Act 357, Eff. Jan. 1, 1982;—Am. 1985, Act 103, Imd. Eff. July 30, 1985.

Constitutionality: The statutory limitation in subsection (2)(g) of this section is not unconstitutional. Johnson v Harrischfeger Corp, 414 Mich 102; 323 NW2d912 (1982).

Compiler's note: For legislative intent as to severability, see Compiler's note to MCL 418.213.

Popular name: Act 317

Popular name: Heat and Lung Act

Rendered Thursday, June 11, 2009 **Page 2** **Michigan Compiled Laws Complete Through PA 37 of 2009**

© Legislative Council, Station of Michigan *Courtesy of www.legislature.mi.gov*

FIGURE 10.6 (continued).

1. Back Injury
   - Subject is carrying bundles (such as groceries) in a normal fashion.
   - Subject is carrying anything of moderate weight in an awkward position (such as a large container of water in front of him with both hands).
   - Subject is leaning in an awkward position (such as out a window to clean an upper pane of glass).
   - Subject is using his body to hold a heavy object in place or to apply pressure (such as applying pressure to an electric drill to bore a hole at the level of his head or above).
2. Head Injury
   - Subject is extremely active, physically, in extreme heat (such as working on a roof laying shingles).
   - Subject continuously moves his head in a quick, jerky fashion (such as one does in some strenuous dances).
   - Subject is involved in strenuous running.
3. Leg Injury
   - Subject is walking in a quick, carefree manner (such as skipping or quickly crossing the street).
   - Subject is running.
   - Subject is freely and quickly climbing stairs without the assistance of a railing or cane.
   - Subject is found carrying a heavy object up stairs.
   - Subject gets up from an extended crouching position (such as when washing a car or weeding a garden).
   - Subject remains in a crouching position for some time.
4. Arm Injury
   - Subject is carrying something heavy at arm's length (such as a car tire).
   - Subject is seen grasping or pulling something (such as a large rock or root from the ground).
   - Subject is propping something of weight up (such as an extension ladder).
   - Subject is twisting something (such as wringing out a wet towel).
   - Subject is lifting something above the belt (such as loading luggage, groceries, or boxes into a vehicle).
5. Whiplash
   - Basically the same activities shown in 1. and 2. above, with the addition of unusual movement of the neck.[9]

Figure 10.7 includes detailed data on types of information to gather, pertinent medical information to find, and surveillance to report, as well as a summary of the investigator's findings.

Worker's Compensation Investigation
Final Report

Client: [Name]	File No:
[Title]	Date:
[Company Name]	Report by:
[Address]	

Report of Investigation

Re: [Subject's name or other pertinent information]

Synopsis:

As requested by [client and address], a [type of investigation] was conducted on [subject's name] to determine.... The [investigation] and/or [activity] included [photographs or videos]. These efforts revealed....

Details

A. Personal Information:
Name of subject and any aliases
Address of Subject
Telephone Number
Date of Birth
Social Security Number
Height/Weight
Hair/Eye color

B. Intelligence Information
A check of the [state] Department of Motor Vehicle Records revealed that the subject has a [current/expired/suspended] [state] driver's license, OLN [number], expiration [date].
Subject owns and/or uses the following vehicles:
[year/make/model/color of car]
[registration]

C. Interview Results (if any)
On [date] [name of interviewee] was interviewed. [name] is the [relationship] of the subject. The interview took place at [location]. The Agent learned that [results of interview].

or

Interviews were not conducted [reason].

D. Medical Information
According to [source: include name, title and address], the subject's medical condition is [explain].

E. Surveillance Results

July 8, 2009
7:00 am – 10:00 am

7:35 am On Wednesday, July 8, 2009, at 7:35 am Agents arrived at 456 East Main Street, West Hills, PA and initiated a surveillance on subject. Agents observed a 1999 black Buick (PA registration ABC-1234) parked in front of the residence. Agents observed the residence to be a side-by-side duplex, orange brick, subject residing in the left side facing the house. The right side is unoccupied.

9:35 am Agents unsuccessfully attempted to contact the subject by telephone. Agents listened to a recorded message indicating that subject was not at home. Agents terminated surveillance at approximately 10:00 am.

July 9, 2009
6:00 am – 12:00 pm

6:00 am On Thursday, July 9, 2009 at 6:00 am Agents arrived at 456 East Main Street, West Hills, PA and initiated a surveillance on subject. Subject's vehicle (1999 Black Buick, PA registration ABC-1234) was parked on the street in front of the residence.

At approximately 9:00 am, a pretext telephone call was placed to subject to verify her presence at the residence with positive results. Agents maintained surveillance until 12:00 pm and observed no movement. Surveillance was terminated at approximately 12:00 pm.

FIGURE 10.7 Final report in Worker's Compensation investigation.

July 10, 2009
2:30 pm – 6:00 pm

2:30 pm	On Friday, July 10, 2009 at 2:30 pm Agents arrived at 456 East Main Street, West Hills, PA and initiated a surveillance on subject. Agents observed subject enter vehicle (1999 Black Buick, PA registration ABC-1234) and proceed to the West Hills Shopping Center where the subject entered the deli.
2:45 pm	At 2:45 pm the subject exited the deli with an unidentified white female, entered her vehicle and proceeded to the Richmond Shopping Center located at 123 East Main Street, Mars, PA. Subject parked in front of a MAC Banking Machine and made what appeared to be several transactions.
3:10 pm	At 3:10 pm the subject and companion returned to the West Hills Shopping Center and entered the Food King Supermarket.
3:55 pm	At 3:55 pm the subject exited the supermarket with one bag of groceries and proceeded to her vehicle and placed the groceries in the trunk of the car (Photograph #1) Subject then proceeded into the ice cream store.
4:05 pm	At 4:05 pm the subject exited the ice cream store, eating an ice cream cone, entered her vehicle and finished eating the cone. (Photograph #2)
4:10 pm	At approximately 4:10 pm subject proceeded to a MAC Banking Machine located at 456 East Main Street. Subject made a transaction on the machine and proceeded home. Surveillance was terminated at approximately 5:45 pm.

F. Summary
Agents observed no apparent physical disability that would impair movement.

or

Agents observed....

End of Report

FIGURE 10.7 (continued)

C. Disability Claims

Insurance companies that issue disability policies have a recurring need for verification of disability claims in the same way that the Social Security Administration must verify the legitimacy of a claim. At the government level, particularly the Social Security Administration, outside review and analysis by investigators is standard operating procedure. The following elements are crucial to determine whether the claimant is really disabled:

1. Was claimant hospitalized?
   - Where, when, and for how long?
   - Name of attending physician.
2. Is claimant confined to his house?
   - For what period of time is claimant bedridden?
3. Is claimant wearing any braces, aided by orthopedic equipment or other medical accoutrements as a result of the injury? Give description and names of medical aids, if possible.
4. What injuries can be documented?
5. Is the claimant restricted in his activities?
   - Is the claimant working? Confirm status.
6. Has there been any time lost from work due to the accident?
   - Give confirmation and facts.
7. Are there any previous accidents?
   - Does the claimant have a significant past medical history?
8. Does the claimant drive?
9. In what activities is the claimant presently engaged?[10]

In addition to standard surveillance techniques discussed throughout this text, a disability claim investigation relies heavily upon an onsite claimant interview. The investigator need not fear

NEIGHBORHOOD INVESTIGATION CHECKLIST

1. How long have they known the subject?
2. Does a family relationship exist between the subject and neighbors (or reference)?
3. Present address (how long there); previous address.

   How frequently is subject seen?
4. Age, race and marital status (spouse's name).
5. Dependency status (include relationship, names, and approximate ages of dependents).
6. Is the subject employed? If so, where? If place of employment is not known, what time does he leave for work and what is his mode of travel? (Also, if employment status is unknown, does the subject leave his residence at about the same time every day?)
7. If unemployed, when and where did he last work; what were his duties and why did he leave this employment? Does he appear able to work? What is his source of income? His normal occupation?
8. Are neighbors aware of any injuries or hospitalization? (Details, where, when, how long ago, etc.)
9. Health and prior to and subsequent to the injury in question.
10. Did the injury in question affect his normal activities? (yard work, house repairs, car repairs, etc.)
11. Present activities (golf, bowling, dancing, etc.)
12. Is spouse or are children employed? If so, where, how long, etc.
13. Property owned (residence, automobile, boat, truck, machinery, etc.)
14. Desirability as a neighbor and reputation (does subject drink alcohol, fight, gamble, use drugs, file suits, etc.)
15. Names and addresses of personal references, friends, and relatives.

FIGURE 10.8 Neighborhood investigation checklist.

personal confrontation or discussion with the claimant unless the insurance company has a strong certainty of subterfuge and fraud. A pretext of some kind is advisable, and a neighborhood investigation is likely to be the most informative.

> With very few exceptions, the neighborhood investigation is performed under a pretext. A pretext means we do not identify ourselves as a representative of the client or of our own company, and we do not state the actual purpose of our inquiries.[11]

When questioning people, the investigator should be thoroughly prepared, orderly in presentation, and not appear intense or driven to a given end. The information elicited should come forth naturally from these third parties. Use of a checklist, such as that shown in Figure 10.8, will ensure that the investigator focuses on appropriate lines of questioning.

D. Auto Liability Claims

Due to escalating rates of auto litigation, the services of the private security industry are in high demand. Some insurance companies have adopted hardball strategies in contesting the claims and losses filed by lawyers. The typical automobile case arises from the auto insurance contract, that is, the agreement entered into between an insurer (the insurance company) and an insured (the claimant). A sample of a page of an auto insurance contract is provided in Figure 10.9.

FIRST PARTY BENEFITS COVERAGE—PENNSYLVANIA

The Definitions and General Provisions of this policy apply unless modified by this endorsement.

SCHEDULE

BASIC FIRST PARTY BENEFITS

Benefits	**Limit of Liability**
Medical Expense Benefit	Up to $10,000
Work Loss Benefit	Up to $4,000 subject to a maximum of $1,000 per month
Funeral Expense Benefit	Up to $1,5000

The following options apply instead of Basic First Party Benefits as indicated below or in the Declarations:|

☐ ADDED FIRST PARTY BENEFITS

Benefits	**Limit of Liability**
Medical Expense Benefit	Up to $_________
Work Loss Benefit	Up to $_________subject to a maximum of $_________per month
Funeral Expense Benefit	Up to $_________
Accidental Death Benefit	Up to $_________

|☐ COMBINATION FIRST PARTY BENEFITS

Benefits	**Limit of Liability**
Maximum total Single Limit	Up to $_________
Subject to the following individual limits:	
Medical Expense Benefit	No specific dollar amount
Work Loss Benefit	No specific dollar amount
Funeral Expense Benefit	Up to $2,500
Accidental Death Benefit	$25,000

NOTE: IF ADDED FIRST PARTY BENEFITS or COMBINATION FIRST PARTY BENEFITS are not shown as applicable in the Schedule or Declarations only BASIC FIRST PARTY BENEFITS apply.

The following exclusion applies as indication below or in the Declarations:
☐ EXCLUSION OF WORK LOSS BENEFIT
The Work Loss Benefit does not apply

I. DEFINITIONS

With respect to First Party Benefits Coverage:

"the Act" means the Pennsylvania Motor Vehicle Financial Responsibility Law of 1984, as amended.

In addition, the following words and phrases are defined for first party benefits coverage. They are bold-faced when used.

"**Bodily injury**" means accidental bodily harm to a person and that person's resulting illness, disease or death.

"**Insured**" means:

1. You or your **family member**.
2. Any other person:

a. while **occupying your covered auto**; or

FIGURE 10.9 Sample auto insurance contract.

1. Policy Declaration

The economic basis of the contractual obligation between the insured and the insurer is listed on a policy declaration page. Most policy declaration pages are uniform in content and comprise these categories:

- Bodily injury liability
- Collision protection
- Property damage liability
- Towing and labor costs
- Medical payments and benefits
- Funeral expenses
- Comprehensive coverage regarding personal effects
- Fire and theft
- Uninsured and underinsured motorist

Although dollar amounts influence the parameters of a potential lawsuit, the policy itself includes contractual provisions that guide the obligations of the insured and the insurer. Three initial components are described in the insurance contract:

1. Specific agreements and coverage. (See the example shown in Figure 10.9.)
2. Exclusions to coverage. (See Figure 10.10.)
3. Covenants and other contingencies. (See Figure 10.11.)

The investigator may have many functions within auto liability claims investigation, but the primary function is to determine the facts by obtaining an unbiased, factual recitation of what occurred. Decisions regarding liability, claims damages, and litigation are matters beyond the scope of investigative practice. Pinkerton's, Inc. emphasizes this fact in its handbook, *Investigation-Insurance Claims*:

EXCLUSIONS TO COVERAGE

We do not provide benefits for bodily injury:

1. Sustained by any person while intentionally causing or attempting to cause bodily injury to:
   a. himself;
   b. herself; or
   c. any other person;

   nor will we pay an Accidental Death Benefit on behalf of that person.
2. Sustained by any person while committing a felony.
3. Sustained by any person while seeking to elude lawful apprehension or arrest by a law enforcement official.
4. Sustained by any person while maintaining or using a motor vehicle knowingly converted by that person. However, this exclusion (4) does not apply to:
   a. you; or
   b. any family member.
5. Sustained by any person who, at the time of the accident:
   a. is the owner of one or more registered motor vehicles and none of the motor vehicles have in effect the financial responsibility required by the Act; or
   b. is occupying a motor vehicle owned by that person for which the financial responsibility required by the Act is not in effect.
6. Sustained by any person maintaining or using a motor vehicle while located for use as a residence or premises.
7. Sustained by any person injured as a result of conduct within the course of the business of repairing, servicing or otherwise maintaining motor vehicles. This exclusion (7) does not apply if the conduct is off the business premises.

FIGURE 10.10 Sample exclusions section of auto insurance contract.

LIMIT OF LIABILITY

The limit of liability shown in the Schedule or in the Declarations for the first party benefits that apply is the most we will pay to or for each insured as the result of any one accident. This is the most we will pay regardless of the number of:

1. Claims made;
2. Vehicles or premiums shown in the Schedule or in the Declarations;
3. Vehicles involved in the accident; or
4. Insurers providing first party benefits.

If Combination First Party Benefits are afforded, we will apply the total limit of liability to provide any separate limits required by the Act for Basic First Party Benefits. This provision will not change our total limit of liability.

Any amount payable under First Party Benefits Coverage shall be excess over any amounts paid, payable or required to be provided to an Insured under any workers' compensation law or similar law.

FIGURE 10.11 Sample limit of liability section of auto insurance contract.

> We are not experts in determining liability, but we are experts in investigation, in obtaining the facts. Once we have the facts, it is up to the client to take it from there.[12]

Investigators assist the insurance company in the compilation of facts that lead to strategic policy relative to litigation. In an automobile accident case, multiple remedies and causes of action may exist. The negligence action is not mutually exclusive but is predictably the cause of action first pled. Traditional negligence law asserts that certain careless acts, breaches of due care, result in actual injury and damage. The person who runs a stop sign or a red light, falls asleep at the wheel, or has his or her eyes distracted from the roadway, thereby causing injury, will be deemed to have breached the standard of care and conduct owed others in the operation of an automobile. Beyond negligence, other remedies must not be overlooked, such as:

1. First Party Benefits—Under contemporary no-fault provisions, an insured in a contractual capacity with his insurance company may collect benefits for injuries arising out of the ownership, operation or utilization of a motor vehicle.
2. Intentional Torts—Individuals who are not simply careless but intentional in their conduct, who inflict bodily injury, or who destroy property, can be sued on intentional tort theories such as assault, battery, trespass, or intentional infliction of mental distress.
3. Underinsured or Uninsured Benefits—If the tortfeasor's policy limits do not adequately compensate for injury, or the tortfeasor has no insurance (this is labeled "uninsured"), the insured's own policy may make up the inadequacy through its underinsurance or uninsured coverages. Frequently, competing carriers will insist on a right to consent to any settlement before payment of any underinsurance.

Web Exercise: Visit one of the many firms that operates in the auto claims portion of the insurance industry at: http://www.theeyewitness.com/auto-liability-investigations.html

2. Processing the Auto Liability Case

Governing investigative action in auto accident and liability cases is the need to discover the sequence, chain of events, and flow of conditions that led to the collision or other injury. The chain of events leading to the accident consists of:

1. Principal event, the time, the place, and type of accident—for example, running off the road; collision on the road with a pedestrian.
2. Perception of a hazard—the seeing, sensing, or hearing the unusual or unexpected movement or condition that could be taken as a sign of an accident about to happen;

3. The point of perception—the time and place at which the unusual or unexpected movement or condition could have been perceived by a normal person;
4. The point of no escape—the time and place beyond which the accident can no longer be prevented by the person who is watching;
5. Maximum engagement—the time and position in which the objects in a collision are pushed together as far as they will be; and
6. The final position—the time and place when objects involved finally come to rest; this is the position before anything is moved.[13]

Auto accident investigators must do all they can to maintain the final position of the persons or objects involved in the accident. Except for lifesaving issues and the minimization of property destruction, objects should remain in their final position to provide the most untainted picture of the accident scene. Insurance companies realize profits based on their capacity to analyze and reconstruct accident cases. Investigators, working on behalf of either the insured or the insurer, must possess the same level of dedication and proficiency. Where contributory negligence operates as a pure defense, reconstruction of the accident scene becomes an even more critical step in the investigative process.

Investigators need to document and complete memoranda outlining accident fact patterns because police reports and diagrams, as discussed in earlier sections of this text, serve as foundational pieces of evidence in the investigation of accident cases. Two types of forms regularly used to gather data are medical information sheets and accident data sheets. Samples of these types of forms are shown in Figures 10.12 and 10.13.

MEDICAL DATA

Please summarize the following items:____________________

Description of Injuries: ____________________

____

____

History of Accident: ____________________

____

____

Progress: ____________________

____

____

Past Medical History: ____________________

____

____

Present Complaints:

Date	Nature	Permanency

FIGURE 10.12 Summary of medical data.

Accident Data Form

Your name ____________________

Accident date ____________________ Time ______ am/pm

Address ____________________ City ____________________ State ______ Zip ______

Police Dept. ____________________ Case # ____________________ Tickets Issued? ☐ Yes ☐ No

If yes, to whom? ____________________ Charges ____________________

Other Vehicle:

Year ____________________ Make ____________________ Model ____________________

Color ____________________ License Plate # ____________________ State ____________________

Driver of Other Vehicle:

Name ____________________ Apparent injuries? ☐ Yes ☐ No

Home Address ____________________ City ____________________ State ______ Zip ______

Home Phone ____________________ Business Phone ____________________

Drivers License # ____________________ State ______ Insurance Carrier ____________________

Age ______ Sex ______ Ht ______ Wt ______

Injury type ____________________

Registered Owner of Other Vehicle:

Name ____________________ Apparent injuries? ☐ Yes ☐ No

Address ____________________ City ____________________ State ______ Zip ______

Drivers License # ____________________ State ______ Insurance Carrier ____________________

Passengers in Other Vehicle:

Name ____________________ Apparent injuries? ☐ Yes ☐ No

Home Address ____________________ City ____________________ State ______ Zip ______

Home Phone ____________________ Business Phone ____________________

Drivers License # ____________________ State ______ Insurance Carrier ____________________

Age ______ Sex ______ Ht ______ Wt ______

Injury type ____________________

Position in vehicle at time of accident ____________________

Name ____________________ Apparent injuries? ☐ Yes ☐ No

Home Address ____________________ City ____________________ State ______ Zip ______

Home Phone ____________________ Business Phone ____________________

Drivers License # ____________________ State ______ Insurance Carrier ____________________

Age ______ Sex ______ Ht ______ Wt ______

Injury type ____________________

Position in vehicle at time of accident ____________________

Witnesses:

Name ____________________ Apparent injuries? ☐ Yes ☐ No

Home Address ____________________ City ____________________ State ______ Zip ______

Home Phone ____________________ Business Phone ____________________

Name ____________________ Apparent injuries? ☐ Yes ☐ No

Home Address ____________________ City ____________________ State ______ Zip ______

Home Phone ____________________ Business Phone ____________________

FIGURE 10.13 Form used to gather accident data.

a. Scene Sketch

The investigator should ask the client to diagram the accident as he or she remembers it. This type of active, graphic participation will help the client get the facts straight, and the investigator should then verify and authenticate a client's story.

b. Photographing the Accident Scene

Although reports and documentation are necessary parts of investigative technique, photographs of the accident scene are vital pieces of evidence. Investigators should become proficient photographers or develop strong relationships with police photographers or private photographers who work as independent contractors. Photographic coverage of an accident scene should include:

1. *Approach to the scene* from the viewpoint of the driver or drivers involved. It may be necessary to make several photographs of the scene at different distances. Make these from the driver's eye level as he or she would be seated in the vehicle. Remember that the high cab of a tractor-trailer rig may place the driver as much as eight feet from the ground. Climb on a tow truck or station wagon tailgate to get the needed height.
2. *Eyewitness' viewpoint.* To corroborate eyewitness statements, make pictures of the scene from the eyewitness' position and eye level.
3. *Position of the vehicles.* Try to get shots of the final position of vehicles before they are moved. If they must be moved before they can be photographed, mark their positions with chalk or tape.
4. *Position of victims.* Where victims are thrown clear of the vehicles, get photographs of the position of a body or mark the position of an injured victim who is being removed for treatment.
5. *Point of impact.* If it is possible, determine and photograph the point of impact of the vehicle or vehicles involved in the accident. This may correspond to the final position of the vehicles, or it may be some distance from that point. Relate the vehicles in a photograph if possible.
6. *Overall view of scene.* One or several pictures that relate the overall scene elements can be useful to the accident investigator. One viewpoint for such photographs is a high position overlooking the scene; a rooftop, an embankment, a bridge, or even a truck can provide a commanding position. Other overall shots can be made with the camera at eye level in the direction of vehicle travel and then by looking back through the scene from the opposite direction to show the area of approach.
7. *Close-ups of accident details.* Details of vehicle damage, skid marks, tire marks, worn or damaged tires, registration plates, oil-water-gasoline spills, and broken parts provide key information to aid the accident investigator. Photograph questionable items within the car such as wine, beer, and liquor bottles; narcotics; or firearms.[14]

The Center for Public Safety at Northwestern University has the following suggestions on what to photograph at an accident scene:

1. Vehicle identification
   a. Vehicle license plate
   b. Vehicle identification plate
   c. Vehicle's make and model
2. Contact damage area
   a. Overlap
   b. Collapse
   c. Direction of thrust

3. Induced damage area
4. Undamaged area
5. Interior—when needed
6. Vehicle lamps (if there is a question regarding #6 and #7, take picture)
7. Vehicle tires
8. Close-up photographs[15]

The Traffic Institute also recommends that each picture be charted as to shutter speed, focal point, distance, and depth of field.

c. *Auto Accident Reconstruction*

Investigators involved in a traffic accident investigation will be confronted with problems from the simple to the complex. "Like many other specialized activities, traffic accident investigation may be done at various levels or degrees of technology depending on the needs and the resources available."[16] Northwestern University's Traffic Institute,[17] now known as the Center for Public Safety, a private, nonprofit organization founded in 1936, has provided accident reconstruction services to law enforcement, criminal justice, private security, and highway transportation agencies. Private investigators who wish to enhance their professional standing in accident reconstruction should consider participation in one of the Traffic Institute's many educational programs. Its web page that explains its Accident Reconstruction Course is shown in Figure 10.14.

The Center distinguishes five levels of traffic accident investigation:

1. Reporting
2. Supplementary Data Collection
3. Technical Preparation
4. Professional Reconstruction
5. Cause Analysis

At the first level, the investigator *identifies* and *classifies* the accident conditions, persons, and property involved. Reports and other documents discussed throughout this text are filled out indicating time of day, location, environment, damage to vehicles and drivers, pedestrians, passengers, witnesses, and officials on the scene.

Companies such as Smart Draw deliver virtual reconstructions such as that shown in Figure 10.15.[18]

At the second level, the *supplementary data collection* phase, the initial accident report is supplemented by the following:

- Measurements to locate final positions of vehicles and bodies of persons killed or injured.
- Measurements to locate tire marks, gouges, debris left on the road.
- Photos of final positions of vehicles.
- Photos of tire marks, gouges, and debris left on the road.
- Descriptions of damage to vehicles and measurements of collapse.
- Photos of damage to vehicles.
- Blood samples for alcohol tests.
- Informal statements of people involved and other witnesses.
- Preliminary matching of contact damage between vehicles and between vehicles and road surface or fixed objects.
- Descriptions and photos of damage to such equipment as lamps, tires, batteries, safety belts, and obtaining these for test if possible.

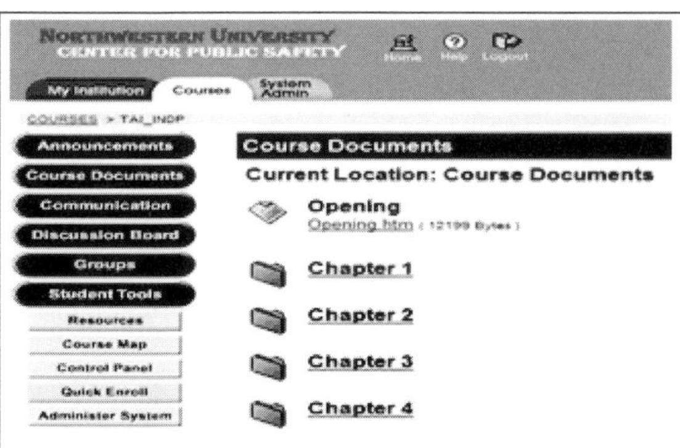

Accident Investigation 1 Online is a self-paced course that is taught online using Blackboard, a password-protected course management system, and can be accessed anywhere an internet connection is available.

Accident Investigation 1 Online provides the same information and comprehensive study of accident investigation as presented in the on-campus courses with the convenience and flexibility of accessing the course sites at a time that works best for you. Once you have registered and received your login information, you can begin your course at any time. Because the courses are self-paced, there are no scheduled course start dates.

Students will learn to take measurements and photographs of the accident scene and to make sketches and after-accident diagrams. Students are expected to complete field projects similar to those completed in the on-campus version of the course.

After successfully completing the projects and tests, you will receive a certificate of completion from the Northwestern University Center for Public Safety. You will then be prepared to attend the Accident Investigation 2, either online or on campus.

Upon registration, you will receive a copy of the revised edition of J. Stannard Baker's accident investigation manual, *Traffic Collision Investigation*, as well as instructions for accessing the online course site.

To order instructional materials, or for help accessing your online course site, please contact Janet Hundrieser at (800) 323-4011.

Additional shipping charges will be applied to international addresses.

COURSE CONTENT

- Preparation for traffic collision investigation
- Information from and about people
- Information from vehicles
- Information from roads
- Measuring and mapping the collision scene
- Photographing the collision scene and damaged vehicles

FIGURE 10.14 Based on changes made to replace Accident with Crash and Janet Hundreiser with Crash Investigation from Online Accident Investigation course webpage at http://nucps.northwestern.edu/course/crs_detail.asp?id=1065. With permission.

- Samples of paint and glass for examination.
- Chemical tests for intoxication.
- Autopsies to determine cause of death.
- Medical descriptions of injuries.[19]

Proceeding to the third level, *technical preparation*, the investigator begins to map out or graphically portray the incident. It may involve activities such as:

- Elementary ground photogrammetry.
- Mapping from perspective template photos.
- Matching vehicle damage areas and preparing maximum engagement, first contact, and disengagement diagrams.
- Preparation of after-accident situation map.
- Simple speed estimates from skid marks, yaw marks, and falls.
- Determination of design speed and critical speed of curves and turns.[20]

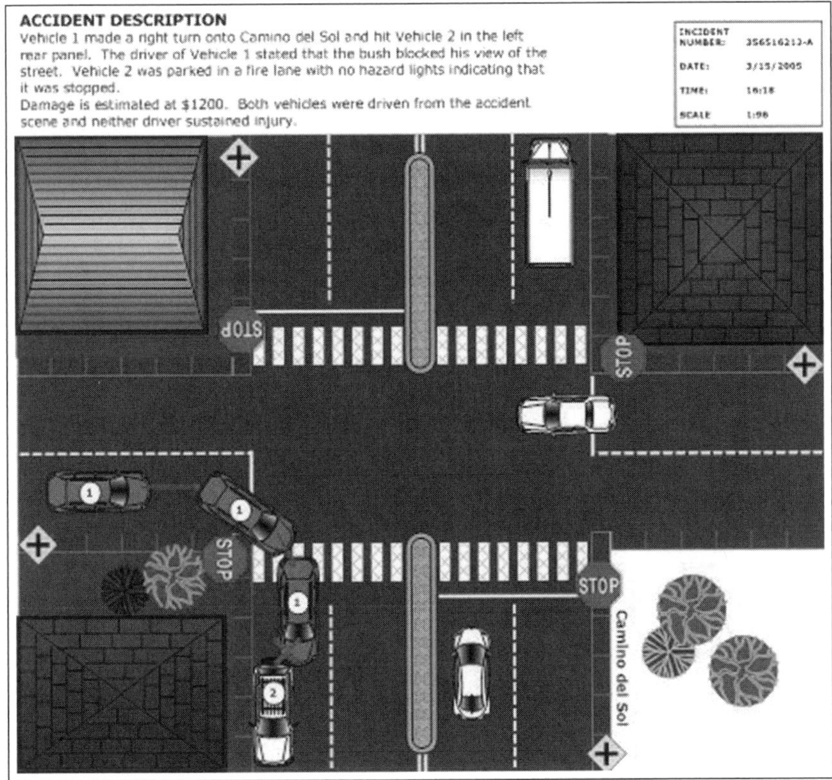

FIGURE 10.15 Auto accident reconstruction graphic. Reproduced with permission from SmartDraw.com. http://www.smartdtaw.com.

Yaw marks and other reference points can be photographically examined.

As discussed earlier, the investigator's comprehension of the accident site will be fostered by a scene sketch or other descriptive means. To construct an accident map, the investigator should follow the step-by-step instructions below.

1. Decide detail needed based on how map will be used:
   a. for *working* (reconstruction) *purposes*, minimum detail;
   b. for *display* (court) *purposes*, additional detail for realism.
2. Determine layout of roadways by inspection.
   a. Single roadway:
      (1) straight or curved;
      (2) number of lanes.
   b. Junction of two or more roadways:
      (1) number of legs;
      (2) number of lanes in each leg;
      (3) which roadway edges align without offset or angle;
      (4) what angles between roadways are not right angles.
3. Draw on field sketch basic layout of roadways. Use light lines. Show approximate widths, angles, and curves (freehand).
4. Connect all edges which align by dashed line on field sketch.
5. If any leg is not square with the others, project one edge of it until it intercepts the edge of another leg to form an intercept.
6. Select RP (reference point or points). Mark it on field sketch. Write description of RP on field sketch.

7. Mark accident RPs on field sketch if they are known.
8. Draw in edge returns (curves between edges of roadways), shoulders, sidewalks, etc., which may be needed.
9. Draw roadside objects which may be needed (fixed objects, etc.)
10. Draw in other things (buildings, fences, etc.) needed for display.
11. Indicate measurements to be made by dimension lines from coordinates or RPs to Items 3, 5, 7, 8, 9, and 10 above. Show measurements in series as much as possible (a series of measures from one point along a line).
12. Show additional measurements for curves and angles.
13. Add check measurements between important points.
14. Mark road surface (RP, etc.) if needed. Use yellow crayon.
15. Make measurements indicated. Record on field sketch.
16. Note grades, elevations, and character of surface. Record if needed.
17. Show north by arrow. (Add accident identifiers.)
18. Identify location by road name and, if needed, distance and direction to recognizable landmark. Give city or county and state.
19. Sign and date field sketch.[21]

At the fourth level of accident scene investigation, *professional reconstruction*, the investigator—after gathering all information and graphically reproducing it—attempts to define the accident in order to pose an explanation. Although a specific cause is not determined or enough evidence amassed to deduce legal causation, the fourth level of accident analysis seeks "opinions, deductions, and inferences … usually in the form of estimates of speed, position on the road, and visibility; descriptions of driving tactics (evasive action), strategy, communications, and how injuries were received; or proof of law violations and who was driving."[22]

In the final stage of accident reconstruction, *cause analysis*, a conclusion as to the actual cause is determined. Conceptually, the accident reconstruction now defines circumstances and events, relays why the accident occurred, and gives direct or conditional explanations. The investigator's position can include, but is not limited to, the following findings:

- Probable contribution of road or vehicle design deficiencies to accident, injury, and damage occurrence.
- Probable contribution of third parties to accident and injury occurrence.
- Probable contribution of temporary road or vehicle conditions, accident and injury, and damage occurrence.
- Probable contribution of temporary driver conditions (such as intoxication) to accident and injury occurrence.
- Complete combination of probable and possible factors contributing to tactical (evasive action) failures in the highway transport system.
- Complete combination of probable and possible factors contributing to strategy (precautionary measures) that prevented successful tactics or otherwise influenced the outcome of events.
- Recommendations for prevention of future accidents with some of the same factors as the one under study.[23]

Even a lifetime of field experience will not enable the investigator to claim perfection in auto accident analysis and reconstruction. As insurance companies seek ways of defending the onslaught of accident litigation, private security serves as the objective third party that provides information without bias or prejudice.

III. SPECIAL PROBLEMS: AUTO THEFT, FRAUD, AND PARTS PILFERAGE

Crime statistics point to a staggering rate of auto theft, illegal trafficking in auto parts, and the establishment of chop shops, underground operations that steal cars, strip them, and sell individual parts. The National Crime Insurance Bureau was formed in 1992 from a merger between the National Automobile Theft Bureau (NATB) and the Insurance Crime Prevention Institute (ICPI), both of which were not-for-profit organizations. The NATB, which managed vehicle theft investigations and developed vehicle theft databases for use by the insurance industry, dates to the early twentieth century, while the ICPI investigated insurance fraud for approximately twenty years before joining with the NATB. The primary purpose of the NCIB is to lead a united effort of insurers, law enforcement agencies, and representatives of the public to prevent and combat insurance fraud and crime though data analytics, investigations, training, legislative advocacy, and public awareness.

> **Web Exercise:** See the NCIB poster at https://www.nicb.org/cps/rde/xbcr/nicb/HotlinePosterFNL.pdf

To combat this plague of fraud, collusion, and thievery, the insurance industry, auto dealers, manufacturers, and legislative agencies have called upon the services of private investigators to pinpoint the location and identification of suspect motor vehicle practices. Investigators should cautiously evaluate an affidavit of vehicle theft, filed at either the local police department or insurance company, for the purpose of claim reimbursement. Figure 10.16 shows one such form.

Investigators must be wary of many claims and allegations, especially when certain insured profiles and other mitigating factors appear. Be skeptical of an insured, a claimant, who:

- Gives an address and phone number of a bar, hotel, or motel as a place where he or she can be contacted;
- Is unavailable or difficult to contact;
- Has family members or household who know nothing about the loss;
- Avoids the use of the U.S. mail;
- Has income incompatible with the amount of the car payment;
- Is a single male under twenty-eight years of age;
- Is unemployed;
- Is in arrears with lienholder;
- Has no prior business with the insurer;
- Is in an extreme hurry to settle the claim;
- Has made recent inquiry into policy coverage;
- Wishes to retain title on a total loss.

The type of vehicle is also instructive regarding potential fraud, theft, or collusion. Consider these queries:

- Is it a late model, expensive auto?
- Is the vehicle expensively customized?
- Are there expensive extras and accessories?
- Has the vehicle been rebuilt from a prior major collision claim?
- Is the vehicle inefficient on fuel?
- Is the vehicle identification number (VIN) suspect?
- Is there no collision damage on the recovered vehicle?
- Has the vehicle been stolen, subsequently recovered, and then shortly thereafter burned?

Received	
Dispatched	
Arrived	

Phoenix Police Department
Property Crimes Bureau
Auto Theft Detail
Stolen Vehicle Agreement & Affidavit

Case/Report number:______________________________

Name of registered owner of stolen vehicle (printed): ______________________________
Name of reporting person (printed): ______________________________
ID type: ________________ID #:________________DOB: ____________

Description of stolen vehicle:

MAKE______________MODEL__________YEAR____________
STYLE______________ COLOR__________VIN ____________
LICENSE______________ STATE__________LIEN HOLDER ____________
INSURANCE COMPANY____________________ POLICY#____________
FURTHER VEHICLE DESCRIPTION:______________________________

I ____________________ certify that the above-described vehicle was taken without my knowledge or permission from________________________ between the time span of ______________________________.

Due to the number of stolen vehicle reports the Phoenix Police Department receives, it is necessary that:

- I immediately notify the Phoenix P.D. if I become aware of the location of the stolen vehicle. ____(INITIAL)
- I agree to assist in the prosecution of the theft of my vehicle.______(INITIAL)

Under ARS 13-2907.01, it is unlawful for a person to knowingly make to a law enforcement agency of either this state or a political subdivision of this state a false, fraudulent or unfounded report or statement or to knowingly misrepresent a fact for the purpose of interfering with the orderly operation of a law enforcement agency or misleading a peace officer. False Reporting to a law enforcement agency is a **class 1 misdemeanor** punishable up to six months in jail, $2,500 fine and three years probation. Furthermore, under ARS 13-2204, it is unlawful for a person to knowingly destroy, remove, conceal, encumber, convert, sell, transfer, control, or otherwise deal with property subject to a security interest with the intent to hinder or prevent the enforcement of that interest. Defrauding Secured Creditors is a **class 6 felony** punishable up to 1.5 years in jail, and up to a $150,000 fine.

IF THE AFFIDAVIT IS NOT TAKEN IN PERSON BY A LAW ENFORCEMENT OFFICER OR AGENCY, THE PERSON WHO ALLEGES THAT A THEFT OF MEANS OF TRANSPORTATION HAS OCCURRED SHALL MAIL OR DELIVER THE SIGNED AND NOTARIZED AFFIDAVIT TO THE APPROPRIATE LOCAL LAW ENFORCEMENT AGENCY WITHIN SEVEN (7) DAYS AFTER REPORTING THE THEFT. IF THE APPROPRIATE LAW ENFORCEMENT AGENCY DOES NOT RECEIVE THE SIGNED AND NOTARIZED AFFIDAVIT WITHIN THIRTY (30) DAYS AFTER THE INITIAL REPORT, THE VEHICLE INFORMATION SHALL BE REMOVED FROM THE DATABASES OF THE NATIONAL CRIME INFORMATION CENTER AND THE ARIZONA CRIMINAL JUSTICE INFORMATION SYSTEM.

____
Signature of Reporting Person Date/Time

____
Complete Address

____
Home Phone Cell Phone Work Phone

____
Officer Signature Serial # Date/Time

Subscribed and sworn to me on this_______day of ________________, 20____.
Notary Public______________________________

My Commission Expires:______________________________

80-96D Rev. 8/07

FIGURE 10.16 Stolen vehicle affidavit.

The whole essence of effective auto theft, fraud, and collusion investigation involves the search for patterns, trends, special characteristics, and factors, such as:

- Type of car
- Time of the theft
- Day of the week
- Location of vehicle when stolen
- Suspects or vehicles seen
- Location of vehicle when recovered
- Condition of vehicle when recovered

Use the auto theft fraud indicator checklist in Figure 10.17 as a guide to this type of investigation.

AUTO THEFT FRAUD INDICATORS

1. Policy in effect ninety (90) days or less, or recent vehicle purchase.
2. Auto stolen while not in possession of insured.
3. In arrears with lienholder.
4. The vehicle was a previously recovered theft or the subject of a prior major collision claim.
5. Insured furnished address and phone number of a bar, hotel or motel as a place to be contacted by the claims adjuster.
6. The insured has failed to report the theft to the police.
7. The insured is unable to identify himself (i.e., does not know his own social security or driver's license number).
8. Late notice of theft to insurance company or police.
9. Any discrepancy in VIN or license plate numbers.
10. Cash purchase from an individual rather than a dealer.
11. The vehicle was alleged to have been stolen prior to titling and registration.
12. The previous owner cannot be located or is unknown to the insured.
13. Mail address differs from garaging address on policy.
14. Date of coverage and date of claim are closely related.
15. Title or proof of ownership is a duplicate issue or from a distant state.
16. The insured has just recently titled the vehicle in his name.
17. The insured presents an assigned title, still in the name of the previous owner, as proof of his ownership.
18. The insured is unable to produce title or proof of ownership.
19. Time and location of loss are suspicious – usually away from insured's premises and in the evening.
20. The vehicle is reported to be expensively customized or a show model.
21. The vehicle has become unpopular for any reason (i.e., inefficient to operate, difficult to find repair parts, has received unfavorable press coverage concerning safety, etc.).
22. Members of the insured's family or household know nothing about the loss.
23. Insured has little or no liability coverage.
24. Insured quickly pressures for claim settlement including threats of complaints to Insurance Commissioner.
25. Demands car settlement in lieu of replacement.

FIGURE 10.17

Aside from auto theft, auto fraud, which involves deceit, trickery, and intentional perversion of the truth, is another rampant activity. Simple fraud includes reporting a stolen vehicle to accomplish these ends:

1. To cover up a hit-and-run accident.
2. To cover up a one-car accident to beat the deductible.
3. To cover an accident in which operators are under the influence of alcohol or drugs.
4. To cover the need for extensive repairs such as new transmission, new motor, or new paint job.
5. To receive money in order to replace a large vehicle that has a large gasoline consumption.
6. To purchase a good vehicle, export it by selling to foreign country, then report as stolen.
7. To allege purchase of a vehicle from outside the United States, obtain the vehicle, then report as stolen (import fraud).
8. To purchase a vehicle, strip unit of most of its parts, return it, and claim it was recovered in stripped condition (strip fraud).

At a minimum, the investigator should always be dubious of auto theft claims when these factual scenarios exist:

- Ownership of the vehicle is very recent.
- Vehicle was purchased from a private individual.
- Vehicle was purchased out of state.
- The insured presents an assigned title with the previous owner's name still on it.
- Previous owner cannot be located.
- Payment for vehicle is made in cash.
- Duplicate title or no title is available.
- The loss occurred shortly after obtaining an insurance policy.
- Fire loss occurred at night in an out-of-the-way location.
- Notice of loss was not timely.
- Recovered vehicle had heavy collision damage.
- Reported to police rather than through insurance agency.
- Not reported to police at all.
- Loss occurred prior to issue of title and registration.

A. Auto Identification Systems

1. VIN Systems

Automobiles are identified by several methods, including insurance identification number, title, registration, and other motor vehicle documentation. Identification of a vehicle at its point of manufacturing origin is accomplished through the vehicle identification numbering (VIN) system. The VIN method of vehicle marking and identification is an impressive defense mechanism because foreign and domestic automakers make a concerted effort to inscribe, without chance of alteration or obliteration, identification numbers at selected points on a vehicle. These identification numbers are stamped and registered at the factory. The engine and vehicle identification numbers are used on legal documents and recorded upon transfer.

Web Exercise: Visit a District of Columbia Metropolitan Police Department web page that lays out the intricacies of the VIN program at: http://mpdc.dc.gov/mpdc/cwp/view,a,1240,q,547830,mpdcNav_GID,1552,mpdcNav,%7C.asp

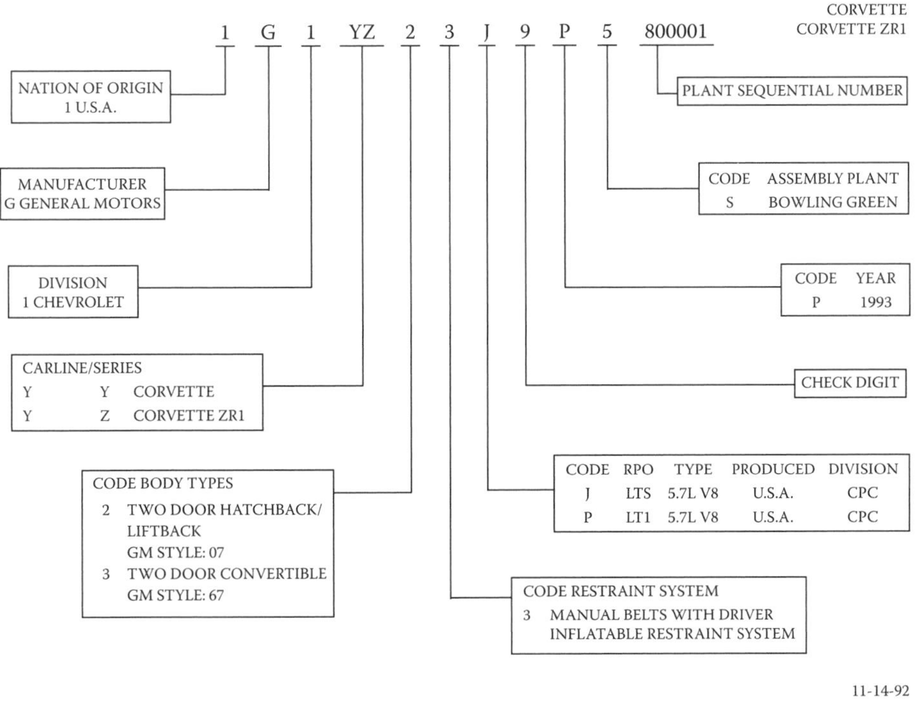

FIGURE 10.18 The Vehicle Identification Numbering (VIN) system.

Under rules established by the National Highway Traffic Safety Administration, specifically Federal Motor Vehicle Safety Standard 115, commencing in 1981, all motor vehicles must adopt a vehicle identification numbering system. The VIN is a series of seventeen alphanumeric characters. For vehicles with a gross vehicle weight of 10,000 pounds or less, the VIN must be located inside the passenger compartment adjacent to the left windshield pillar and readable from the outside of the vehicle. For vehicles with a gross vehicle weight rating of more than 10,000 pounds, location and visibility requirements are not specified. All VINs shall appear clearly and indelibly upon either a part of the vehicle, other than the glazing, that is not designed to be removed except for repair or upon a separate label or plate which is permanently affixed to such a part. Figure 10.18 illustrates the basis of the VIN numbering system. Auto manufacturers designate specific areas on each model for identification number placement, as shown in Figure 10.19.

2. Parts

Identification numbers are also placed on certain parts of a vehicle. Because of the high cost of parts replacement, the crude practices of chop shops, and the ease with which engines, transmissions, and other selected parts can be sold, manufacturers have inscribed identification numbers on engines and transmissions. As a rule, the number is derivatively based upon the VIN.

As the price of replacement parts has risen, automobile manufacturers have embarked on parts identification programs. Probably the most advanced contribution is from General Motors Corporation, which, in 1980, established a special parts marking program by which parts such as luggage lids, fenders, doors, and other body panels are labeled. The labels consist of a special brand of security film, approximately 2.25 inches wide by 6.25 inches high. The label is designed so that once it is affixed to the surface, any attempt to remove it will result in the border pulling away from the window, which will destroy the integrity of the label. Under ordinary light, the label will appear light blue in color. It can be authenticated by examination under retroreflective light. This

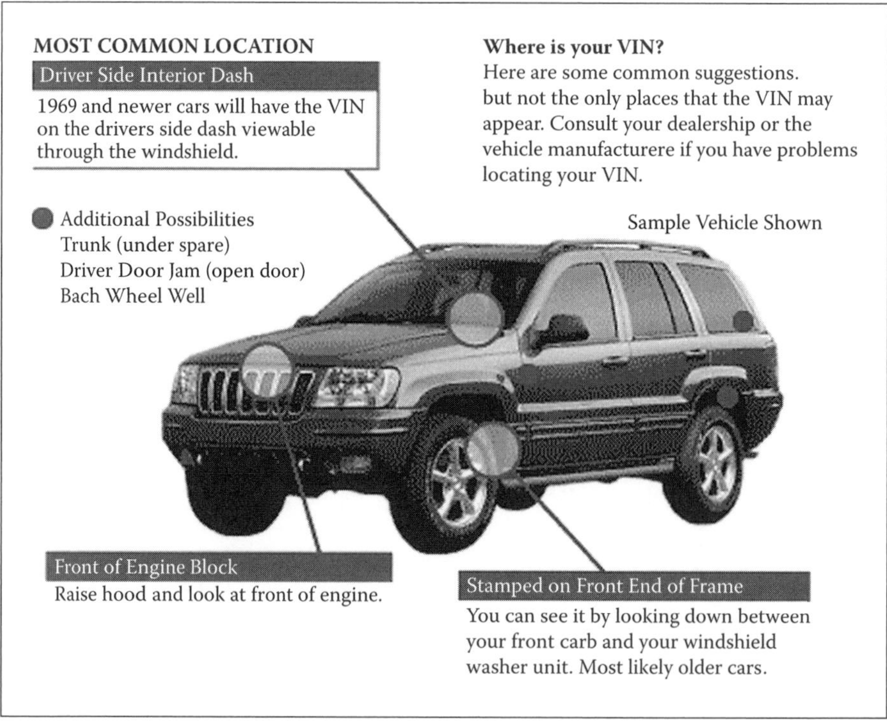

FIGURE 10.19 Locations of VIN placement.

is accomplished by using an inexpensive retroreflective viewer, available from several commercial sources, or by holding a flashlight parallel to and at the same level as the viewer's eye. Under retroreflective light, an authentic label will display a pattern of the GM logo across the entire face of the label. The lack of such a pattern or discontinuity in the pattern will indicate counterfeit products.

To stay on the cutting edge of this complex field, private investigators should strongly consider membership in the International Association of Auto Theft Investigators (IAATI).

Web Exercise: Visit the web page for the IAATI at: http://www.iaati.org/aboutiaati.asp

NOTES

1. Pinkerton's, Inc., *Investigation—Insurance Claims* (1990), 3.
2. National Institute of Justice, *Sourcebook of Justice Statistics* (1988).
3. Richard N. Kocsis, "Arson: Exploring Motives and Possible Solutions," *Trends and Issues in Crime and Criminal Justice.* (August 2002), 1.
4. Mary R. Williams and Michael Sigman, "Performance Testing of Commercial Containers for Collection and Storage of Fire Debris Evidence," *J. Forensic Sci.* 52 (2007), 579.
5. "'Loss' from Employer's Fraud on Insurers Is Unpaid Workers' Compensation Premiums," *Crim. L. Rep.* 83 (2008), 752.
6. North Carolina Bar Foundation, *VI Practical Skills Course, Workers' Compensation* (1988), 36.
7. See Mich. Stat. Ann. § 17.237.301.
8. *Id.*
9. Pinkerton's, *supra* note 1, at "Using Your Camera on an Insurance Investigation."
10. *Id.* at 4.
11. *Id.*
12. *Id.* at 7.
13. W. Strobl, *The Investigator's Handbook* (Butterworth-Heinemann, 1984), 90.
14. Eastman Kodak Co., *Photography in Traffic Accident Investigation* (1979), 4.

15. The Traffic Institute, *Vehicle Damage Photography* (SN 7717), 2–3.
16. The Traffic Institute, *Level of Traffic Accident Investigation* (SN 8000), 1.
17. Northwestern University, The Center for Public Safety, 555 Clark St., Evanston, IL 60204.
18. SmartDraw, 4-Way Intersection Accident Diagram at http://www.smartdraw.com.
19. Traffic Institute, *supra* note 16, at 4.
20. *Id.* at 5.
21. The Traffic Institute, *Measuring for Maps* (SN 1097), 2.
22. Traffic Institute, *supra* note 15, at 6.
23. *Id.* at 7.

11 Investigative Method and Technique
Background Investigations

I. INTRODUCTION

A large portion of private security assignments consist of background investigation. Due to rising concerns about alcohol and drug addiction, the ease of document forgery, transcript alteration, assumption of false names and backgrounds, and the threat of espionage and terrorist activities, background investigations are increasingly important to businesses, institutions, and individuals.

Within corporate settings, personnel departments greatly rely on background reviews. According to William Cunningham and Todd Taylor, authors of the first *Hallcrest Report*:

> It is essential that a person hired for a specific position possesses the background, training, and skills stated in his or her résumé and employment application. Certain positions have special requirements for trust, deportment, confidentiality, and other character traits. For these positions, the organization must be able to verify that there have been no previous adverse reflections on the candidate's character and that there are no tendencies toward inappropriate conduct.[1]

Business's natural hesitancy in believing an applicant's stated background is intelligent discretion, especially when one considers the civil actions that can be brought against an employer who negligently retains and fails to terminate an employee.[2] As J. Kirk Barefoot remarked:

> It is absolutely essential in building a healthy company to begin with the selection of persons who are inherently honest, or at least basically honest if the proper controls and procedures are in effect. Hiring persons who have a history of consistent employee theft only insures that security problems will continue to develop and that there will always be plenty of work to occupy the investigation section of the security department.[3]

In this framework, background investigation serves a major function in employee screening. The philosophy extends not only to the initial date of hire but also to the ongoing evaluation and assessment of an employee. Background assessment can take many forms, including but not limited to personal and community interview, polygraph tests, and psychological examinations designed to measure various personality characteristics. "Screening procedures used should be based on the nature of the business, its resources for carrying out the procedures, and the security needs of the business."[4]

The ability to determine the background of an individual in employment settings, surveillance operations, skip/trace analysis, or other matter depends on access to the following types of records:

- Educational and school materials
- Employment information
- Neighborhood information
- Criminal background and court records
- Civil litigation and court records

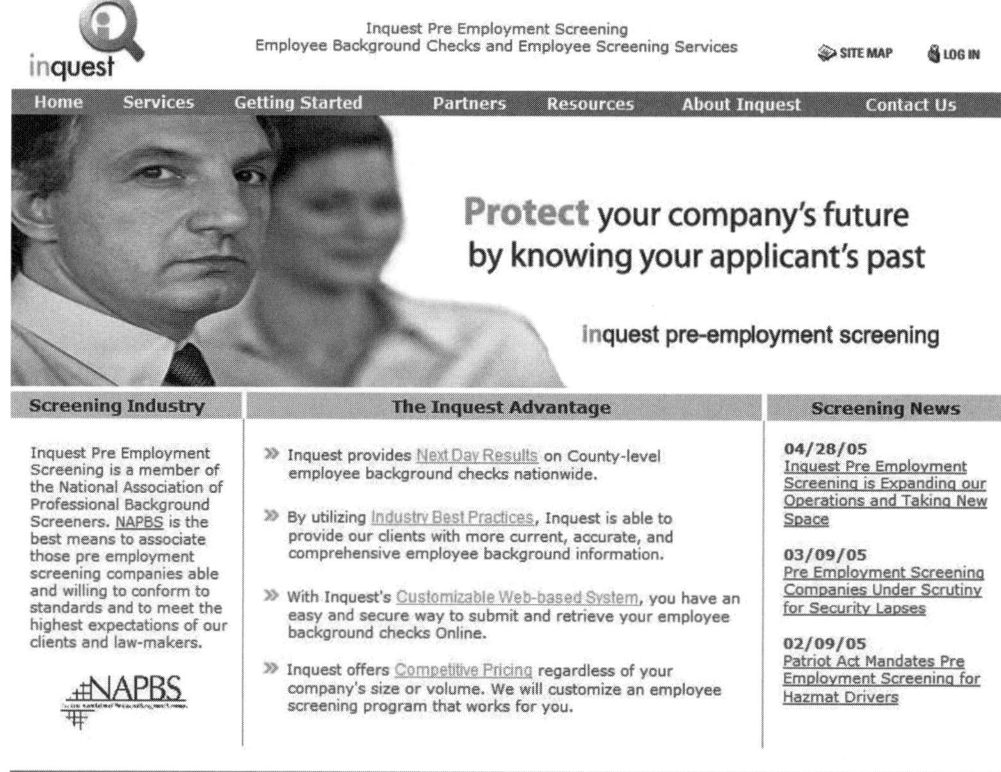

FIGURE 11.1 Inquest website. Reproduced from www.cisworldservices.org/investigations.html. With permission.

- Credit and financial resources
- Personal references

Many security firms solely focus on this aspect of practice. See Figure 11.1.[5]

These sources of information have been discussed comprehensively in Chapter 5. This chapter's focus is a generic discussion of the investigative sequence used in establishing background history with specialized suggestions, forms, documents, and checklists of practical use to the private investigator. Figure 11.2 reviews the areas of a background investigation and can help the investigator refine the search process. An investigator's checklist, guiding the security professional through the facets of background check, is shown in Figure 11.3. The investigator is reminded to adhere to federal, state, and local legislation bearing on background investigation practices and access to background information.

II. BACKGROUND ISSUES

Exactly what constitutes the idea and concept of a person's background is the first order of business for the investigator. Background encompasses a history of identity or residence, employment or military background, and economic ownership. A summary review follows.

REQUEST FOR INVESTIGATION

To: ______________________________

From: ______________________________

____

____

Phone Number: ______________________________

SUBJECTS TO BE SEARCHED:

NAME ____________	NAME ____________
DOB ________ SSN ________	DOB ________ SSN ________
LAST KNOWN ADDRESS ____________	LAST KNOWN ADDRESS ____________
____________	____________
NAME ____________	NAME ____________
DOB ________ SSN ________	DOB ________ SSN ________
LAST KNOWN ADDRESS ____________	LAST KNOWN ADDRESS ____________
____________	____________
COMPANIES ____________	COMPANIES ____________
____________	____________
____________	____________

COUNTIES TO BE SEARCHED			
	1) ________	3) ________	5) ________
	2) ________	4) ________	6) ________

TYPE OF SEARCH REQUESTED:

________	UCC's (County and Secretary of States	COPIES	☐ YES	☐ NO
________	Property (Real & Personal)	COPIES	☐ YES	☐ NO
________	Judgments/Liens	COPIES	☐ YES	☐ NO
________	Bankruptcy (specify County ________)	COPIES	☐ YES	☐ NO
________	Federal Civil Actions	COPIES	☐ YES	☐ NO
________	Motor Vehicles (including boats/planes)	COPIES	☐ YES	☐ NO
________	Assumed Names	COPIES	☐ YES	☐ NO
________	Incorporation Info. Ltd. Partnerships	COPIES	☐ YES	☐ NO
________	All of the Above	COPIES	☐ YES	☐ NO

FIGURE 11.2 Request for investigation form.

A. Establishing Identity

The task of checking an individual's background, as in all facets of investigation, requires an orderly process of thinking and action. Figure 11.4 lists the appropriate investigation sequence.

Access to records and information will vary by the locality, but access, in every circumstance, is essential to success in the background investigation process. States and counties are somewhat more liberal than federal agencies in granting access to records. According to Bottom and Kostanoski:

> Many public records are available to personnel directors and to security and loss control personnel. Each state has its own repository for workers' compensation claims. Each state has a central driver's

INVESTIGATOR'S CHECKLIST

Subject:____________________________________ Date received: ____________________

Position applied for: ____

Application review

1. Handwriting: Note any areas requiring further attention:
2. Area number-social security number:
3. Address and telephone number: note any discrepancies:

Previous employers

1. Verify dates of employment, job responsibility, etc.
2. Employers' comments:

Schools and/or colleges

1. Correspondence-response received?
2. Results of personal visit, if required:

Licenses held

1. DMV check
2. Department of State-Division of Licensing
3. County, town, and/or city clerk
4. Police Department
5. Education Department
6. Coast Guard
7. Insurance Department
8. Health Department
9. Other

County clerk (town or city registrar's) office

1. Criminal Index
2. Civil Index
3. Judgment & Liens Index
4. Mortgage Index
5. Filings under UCC

District Court

1. Criminal Clerk's Index
2. Civil Clerk's Index

U.S. District Court

1. Criminal Index

Summary of interview with references: Verify how long reference has known subject, and how reference came to know the subject:

Police Department

1. Any field interrogations
2. Other information given by police sources

Results of neighborhood investigation

1. Indicate who was interviewed, and where they live in relation to the subject
2. Substance of the interview:

Attach consumer report (if needed).

FIGURE 11.3 Investigator's checklist.

1. Name Verification
   a. Telephone directory (either print or online)
   b. Credit records
   c. Pretext
   2. Address Verification
   a. Telephone directory (either print or online)
   b. Credit records, etc.
   c. Pretext
   d. Utility Bills
3. Voter Registration
   Check principals to identify full name, confirm address, place and date of birth, social security number (if available), spouse, and other residents of household.
4. Assumed/Fictitious Business Names
   In some states, this may be referred to as Fictitious Name, DBA (doing business as), or Fictitious Business Name.
5. Secretary of State
   Check Secretary of State records to confirm ownership of corporations and limited partnerships.
6. Property Tax Records
   Identify all properties, real and personal, owned by the individuals or companies at the time of the last tax roll, and obtain copies, if necessary.
7. County Clerk Records
   a. Pull all documents identified in the Appraisal/Assessor's Office.
   b. Obtain copies of all Warranty Deeds and Deeds of Trust for those properties identified.
   c. Check the Indexes for any property transactions since the last tax roll up to the present date.
   d. Check Indexes for properties sold in the last two years and obtain copies of the documents.
   e. Check Indexes for liens and abstracts of judgments, to include releases, for the past five years, and obtain copies. Make note of any other information identifiable with principals.
   f. Check for oil and gas information.
8. Filings
   Check Uniform Commercial Code filings (financing statements) at County and State levels, to identify assets other than real property.
9. Divorce Records
   Check divorce records at county level to obtain list of property (assets) awarded in proceedings.
10. Bankruptcy
   Check bankruptcy records at servicing Federal courts to obtain list of assets and creditors, and statement of filings.
11. Federal Civil Cases
   Check Federal civil records for judgments, pending cases, etc.

FIGURE 11.4 Investigation outline.

license records center. Criminal records are available at the county level (over 3,000 in the United States) and at all state levels (with the exception of Nevada). Rules of access to these records vary from state to state. The vast majority of counties and/or state agencies will provide some information by telephone or letter. Computerized access to these records is expanding every year. All states and the District of Columbia will make driving records available to the public.[6]

Policies of access will depend on the type of institution as well. For example, educational institutions are guided by a host of privacy and data rules that make easy access impossible. Although colleges and universities will allow confirmation of attendance or a degree granted, access to a transcript without the party's consent is nothing more than a pipedream. Federal agencies are more aggressively guided by "sunshine" or "right to know" policies than their state counterparts. As a result, federal records, such as criminal convictions, civil litigation records, federal tax liens, and bankruptcy filings, are not difficult to acquire. Statutory designs and even internal agency and entity policies will have much to do with how much information can be garnered with or without the permission of the investigative subject.

B. Employment History

From the first day of application to the date of resignation, retirement, or termination, employment history manifests a great deal about the investigative subject. In employment settings, the application form serves as a significant tool in screening applicants and verifying the identities and conduct of present employees. The form should be a detailed document that is sensitive to legal issues. To accomplish its divergent purposes, an application should address these topical concerns:

- Request an applicant to write his/her name and address on an application.
- Ask an applicant if a complaint has been placed against him/her or if he/she has been indicted or convicted of a crime and under what name.
- Ask an applicant's age (only if the information is an occupational qualification).
- Explain to an applicant the hours and days he/she will be required to work.
- Ask if applicant is a U.S. citizen, or if he/she has the intent to become one.
- Ask about schooling, both academic and vocational.
- Inquire about relevant work experience.
- Inquire into his/her character and background.
- Ask for name, address, and relationship of person to be notified in case of an accident or emergency.
- Inquire into applicant's military experience in the U.S. Armed Forces. After hiring, ask to see discharge papers.
- Ask an applicant about memberships in organizations that may indicate race, religion, or national origin.
- Ask an applicant if he/she belongs to an organization advocating the overthrow of the U.S. government.
- Ask the sex of the applicant only where it constitutes a qualification for the job.[7]

Employers who design their own application forms need to be conscious of issues that raise red flags—particularly legal ones. Under some state and federal legislation, certain types of questions from prospective employers are inappropriate, such as:

- Asking an applicant whose name has been changed to disclose the original name.
- Inquiring as to the birthplace of an applicant or applicant's family if outside the United States.
- Requiring an applicant to produce discharge papers from the U.S. Armed Forces (before employment).
- Inquiring into foreign military experience.
- Asking an applicant's age when it is not an occupational qualification or is not needed for state or federal minimum age laws.
- Asking about an applicant's race or color.
- Requiring an applicant to provide a photograph with the application.
- Asking an applicant to disclose membership in organizations that may indicate race, religion, or national origin.
- Asking a male applicant to provide the maiden name of his spouse or his mother.
- Asking the place of residence of an applicant's spouse, parents, or relatives.
- Inquiring whether an applicant's spouse or parents are naturalized or native citizens.
- Asking an applicant his religion.[8]

Similarly, federal consumer legislation has restrictive guidelines regarding information on these matters:

- Records of arrests, indictments, or conviction of crimes where the disposition of the case, release or parole has been more than seven years prior to the date of application.
- Any bankruptcies that have been more than fourteen years before the application.
- Any paid tax liens, legal suits or judgments, or other such information that has a harmful effect.[9]

From the outset, it is important to determine the breadth of the background investigative request. In Figure 11.5, the client, referred to as subscriber, has placed an order regarding a certain applicant. The items in the lower section of the document, where the subscriber is asked to choose from a menu of services—credit, court, criminal, education, neighborhood, motor vehicle, present employment, previous employment, and industrial accident records—indicates the range of choices the investigator has in deciding the breadth of investigation.

Oral assertions about the applicant's reputation are hearsay (second- or third-hand remarks) and are therefore of little value. Quality and professionalism of a background investigation depend on written documentation. Information regarding the applicant's use of drugs, attendance record, and overall quality of labor can be requested from the applicant's previous

PERSONNEL INVESTIGATION REQUEST

Client____________________ Date __________

Address ______________________________

Report to ____________________ Tel. # __________

Applicant's Name ____________________ Tel. # __________

Home Address______________________________

Previous Addresses ______________________________

____

DOB ____________________ Driver's License # __________

Sex________Nationality __________ Ht_______Wt_______SS# ________

Marital Status ________ Spouse __________ Maiden Name __________

Dependants ______________________________

Education (High School, College, Trade School, etc.)____________________

____

____

____

Employment (past & present)____________________

Name & Address	Position & Supervisor	Date

Services Ordered (please check)

☐ Credit ☐ Education ☐ Present Employment

☐ Court ☐ Neighborhood

☐ (present) ☐ (previous) ☐ Previous Employment

☐ Criminal ☐ Motor Vehicle Record ☐ Industrial Accident Record

FIGURE 11.5 Background investigative request.

REQUEST FOR EMPLOYMENT INFORMATION

Dear

The above named applicant applied to use for a position of considerable responsibility. The applicant has stated you can verify the following information:

[insert data]

Is the above information correct? _____. If not please provide correct information.

From your personal knowledge or available records, would you recommend the applicant for employment with us? _____. If no, please explain on reverse side.

Do you consider the applicant to be of good character? ____. If no, please explain on reverse side.

If the applicant was employed by you, please indicate:

Reason for termination ____________________			
Eligible for re-employment	Yes	No	
Quality of Work	Good	Satisfactory	Poor
Attendance Record	Good	Satisfactory	Poor
To your knowledge, does the applicant use illegal drugs?	Yes		No
Or associate with anyone involved with illegal drugs?	Yes		No

Please use the reverse side of this letter to inform us of any additional comments concerning this applicant. If you prefer, you may contact me personally at the phone number below.

This applicant is aware of this inquiry and has voluntarily authorized us to conduct a background investigation. Your reply will be kept confidential.

FIGURE 11.6 Request for background information.

employer (Figure 11.6) and is a mandatory attachment to a finalized report on the applicant's employment background.

C. Credit History

Some security professionals hold that a subject's credit history, whether good or bad, is a reflection of character. Individuals who properly handle financial affairs, who intelligently weigh assets and liabilities, who do not take undue risk, or who do not show a history of impulsive buying are usually considered reliable. Regulatory acts, such as the Fair Credit Reporting Act, limit inspection of these records. However, documents such as the authorization permit shown in Figure 11.7 allow access.

Unless consent is given or there are statutory exemptions in federal and state laws, investigators have restricted access to credit reports. Typically, the reverse side of a credit report explains the terms, conditions, and rules of construction for the interpretation of the credit report. The investigator should check local telephone directories for addresses and phone numbers of companies that specialize in tracking and reporting credit histories. Some of the more prominent companies engaged in the business are:

- Equifax
- Experian
- TransUnion Credit Information Co.
- Dun & Bradstreet
- National Association of Credit Management

Name and Address or Guarantor

Full name of Guarantor (1): ______________________________

Signature: ______________________________

Date: ______________________________

Address: ______________________________

Full name of Guarantor (2): ______________________________

Signature: ______________________________

Date: ______________________________

Address: ______________________________

FIGURE 11.7 Authorization to check creditors.

At a minimum, a credit report makes an honest, though not perfect, attempt to reflect the overall credit history of an individual. Although the report deals mostly with forms of public credit, such as that reported by banks, investment companies, credit card companies, or other personal grant of credit, the results are not all-encompassing. Investigators should realize some of the more obvious omissions:

- Credit acquired under an assumed or changed name.
- Credit not publicly reported, such as a loan between parent and child.
- Mortgages/personal loans provided by owners of property in a land transaction.
- Temporary lines of credit or corporate loans for key executives.

Weighing credit worthiness calls for an examination of many other sources and documents. Access to courthouse records is essential for an investigator reviewing an individual's credit background and financial stability. According to the American Society for Industrial Security:

> Information on real estate transactions or occupational or business licenses applied for by the subject or his spouse are a matter of public record. Information on divorces, civil litigation, suits, judgments, and other pertinent matters may be found in the files of the county. Both the subject and his spouse may be checked.[10]

Direct or inferential evidence regarding financial data and credit-worthiness can be collected from numerous sources:

- Credit bureaus
- Banks and financial institutions
- Employment records
- Local sources
- Public records
- Collection agencies
- Directories
- Key informants
- Newspapers
- Investment manuals
- Landlords
- State authorities
- Collection services
- Federal government

- Post offices
- Stock exchanges
- Company or person being investigated
- Investment firms
- Creditors
- Insurance companies
- Trade references[11]

To determine the exact scope of the financial investigation, the investigator should rely on a document such as that shown in Figure 11.8. The assignment form has a "confirm/verify" section and a courthouse record search section to pinpoint the types of activities the client wishes to undertake.

Often, the search for credit worthiness deals with the subject's assets and overall net worth. The investigator requests a review of the applicant's credit, businesses or corporations owned, real property, security interests, and other personal information. The hours, expenditures, and authorization rates for fees and expenses are also calculated. See Figure 11.9 for a sample form.

Information on real property can be found in courthouse records. The review of real property can also determine the liens and liabilities currently attached against the property, such as mortgages,

ASSIGNMENT FORM

To ______________________ From ______________________ Date Assigned__________

Assigned to ______________________ Requested by ______________________

Cost Limitation ______________________ Completion date ______________________

Request is made for your office to conduct an asset search, or other specified investigation on the following individuals and/or businesses

Name Address

____

____

____

____

Please search the following areas covering a period of at least five years unless requested otherwise. Provide telephone numbers for each subject and/or business assigned and verify all possible information through pretext calling. Obtain copies of all complete documents pertinent to this investigation.

Please direct your research to the following counties and include the following search areas for each of the subjects and/or businesses assigned.

Counties: ______________________

____

CONFIRM/VERIFY

Resident address – resident telephone number – present ownership of residence –
Market value – marital status – business status – business telephone number

COURTHOUSE RECORDS SEARCH

Deed records – UCC filings – assumed names – tax assessor – tax liens –
Criminal and civil records – bankruptcy – divorce – probate – voter registration – motor vehicles

Other ______________________

Special instructions ______________________

FIGURE11.8 Assignment form.

ASSET INVESTIGATION AUTHORIZATION

Date Rec'd__________ Due Date__________
Subject__________ Investigator__________
Address__________ Completed__________
__________ Date Mailed__________
SS#__________ Auth. Hrs.__________
SS#__________ Auth. Rate__________
Employer__________ Mileage__________
__________ County__________ State__________

Summary of report__________

Daily Progress of investigation

Date	Description	Hrs	Exp
	Credit		
	Corp.		
	CPF		
	Real Property		
	UCC		
	SS# Trace		
	Address Update		
	Neighborhood Search		

FIGURE 11.9 Authorization for release of asset information.

promissory notes, judgments, and other secured or liened interests.[12] Figure 11.10 has the necessary language and clauses to thoroughly document the current state of liabilities against specific real property.

The investigator must also be aware of personal property information recorded at the offices of tax assessors, recorders of deeds, or registers of wills. In some jurisdictions, personal property tax forms that list stocks, bonds, other negotiable instruments, and even jewelry and other delineated personal property must be filed annually. An excellent worksheet for recording this information is included in Figure 11.11.

A search of motor vehicle records through the Division of Highway and Public Safety or other government authority provides another insight into the asset and liability quotient of an investigative subject. Primary and secondary liens on the title of a vehicle suggest overextended credit or larger-than-normal liabilities. Boats and aircraft are also reportable in a central registry such as the Department of Marine Resources or the Federal Aviation Administration. This type of information can be recorded on a form such as that shown in Figure 11.12.

Uniform Commercial Code (UCC) filings or financing statements, evidencing a secured interest in another person's property, are centrally stored at the Secretary of State's office or other office of corporate and consumer business filings. Owners who have property and tangible assets that have

Real Property

______________________	______________________	______________________
Date Searched	Subject	County, State

Our investigation in______________________County,______________________(State) revealed

The following information pertaining to______________________

Type of Deed: ______________________

Date Filed:______________________

Volume & Page No. ______________________

Grantor:______________________

Grantee:______________________

Property Location: ______________________

Property Description: ______________________

____

A promissory note dated______________________in the amount of ______________________

is payable to______________________(Lender & City).

The current assessed value of property is ______________________

Type of Deed: ______________________

Date Filed:______________________

Volume & page No.______________________

Grantor:______________________

Grantee:______________________

Property Location: ______________________

Property Description: ______________________

A promissory note dated______________________in the amount of ______________________

is payable to______________________(Lender & City).

The current assessed value of the property is ______________________

____

Initials

FIGURE 11.10 Real property search form.

sizable or inordinate financing statements on record often evidence a troubled financial situation. According to O'Block:

> Serious indications of financial instability, which could lead to employee dishonesty, include a history of declared bankruptcies, defaults, and repossessions. Financial strains of this type may induce an employee to steal from the employer as a means of getting additional income or could force the employee to take a second job, which could cause decreased proficiency in the first job.[13]

The party who owes money is the debtor and the party who has extended credit is the secured party. Collateral is the property pledged as security during the life of the loan.[14] Figure 11.13 is a sample of a form that can be used to record UCC filings.

Although documents to record information related to judgments, liens, and bankruptcies were reviewed in Chapter 5, the forms shown in Figures 11.14 through 11.16 are provided for added insight. A variety of security enterprises exclusively emphasize these types of service.

Personal Property

Date Searched ______ Subject ______ County, State ______

Year of Tax Roll: ______

Obtained from: ______ Tax Assessor's Office

______ Tax Appraisal District

Owner ______

Property Location: ______

Property Description: ______

______

Valuation ______

Volume & page No. ______

Owner ______

Property Location: ______

Property Description: ______

______

Valuation ______

Volume & page No. ______

Owner ______

Property Location: ______

Property Description: ______

Valuation ______

Volume & page No. ______

______

Initials

FIGURE 11.11 Personal property search form.

Because private individuals often funnel assets through corporate and partnership enterprises, the investigator cannot acquire a true and accurate representation of overall net worth or credit worthiness without consideration of other business entities. Through various legal maneuverings and other corporate machinations, a subject may have transferred personal assets into corporate entities to render them untouchable. With this in mind, the investigator must always undertake an assessment of the subject's companies or corporate interests. The information regarding a company's officers, shareholders, and the like are accessible through the Secretary of State or other delegated agency. A sample of a form to record this type of data is shown in Figure 11.17.

III. ALTERNATIVE METHODS OF BACKGROUND REVIEW

A. References

References were once the chief means of personal evaluation and assessment, but as a result of the rise of technology, information sharing, and the polygraph machine, references have taken a back

Vehicles

Date Searched	Subject	County, State

Owner ______________________

Year, Model, Make: ______________________

License #, State: ______________________

Vehicle ID Number: ______________________

Lien Date: ______________________

Lien Holder & Address: ______________________

____

Value (Approx): ______________________

Remarks: ______________________

____

Owner ______________________

Year, Model, Make: ______________________

License #, State: ______________________

Vehicle ID Number: ______________________

Lien Date: ______________________

Lien Holder & Address: ______________________

____

Value (Approx): ______________________

Remarks: ______________________

____
Initials

FIGURE 11.12 Vehicle search form.

seat.[15] Nevertheless, reference documents, such as that at Figure 11.18, are still reliable methods for assessing a person's character.

The reference system has come to be viewed as a cumbersome, difficult, and unreliable process for many reasons: (1) the investigator had to track down the author of the reference to assess the integrity of the information, (2) the content and quality of the references is never uniform, and (3) the fear of lawsuits for falsehoods or misinformation, even when innocently made, make an honest evaluation unlikely. "Consequently, employers have come to put little faith in the traditional reference letters because they themselves refuse to be candid in responding when such questionnaires reach their own desks."[17]

Investigators who have read enough of these documents to understand their language and the implications that come forth recognize a good evaluation at once—the author is unequivocal in commendation. Mediocre or even negative assessments often are presented in a bland or neutral commendation, such as: "The applicant really tries hard," or "It's a shame the applicant has to leave, but he feels there are better opportunities elsewhere." Experienced investigators can differentiate the language of commendation versus the language of mediocrity.

Uniform Commercial Code Filings
(Financing Statement)

________________ ________________ ________________
Date Searched Subject County, State

Instrument Number: ________________
Date Filed: ________________
Debtor: ________________
Secured Party: ________________
____
Collateral: ________________
____
____
This UCC is also filed with the: ________________
(Secretary of State/County)
under number ________________ dated ________________

Instrument Number: ________________
Date Filed: ________________
Debtor: ________________
Secured Party: ________________
____
Collateral: ________________
____
____
This UCC is also filed with the: ________________
(Secretary of State/County)
under number ________________ dated ________________
____

____
Initials

FIGURE 11.13 Uniform Commercial Code filing search form.

B. Consultative Services

Social and behavioral scientists are increasing their visibility in background investigations by creating tests and other evaluative methodologies for the workplace. Tests of various forms and construction have been devised in the following areas:

- Personality
- Minnesota Multiphasic Personality Inventory
- The Glueck Predictability Table
- The Kvaraceus Delinquency Scale and Checklist
- The Rorschach Test

Judgments

Date Searched	Subject	County, State

Case Number: ____________________
Court of Record: ____________________
Volume & Page Number: ____________________
Date Filed: ____________________
Petitioner vs. Defendant: ____________________
Amount of Judgment: ____________________

Case Number: ____________________
Court of Record: ____________________
Volume & Page Number: ____________________
Date Filed: ____________________
Petitioner vs. Defendant: ____________________
Amount of Judgment: ____________________

____
Initials

FIGURE 11.14 Judgment record search form.

Liens

Date Searched	Subject	County, State

Document Number: ____________________
Date Filed: ____________________
Amount of Lien: ____________________
Petitioner vs. Defendant: ____________________

Document Number: ____________________
Date Filed: ____________________
Amount of Lien: ____________________
Petitioner vs. Defendant: ____________________

Document Number: ____________________
Date Filed: ____________________
Amount of Lien: ____________________
Petitioner vs. Defendant: ____________________

____
Initials

FIGURE 11.15 Lien search form.

Bankruptcy

Date Searched	Subject	County, State

Name of Bankrupt: ______

Case Number: ______

Date Filed: ______

Type of Bankruptcy: ______
(Voluntary/Involuntary—Chapter 7, 11, or 13)

U.S. Bankruptcy Court: ______ (District) ______ (Location)

Status (Choose one): ☐ Pending ☐ Closed

If closed, disposition: ______

List or provide copies of assets, debts and creditors.

______
Initials

FIGURE 11.16 Bankruptcy search form.

- Honesty or integrity
- Drug or alcohol usage
- Productivity and efficiency
- Work history
- Service capacity and relations
- Conduct and personal habits

One of the leaders in consultative background screenings and evaluations is Vangent Human Capital Management, formerly Reid Psychological Services, established in 1947, and located in Chicago. Through a series of surveys and testing instruments—mainly in a yes-and-no format—multiple areas of character and personality development like integrity or honesty can be measured. In the service test, a party's abilities to establish effective and helpful relationships with customers, peers, and supervisors are the measurable factors. Specifically, the Reid report assessment helps identify job applicants with high levels of integrity who are likely to become productive employees by assessing and measuring the following dimensions:

- Integrity
- Social behavior
- Substance
- Work background[18]

C. The Polygraph Test

Before the passage of the Polygraph Protection Act of 1980, the provisions of which became effective in the later part of 1988,[19] the polygraph was considered by many American businesses as the instrumental means of background investigation and review. Thus, before 1989, there were "tens of thousands of companies ... that utilize[d] polygraph screening for job applicants."[20] State and other federal laws have placed extensive limitations on preemployment screening. As

Companies/Corporations
Incorporation

_______________ _______________ _______________

Date Searched Subject County, State

Our search of the records of the _______________Secretary of State Office revealed the following
(State)
information pertaining to

Corporation Name: _______________
Address: _______________
Charter Number: _______________
Date of Incorporation:_______________
Registered agent:_______________
Officers:_______________ Title: _______________
Officers:_______________ Title: _______________
Officers:_______________ Title: _______________
Status: _______________

Corporation Name: _______________
Address: _______________
Charter Number: _______________
Date of Incorporation:_______________
Registered agent:_______________
Officers:_______________ Title: _______________
Officers:_______________ Title: _______________
Officers:_______________ Title: _______________
Status: _______________

____
Initials

FIGURE 11.17 Form used to request corporate information from the secretary of the state where corporation is registered.

a result, individual internal investigations are encumbered, which causes employers and security vendors to be uncertain about the future role of the polygraph.[21] Even so, public employees still engage security firms to conduct such tests. For example, the polygraph is still regularly utilized in police applicant screening since consent must be given by an applicant.[22]

In addition, the polygraph is a tool for the prosecutor's office as it seeks to screen and test the veracity of a defendant's claim of innocence. Here too the defendant must consent. The admissibility of the polygraph results, except in the restrictive case of stipulation of the parties, has yet to be witnessed in the American legal system.

IV. COMPREHENSIVE BACKGROUND REPORT

The final responsibility of the investigator who has amassed and collected background information is to compose the background investigative report.[23] It should include:

To Whom It May Concern:

I have known ________________ for approximately two years. As the Director of the Criminal Justice Program, I am responsible for the evaluation of all faculty teaching within the program. In fulfilling this responsibility I am able to develop an awareness of the abilities demonstrated with the classroom. I have found ________________ to be a mentally mature, emotionally intelligent, and highly sensitive professional person who works very well with people. He represents his ideas articulately and with enthusiasm. He certainly has had a profound effect upon my perception of the role of educator; he is able to combine research, intellectual concern, and communication arts into a very practical and understandable reality for the student.

Over the past year ________________ has developed a sustained record of academic excellence in teaching, professional development, and service to the college. His consistently positive student evaluations reflect a unique ability to relate complex abstract material to the daily experiences of students' lives and a capacity to maximize the motivation of the students with diverse needs and varying histories of academic anxiety. As such, ________________ has scheduled classes at times inconvenient to himself so as to accommodate the needs of shift workers who must change schedules from day to evening classes over the course of a semester. He has successfully instilled a love for learning in housewives, police officers, plant workers, and younger students with a history of academic failure.

________________ has an excellent basic understanding of the nuances of everyday living which gives him a rather remarkable ability to work effectively with the more difficult pragmatic realities of life. In addition, he works well within our social system and confronts issues and problems rationally and intelligently within a professional framework.

________________ is a superior member of the teaching profession and a dedicated force to the professionalism of our criminal justice system. I recommend him with the highest respect I can hold for an individual.

FIGURE 11.18 Sample reference letter.

- Identification information
- Records of conviction
- Proof of civil actions and other litigation
- Credit and financial history
- Educational records
- Neighborhood information
- Personal and business references
- Previous and current employment
- Opinions of previous and current employers
- Other financial data

A sample background investigation report is outlined in Figure 11.19.

Carefully review the document. The following sample questions can be answered by such a report:

1. How many children does the subject have?
2. Where has the subject worked?
3. What is the subject's name?
4. What is the subject's credit record?
5. Has the subject ever been convicted of a crime?
6. What is the subject's address?
7. Has the subject attended any colleges or universities? If so, did he graduate?
8. Who is the investigator's client?

1. CRIMINAL INVESTIGATION:
Search Type: Tennessee Statewide
Status: Criminal Record Found
CASE NUMBER: 99-CR5500403
COUNTY: Davidson
OFFENSE: Bad Checks
LEVEL: Misdemeanor
SENTENCE DATE: 9/13/1999
DISPOSITION: Guilty on single count
COMMENTS: Wrote a check for $404.45 to Wal-Mart which was returned. Did not pay the amount within 30 days as directed. Sentenced to pay restitution plus $65 fines, and placed on 1-year probation, which was completed without violations.

2. EDUCATION VERIFICATION: Davidson County Community College
GRADUATION CLAIMED: 6/76
GRADUATION VERIFIED: None
DEGREE CLAIMED: A.A.
DEGREE VERIFIED: None

3. EMPLOYMENT VERIFICATION: Fast and Speedy Trucking
ACCIDENTS

DATE	TYPE	COST	CHARGEABLE	FATALITIES	INJURIES
06/23/00	Backing	$3,400	Yes	No	Yes

4. MOTOR VEHICLE RECORD:
SEARCH TYPE: Tennessee
STATUS: Results Received

RESULTS:
LIC NUMBER: 888-11-8888
ISSUED DATE: 7/24/99
EXPIRES: 7/24/05LIC STATUS: Valid
TYPE/CLASS: Operator
RESTRICTIONS: None

VIOLATIONS

1. Speeding 83/55	6/12/01	Lowndes County SO, MS
2. Ignore Traffic Signal	1/3/03	Nashville PD, TN

ADDRESS SEARCH

RESULTS:
1. 11/2003 - 03/2004 APPLICANT, SAMPLE SSN: 888-11-8888 DOB: 03/1956 AGE: 47
   231 Peachtree Rd. SW
   ATLANTA, GA, 30303
   COUNTY: Fulton
   SSN VALID: yes ISSUED: TN

FIGURE 11.19 Background investigation report.

2. 09/1997 – 10/2003 APPLICANT, SAMPLE SSN: 888-11-8888 DOB: 03/1956 AGE: 47
   1641 Apple Orchard Dr.
   NASHVILLE, TN 37201
   COUNTY: DAVIDSON
   SSN VALID: yes ISSUED: TN
3. 01/1989 – 06/1997 APPLICANT, SAMPLE SSN: 888-11-8888 DOB: 03/1956 AGE: 47
   32B SUMMIT AVENUE
   CORAL GABLES, FL 33133
   COUNTY: DADE
   SSN VALID: yes ISSUED: TN
4. 08/1991 – 01/1989 APPLICANT, SAMPLE SSN: 888-11-8888 DOB: 03/1956 AGE: 47
   PO BOX 13A
   PICKENS, MS 39146 00879
   COUNTY: HOLMES
   SSN VALID: yes ISSUED: TN
5. 01/1980 - 01/1989 APPLICANT, SAMPLE SSN: 888-11-8888 DOB: 00/1957 AGE: 47
   347 PINE STREET
   NASHVILLE, TN 39095 98039
   COUNTY: DAVIDSON
   SSN VALID: yes ISSUED: TN

CRIMINAL INVESTIGATION

Search Type: Florida DOC
Status: No Records Found

Search Type: GA Statewide
Status: No Records Found

EDUCATION VERIFICATION

INSTITUTION

Davidson County Community College
100 Education Way
Nashville, TN 37201
PHONE: 615-444-3333 FAX: 615-555-6666

STATUS: Research Complete

	DATA SUPPLIED	DATA CONFIRMED	ALERT
Dates Attended	9/74 - 6/76	9/3/74- 6/15/76	No
Graduated Date	6/72	None	Yes
Degree	A.A.	None	Yes
Major	Liberal Arts	Liberal Arts	No
Minor	n/a	n/a	No
G.P.A.	3.0	3.0	No
Curr. Attend.	No	No	No

FIGURE 11.19 (continued).

COMMENTS: Did not graduate or earn a degree of any kind.
VERIFIED BY: S. Kann
DATE VERIFIED: 2/19/04

EMPLOYMENT VERIFICATION

EMPLOYER
ABC Manufacturing
1200 Metal Gear Avenue
Bigtown, GA 30303

STATUS: Research Complete

	DATA SUPPLIED	DATA CONFIRMED	DISCR.
Dates Of Employment	1/97 - 4/98	1/4/97 - 4/30/98	No
Supervisor / Title	Mr. Smith/Warehouse Manager	Mr. Smith (no longer there)	No
Job Title	Forklift driver	Forklift driver	No
Job Description	Drove forklift and kept stock neat	Forklift operations and stocker	No
Salary	$7.65/hr	$7.65/hr final	No
Currently Employed	No	No	No
Reason For Leaving	Learned to drive a truck	Left to drive a truck	No

CUSTOMIZED QUESTIONS

QUESTION	INFORMATION VERIFIED
Did this person get along well with coworkers?	"Always. Very friendly and helpful."
Was this person's attendance satisfactory?	"Missed time like others. Nothing unusual or problematic."

ELIGIBLE FOR REHIRE: Yes
EXPLANATION:"He was a fine worker. We were sorry to see him go."

COMMENTS: NO ADDITIONAL COMMENTS PROVIDED.

VERIFIED BY: D. Lewis
DATE VERIFIED: 03/11/04

EMPLOYER
Fast and Speedy Trucking
123 East Main St.
Nashville, TN 37201

STATUS: Research Complete

	DATA SUPPLIED	DATA CONFIRMED	DISCR.
Dates Of Employment	2/97 - 2/02	2/1/97 - 2/14/02	No
Supervisor / Title	Ms. Adams/Safety Director	Ms. Adams/Safety Director	No
Job Title	Truck driver	Truck driver	No
Job Description	Drove 18-wheeler	Drove OTR	No
Salary	32 cents/per mile	n/a	No
Currently Employed	No	No	No
Reason For Leaving	Sought new position with city	Left with appropriate notice	No

FIGURE 11.19 (continued).

CUSTOMIZED QUESTIONS	
QUESTION	**INFORMATION VERIFIED**
Did this person get along well with coworkers?	"Yes."
Was this person's attendance satisfactory?	"He rated very well in this category."

ELIGIBLE FOR REHIRE: Yes
EXPLANATION: "Would need to be retested for drug and alcohol."

COMMENTS: NO ADDITIONAL COMMENTS PROVIDED.

VERIFIED BY: Ms. Adams
DATE VERIFIED: 03/12/04

DOT EMPLOYMENT VERIFICATION

STATUS: Research Complete

CAUSE FOR SEPARATION: Voluntary
TYPE OF COMPANY: Small Trucking
EQUIPMENT TYPE: Tractor-semi
TRAILER TYPE: Dry Van
TYPE OF FREIGHT HAULED: Appliances and auto parts
GEOGRAPHIC AREA: 48 states
FULL OR PART TIME: Full Time
OVER THE ROAD OR LOCAL: Over The Road
QUALIFIED FOR SINGLE OPERATION: Yes
QUALIFIED FOR TEAM OPERATION: No
HAZARDOUS MATERIALS: Yes

ELIGIBLE FOR REHIRE: Yes
DETAILS: Would need to be retested for drug and alcohol.

TESTED POSITIVE FOR A CONTROLLED SUBSTANCE IN THE LAST 3 YEARS: No
DETAILS: N/A

ALCOHOL TEST WITH A BREATH ALCOHOL CONCENTRATION OF 0.04 OR GREATER IN THE LAST 3 YEARS: No
DETAILS: N/A

REFUSED A REQUIRED TEST FOR DRUGS OR ALCOHOL IN THE LAST 3 YEARS: No
DETAILS: N/A

VIOLATED OTHER D.O.T. DRUG/ALCOHOL REGULATIONS: NO

IF SO, IS THERE DOCUMENTATION OF SUCCESSFUL COMPLETION OF D.O.T. RETURN-TO-DUTY REQUIREMENTS, INCLUDING FOLLOW-UP TESTS: N/A

SUBSTANCE ABUSE PROFESSIONAL:N/A
LOCATION: N/A

NUMBER OF ACCIDENTS: 1

ACCIDENTS

DATE	TYPE	COST	CHARGEABLE	FATALITIES	INJURIES
06/23/00	Backing	$18,000	Yes	No	Yes

FIGURE 11.19 (continued).

NOTES

1. W. Cunningham and T. Taylor, *The Hallcrest Report: Private Security and Police in America* (Chancellor, 1985), 43. See also Peter Psarouthakis, "Business Background Investigations: Tools and Techniques for Solution Driven Due Diligence," *Security Management*. (June 2008), 120.
2. See Charles P. Nemeth, *Private Security and the Law*, 3rd edition (Butterworth-Heinemann, 2005).
3. J. Kirk Barefoot, *Employee Theft Investigation* (Butterworth-Heinemann, 1979), 190.
4. Robert O'Block, *Security and Crime Prevention* (Mosby, 1981), 191.
5. Inquest Pre Employment Screening, at http://www.inquestscreening.com
6. N. Bottom and J. Kostanoski, *Introduction to Security and Loss Control* (Prentice Hall, 1990), 158; see also, The National Employment Screening Services, *The Guide to Background Investigations* (1990).
7. T. Ricks, B. Tillett, and C. Van Meter, *Principles of Security*, 2nd edition (Anderson Publshing Co., 1988), 204–205.
8. *Id.* at 205–206.
9. *Id.* at 206.
10. American Society for Industrial Security, *Basic Guidelines for Security Investigations* (1981), 71.
11. Pinkerton's, Inc., *Investigations Department Training Manual* (1990), 97.
12. See Charles P. Nemeth, *The Reality of Real Estate* (Prentice Hall, 2007).
13. O'Block, *supra* note 4, at 193.
14. See Charles P. Nemeth, *The Paralegal Resource Manual*, 3rd edition (McGraw-Hill, 2007), 226.
15. Peter Mirfield, "Character and Credibility," *Crim. L. Rev.* (March 2009), 135.
16. Barefoot, *supra* note 3, at 191.
17. Vangent, The Reid Report at http://www.vangent-hcm.com/Solutions/SelectionAssessments/GeneralAssessments1/ReidReport, visited September 3, 2009.
18. See Congressional Record, Vol. 131, No. 148, S. 1815 (1988).
19. Barefoot, *supra* note 3, at 192.
20. Charles P. Nemeth, "Erosion of Privacy Right and Polygraphs," *Forensic Sci. Intl.* 21 (1984), 103.
21. Mark Handler et al., "A Focused Polygraph Technique for PCSOT and Law Enforcement Screening Programs," *Polygraph.* 38 (2009), 77; Amy-May Leach et al., "The Reliability of Lie Detection Performance," *L. Human Behav.* (February 2009), 96.
22. Laura P. Worsinger, "Tips for Background Checks," *Sec. Mgmt.* (October 2006), 85.

12 The Security Office
Administrative Issues

I. GENERAL PRINCIPLES OF OFFICE ADMINISTRATION

Security investigators will quickly discover that an organized method of investigation will make life easier and more productive for themselves and their supervisors. Being organized is an enviable trait for the security professional. At its base, the security industry is a business that seeks a profit; it engages its clients in a manner so that cost will not exceed benefit while ensuring the security operative and his or her business will be fruitful. Hence, there is an ongoing need for internal processes that track and trace the business. It is important to learn, early on, to organize and document. When in doubt, create a form, an exhibit, a checklist, a document, a chart, a graph—some system for controlling the ebb and flow of the investigative process. A failure to be administratively efficient is one of the chief causes of a loss in corporate profits. The security business is no different; without a routine, standardized operational procedure, the company for which the security operative works will suffer. Robert Half, president of Robert Half International (a personnel service center with many offices worldwide), refers to this phenomenon as "time theft," a sort of unintentional, even normative, behavior that regularly occurs at offices in the business and industrial sectors and results in an inefficient administrative operation.[1] Standard Time, a software company that develops tools for the elimination of time wasting, sees the impact of lost time in the business enterprise. Its ten most common methods for wasting time include:

1. Surfing the Internet for personal use
2. Checking personal email
3. Socializing with colleagues
4. Conducting personal business
5. Spacing out
6. Running errands
7. Making personal phone calls
8. Applying for jobs
9. Planning personal events
10. Arriving late or leaving early[2]

Security firms are just like any other businesses: time wasted is money evaporating. Dominic Deeson describes time wasting as a form of theft and surely bad management practice that must be controlled.[3] Pinkerton's, Inc., has determined nine universal ways of wasting time:

1. Excessive time in briefing or assigning investigators.
2. Excessive time engaging in lengthy telephone conversations.
3. Excessive time to edit a report, prepare paperwork, or answer a piece of correspondence.
4. Excessive time spent in meetings and consultation with the manager, other officials, and investigators.
5. Improper or lack of planning ahead for the following day's activities.
6. Inefficiency caused by failure of handling official to dictate correspondence, journals, etc.
7. Lack of full coordination between handling officials as to the assignment of investigators.

TOP 40 TIME WASTERS WORLDWIDE

PLANNING
1. Lack of Objectives/Priorities/Planning
2. Crisis Management, Shifting Priorities
3. Attempting Too Much at Once/Unrealistic Time Estimates
4. Waiting for Planes/Appointments
5. Travel
6. Haste/Impatience

ORGANIZING
7. Personal Disorganization/Cluttered Desk
8. Confused Responsibility and Authority
9. Duplication of Effort
10. Multiple Bosses
11. Paperwork/Red Tape/Reading
12. Poor Filing System
13. Inadequate Equipment/Facilities

STAFFING
14. Untrained/Inadequate Staff
15. Under/Over Staffed
16. Absenteeism/Tardiness/Turnover
17. Personnel with Problems
18. Over-Dependent Staff

DIRECTING
19. Ineffective Delegation/Involved in Routine Details
20. Lack Motivation/Indifference
21. Lack Coordination/Teamwork

CONTROLLING
22. Telephone Interruptions
23. Drop-in Visitors
24. Inability to say "No"
25. Incomplete/Delayed Information
26. Lack Self-Discipline
27. Leaving Tasks Unfinished
28. Lack Standards/Controls/Progress Reports
29. Visual Distractions/Noise
30. Overcontrol
31. Not Being Informed
32. People Not Available for Discussion

COMMUNICATING
33. Meetings
34. Lack/Unclear Communication, Instructions
35. Socializing/Idle Conversation
36. "Memo-itis"/Over-Communication
37. Failure to Listen

DECISION-MAKING
38. Procrastination/Indecision
39. Wanting All the Facts
40. Snap Decisions

FIGURE 12.1 Top 40 time wasters worldwide.

8. Insufficient use of consolidated reports.
9. Reports and other paperwork more lengthy than necessary because of extraneous material and redundancy.[4]

Pinkerton's has also compiled a list of the "Top 40 Time Wasters Worldwide" (Figure 12.1[5]).

Aside from the economic disadvantages of inefficiency, any professional approach insists upon high-level organizational and administrative skills. Intelligent management dictates enlightened administrative practice.

II. TIME-KEEPING METHODS

From the outset of any security service, the tracking of time becomes a crucial step for the security professional. Clients are rightfully impressed with a well-organized security professional and just as rightfully distressed over the inefficient and bungling operative. As an example, missed, confused, or conflicting appointments cause a poor impression from the outset for any security firm. Track and memorialize appointment dates by using either manual or software systems to monitor the calendar. Numerous companies worldwide deliver software programs that address appointment tracking and time and task management for the busy security professional.

Web Exercise: Check out software for time keeping expressly developed for the security industry at: http://www.guard1.com/en/home.htm

SCHEDULE	Effective Date:	
Client Name:	Subject:	**Page of**

SUNDAY	MONDAY	TUESDAY	WEDNESDAY	THURSDAY	FRIDAY	SATURDAY
Shift 1:	Shift 1:	Shift 1:	Shift 1:	Shift 1:	Shift 1:	Shift 1:
Shift 2:	Shift 2:	Shift 2:	Shift 2:	Shift 2:	Shift 2:	Shift 2:
Shift 3:	Shift 3:	Shift 3:	Shift 3:	Shift 3:	Shift 3:	Shift 3:

Officer:	Rank:	Badge:	Assignment:	Hours:
			Total Scheduled Hours	

FIGURE 12.2 Employee work schedule.

To avoid overlapping appointments, the investigator should make certain that he or she has some understanding or awareness of the depth and breadth of the case being investigated. Fifteen minutes is not long enough for a case at first visitation. On the other hand, a relatively easy case, for which a portion can be handled by secondary personnel, such as the office secretary, should not be scheduled for a long period of time.

One method of assuring client awareness as to date and time of an appointment is the use of a reminder card. Historically, lawyers, doctors, and other professionals have used this method to jog a client's memory. Private security offices should give this practice consideration, particularly when the volume of appointments is steadily increasing.

Scheduling both personnel and assignments clearly produces internal office efficiency. It is a good idea to use schedule systems to keep track of upcoming appointments and field assignments (see Figure 12.2[6]). For those clients who fail to keep appointments, a memo, usually in the form of a postcard or letter, can be a courtesy, but it should have a positive personal flavor to maintain goodwill.

III. THE VALUE OF ADMINISTRATIVE DOCUMENTS

The initial client interview, claim evaluation, and maintenance of client contact have been covered in other portions of this text. As a case progresses, assuming that fee contract agreements and other

INSURANCE INVESTIGATION REQUEST

File No: ________________________________

Subject's Name ______________________________________ Date of request________________

Current Address ______________________________________ Phone Number________________

Previous Address____

Employer______________________ Job title________________ Phone Number________________

Client________________ Client file number__________________________

Address ________________ Phone number__________________________

Requested by Letter ☐ Phone ☐ Email ☐ New Case ☐ Rework ☐

Type of Case

- ☐ Worker Compensation
- ☐ No-fault
- ☐ Liability
- ☐ Medical Malpractice
- ☐ Other ________________
- ☐ Accident
- ☐ Uninsured motorist
- ☐ Location

Budget/Time allocation____

Nature of investigation ____

Subject description DOB________________ Race________________ Sex ________________

Height ______________ Weight ______________ Hair ______________ Eyes ______________

Glasses ________________ Mustache/Beard ________________ Build ________________

SSN ________________ Other comments____

Attorney ____

Spouse/dependents ____

Other parties involved____

Vehicle information____

Client special requestsl ____

FIGURE 12.3 Insurance investigation request.

preliminary matters have been cleared up, some type of memory notation system should be adopted by the investigator and his or her employing firm. Forms for an insurance investigation request and for reporting the facts of an interview are presented in Figures 12.3 and 12.4, respectively. By using forms of these types, the security investigator has convenient, though admittedly abbreviated, information that can be inserted in the beginning of the file.

The investigator should not merely collect information, but rather adopt methods that make the information meaningful and understandable at a later date. One of the recurring flaws in security practice and procedure is the duplication and haphazard maintenance of the information collected. In order for information gathering to be a profitable exercise, the investigator must pare down information and employ language that is universally understood by all parties who may be granted access to the file. Although forms, checklists, and other exhibits focus and cohesively preserve a wealth of information, the content of these documents must be prepared in such a way that they benefit the investigative team. The clientele the security firm serves has better things to do than

INTERVIEW REPORT

Case Name: ____________________ Interview Date: ____________________

Case Number: ____________________ Interview Duration: __________ To __________

Interviewer: ____________________

Name of Person Interviewed: ____________________

Location of interview: ____________________

Relationship to subject: ____________________

Detailed summary of interview: ____________________

FIGURE 12.4 Interview report.

to wade through pages of redundant material or decipher long-winded reports. The importance of selecting the correct facts to include in a report cannot be emphasized enough:

> There was a time when investigators were encouraged to write as much as possible; that time has passed. Our clients today do not have the time to wade through pages and pages of chitchat prepared by an investigator on a daily basis. Our clients are paying good money for cold, hard fact[s]. They have learned to expect it, and they are determined to get it. This does not mean investigators should be told to use their own initiative as to what should and what should not go into a report. Quite often, neither you nor the investigator can evaluate the importance of a piece of information to your client. The facts should be in, but the report need not finish off like the great American novel![7]

At the conference or personal visitation level, some formal notation should be made regarding results. The security officer should be allowed to write out impressions and obligations resulting from those discussions on a conference note form. As the investigation progresses, the security officer may wish to use the same form for jotting down specific factual or legal issues as well as mental impressions that may become a part of the greater picture.

Aside from documenting facts, circumstances, and conditions in the investigation, these forms and documents serve another critical purpose: protecting the security firm and operative from the accusations of professional malpractice and negligence. The problem of malpractice is substantial in private security, so thorough, accurate record keeping is an intelligent defense mechanism. For instance, private security firms and individuals are coming under threats of litigation for their failure to perform their jobs in a professional manner. Correspondence and solid, written documentation, if adopted and routinely employed, can refute allegation and innuendo. The forms and documents become part of the case's permanent record and adequately defend an accusation of professional incompetence.

IV. FILING SYSTEMS

A. Set-Up and Maintenance

An effective filing system is mandatory to promote a competent investigation. Just imagine the security professional, operating under a deadline, who cannot locate the necessary information regarding parties, places, and conditions. Envision the security investigator who receives a call from a client inquiring about case status, and the file is buried deeply beneath a stack of papers or other documents arranged without rhyme or reason. In any office, time spent searching is time wasted.

First, the filing system should be centralized—that is, in one location, with one person appointed to ensure the integrity and organization of the system. When a file has been removed, it should be returned to that location for refiling.

The filing classifications depend on the scope, type, and style of investigation but should follow the guidelines outlined in Figure 12.5.

If correspondence with several parties is anticipated, individual folders are suggested. Various techniques for filing systems exist. An example of a subject matter filing system is reproduced in Figure 12.6.

As the form indicates, subjects have been designated by numerical code. A numerical coding system saves space, offers quick reference, and can be easily integrated in a computerized filing system. The numerical system can be further enhanced by the use of color coding. The numerical filing system should also be as informative as possible to help persons unfamiliar with the case to know its dynamics at a glance. A numerical system provides a quick reference guide for storage and disposal techniques. The system should indicate the name of the client; the year the file was opened; the number of the case for that year; and the number code assigned to the type of investigation. As an example:

✓ Current Matters
✓ Correspondence
✓ Billing
✓ Drafts
✓ Extra Copies
✓ Invoices/Receipts (Paid)
✓ Invoices/Receipts (Unpaid)
✓ Memoranda (internal)
✓ Research
✓ Telephone Calls
✓ Work Papers
✓ Photographs
✓ Investigative Reports
✓ Witness Statements

FIGURE 12.5

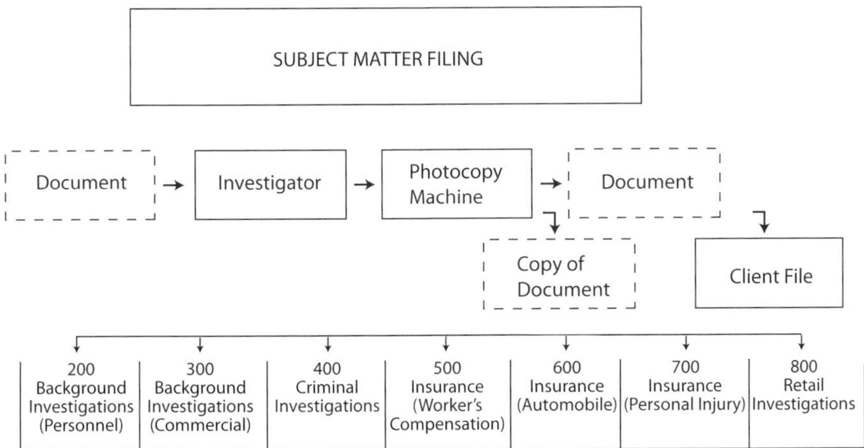

FIGURE 12.6 Subject matter filing.

New client Sam Brown meets with investigator John Lee in January 1990 desiring surveillance of employees suspected of theft activities. The file then could be identified in this manner:

Brown, Sam 09-0005.200

The coding indicates Brown, Sam (client); 09 (year file opened); 0005 (case number for year opened); 200 (number code for theft).

The folders should have tabs extending a little above the expanding files so that they are quickly visible, and documents should be contained within the folders with the use of some form of clip to prevent loss. Generally, insertion should be chronological with the latest information on top. Insertion arrangements depend on the particular documents being filed and should be mutually agreed upon by security personnel and the file maintainer.

B. Tickler Files

The security profession is regulated by both clock and calendar. Clients have a natural expectation for their time to be used wisely regarding both the end result and related costs. Therefore, it is essential to have a tracking system that comprehensively outlines upcoming events in each case. One such system is a tickler system, which is very effective and consists of:

- three-by-five-by-twelve-inch cardboard index card box
- several sets of numbered one through thirty-one daily index card dividers
- one set of January through December monthly index card dividers
- yearly index card dividers
- supply of index cards in several colors

The dividers and cards should be arranged as follows, from the front of the index card box to the back:

- Current year
- Current month
- Set of daily dividers

- Next several months with daily dividers
- Remaining months to December
- Next year
- January to prior month divider
- Remaining years
- Blank cards

The cards may also be color coded, for example:

White:	Client billable matters
Green:	Nonbillable matters
Yellow:	Personal
Blue:	Names of people you meet, per occasion, by date
Orange:	Quotations
Red:	Important Deadlines[8]

A simple reminder method is to use a special memo form such as that shown in Figure 12.7. The security operative needs only to check the matter to be performed and to place it in numbered files, which should be checked on a daily basis.

Other types of reminder systems such as a large calendar or a desk date book can also be used. The choice of systems generally depends on the size of the security firm and corresponding workload of its personnel.

TICKLER MEMO

Client Name:____________________ Client No.: ____________________

Investigator:____________________ Date: : ____________________

Reminder: ____________________

Appointment with: ____________________

Meeting scheduled with:____________________

Place:____________________

Date:__________ Time:__________, Confirmed (Y/N)

Interview with (witness name):____________________

Statute of Limitations expires: ____________________

File Report. ____________________

Bill Client.____________________

Close file. ____________________

Follow-up.____________________

Notes: ____________________

FIGURE 12.7 Tickler memo used as reminder.

V. SOFTWARE CONSIDERATIONS

Software systems are now normal for the security office. Software packages are readily available to the industry, although there are a bevy of consultants and support companies that can assist. A variety of companies have set out to assist businesses in the coordination of all activities related to the complexities of file and case management. Some of these software products have been examined previously in this text. If the software system accomplishes the following ends, it is worth consideration:

1. Generates form letters for contact with clients, witnesses, and experts with corresponding authorizations.
2. Provides either a chronological or sequential review of documents, witnesses or events, and conditions involving the case at hand.
3. Has document indexing capacity.
4. Is a compatible system with a run-of-the-mill PC rather than some sophisticated, avant-garde system that is not interchangeable.
5. Is easy to edit.
6. Produces a simple display screen.
7. Can search simple to complex ideas and issues.
8. Can provide document coding.
9. Has data files that are flexible in that titles can be changed easily.
10. Provides information that is relevant to the firm's most usual form of investigation.
11. Is easily learned.

Of course, as the firm's investigative practice becomes more sophisticated and the experiential base of all participating investigators expands, the software should have the capacity to archive information. One of the beauties of technology is its ability to store repetitive information and to compare and contrast cases with similar or different fact patterns. It pays to have software that creates a database that is easily accessible, not only for use in the present case, but also cases that will occur in the future. Tracking of documents, witnesses, and fact analysis is most helpful. See Figures 12.8[9] and 12.9[10] for a few sample advertisements.

VI. BILLING

Of all the administrative tasks a security professional performs, calculation of expenses and recording of billable time are decidedly priorities. The security professional must be diligent in these endeavors because clients, no matter how friendly or well intentioned, may be slow to pay their bills. Figure 12.9[10] charts the progression of a legal case. The diagram show that all billings must be completely calculated and sent to the client expeditiously because there is a natural decrease in a client's willingness to pay bills as time passes. A comparable pattern is applicable in the private security setting.

Financial responsibility and bill collection are certainly not favored activities in the security office. However, without sound economic practices and client fiscal responsibility, the office is placed in jeopardy. Pinkerton's, Inc., urges its employees to act with sound business judgment.

> You have all been called to the office of a prospective client with whom you are unfamiliar. You do not know the man, you are not fully acquainted with his business, and common sense tells you that you must take precautions. Are you really embarrassed when you ask this man to prove his financial stability? Do you really think that he is going to be embarrassed when you put the question to him? The answer to both questions, gentlemen, is negative. If your client is a businessman, he will respect your concern. If you are tactful and polite, no harm is done, and you will have safeguarded your position. At this particular point, you must make a decision. Is this man going to pay his bill when you want him to pay it? If you believe the answer is "No" you must ask for a retainer. A retainer in full, covering all

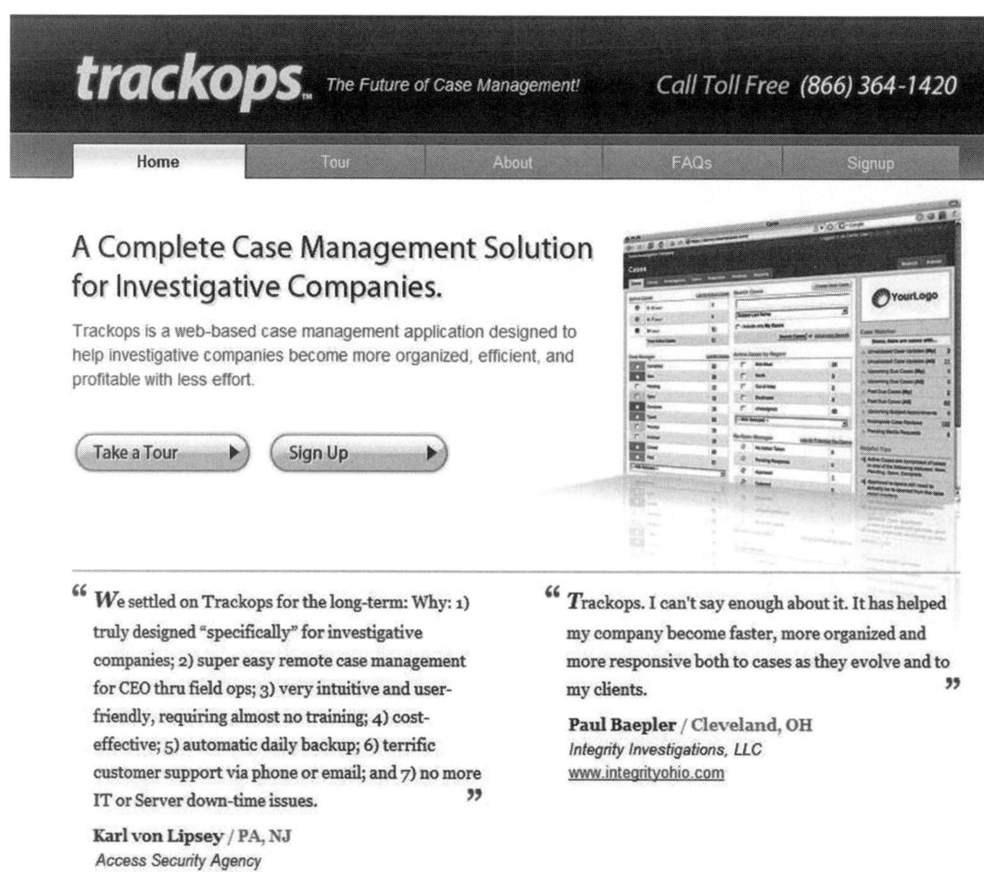

FIGURE 12.8

> possible time and all possible expenses. If you believe the answer to be "Yes" may I advise you still to take certain elementary precautions. Ask with whom your client's business does its banking. You will have no problem; he'll willingly tell you, and from then on it is a simple matter to have your own bank make a credit check for you, to ascertain if your client is good for the amount estimated by you as being the final bill.[11]

The security guard or investigator should adhere to company directives and policies in setting fees. The costs of undertaking any security activity should be planned, weighed in advance of performance, and calculated for costs. Figures 12.10 and 12.11 are good models to follow in recording preliminary and ongoing facts.

Of greater relevance is the investigator's responsibility to keep track of the time spent on billable tasks. The investigator may use a time and expense report to fully track dates of service, correspondence, and related expenses, such as transportation fares, telephone, meals, lodging, and other miscellaneous expenses (Figure 12.12) or a general expenses form such as that shown in Figure 12.13. Another way is to use a credit card for expenses and record them on a verification form (Figure 12.14).

Something else that should not be overlooked is the meticulous tracking of telephone charges, especially long-distance calls and cell phone charges. Figure 12.15 is a sample telephone record that plots the exact number of the telephone exchange and an appropriate case name reference.

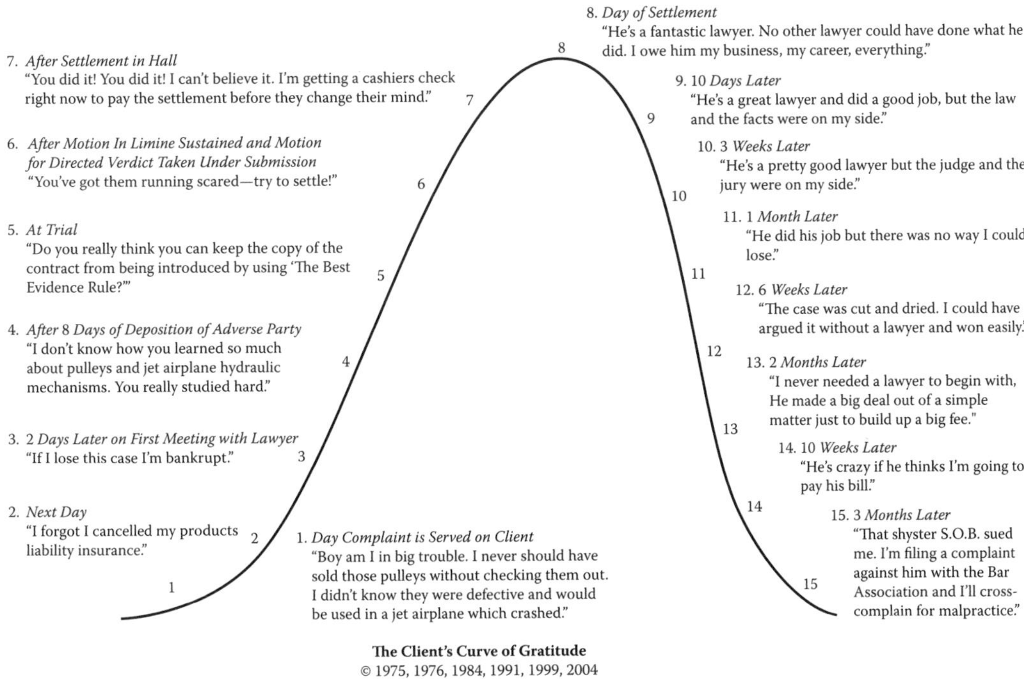

FIGURE 12.9 Client's curve of gratitude. Reproduced from https://www.tracktops.com/. With permission.

Out-of-pocket expenses for travel and travel-related matters such as client entertainment, tolls, parking, and so forth can be recorded on forms such as those presented in Figures 12.16 and 12.17. These expenses noticeably influence the profit and loss statement of any investigative practice. Some firms track both the traveler's expenditures and original acquisition costs. (With the differences in the fees charged by airlines and other transportation carriers, proper preliminary planning and selection should be substantial considerations.) Other security firms often make available to their agents and investigators an advance of funds or an expense account from which they may draw funds. The security professional should realize that the advance is neither salary nor wages but is a loan of the company's money to cover expenses. Any amount beyond ordinary and reasonable expenditures should be returned to the firm.

Another type of form is a general time slip to track various types of services. An ongoing record can outline for a client the bills that might otherwise result in a form of "sticker shock." This type of form is shown in Figure 12.18. The forms in Figures 12.17 and 12.18 are particularly complementary to record expenses. Regular completion of such documents creates a record upon which the investigator and client can rely. It also increases dramatically one's ability to collect such expenses.

After all billable hours have been calculated, expenditures have been surveyed and accounted for, and expenses related to travel, telephone, and other ordinary and reasonably related matters have been tabulated, an invoice should be submitted to the client. A basic billing format is given in Figure 12.19. Figures 12.20, 12.21, and 12.22 present other pertinent forms that aid in the billing process.

Finally, legitimate office procedures can be careless about documenting incidents and/or injuries at the work location. A formal report should recount how the injury occurred, what the function or task of the employee was, and what level of benefits exist.

Preliminary Fact Investigation	
Timekeeper	**Hours**

Task Assumptions

State Date__________________ End Date__________________ Approximate Duration__________________

Tasks to consider:
* Conduct client interviews
* Conduct witness interviews
* Prepare memos to file
* Review public documents
* Analyze documents

Assumptions:

Cost Assumptions

Costs to consider:
* Copying
* Document processing
* Online research
* Investigator fees
* Travel

Assumptions:

FIGURE 12.10 Report form used to file results of preliminary investigation.

VII. CONCLUSION

Private security plays an integral role in the legal, economic, and social fabric of this nation. From insurance investigations to asset protection, private security personnel involve themselves in most major institutions, including schools, universities, museums, entertainment complexes, Fortune 500 companies, and the majority of the retail and commercial marketplaces. It is hoped that this book has given the reader an eclectic impression of the functions of private security and, perhaps, a sense of awe for the future of this great undertaking.

Ongoing Fact Investigation	
Timekeeper	**Hours**

Task Assumptions
State Date____________________ End Date____________________ Approximate Duration____________________
Tasks to consider: * Conduct client interviews * Conduct witness interviews * Review selected client documents * Review publicly available documents * Analyze and organize documents Assumptions:
Cost Assumptions
Costs to consider: * Copying * Document processing * Online research * Investigator fees * Travel Assumptions:

FIGURE 12.11 Ongoing fact investigation report.

TIME AND EXPENSE REPORT

Client________________________ Operation________________________

Billing address ________________________ Client Account No. ________________________

________________________ Phone________________________

Services					
Inv.	**Dates**	**Hours/day**	**Rate**	**Amount**	**Total amount**
				Total →	
	Expenses:		Local & Bus fares Telephone Auto expense Meals Other travel expense Lodging		
		Miscellaneous: (Itemize)	____________ ____________ ____________ ____________	Total →	
				Grand total	____________

Attach all items to support expenses

FIGURE 12.12 Sample form used to list expenses and track time on each individual investigation.

OFFICE EXPENSE MEMORANDUM

Client ______________________ Client Account No. ______________________

Operation ______________________ For the month of ______________ 20 ______

Investigator ______________________ Date submitted ______________________

Date	Description	Expense		Surcharge		Total billable	
	Totals						

____
Investigator

FIGURE 12.13 Form on which expenses are listed.

VERIFICATION OF CHARGE CARD PURCHASE

Employee______________________________ For month of ______________________

Date	Description	Amount		Billed to	Client No.
	Total				

____
Employee

FIGURE 12.14 Verification of charge card purchase form.

LONG-DISTANCE TELEPHONE RECORD

Employee: ______________________________ ID Number: ______________________

Date	Phone # dialed from	Name of Person Called	Number Dialed	Case Name & Number	Length of Call

FIGURE 12.15 Sample form on which long distance telephone calls are recorded.

EXPENSE REPORT

Name|||Period Ending|

Name______________________ Period Ending ______________________

Day/Date	Case #	Mileage	Lodging	Per Diem	Entertainment	Tolls/Parking	Miscellaneous	Daily Totals
Sunday								
Monday								
Tuesday								
Wednesday								
Thursday								
Friday								
Saturday								
Sub-Total								
Other								
Total Expenses Reported								
Total Expenses Due								

PURPOSE OF TRIP	SUMMARY	
	Total Expenses	
	Less Cash Advance	
	Less Company Charges	
	Amount Due Employee	
	Amount Due Company	

Prepared by ______ Date ______ Approved by ______ Date ______

FIGURE 12.16 Sample of expense report form.

EXPENSE STATEMENT

Client Name	Case Number	File Number
Date	Expense Total	
☐ Travel		
From	To	
Starting Mileage	Ending Mileage	Total Mileage
☐ Personal Auto		☐ Business Auto
☐ Air ☐ Taxi ☐ Bus	☐ Train ☐ Subway	Total:
☐ Phone Calls		
To:		
City:	State:	Phone Number:
Made by:		
☐ Personal Phone Bill	☐ Credit Card	☐ Collect
☐ Entertainment		
Where		
Client Name		
Purpose		
☐ Other		
☐ Postage ☐ Parking	☐ Photocopies: Number _____	☐ Other
Signature:	Date:	

FIGURE 12.17 Sample expense statement.

TIME SLIP

Client Name:	Case Number:
Concerning	
Type of Activity	Total Time Charged:
Notes:	
Signature:	Date:

FIGURE 12.18 Sample time slip.

NAME OF SECURITY COMPANY
123 ABC Street
Anytown, USA 00000

TO:

FOR SERVICES RENDERED:

FIGURE 12.19 Sample invoice.

DAILY TIME RECORD AND EXPENSE SUMMARY

Subject____

Case Number__________________________________ Date ____

Investigator ____________________________________

Travel time ____________________________________ Surveillance Time ____________________________

Mileage _______________________________________

Expenses: Please list and attach receipts.

____

____

____

Vehicle Driven____

Cell Phone Charges. Please attach phone log and list of charges

____

____

Report Time ____

SUMMARY OF ACTIVITIES

____

____

____

FIGURE 12.20 Sample daily time and expense record.

Cash Statement									
Date Submitted			Office		Name (Print)			Period Ending	
Date		Supervisor's Initials	Amount		Date		Supervisor's Initials	Amount	
Month	Day		Advances	Expenses	Month	Day		Advances	Expenses
					Totals Forwarded				
Totals Forward					Grand Totals				

FIGURE 12.21 Sample record of advances and cash expenditures.

Weekly Time Sheet						
Employee Name		Employee Number		From		To
Date	Case#	Office	Travel	Surveillance	U/C	Total Hours
Total by Activity Type						
					Grand Total	
Employee Signature:					Date:	
Supervisor Signature:					Date:	

FIGURE 12.22 Sample weekly time sheet.

NOTES

1. R. Half, "Time Death: How Bosses Can Reduce Ranks of Goof-Offs," *USA Today*. (January 3, 1985); See also Jack Gordon, "Wasting Time on the Company Dime," *Training*. (May 2006), 6-6; George M. Naimark, "Stop Wasting Valuable Time," *Harv. Bus. Rev.* (December 2004), 143.
2. You may also take a video tutorial that outlines the software program at http://www.stdtime.com
3. Dominic Deeson, "Time Wasting Is Theft and Bad Management," *Management Services*. (Spring 2005), 3.
4. Pinkerton's, Inc., *Administration of the Investigations Department* (1990), 1–2.
5. *Ad.*
6. For a flowchart that tracks client and case, see Charles P. Nemeth, *The Paralegal Resource Manual*, 3rd edition (McGraw-Hill, 2008), 319.
7. Pinkerton's, *supra* note 4, at 4.
8. Pennsylvania Bar Institute, *The Pennsylvania Young Lawyer's Handbook* (1984), 28.
9. Trackops, LLC, https://www.trackops.com/
10. Jay G. Foonberg, *How to Start and Build a Law Practice*, 5th edition (American Bar Association, 2004), 309.
11. Pinkerton's, *supra* note 4, at 12.

Index

D

E

F

G

H

I

J

K

L

M

O

P

Q

R

S

T

U

V

W